BROTHERS

OF THE

GUN

ALSO BY MARK LEE GARDNER

The Earth Is All That Lasts: Crazy Horse, Sitting Bull, and the Last Stand of the Great Sioux Nation

Rough Riders: Theodore Roosevelt, His Cowboy Regiment, and the Immortal Charge Up San Juan Hill

Shot All to Hell: Jesse James, the Northfield Raid, and the Wild West's Greatest Escape

To Hell on a Fast Horse: Billy the Kid, Pat Garrett, and the Epic Chase to Justice in the Old West

George Armstrong Custer: A Biography

Geronimo: A Biography

Wagons for the Santa Fe Trade: Wheeled Vehicles and Their Makers, 1822–1880

The Mexican War Correspondence of Richard Smith Elliott (with Marc Simmons)

Brothers on the Santa Fe and Chihuahua Trails: Edward James Glasgow and William Henry Glasgow, 1846–1848

BROTHERS

OF THE

GUN

Wyatt Earp, Doc Holliday, and a
Reckoning in Tombstone

MARK LEE GARDNER

DUTTON

DUTTON

An imprint of Penguin Random House LLC
1745 Broadway, New York, NY 10019
penguinrandomhouse.com

Copyright © 2025 by Mark Lee Gardner
Penguin Random House values and supports copyright. Copyright fuels creativity,
encourages diverse voices, promotes free speech, and creates a vibrant culture. Thank you
for buying an authorized edition of this book and for complying with copyright laws by
not reproducing, scanning, or distributing any part of it in any form without permission.
You are supporting writers and allowing Penguin Random House to continue to publish
books for every reader. Please note that no part of this book may be used or reproduced
in any manner for the purpose of training artificial intelligence technologies or systems.

DUTTON and the D colophon are registered trademarks of
Penguin Random House LLC.

Book design by Daniel Brount
Map of Wyatt and Doc's Tombstone by David Lindroth Inc.

LIBRARY OF CONGRESS CATALOGING-IN-PUBLICATION DATA
has been applied for.

ISBN 9780593471890 (hardcover)
ISBN 9780593471913 (ebook)

Printed in the United States of America
1st Printing

The authorized representative in the EU for product safety and compliance is
Penguin Random House Ireland, Morrison Chambers, 32 Nassau Street,
Dublin D02 YH68, Ireland, https://eu-contact.penguin.ie.

To Roy B. Young
Chronicler of the Wild West

Some ten or twelve old friends of yours and mine,
If we spoke truly, are not friends at all.
They never were. That accident divine,
A friendship, not so often may befall.

DON MARQUIS

Some is sad and some is quite laughable,
but such is life any way we take it.

BIG NOSE KATE

CONTENTS

PREFACE

I cons never die. Such is the fate of Wyatt Earp and Doc Holliday, friends in life and friends in immortality, forever facing down "the Cowboys" at the O.K. Corral. We revel in their legends at Dodge City and Tombstone, once booming towns with a wide-open future now clinging to a six-gun past. And we chase relics, pieces of the True Cross, that prove Earp and Holliday once walked this Earth as men. Wyatt Earp guns, nearly always of questionable provenance, have fetched astronomical prices from collectors while legal documents Earp signed as a lawman—most pilfered from unsecure county courthouses—continue to surface from time to time, invariably commanding thousands. A crude map Wyatt drew in 1926 of the O.K. Corral gun battle (which he referred to as the "street fight") brought $115,000 in 2004—and it wasn't even signed.

In Tombstone, Arizona, thousands of pounds of black powder have been burned up over the decades in daily reenactments of that thirty-second gunfight. And in countless articles, books, songs, films, and documentaries, Wyatt's and Doc's stories have been told again and again for well more than a hundred years. Over and over, the two have been celebrated and despised, their lives mythologized and, in more recent times, demythologized.

Does anything remain to be written about these western protagonists, any aspects of their lives and loves that haven't already been examined ad infinitum? The answer, maybe surprisingly, is yes. There's nearly always a hidden historical path to explore, a stubborn question in search of an answer, a forgotten verse of an ancient ballad to be discovered and *sung*.

When we do ostensibly know everything there is to know about a person or event from the past, that history loses something. The tale becomes dull and dusty, a case closed instead of an ongoing investigation. No true history lover wants that. Thank goodness, as I gladly discovered while researching this book, there is indeed more to the lives of Wyatt Earp and Doc Holliday and their odd but endearing friendship, a bona fide saga if there ever was one.

The pursuit of these two men's stories took me from the rolling hills of Barton County, Missouri, to the stately gardens of the Huntington Library in San Marino, California; from a hilltop cemetery overlooking Glenwood Springs, Colorado, to a narrow, fenced-in lot near (not at) the old O.K. Corral. In Dodge City, Kansas, I secured a copy of a typescript manuscript of Wyatt Earp's own story of his life from a local historical society operating out of a former department store. At the Arizona Historical Society in Tucson, I held a small bible gifted to Earp by a Dodge City law firm "as a slight recognition of his many Christian virtues." That bible, by the way, did not appear to have seen much use.

Firsthand observation at historic sites (more like shrines in some cases), weeks spent poring over letters and manuscripts in various archives, countless hours reading contemporary newspaper reports, not to mention the creation of a personal library of Earpiana that has grown to startling proportions, have all contributed to the book in your hands. And in case there's been any question up to now, this is nonfiction, where the discernible facts supersede legend. (Sorry, John Ford, but not really, as I've never cared for your oft-quoted line.) All the dialogue within quotes came directly from primary sources; nothing has been made up or altered. And those sources are fully cited in my extensive endnotes.

Wyatt Earp and Doc Holliday, like anyone else then and now, have their fair share of contradictions and failings. They made their way not in the Old West but in the New West, young towns and camps on the fringe of morality, where money flowed through gambling, prostitution, and rampant speculation. In this New West, a sordid history or lifestyle didn't preclude respectability. A onetime pimp and horse thief could become an upstanding peace officer. A boozing, gun-toting gambling addict could also be a successful dentist—for a time, anyway—with plenty of satisfied customers. And the two could be friends without anyone giving it a second thought. Wherever Wyatt Earp and Doc Holliday found themselves, though, there was one constant. Trouble seemed to follow Wyatt. Doc made his own.

ONE

THE WAY WEST

And the world began when I was born
And the world is mine to win.

CHARLES BADGER CLARK

Vidal, California
March 1927

Feeling his years at the age of seventy-eight, Wyatt Earp was tired, exasperated, and broke. His big mustache had been white for a long time now, and he was practically bald, but his six-foot frame remained slim and straight as a board. Wyatt lived with his common-law wife, Josephine, in a tiny cottage that sat just 216 feet from the tracks of the Atchison, Topeka & Santa Fe Railway. From their front door, unbroken desert peppered with clumps of greasewood stretched for eight miles to the foot of the Whipple Mountains, where Wyatt would spend most days digging and scratching the earth for gold and copper ore at his Happy Day Mine.

But even in this two-bit town in the Sonoran Desert, Wyatt was having to deal with his distant—and controversial—past. On March 15, the old lawman reached back into his memory as he composed a long letter to bestselling author Walter Noble Burns. Burns had requested information from Wyatt on Doc Holliday for a planned biography. The author was originally keen on writing Earp's story, but he'd settled on Doc, or so he claimed, after Wyatt told him that a friend had already completed a manuscript of his life, and they were currently looking for a publisher.

Wyatt wrote Burns that he was happy to tell him what he wanted to know, but he asked the author not to mention his name too freely in the book. "I am getting tired of it all," Wyatt explained, "as there have been so many lies written about me in so many magazines in the last few years that it makes a man feel like fighting." Referring to a research trip Burns had made to Tombstone, Wyatt commented that, "No doubt you were filled up with lots of things which never happened about me." Wyatt had indeed had more than enough of the stories from blowhards and journalists who weren't even there. "I can't understand why they don't let me alone," he wrote, "and I think it time to put a stop to it all."

That wasn't necessarily an idle threat. In 1922, he'd been enraged by a "nasty and ugly article" in the *Los Angeles Times* that described Wyatt, his brothers, and Doc Holliday as part of a gang of stage robbers. They'd made Tombstone their headquarters, the story went, after being driven out of Dodge City by "Chief of Police" Bat Masterson. Not only that, but the writer, a John M. Scanland, had Wyatt being killed in Colton, California, some years later.

The silent-film star William S. Hart, an unabashed Earp admirer, came to the old lawman's defense in a subsequent issue of the newspaper, but Wyatt wasn't satisfied. He was determined to find the offending writer and set the man straight himself. It took two years, but Scanland, then age seventy-nine, was finally located, boarding with a couple in Los Angeles and about as broke as Wyatt. Wyatt showed up at the front door along with John Flood Jr., the man who was writing Earp's autobiography, and Wyatt was in no mood for introductory pleasantries.

Just how startled Scanland was to see the famed Wyatt Earp towering over him can only be imagined, but Earp later wrote Hart that the journalist expressed real regret and readily apologized for his two-year-old story. Scanland even typed up a retraction and signed it—anything to get Earp on his way.

"It does beat the band how the truth will be warped and misstated over a period of years," Earp wrote Hart, which was a big reason why Wyatt was dictating his life story to John Flood. Another reason was that authors were making money off those faulty newspaper and magazine articles, and Wyatt felt that if anyone should be making money off his exploits, real or imagined, it should be him.

The old lawman had high hopes for the manuscript John Flood was preparing, which they would tout as the "first and only authentic story" of Wyatt Earp. He was eager that that story be told right not only for himself, but for the sake of those no longer living and unable to defend their reputations: brothers Virgil, Morgan, and Warren—and Doc Holliday. They'd all backed Wyatt when he needed backing. It was a debt that could never be fully repaid, but Wyatt would try. His story, then, Wyatt instructed Flood, was to be about truth, correctness, and vindication.

Especially vindication.

———

THE TRUTH OF WYATT EARP BEGINS IN ILLINOIS IN THE SPRING of 1848. He came into the world on March 19 of that year in the rural village of Monmouth, the third son of Nicholas and Virginia Ann Earp. Six months earlier, thirty-four-year-old Nicholas had ridden off to Mexico with one hundred recruits from the town and surrounding area, eager to win laurels fighting the soldiers of Antonio López de Santa Anna. They called themselves the Monmouth Dragoons, and their commander was a well-liked attorney and merchant named Wyatt Berry Stapp. However, a mule kick to the groin abruptly ended Nicholas's soldiering south of the Rio Grande. He was discharged in Vera Cruz in December 1847 and arrived home four weeks before the birth of his son, whom he named for his former captain: Wyatt Berry Stapp Earp.

Young Wyatt joined three brothers, Newton (a half brother), James (Jim), and Virgil, and a sister, Martha, in the Earp family's small two-story home. But it wouldn't be their home for long. Just one year after Wyatt's birth, Nicholas sold the house for $300 and moved his family one hundred and twenty-three miles northwest to the new settlement of

Pella, in Marion County, Iowa. Like Monmouth, Pella was surrounded by lush prairie land with rich, black soil just beneath the surface. The settlement had been founded by emigrants from Holland seeking religious freedom in the United States. Their colony numbered some nine hundred individuals with more on the way.

Nicholas wasn't Dutch, nor was he fleeing religious persecution, but he was a cooper (barrel maker) by trade, and there was surely money to be made serving these newcomers. In fact, one newspaper article about the Hollanders observed that they had "considerable pecuniary means." Nothing is known of Nicholas's initial dealings with the Hollanders, but it's apparent that the bearded five-foot-eleven Mexican War vet quickly took to his new surroundings and neighbors. When the federal census taker visited Marion County's Lake Prairie Township in September 1850, he recorded Nicholas as engaging in both coopering and farming, with land holdings valued at $500. The following year, Nicholas added flatboat captain to his résumé of skills, floating a load of corn down the Des Moines and Mississippi rivers to St. Louis.

Wyatt remembered his father as having a "love for the soil and for making things grow," but that didn't mean he wouldn't give up that passion if something more lucrative came along. Intoxicating stories of easy riches coming from the California gold fields spread like a contagion among Iowa's farmers and tradesmen. "Even the most thoughtful and sober-minded," stated an early Marion County history, "found it difficult to resist the infection." Nicholas was one of the many who succumbed. He'd earned 160 acres of bounty land for his wartime service and sold it in June 1852, possibly to raise funds for his overland journey. The exact date of his trip is uncertain, but the fabled bonanzas were as elusive to Nicholas as they were to thousands of other Argonauts. He returned to his family after a few months, with nothing to show for his weary adventure but the experience of crossing the Great Plains and Rocky Mountains and some fireside tales to delight Wyatt and his siblings.

Wyatt gained two brothers while the family lived in Marion County: Morgan in 1851 and Warren in 1855. In March 1856, however, Nicholas sold his Iowa land at a good profit and moved Virginia Ann and the kids back to Monmouth, the Warren County seat, which had grown to a population of about three thousand. Nicholas purchased three lots in town and opened a grocery store. He also ran for the office of constable, one of three in Monmouth, and won. In July of 1857, the Mercantile Agency, a credit-reporting firm based in New York City, observed that although Nicholas was doing a "small business," he was industrious, sober, and was good for his debts. He was also a member in good standing of the Warren chapter of Masons.

From all accounts, then, Nicholas was one of the community's leaders, but less than a year later, things suddenly took a turn for the worse: Earp was charged with selling liquor out of his store. At that time, only druggists could legally sell alcohol in Monmouth, although that restriction hardly stopped the flow of ardent spirits. "The roudyism, and drunkenness and revellings which are carried on in our streets at night are [becoming] next to intolerable," complained the town's newspaper editor, "and the sooner it is suppressed the better it will be for the morals and good name of Monmouth." Earp, though a town constable, enjoyed the occasional drink himself, but helping to supply the townsfolk with booze, regardless of the fact that numerous Monmouth citizens were clearly opposed to prohibition, was an egregious violation of the public trust.

Thus began several months of court appearances, fines that he avoided paying, and because Constable Earp continued to believe he was above the law, two additional charges of selling alcohol. Nicholas sold out to his brother Walter, who had his own indictment and conviction for peddling liquor. The Mercantile Agency wasn't nearly as confident about Walter and reported that he was "not worth anything." Worthless brother Walter skipped town without paying his fines.

Nicholas also concluded that it was time to leave his Monmouth woes behind. The Earp family, young Wyatt now eleven, returned to Pella, Iowa, in November 1859. They'd suffered the loss of a daughter while in Monmouth: young Martha, who died at the age of ten. But another daughter had been born to Nicholas and Virginia Ann in 1858 and named for her mother, bringing the Earp tally to six boys and a girl. Clearly, that mule kick to the groin did Nicholas no lasting harm.

THERE ARE HARDLY ANY STORIES OF WYATT EARP AS A BOY, NO reminiscences from doting parents and, other than yarns of a schoolyard fight or two, no revealing tales from childhood friends or classmates. This seems odd. What neighbors, either in Illinois or Iowa, wouldn't recall the time they lived next to the family that had three sons in the legendary Tombstone gunfight? And yet the record is largely silent. The only detailed stories we have of Wyatt's youth take place when he was in his teens—and they come from Wyatt himself.

Following the outbreak of the Civil War in 1861, three of Wyatt's brothers marched off to fight to preserve the Union. Wyatt's father, then forty-seven, didn't enlist, but he did his part—for a time. Nicholas helped to recruit and drill troops in the county and was later appointed a deputy provost marshal. As a deputy provost marshal, Nicholas's primary charge was chasing down and arresting deserters. On top of that, he also served as Pella's town marshal from 1862 to 1864.

With his father so busy, Wyatt was left to tend the corn crop in an acre field just outside Pella. It was then, Wyatt recalled, "I gained my lifelong sympathy for the man with a hoe. . . . I was barely thirteen, but I was warned that if I didn't bring that corn crop through, my brothers in the army might go hungry." Wyatt's younger brothers, Morgan and Warren, helped in the field as much as small boys could, but that didn't make the task any more pleasant. Nevertheless, Wyatt got the 1861 crop harvested, but when springtime came the next year, he couldn't stand the idea of more days in the Iowa sun and humidity. If his brothers in the army went hungry, so be it, but he'd be hungry with them. He was going to fight the Rebs, too.

On a day when he believed his father would be away from home for a good length of time, the fourteen-year-old Wyatt started for Ottumwa, forty-five miles southwest of Pella, where he hoped to enlist. It wasn't an easy journey, for rail lines had yet to reach Pella. Wyatt either caught a stagecoach or hoofed it to Eddyville, twenty-seven miles away, where a train left at 11:30 each morning for Ottumwa. By the time Wyatt reached his destination, he would have spent most of two days looking over his shoulder for his father. But as he stepped off the train at this bustling town on the banks of the Des Moines River, he could finally relax. All that remained was to find a recruiting officer and convince him he was of age for the service. That is, until Wyatt entered a hotel lobby and recognized his father across the room.

Nicholas Earp, who'd not been away from home as long as expected, had immediately started after his son and actually beaten the boy to Ottumwa. But while Wyatt couldn't help but make out the figure of the man he most feared seeing, he wasn't certain his father had spotted his son. Wyatt made a quick about-face, dashed into the street, and started back for Pella, this time outpacing his father. But Wyatt was wrong about his father not observing him in the hotel, and, as Wyatt told the story years later, he narrowly escaped a whipping when his father arrived home. The matter was settled after Wyatt made a solemn vow that he wouldn't run away again, nor attempt to enlist without his mother's permission.

And he would tend to that dreaded cornfield.

EXCEPT FOR A DALLIANCE AS A SUPPORTER OF REPUBLICAN John C. Fremont in the 1856 presidential election, Nicholas Earp was a strong Democrat. And for Nicholas and many of his fellow Democrats in the North, the nature of the war with the South had changed into something alarming. "It was begun with the declaration that it was simply and only a war for the Constitution and the Union of our fathers," spouted a Democrat orator early in 1864. But now, he continued, the war was "declared unblushingly 'an abolition war.'"

Nicholas was said to have at one time been a slave owner himself. Whether this was true or not, he held an ingrained racist bias that led him to question why his sons and other young men were fighting and dying in an endless war to free a people he believed were unsuited for anything but servitude. It wasn't just the possible wholesale emancipation of the South's slave population that Nicholas and others of his party were opposed to, however. There was the controversial suspension of habeas corpus by President Abraham Lincoln in 1862, and the passage of the

Conscription Act by Congress the following year. Liberties taken for granted were no longer certain, and a government "of the people" appeared, to many Democrats, more like a people governed by tyrants. These Democrats pushed for an immediate end to the war. They were known as Copperheads, and Nicholas readily cast his lot with them.

Nicholas's political leanings were on full view in January 1864 when he came to the aid of a fellow Copperhead, John B. Hamilton, in a contested election for the office of Marion County clerk of the courts. Hamilton's opponent, a man named Kruck, had cleverly slipped into the county building just before midnight on December 31 and ensconced himself in the clerk's office. A few days later, Earp, as Pella's marshal, and Hamilton arrived at the office to forcefully take possession of the county seal. A scuffle broke out, but as strong as Earp was, he couldn't wrest the seal from Kruck's hands. The noisy tug-of-war finally ended with the arrest of both Marshal Earp and Hamilton, presumably by the county sheriff. In the end, Kruck retained the seal and the office.

This altercation seems to have been the tipping point for Earp and some of his fellow Copperheads in Marion County; they began making plans to emigrate to California in the spring. Nicholas resigned as Pella's marshal on April 1, 1864, and six weeks later, the Earp family was on its way west with all their possessions crammed into a horse-drawn carriage and a prairie schooner pulled by three yoke of oxen. Little Virginia Earp had died in Pella three years earlier, but another daughter, Adelia, had been born in 1861. Twenty-two-year-old Jim Earp, his left arm unusable after being wounded early in the war, was making the journey with his family. Wyatt, now sixteen and standing close to six feet tall, was the ox team's driver, known on western trails as a bullwhacker.

Nicholas had also given Wyatt the role of meat hunter for the family. An excellent shot, Wyatt never had a firearm he could call his own. That changed for this trip when his father gave him a two-barreled muzzleloader: The top barrel was a .40-caliber rifle and the bottom a smoothbore for firing bird shot. "It was a cumbersome weapon," remembered Wyatt, "but I thought more of it than any other I owned in later years. . . . The range of the rifle was not much greater than that of the shotgun; one hundred yards was certainly its limit for accurate work. But I was proud of that gun."

The Earps and the other families in their caravan ferried across the Missouri River at Omaha, Nebraska, at which time the train counted some forty wagons, a mere fraction of the more than five thousand teams—horses, mules, and oxen pulling all manner of wheeled conveyances—estimated to have crossed the Missouri so far that season. And the man elected to captain the train and its roughly 150 men, women, and children, was a fellow who could claim experience, who'd already made the trip to California: Nicholas Earp.

The journey took seven long, grueling months, but the part that remained vivid in Wyatt's mind more than sixty years later occurred west of Fort Laramie over nine days in July. Lakota, Cheyenne, and Arapaho warriors, angrily opposed to the thousands of emigrants passing through their lands, shooting their game, denuding their grasslands, and exhausting the wood fuel along their streams, attacked train after train. On July 12, they struck the Pella train shortly after it stopped to noon on the banks of the North Platte River.

Forty-nine-year-old Sarah Rousseau, her husband, and three children were members of the train, and Sarah described the terrifying first moments of the attack in a diary: "Every man was for his gun and revolver, and to try to get the horses, as there was a regular stampede among them. They were terrified and running in every direction. The Indians would rush by on the bluffs, firing, and our men firing on them as they passed. Bullets flying in every direction, and horses frantically running as hard as they could."

Nicholas Earp shouted at Wyatt and Jim to round up the family's stock. The brothers jumped on their horses and raced into the dust and confusion. As they attempted to drive what animals they could to the wagons, several warriors charged them. Wyatt and Jim slid off their mounts and began firing at their attackers, holding them off. The warrior party eventually galloped away with about fourteen of the train's horses, and the Earps and several others pursued them. Their party followed for about three miles until, worried about being ambushed, they turned back.

Two days and about twenty-seven miles later, Sarah Rousseau wrote in her diary that, "We are in the most dangerous part of the country now." The train had made camp, and Wyatt and a companion were chosen as lookouts. The pair rode to a high bluff above the Platte, from where they soon heard voices coming from the stream. Wyatt and his fellow lookout carefully moved down toward the sounds until they spotted a dozen warriors on horseback riding in the middle of the river. Wyatt instantly brought up his gun to shoot, but his companion, fearful of initiating a fight when they were so outnumbered, grabbed Wyatt's weapon. The warriors, however, were clearly heading to the camp, and they were likely part of a larger force. Wyatt knew he must warn the train. He jerked the gun away from his friend and fired. The crack of the rifle was plainly heard by Wyatt's father, who immediately ordered the livestock driven into the wagon corral.

Because of Wyatt, the emigrants were ready for the warriors' charge. The men of the train waited until the warriors were well within range and, as Nicholas Earp described the affair in a letter some months later, "we commenced popping away at them and putting them to flite." Nicholas then mounted a horse and led a pursuit of the warriors. It was a running skirmish for close to four miles before Earp and his men finally halted. Wyatt recalled that they succeeded in killing one of the attackers.

In these fights on the Platte, young Wyatt Earp displayed the fearlessness that would come to define him as an adult. His violent encounters with Plains Indian warriors also marked the first time he fired a gun at a fellow human with the intent to kill, although, to be sure, few Euro-Americans at this time considered the Indigenous peoples of the West human. In fact, an army lieutenant coldly instructed Sarah Rousseau's husband to "kill every Indian he saw, friend or foe."

The Pella train arrived at its California destination in mid-December 1864. In the final entry of her diary, Sarah Rousseau offered no celebratory statement, writing simply, "Reached San Bernardino about sundown." Sarah's daily jottings contain no mention of Wyatt—only occasionally did she make note of a fellow traveler's name—but Nicholas Earp does appear from time to time, and not always in a positive light. From Sarah we learn that the Earp patriarch was quick-tempered, could curse as well or better than any man, liked his liquor, and was hard, even cruel, with the horses they depended upon. Nevertheless, Nicholas Earp, with all his flaws, did get his family and his Pella neighbors to Southern California.

———————

BEFORE THE MULE KICK TO THE GROIN SENT NICHOLAS EARP home from the Mexican War, he just may have crossed paths with a twenty-eight-year-old lieutenant from Griffin, Georgia, named Henry Burroughs Holliday. Both saw duty in and around the city of Xalapa, some seventy miles northwest of Vera Cruz, in November 1847. So did thousands of other American soldiers, of course, but, who knows, fate may have placed the two men in the same cantina—or brothel. Even if they didn't rub shoulders, the father of Wyatt Earp and the father of John Henry "Doc" Holliday were never again so close as they were in Mexico.

Like Nicholas Earp, Henry Holliday tried his hand at many things to make a living. In May 1840, he was one of forty Georgians to take out a peddler's license. The license stated that young Henry was five feet, eight and one half inches tall with dark hair and blue eyes, a Holliday family trait. Ten years later, he was listed in the US census as a druggist. He would also dabble in real estate, buggies and furniture, and various types of horticulture, from grapes to pecan trees. Whether in Griffin or his later home of Valdosta, Georgia, Henry Holliday was always a respected member of the community, even serving a year's term as Valdosta's mayor. In later years, however, it was a different story behind that facade of success. Credit reports from the 1870s identify Henry as a failed businessman, having "no means" and "unreliable, not to be trusted."

Unlike Nicholas Earp, Holliday had no wife or children waiting for him when his Mexican War service ended. However, he did bring home to Griffin an eleven-year-old Mexican orphan to raise: Francisco Hidalgo. How many American soldiers returned from Mexico with an orphan is impossible to know, but it's safe to say it was a highly unusual act. Then, on January 8, 1849, Holliday married Alice Jane McKey, age nineteen. The couple's first child, Martha, died after living just six months. Their second, John Henry, was born in Griffin on August 14, 1851. Like his father, the boy had blue eyes.

John Henry had been delivered by his father's brother, Dr. John Stiles Holliday, a graduate of the Medical College of Georgia. And John Stiles was the first to notice that baby Holliday was born with a cleft palate. To repair the defect would necessitate a delicate and dangerous operation for the time. According to family lore, John Stiles sought the assistance of renowned Atlanta surgeon Crawford Long, a relative through marriage and a pioneer in the use of anesthesia. Together, John Stiles and Dr. Long performed the operation, and it could not have gone better. Young John Henry would have a mild speech impediment, but through frequent practicing of his words with his determined mother, he eventually overcame it.

Described as a "quiet, well-mannered child," John Henry grew up in a household bustling with relatives—particularly three doting aunts, sisters of his mother—and the enslaved. In 1850, the census taker recorded Henry Holliday as owning one slave. A decade later, he owned six, ranging in age from ten to forty-one. Henry's brother, John Stiles Holliday, who lived in neighboring Fayette County, owned thirteen in 1860. And, according to the census, John Stiles's place included two "slave houses" where they were quartered.

It's very likely that little John Henry's view of slavery was similar to that of another boy born and raised in a slave state: Samuel Clemens, later to become famous as Mark Twain. "I was not aware that there was anything wrong about it," Twain recollected about the "peculiar institution." "No one arraigned it in my hearing; the local papers said nothing against it; the local pulpit taught us that God approved it, that it was a holy thing and that the doubter need only look in the Bible if he wished to settle his mind."

But while slavery might have seemed an accepted fact of life in the eyes of a white child in Georgia, the buying and selling of human beings, deeming them nothing more than chattel, had long been a source of divisiveness between North and South and would soon have fateful consequences. "Slavery was at the bottom of the trouble, no matter who may delude himself to the contrary," admitted a former Confederate soldier about the Civil War. To this veteran's mind, the quarreling between Northerners and Southerners, abolitionists and pro-slavery advocates, had lasted for so long and been so bitter that "a good blood-letting was the only way to put an end to it."

John Henry was just shy of his tenth birthday when the bloodletting began, and, like young Wyatt Earp, he witnessed close family members succumb to the war spirit, including his father and several uncles and cousins. Henry Holliday, now age forty-two, received a commission as a major and an appointment as an assistant quartermaster in the Twenty-Seventh Georgia Infantry. He left Griffin for the front in December 1861, but by the end of the following year, he was back home. Like numerous soldiers on both sides, it wasn't a bullet that knocked Henry Holliday out of the war; it was disease. In his case, "Chronic Diarrhea and general disability."

By the spring of 1864, it was no secret that Union general William T. Sherman was preparing to launch a massive campaign to capture Atlanta, which was too close for comfort for Henry Holliday, who'd recovered his health. That April, Henry moved his family nearly two hundred miles south to Lowndes County. They took up residence a few miles north of the small town of Valdosta, in a gently rolling countryside checkered with croplands and forests of tall loblolly pines.

John Henry doesn't seem to have been happy about leaving Griffin, and their new home was hardly a joyful place because his mother was desperately ill. Alice Jane suffered from tuberculosis, the scourge of the nineteenth century, and was mostly bedridden. The disease finally killed her in September 1866. A religious woman, her last thoughts were for John Henry. Her lengthy obituary stated that she was "deeply anxious about the faith of her only child," and that she'd had her "faith written so her boy might know what his mother believed."

Unfortunately, Henry Holliday seems to have been indifferent to his fifteen-year-old son's emotional state following the death of his mother. Alice Jane had been in the dark ground but three months when Henry married the twenty-three-year-old daughter of a neighbor. Clearly, Henry had been aware of the young lady for some time, but failing to observe a widower's customary twelve-month mourning period was, at best, disrespectful to his dead wife—at worst, scandalous. Next Henry moved his family to Valdosta, into a house owned by his new wife's father. All of this, according to a family member, made John Henry "quite sullen."

John Henry's relationship with his father and stepmother was strained to be sure, but townspeople and schoolmates at the pretentious-sounding Valdosta Institute fondly recalled a different side of the young man. They said he was "mischievous but not mean; he was polite, good-natured, well reared, but firm and brave. He never receded from any position taken by him. He was slow, but sure, and when the pinch came he was ready for the last inch."

JOHN HENRY GREATLY ADMIRED HIS UNCLE, JOHN STILES, AND expressed a desire to become a physician like him. His uncle, however, dissatisfied with the state of the study of medicine at that time, encouraged his nephew to take up dentistry. That decided it. John Henry chose one of the best dental schools in the country, the Pennsylvania College of Dental Surgery in Philadelphia, where he began his studies in September 1870. Among the several requirements to graduate, dental students needed to complete a minimum of two full courses of lectures (at $100 per course), serve an internship with a private practice, and write a thesis.

A year and a half later, having submitted a thesis titled "Diseases of the Teeth," John Henry Holliday received the degree of Doctor of Dental Surgery. Sometime before his graduation, perhaps to commemorate the important occasion, John Henry visited the Philadelphia photographic gallery of Oliver B. De Morat and had his image made. Only one carte de visite photograph of the twenty-year-old Georgian survives from that visit. On the reverse of the photo, written in the proud graduate's own hand, is "J. H. Holliday D.D.S./Valdosta Georgia." It's the earliest known portrait as an adult of the man who would eventually become known throughout the American West as Doc Holliday.

With degree in hand, John Henry chose to begin his dental career in

The Pennsylvania College of Dental Surgery, Philadelphia, where Holliday obtained his dental degree.
(PUBLIC DOMAIN IMAGE, AUTHOR'S COLLECTION)

John Henry Holliday from a carte de visite by Philadelphia photographer Oliver B. De Morat, circa 1872.
(PUBLIC DOMAIN IMAGE, AUTHOR'S COLLECTION)

Atlanta. His favorite uncle, John Stiles, had relocated with his family to the state's capital, and John Henry was warmly welcomed into their household. By the summer of 1872, he'd secured a position in the office of Atlanta dentist Arthur C. Ford, but it wasn't long before he began exhibiting a number of the symptoms of a consumptive: persistent coughing, fever, fatigue, weight loss, and night sweats. After a careful examination, John Stiles confirmed that John Henry was indeed suffering from tuberculosis, which he'd almost certainly contracted from his mother.

This was disturbing news for the Holliday family. A macabre joke published in the *Atlanta Constitution* that same year aptly conveyed the sad reality for many of those afflicted with the disease:

A gentleman meeting a friend who was wasting away with consumption, exclaimed:
"Aw, my dear fellow, how slow you walk."
"Yes," replied the consumptive, "I walk slow, but I am going fast."

John Henry, of course, had witnessed firsthand his mother painfully wasting away. He had few options for treatment, but if he did nothing, that nightmare was unquestionably his future.

With the discovery of penicillin still decades in the future, the most commonly recommended treatment for consumptives in the nineteenth century was a sojourn in the West. Sometimes called the "prairie cure," it was believed that the abundant sunshine and rarified atmosphere of the western plains and mountains were a true panacea for nearly any illness. John Stiles offered that California would be a good place for his nephew to seek his health. However, Henry Holliday wanted his son to try Texas.

Texas was an odd choice—the Lone Star State's climate, especially the eastern half, wasn't that much different from Atlanta's—and why Henry Holliday argued for it is unknown. It may have been little more than the fact that Texas was another southern state and not nearly as far away from home as California. In any event, early in the summer of 1873, Dr. John Henry Holliday packed his wardrobe and dental tools and started west, destination Dallas.

Another story exists in Holliday lore, however, that purports to explain why the young dentist left Georgia, and it has nothing to do with tuberculosis. The most well-known version was related by none other than William Barclay "Bat" Masterson, who was more than just an acquaintance of Doc Holliday. According to Masterson, Holliday and his friends had a favorite swimming hole on the Withlacoochee River just outside Valdosta, a swimming hole that was also popular with local Black youth. One day, Holliday and his buddies decided it wouldn't do to share the spot with the Black swimmers, and they let it be known that in the future the Black swimmers would have to do their frolicking somewhere downstream. Not surprisingly, the Black men weren't about to go along with this plan, and they told the Holliday party that if they didn't like sharing, they themselves could find a new spot.

This defiant response, the story goes, enraged John Henry and his friends. John Henry bided his time for a few days until a Sunday afternoon when the swimming hole was crowded with Black swimmers, splashing and laughing. Suddenly, a menacing-looking John Henry appeared on the riverbank, a double-barreled shotgun gripped in his hands.

"Get out and be quick about it," John Henry shouted.

As he brought the gun to his shoulder, the swimmers scrambled out of the water, some slipping and falling into one another. John Henry waited until several of the swimmers were bunched together and jerked both triggers. Flame and smoke belched from both barrels, and two young men dropped lifeless into the mud. Several others continued running and yelling, blood oozing from multiple buckshot wounds. According to Masterson's tale, the local authorities weren't overly concerned about the dead Black men, but John Henry's family thought it wise for the young man to absent himself from the area for a time to let things quiet down.

No contemporary newspaper reports or legal documents have been found that confirm this horrifying episode, which supposedly occurred sometime in 1872. However, slightly different versions of the incident did circulate among John Henry's kin, with some claiming that Holliday only fired over the heads of the swimmers to scare them. In any event, the truth of what happened that day on the Withlacoochee River will likely never be known, but it's probably safe to say that John Henry Holliday, unlike Mark Twain, never rose above the prejudices of his youth. Few Southerners did.

He would feel right at home, then, in the Dallas of 1873.

TWO

THE PEORIA BUMMER AND THE DISSIPATED DENTIST

There are different kinds and qualities of the bummer species. Some are whiskey bummers, some are boardinghouse bummers, and some are bummers on general principles.

ROCKY MOUNTAIN NEWS, MAY 23, 1862

Lamar, Missouri
January 16, 1870

It was a Monday, and Wyatt Earp, twenty-one years old, stood before the township's justice of the peace, who happened to be his father. Next to Wyatt stood his bride, Arella Sutherland, age twenty and the daughter of the owner of the town's Exchange Hotel. How the couple met wasn't preserved in family lore, nor is much of anything known of the newlyweds' short time together. In the first book-length biography of Earp, author Stuart Lake wrote that Wyatt was "loyal to the young love, in a manner and from a sentiment which few of his casual associates could have fathomed." How Lake came to know this is another mystery, for Wyatt was tightlipped when it came to his time in Lamar, and there is no mention of Arella in either Wyatt's recollections given to John Flood or his limited correspondence with Lake.

Nevertheless, Wyatt's wedding day marked an early high point in his life, and it had come quickly. Just a year and a half earlier, Nicholas Earp uprooted his family yet again and traveled overland from California to the

Lamar, Missouri, 1886. Although this stereo view was made several years after Wyatt's departure, the town had changed little in that time. Note the dirt street. (AUTHOR'S COLLECTION)

western edge of the Missouri Ozarks, where he owned a piece of land. The Earps settled in the small town of Lamar, the Barton County seat. Bushwhackers burned the town during the Civil War, but the population had rebounded to about eight hundred by the time the Earps arrived. Nicholas opened a combination bakery and small grocery on Lamar's square, and, just like he'd done in other towns, he speedily inserted himself as a community mover and shaker.

Sometime in 1869, Nicholas had been appointed Lamar's only lawman. But in November of that year, he resigned the constable position to accept the office of the township's justice of the peace. Immediately after accepting Nicholas's resignation, the Barton County Circuit Court appointed Wyatt Earp to fill the vacancy of town constable. It was the beginning of Wyatt's off-and-on career as an officer of the law. He had absolutely no experience, of course, but he'd observed his father perform the duties of constable and marshal in Monmouth, Pella, and, more recently, Lamar—although an argument could be made that maybe Nicholas Earp wasn't the best example of a lawman to emulate. But there was something about young Wyatt, a certain sureness, perhaps, that suggested he was fully suited for the task. The town's newspaper, the *South-West Missourian*, offered that it was a good appointment and that "law-breakers had better look out."

Lamar was situated in a beautiful country, a mixture of hardwood forests; prairie lands; small, tilled fields, and orchards. It wasn't a hotbed of crime, but Wyatt had plenty to keep him busy. Stolen horses, public drunkenness, and fistfights weren't uncommon, and the area did indeed experience the occasional murder. Wyatt made arrests, served summonses on witnesses for court cases, and, if needed, was present in the courtroom. He also collected taxes as called for by both county and town ordinances. One such ordinance stipulated that a tax of fifty dollars be levied upon circuses performing within the county and ten dollars for juggling and sleight of hand shows, with the monies earmarked for the county's Common School Fund. Two circuses came to Lamar in 1870: James T. Johnson & Co.'s circus that July and the Hemmings, Cooper, & Whitby circus and menagerie in September. Both circuses featured juggling or sleight of hand shows, and Wyatt took in a total of $130 in taxes.

In August 1870, Constable Wyatt Earp bought a house in Lamar for $50, just one house down from that of his parents. His next-door neighbors were his half brother, Newton, and family. That ended up being a very interesting, and presumably very awkward, arrangement, for in the November election, Newton inexplicably ran against brother Wyatt for town constable. Wyatt won with 137 votes to Newton's 108.

Things couldn't have been going better for Wyatt, it seems—until they weren't. Arella Earp died suddenly. Possibly of typhus, but no one knows for sure. On November 7, Wyatt sold his house, and some weeks later, he became a ghost. Not only did Wyatt go missing, but so did the tax money he'd collected from the circuses. The following March, the Barton County attorney filed for a judgment not only against Wyatt but also his three sureties, the men who'd pledged to back a $1,000 bond required the moment Wyatt took office. That $1,000 was payable if Wyatt failed to faithfully perform his duties, which, obviously, included remitting all tax monies he collected. This created quite the predicament for

The Hemmings, Cooper & Whitby Circus was one of two circuses to perform in Lamar in 1870. Wyatt, as Lamar constable, collected taxes from both shows but failed to turn the monies over to the county treasury. This advertisement is from the *South-West Missourian*, August 25, 1870. (PUBLIC DOMAIN IMAGE, AUTHOR'S COLLECTION)

the Earps, as one of the sureties was Wyatt's father, and another was Wyatt's uncle, Jonathan.

The county attorney offered up another revelation when he asserted in his filing that Nicholas Earp was preparing to skip town. He was right. Nicholas owed money he couldn't pay, and lawsuits against him were piling up. So, just like in Monmouth years before, he and his family packed up their things and hurriedly left Lamar, creditors be damned. Several months later, the sheriff sold their home at public auction. It was an inglorious exit for a man who was thought so highly of that, just a year earlier, he'd been charged with hand delivering to the Barton County Circuit Court a citizens petition requesting that the town of Lamar be incorporated.

To be generous, Wyatt Earp's fall from grace may have resulted from difficulty in coping with his wife's death. Yet the circuses' taxes had been collected before Arella died. Another possibility is that Wyatt gave the missing tax money to his debt-stricken father, intending to pay it back when he could. That is, until the death of his dear Arella changed everything. Whatever the circumstances, Wyatt did not leave Lamar with pocketfuls of cash. If he'd had money, one would like to think he would've spent it on a permanent headstone for Arella's grave. Even a simple stone would have signified that she once lived and was loved. But her grave in the town cemetery was forgotten, and Wyatt apparently erased her from his memory as well.

WYATT EARP DIDN'T HAVE ANY BUSINESS IN INDIAN TERRI-tory, and he certainly wasn't Cherokee. But if you were a white man looking to stay clear of certain legal proceedings against you, the Cherokee Nation was a good place to hide, and it was only a three days' ride from Lamar. That's where Wyatt headed, and that's also where he made the mistake of becoming a horse thief.

Particulars of what led up to the crime aren't known, but court documents disclose a good deal of the story. Somewhere near Fort Gibson, at the end of March 1871, Wyatt and two companions stole two horses valued at about a hundred dollars each. On April 1, an arrest warrant for Wyatt and one of his cohorts (the second was already in custody) was issued from the US Court for the Western District of Arkansas in Van Buren. Deputy US Marshal Jacob Owens put together a posse of four men and immediately started west into Indian Territory.

Although Wyatt would one day become adept at evading a posse, that day was a long way off. Marshal Owens easily apprehended the wanted men two hundred miles into the Cherokee Nation and presented them before the court in Van Buren less than two weeks later. They were arraigned on the thirteenth, and as bail was set at an out-of-reach $500 each, Wyatt and his accomplices were given free lodging in the federal jail. There they awaited their day in court. But, as days turned into weeks, Wyatt became less and less interested in leaving his fate to a jury. Some of the prisoners cooped up in the jailhouse with Wyatt didn't care to stick around, either. They devised a plan of escape.

Most jails in the western country were makeshift affairs—newspapers were filled with stories of one jailbreak after another. Even Constable Earp had three prisoners escape from him in Lamar when they climbed up through the collapsed roof of an abandoned building he was using as the town calaboose. And interestingly enough, escaping through the roof was the same plan he and his fellow inmates came up with in Van Buren. On May 3, 1871, then, Earp and six other prisoners housed on the jail's upper floor climbed through a hole in the ceiling rafters they'd made the day before. Passing through the crawl space beneath the roof, they made their way to the back of the building and pried enough stones from the wall to create a gap big enough for a man to squeeze through.

The prisoners had tied several blankets together to make a rope, and they dropped this out through the opening and climbed down twenty feet to the jail yard. A fence surrounded the yard, but the men easily scooped the dirt out from underneath it and gained their freedom. This all took place in broad daylight, and yet it was two to three hours before the lone guard realized his wards were missing. In a statement of the obvious, the *Van Buren Press* commented that, "it is apparent there was general carelessness on the part of the keepers of the jail, for if the guard had been on watch it would have been impossible for them to have made their escape."

The *Press* published the seven prisoners' names, which included one W. S. Earp, and described them as "all desperate characters" and "all bad men." Indeed, two of the escapees had been charged with murder. A posse started on the trail of the fugitives, but only one of the prisoners was later reported recaptured. Wyatt made a beeline for Indian Territory, just five miles distant, and it seems some of his jail mates accompanied him.

More than two decades later, Wyatt related to a Denver journalist an episode from his flight through the Cherokee Nation, although he cleverly set his tale during the Civil War to keep his shameful Van Buren trouble secret. Wyatt told the journalist that he and his companions were making their way north on horseback, traveling only at night, when they halted just south of Vinita, approximately 140 miles from Van Buren. Here they decided to split up. If a posse was on their trail—and they were convinced one was—there wouldn't be manhunters enough to chase each individual fugitive.

Wyatt slipped into Vinita alone and began looking in the darkness for stables or corrals. After several days of hard riding, his horse was completely played out. Wyatt needed another mount. He eventually came to a large corral that held a good number of mules. All were young except "one old fellow that was quiet and gentle." Wyatt saddled and bridled the old mule, climbed aboard, kicked his spurs into the animal's flanks, and galloped off into the darkness.

Two miles out of town, Wyatt pulled on the reins and halted, and that's when he heard them: horses coming up on his back trail. They were maybe a half mile away, but there was no mistaking that sound. It was either the feared posse or the mule's owner and friends giving chase. Wyatt guided the old mule off the road and into some nearby bushes. Fortunately, no moon hung in the sky, and the night was black as ink. Maybe his pursuers would ride past him in the darkness, he thought. Wyatt listened as the sound of hoofbeats grew closer and closer. His heart sank, though, as he guessed how many riders were in the party: perhaps as many as fifty! The riders stopped in the road opposite where Wyatt was hiding, and he thought he heard the low whispers of the men.

"I felt sure I had been discovered," Wyatt recalled, "and did not know exactly what to do. A few of the horsemen started in the direction of me, and then the old mule I was on made a noise. This was the signal for a charge, and the entire company started after me like a flash. I drove the spurs into my mule and went headlong into the darkness, determined to give them a race. Not a word was said and not a shot fired, but I felt that I was in a tight place, and prepared to sell my life dearly."

The chase continued into a patch of woods, which made the night even blacker. Limb after small limb slapped Wyatt's face as he blindly tried to flee, and while the going must have been just as difficult for the party following, they somehow seemed to be surrounding Wyatt. Wyatt abruptly halted and slid down from his mule. There was still a slight chance he could sneak away on foot. But just then Wyatt's mule brayed, and suddenly the woods erupted with a cacophony of braying.

"The whole company of supposed horsemen rushed rapidly in the direction of my mule," Wyatt remembered, "and I was soon surrounded by a gang of young mules. There was not a rider upon any of the animals! They were the mules I had left at the corral, and had followed their leader, which I had appropriated."

In his hurry to get out of Vinita with a stolen mule, Wyatt had neglected to shut the corral gate behind him. This tale may be a "Wyatt whopper," but how he got shed of all those mules, he never said.

WYATT EARP WAS PRETTY GOOD AT COVERING HIS TRACKS when it came to the more sordid parts of his past, or so he thought. Skipping over his shameful horse thief interlude, he told John Flood and Stuart Lake that he next got hired on with a surveying crew in Indian Territory. Then, beginning in the fall of 1871, he became a buffalo hunter on the Kansas plains. "[B]uyers of hides and meat were falling all over one another to pay cash to the hunter for every animal he could kill," he recalled. "My long jaunt through the Indian Nations had shown me the possibilities for a skillful buffalo hunter."

By his own account, Wyatt killed a slew of buffalo, making $2,500 the first winter and roughly the same amount for his winter of 1872–73 harvest, after which he quit the business.

Flood and Lake had no reason to question what Earp told them, and Earp may very well have spent time as a surveyor and a buffalo hunter— just not the *whole time*. Later historians, tediously sifting through city directories and newspaper back issues, tracked Wyatt to Peoria, Illinois, in 1872. As they discovered, Wyatt's older brother Virgil was living in

Peoria as early as 1870 and working a steady job as a bartender. It made sense, then, that Wyatt would go there, and it didn't hurt that it was a good six hundred miles from federal authorities in Arkansas. Wyatt brought along brother Morgan, making the reunion a real family affair.

A prosperous city of approximately twenty-three thousand people, Peoria fronted the slow-moving Illinois River. It was principally known for its several distilleries, producing more than five million gallons of whiskey annually. (Not surprisingly, Peoria acquired the moniker "Whiskey Capital of the World.") But Peoria was also known for something else: prostitutes. Understandably, prostitution wasn't something municipal leaders were especially proud of, and early in 1872, they determined to drive the bagnios ('ban-yōs) from the city, "root and branch." A January 13 report from Peoria published in the *Chicago Tribune* proclaimed that, "Chief of Police [Samuel] Gill 'has commenced pulling houses of ill fame, swooping down on two of them last night with his force, and arraigning the inmates in the Police Court this morning.'"

The following month, the press reported yet another raid by Chief Gill and his men, this time on the bagnio of Jane Haspel on Hamilton Street. Gill arrested three men. Two of the men arrested, the *Peoria Daily Transcript* tells us, were Wyatt and Morgan Earp. A police complaint filed on February 26, 1872, charged the Earp brothers with "keeping and being found at a house of ill-fame." Just how Wyatt fell into the sex trade isn't known, but according to the Peoria city directory for 1872–73, Wyatt was residing in the same dwelling as Madam Haspel, around the corner from her bagnio.

This part of Peoria, its Fourth Ward, is often referred to as the city's red-light district, but that's misleading. Yes, more than one brothel operated in that section of town, but a look at the 1870 US census reveals that also living within the Fourth Ward, side by side with the few brothels, were families with children, tradesmen, dressmakers, mechanics, schoolteachers, merchants, and more. The "social evil" was a part of the everyday life of Peoria (or, rather, nightlife), just as it was in numerous other cities and towns of that era. And while Chief Gill was doing his best to crack down on the houses of ill repute, their proprietors, their women, and their customers weren't going away easily. That included Wyatt, who seems to have become quite taken with the business.

Wyatt and Morgan were again arrested on May 9, 1872, this time at "that hotbed of iniquity, the McClellan Institute." They each received fines of $44.55. The *Transcript* reported that as the Earp brothers "had not the money and would not work, they languished in the cold and silent calaboose." Sometime after this arrest, Wyatt transferred his felonious activities to a river craft known locally as the "Beardstown gunboat," a floating house of ill fame. But even this singular enterprise, perhaps the true definition of a pleasure boat, could not escape the intrepid Chief Gill and his men. The officers raided the brothel on September 7, arresting seven men and six women.

"They were the quietest set of bawds and pimps [the police] ever handled," reported the Peoria *Daily National Democrat*, "they felt so cheap at their unexpected capture. . . . Some of the women are said to be good looking, but all appear to be terribly depraved." The captain of the boat and Wyatt Earp, whom the paper referred to derogatorily as "the Peoria bummer," were each fined $43.15. And there was more. Among the women arrested was one who gave her name as Sarah Earp. She said she was Wyatt's wife.

It's been suggested that Sarah was the eighteen-year-old daughter of Jane Haspel, which would explain Wyatt's living arrangements as revealed in the Peoria city directory. To date, however, no Illinois marriage record for Wyatt Earp has surfaced. Of course, Wyatt would have two more wives in his future, and marriage records don't exist for them, either. As an old resident of the Arizona mining town of Tombstone in the early 1880s explained, "People very seldom got married there. They simply lived together like man and wife. This was the common practice or custom. The man would call her his wife, and she would be called Mrs. so and so."

Wyatt's Peoria sojourn lasted maybe a year. His name didn't appear again in the Peoria papers after his September arrest, nor was he listed in the next city directory. By the summer of 1873, he'd drifted west—with his "wife." They landed in Kansas, where no one knew a federal warrant existed for Wyatt, where no one recognized him as the Peoria bummer. And that's just the way twenty-five-year-old Wyatt Earp wanted it.

————

THAT SAME SUMMER, JOHN HENRY HOLLIDAY STRUCK UP A partnership with Dallas dentist John A. Seegar, a fellow Georgia native who'd been recommended by an Atlanta colleague. Seegar, John Henry's senior by twenty years, had a well-established practice in this booming city of eight thousand, but the addition of a bright young partner gave the firm a leg up on the competition. That October, Seegar & Holliday entered their work at the annual fair of the North Texas Agricultural, Mechanical, and Blood Stock Association, and the judges were duly impressed. They recognized Seegar & Holliday with best set of teeth in gold, best set of teeth on vulcanized rubber, and best display of artificial teeth and dental ware. John Henry Holliday, just twenty-two years old, was an award-winning dentist!

Unfortunately, John Henry was becoming increasingly obsessed with another kind of winning, the kind that took place at a card table. Dallas was "a typical frontier town in everything the term implied," observed Bat Masterson, and gambling was "the principle and best paying industry of the town at the time." Early on, Holliday had done his utmost to resist the temptation of Dallas's saloons and gambling establishments, of which the town was overly blessed. "I attended the Methodist Church regularly," Holliday would say later. "I was a member of the Methodist Church there and also a prominent member of a temperance organization." That lasted, he added solemnly, "till I deviated from the path of rectitude."

According to Masterson, the "hectic Georgian had always shown a fondness for all things in which the elements of chance played an important part." The allure of those gambling halls, then, was simply too much for John Henry to withstand. It was all he thought about. "In a short time, those who wished to consult professionally with the doctor," wrote Masterson, "had to do so over a card table in some nearby gambling establishment, or not at all." It was in the gambling dens and saloons of

Dallas and nearby Fort Worth that the young dentist became known simply as Doc or Doc Holliday.

How much, if any, a notion of fatalism played a role in Doc's descent at this time, cursed as he was with the disease slowly but surely killing him, one can only speculate. Regardless, young men and living fast have been boon companions since time immemorial. Doc's nighttime habits, however, quickly became too much for Dr. Seegar. A notice in the March 6, 1874, issue of the *Dallas Daily Commercial* stated that, "Upon mutual consent, the firm of Seegar & Holliday have dissolved." The notice went on to inform readers that Seegar would continue in the old location, while Holliday would see patients in an office over the Dallas County Bank.

A month later, the Dallas police force conducted one of its periodic sweeps of the gambling district and arrested several men, one of whom was Holliday. He was charged with "betting at a Keno Bank." This arrest, the first on record for John Henry Holliday, marked the beginning of a restless life in one western town after another, consistently running afoul of the law, and, more often than not, running afoul of other humans. Doc didn't completely give up on dentistry, not right away, but gambling became his passion until, eventually, he did nothing else.

Holliday's name didn't appear in the Dallas papers following his arrest, but it's the kind of thing that got around. Soon thereafter, Doc packed his bags and moved seventy-five miles north to Denison, a rowdy town at the end of the tracks of the Kansas and Texas Railroad, and put out his dentist sign. Doc couldn't complain about Denison's nightlife, but business at his office was less than brisk (two dentists already served the community), and then the Panic of 1873 killed one of the town's major employers. Doc returned to Dallas—and its saloons. On New Year's Eve 1874, he was celebrating in Dallas's St. Charles Saloon when he and the saloonkeeper got into some kind of spat. Before the saloon's patrons knew what was happening, the two men suddenly pulled their revolvers and began blazing away at each other.

No doubt inebriated, both men fortunately missed their targets. The *Dallas Weekly Herald* made light of the affair, writing, "The cheerful note of the peaceful six-shooter is heard once more among us." Doc Holliday's first gunfight, interestingly enough, was something of a joke. Both men were arrested, however, and Doc was later charged with assault with intent to murder. He appeared before a judge and jury on January 25, 1875, and was acquitted, another indication that the dustup wasn't taken too seriously.

A few short months later, Doc had abandoned Dallas for Fort Griffin, a little Gomorrah of a thousand souls near the legendary Llano Estacado (Staked Plains). The lively town was mostly saloons and dance halls that catered to soldiers from the nearby military post of the same name. Throw in hordes of cowpunchers, buffalo skinners, freighters, and those running from the law, and you have the perfect storm of opportunity for card sharks and prostitutes.

Money flowed freely, and Doc surely got some of it, or at least tried. We know this because he was arrested twice in the span of a week for breaking an odd anti-gambling law that forbid the playing of cards in an establishment that sold liquor. In other words, a saloon. A grand jury indicted Doc and his fellow gamblers, but Doc didn't stick around for his trial and the paltry fine from the inevitable guilty verdict. Instead, he jumped on a westbound stage, which generated yet another arrest warrant. Catching the scofflaw dentist, however, was another matter, and it doesn't appear that anyone made much of an effort.

———

DOC'S HUNGER FOR THE EXCITEMENT OF THE GAMBLING DENS took him to Denver, Colorado Territory. And the territorial capital (soon to be state capital), with its booming population of twenty-two thousand, was a considerable improvement over Texas. Eight hundred buildings had gone up in Denver the previous year alone. A gasworks lighted the city at night, and the capital boasted a modern water system as well. Several railroads serviced Denver, and residents kept well abreast of national and local news through four daily and six weekly papers. A letter writer described the city in June 1875 as "beautiful, progressive, cosmopolitan, and rich." Rich indeed. Gold and silver shipped express in 1874 amounted to

$1,250,000, and gold received at the branch of the United States Mint was nearly as much.

As progressive as Denver might have been, though, it was also home to the usual undesirable elements, at least as far as city leaders were concerned. "[I]t is almost impossible," an exasperated mayor admitted to Denver's aldermen, "to rid the city of the many gamblers and lewd women in the city." Of course, the mayor's predicament suited Doc, not yet twenty-four, just fine.

Denver boasted no less than nine dentists in 1875, so Doc didn't make an effort to open an office. However, he'd become so skilled at the various games of chance—faro, poker, keno, monte, and the like—that he quickly found employment as a dealer at a "beer hall" on Blake Street called the Canterbury. The Canterbury's proprietor, thirty-eight-year-old John A. Babb, was frequently in court or before the city council answering to violations of one city ordinance or another, including one that prohibited women from being employed as "waiter girls." At one point, the Canterbury's liquor license was revoked, but Babb kept the doors open.

In an editorial bemoaning Denver's "nether side of Western social life," the *Rocky Mountain News* described a typical saloon and dance hall that may very well have been the Canterbury. Whether it was that particular establishment or not, the *News*'s description gives us the sights and sounds that made up Doc Holliday's world:

> *Imagine, if you can, a long, low room, fairly lighted, but by no means il-*
> *luminated, with bare walls and floor and ceiling; chairs and tables ranged*
> *along the walls . . . the chairs and tables crowded with bummers of both*
> *sexes, smoking, drinking, playing cards, and talking all at once and at the*
> *top of their voices; the women no longer young, no longer fair; the men as*
> *various in their appearance as the leaves of a forest; rugged miners from the*
> *mountains rejoicing in their brawny strength; dapper clerks from Larimer*
> *street in shiny hats and faultless linen; long-limbed ranchmen and cattle*
> *boys, hearty and generous to a fault; gamblers high and low degree; young*
> *boys taking their first lessons in lewdness; a noisy but insufficient orchestra*
> *hard at work in one corner adding to the general confusion; waiters calling;*

chairs shuffling; drunken men shouting; women's voices joining in; coming and going feet, and rattle and chink of glasses, and all the noises of the noisy street blending together in one deep, deafening din, and you can have some faint idea of a Denver concert room.

A Denver "sporting man" who claimed to have known Holliday while he was in Denver said that Doc didn't go by his own name but used an alias: Tom Mackey. Maybe. Why Doc would feel the need to use an alias when some seven hundred miles from Fort Griffin is rather puzzling. This same source also said that Doc nearly killed a fellow gambler named Bud Ryan when he took a knife to Ryan's neck, but no such knife attack was reported in the Denver newspapers, which were very good about reporting violent incidents at the notorious Canterbury. Neither the names Tom Mackey nor Bud Ryan make an appearance in the available Denver newspapers during this period, either. In a drunken rage, Doc was quite capable of shooting or stabbing someone, but the existing evidence suggests he stayed out of trouble the short time he was in the Colorado capital.

Additional Doc Holliday lore has him leaving Denver and going to Cheyenne, Wyoming Territory, a distance of only a hundred miles. Gambling was legal in Wyoming, so long as one purchased a gambling license, and Cheyenne was a bustling jumping-off point for miners and freight destined for the Black Hills gold fields. Interestingly enough, John Babb, his Canterbury having gone bankrupt, did turn up in Cheyenne during the winter of 1875, where he formed a partnership in a theater called the Bella Union. It's possible Doc was in Cheyenne, too, but there's no evidence to support his presence, and he didn't mention Cheyenne in later interviews.

Where Doc was during the year 1876 is anyone's guess, and a great many have, but a family account has him briefly visiting his aunt and her family near Louisville, Kansas, where her husband was a Methodist preacher. After that, Doc's movements are unknown until early January 1877. That's when the Dallas police force surprised him and several other knights of the green cloth and placed them under arrest. Doc was charged with not one, but three counts of gambling. "The recent enforcement of the law in this city relative to gambling has been a staggerer to many," reported the *Dallas Daily Herald* that same month. Doc apparently wasn't among those "staggered," though, for he was back at the gambling tables a short time later. Until he got shot.

Details of what led up to the shooting are frustratingly few, but according to a newspaper report, it occurred on June 30 in the town of Breckenridge, Texas, not far from Fort Griffin. Doc walked into a saloon owned by a young man named Henry Kahn and suddenly began beating the hell out of him with a cane. Bystanders separated the two and Doc was arrested, taken away, and fined. Doc paid the fine, after which he made a beeline back to Kahn's saloon, intent on taking up where he'd left off. Kahn, one caning having been enough, yelled several times at Doc to stop, but Doc wasn't having it. Finally, Kahn grabbed a pistol from a saloon patron and fired one shot at Holliday, seriously wounding him. That ended the trouble.

It seems that some onlookers believed Doc's wound was fatal, for the first reports of the shooting to come out of Breckenridge stated that Kahn had killed Holliday. Doc would survive, of course, but he did require time to heal. Somehow, news of the shooting got to Doc's family in Georgia, and a cousin, thirty-year-old grocer George Henry Holliday, traveled to Texas to help care for Doc. George is said to have pleaded with his cousin to come back to Georgia, but Doc was too embarrassed by the shooting, and he certainly didn't want to face myriad questions from relatives and friends about his "career" in the West.

A Texas acquaintance of Doc's recalled that "he was not one who let poor luck get him down and keep him there." Sure enough, by mid-September 1877 Doc had recovered enough to get arrested again in Dallas for gambling. From there it was back to Fort Griffin, where he took a fancy to a petite, 116-pound prostitute with the unflattering moniker Big Nose Kate. Big Nose Kate was only one of her names, however, and she'd bounced from place to place in the West as frequently as Doc. But, also like Doc, she left enough of a paper trail, including her own reminiscences, that we can piece together a good deal of her story.

She'd been born Mária Izabella Magdolna Horony twenty-eight years earlier in Hungary and had moved with her family to the United States in 1860. By 1862, they'd settled in Davenport, Iowa. Three years later, however, her mother and father, a physician, died just seven weeks apart. The children were farmed out, and administrators mismanaged the doctor's estate. Sometime after her eighteenth birthday, Mária, now Mary, left Iowa and never looked back.

At some point, young Mary turned to the social evil to survive. She was using the name Kate Fisher in 1870, when she's found in the US census for St. Louis, Missouri, as living at a brothel operated by a twenty-four-year-old Mollie Hays. The census taker wrote down the occupation of Mollie, Kate, and six other women living in the residence as "whore." In 1874, Kate's surname of choice was Elder. Kate Elder was arrested for prostitution in Wichita, Kansas, in June of that year, and, later that summer, arrested and fined for assault and battery a hundred miles northwest in Great Bend, Kansas. Clearly, getting crossways with the law didn't stop Kate from doing what she wanted to do, something else she shared in common with Holliday.

By the summer of 1875, Kate was working out of Tom Sherman's saloon in Dodge City, doing her best to please Texas cowboys, buffalo hunters, and soldiers. She's one of seven women listed in that year's state census as residing at the saloon. The census taker neglected to record an occupation for these women, but as they're all single and in their twenties, it's not difficult to figure out. Kate's adventures the following two years until meeting Doc in Fort Griffin are unknown. Also unknown is exactly when and how Kate acquired the nickname "Big Nose."

Writers have suggested Kate's nickname came from the obvious: She had a prominent sniffer. But a photograph that's believed to picture Kate in later life doesn't show an unusually large nose. Another theory has it that Kate had trouble minding her own business—she "nosed" into other folks' affairs. The most intriguing explanation, though, is that "Big Nose" is a frontier corruption of the Italian word for brothel: *bagnio*. Bagnio Kate became Big Nose Kate, a playful twist that was probably employed to earn Kate's ire. Whether the nickname was deserved or not, it stuck. Not only that, it became iconic.

MANY GAMBLERS HAD "WIVES" OR CONCUBINES AS SIGNIFI-cant others. Unfortunately, it tended to be an unequal relationship—the money made by the women through romps in bed with cowboys and others invariably went to her gambler lover during stretches of poor luck at the tables. Or, in what may have been the case with Wyatt in Peoria, they simply freeloaded off the woman and did nothing else but offer a little protection.

Kate's recollections, given more than fifty years later, are often untrustworthy. But when it came to Doc, she retained a distinct picture of her on-again, off-again lover. She said he was a consistently sharp dresser, stood six feet tall, and had a fair complexion. And with blond hair, blue-gray eyes, a "very pretty mustache," and a "fine set of teeth," he was "considered a handsome man." As for his character, Kate recalled that Doc was "a gentleman in manners to the ladies and to everyone. Being quiet, he never hunted for trouble. If he was crowded, he knew how to take care of himself. . . . He was not a drunkard. He always had a bottle of whiskey but never drank habitually."

Maybe Kate was being charitable when it came to the "trouble" part, for Henry Kahn, the man Doc bloodied with a cane, saw a very different side of the dentist. And others remembered Doc's drinking quite differently as well. Bat Masterson recalled Doc as having "a mean disposition and ungovernable temper, and under the influence of liquor was a most dangerous man. . . . He was hot-headed and impetuous and very much given to both drinking and quarreling, and, among men who did not fear him, was very much disliked." Doc's drinking can partly be ascribed to his disease—the tonics, cure-alls, and elixirs of the time were loaded with alcohol. But regardless of what drove Doc to drink, it was a problem, a problem that only made bad situations worse.

One day in the fall of 1877, a tall, muscular man of about 160 pounds walked into the Fort Griffin saloon of John Shannsey. The man was, essentially, a bounty hunter, having been hired by the Atchison, Topeka & Santa Fe Railway to track down a couple of outlaws who'd been robbing construction camps near Dodge City, Kansas. The bounty hunter knew Shannsey, and the two stepped into the saloon owner's side-room office, from where he had a good view of the activity at the bar, gambling tables, and dance hall. After a little small talk, Shannsey informed the bounty hunter that the two scamps he was after had left Fort Griffin some time ago. The bounty hunter then asked if anyone knew where the two outlaws might have gone.

"Your best bet in this camp," Shannsey replied, "is Doc Holliday. Know him?"

In a loud voice, Shannsey called over to a group a few tables away, and Doc Holliday stood up and walked to where Shannsey and the bounty hunter were sitting. Shannsey and the bounty hunter got up out of their chairs, and Shannsey started to introduce the men when Doc began coughing uncontrollably. Once the coughing fit subsided, the bounty hunter held out his hand again and Shannsey spoke the man's name a second time: Wyatt Earp.

THREE

IN THE GODLESS HOLES

It has been custom . . . for cattle towns to employ as patrols men as desperate, and even more so, than those they watched.

LEAVENWORTH DAILY COMMERCIAL, JUNE 20, 1875

Main Street, Wichita, Kansas
May 27, 1874

A bout 2 P.M., a large crowd of Texas cowboys began milling about in front of a two-story brick building under construction, the future home of J. H. Miller's tobacco store. The stout hod carrier assisting the masons at work on the walls was one of Wichita's well-known Black residents, Charley Sanders. Charley was climbing a ladder, a small stack of bricks in the wooden hod on his back, when one of the cowboys, a Texan known as Shorty Ramsey, approached the ladder and suddenly jerked his revolver from its holster. Ramsey fired two quick shots at Sanders and watched as the Black man stiffened and fell, his bricks scattering upon the ground.

At least a dozen cowboys drew their revolvers and stood guard as the shooter jumped on a white horse and galloped off. Ramsey turned west on Douglas Avenue and raced toward the bridge over the Arkansas River, two and a half blocks away. His companions ran after him, intent on preventing anyone, including the law, from giving chase. As Ramsey galloped over the bridge, he swung his revolver in the air and shouted a whoop to his friends. He continued his flight across the prairie, his horse creating a thin, yellow dust cloud that followed him until eventually fading into the sky.

When Sanders was shot, Wyatt Earp was on Douglas Avenue, and he'd heard the gunfire. A moment later, he watched as the white horse with the shooter galloped by and across the bridge, followed by the mob of Texans on foot. Wyatt had had some trouble with these same cowboys earlier in the day, and he assumed they were coming after him. He quickly stepped into the door of a livery stable and prepared to defend himself. After a few minutes passed, however, the town marshal, William Smith, appeared in front of the livery, where he had a good view of the mob of cowboys congregated at the bridge. Wyatt cautioned Smith that he was likely to get hit if the cowboys discovered his hiding spot. "They're not after you," he said to Wyatt, and he explained the shooting back on Main Street.

Wyatt was only a bystander, but he immediately urged the marshal to go after Ramsey and arrest him. Wyatt even volunteered to lend a hand. Perhaps it was the thrill of it all, to tempt fate, so to speak, but jumping in headfirst was nothing new to Wyatt. Just a year earlier, again as a private citizen, he helped bring about the surrender of gunman Ben Thompson in Ellsworth, Kansas, following the killing of Sheriff Chauncey Whitney by Thompson's brother. Wyatt now offered to Smith that they could arrest the whole party at the bridge. But the marshal wasn't about to ride through the gauntlet of Ramsey's friends, most of them armed, nor attempt to arrest any of them. They now numbered more than two hundred men! No, someone else would have to take up Ramsey's trail.

The wounded Charley Sanders held on a day and a half before death finally ended his misery. His heinous murder had been the result of a grudge. Some days before the shooting, Sanders and Ramsey had gotten into a fight and both had been arrested. One account, related years later, said that the fight started because Sanders found two of the cowboys at his home harassing his wife, and the muscular hod carrier had gotten the better of the two Texans.

Many in Wichita, as well as a number of nearby communities, were outraged by the murder. The *Wichita Eagle* commented that, "Drunken roughs, thieves and confidence men might indulge in the periodical pastime of sending each other, disappointed and unaneled, to their eternal reckoning without disturbing, perceptibly, the sentiment that sustains and enforces law, but when a man who earns his bread by honest work is shot down in broad daylight upon our principal thoroughfare, be he black or white, the result is widely different."

The *Eagle* called for the mayor to reorganize Wichita's police force and to strictly enforce the city's laws, "else our streets will flow in blood before the ides of November."

And so it was that Wyatt Earp was called before the mayor. Marshal Smith, impressed with Wyatt's boldness, or, rather, foolhardiness, in wanting to chase after Sanders's killer, had told the mayor that he wanted Wyatt on the force, and the mayor ordered Smith to bring Wyatt to his office. Upon getting a good look at Wyatt, though, the mayor was slightly hesitant. He had a rather odd theory that small men were harder to hit with a bullet, and Wyatt was hardly small. Nevertheless, the mayor did offer Wyatt an appointment to the police force, which was accepted. After being handed his badge, Wyatt was instructed to go to the hardware store and select a gun.

As Wyatt remembered it, when he returned from the hardware store, the mayor "noticed that I had only one gun. He said that he was very particular that all of his officers carry two guns, for which I was really glad, so I went back to the store and armed myself accordingly and became a full-fledged policeman."

THERE WAS GOOD REASON FOR TWENTY-SIX-YEAR-OLD WYATT Earp to be in Wichita at the time of the Sanders murder: The town was hopping. Its population numbered only three thousand, but that number exploded during the cattle season, late spring through fall, when scores of dust-caked Texas drovers arrived with immense herds of longhorns. For the months of May through November 1874, longhorns delivered to

Main Street, Wichita, Kansas, mid-1870s.
(COURTESY WICHITA-SEDGWICK COUNTY HISTORICAL MUSEUM)

the stockyards numbered 48,137. These were loaded onto 2,352 cattle cars and shipped off over the Wichita branch of the Atchison, Topeka & Santa Fe Railway. The trail drivers, their job completed, were paid off on the spot, and the town was ready for them—well, at least the saloons and brothels.

"Wichita is a godless hole," wrote a visiting journalist, "drunkenness, prostitution and gambling thrive there. Gambling hells and dance houses are as open as dry goods stores or hotels, and alike invite the passer to patronize." Another reporter observed that, "Every other door opened into a saloon. The first thing heard in the morning and the last at night was that unceasing music at the saloons and gambling houses. The town was headquarters for harlots for two hundred miles around." In other words, Wyatt's kind of town.

It was also the kind of town for Wyatt's brothers. Jim and Virgil were both in Wichita in 1874, and Morgan appears in city records the following year, arrested during a police raid on Madam Ida May's brothel. The Earp women show up in Wichita city records as well—as prostitutes. Bessie Earp, Jim's wife of a year, and Wyatt's wife Sarah, who was now going by

Sallie, were both fined in police court that May, and they were hardly alone. The following month, the *Wichita Weekly Beacon* reported matter-of-factly that thirty "soiled doves" pleaded guilty in police court to being residents of houses of ill repute and paid their fines. Bessie and Sallie faced the court again at the same time, but with a new charge: "Set up and keep a bawdy house or brothel and did appear and act as Mistresses." The bawdy house was on Douglas Avenue, near the river, and but a few steps from the livery where Wyatt had taken cover after the shooting of the hod carrier.

Over the next several months, Bessie and Sallie became familiar faces at Wichita's police court. Like other boomtowns in the West, fines for prostitution served as pseudotaxes that, ironically, funded the city government and its police force. Roughly once a month, offenders were brought before the court and made to pay a nominal fine, and then they went back to work, unimpeded by the constables until the next month.

Kate Elder—Big Nose Kate—made regular monetary contributions to the town of Wichita, too, and, intriguingly, her name was also recorded in police records as "Kate Earb." She must have worked for a time in the Earp brothel, which helps explain why Wyatt, when interviewed in later years, seemed to know quite a lot about the famed prostitute.

Despite the strong objections of some townsfolk to the sex trade, the "harlots" were a considerable attraction for cowtowns competing with one another for the lucrative cattle business—those Texas drovers didn't blow all their money on women and booze. There were saddlemakers, gun dealers, boot makers, clothing dealers, restaurants, hotels, and others who saw their profits spike during the cattle season. Everyone was making money. Wichita, the godless hole, was prospering. Life was good.

THAT FOUR EARP BROTHERS WOULD END UP IN WICHITA AT THE same time was perfectly in keeping with this tight-knit brood, who, no matter the distance separating them at various times, inevitably navigated their way back to one another. Jim, age thirty-three, worked as a bartender in Dagner's saloon while wife Bessie plied her trade at the brothel.

Jim Earp. Artwork by John McCormack. (ORIGINAL SCRATCHBOARD IN AUTHOR'S COLLECTION)

It's uncertain what Virgil, thirty-one, was doing, but years later, he recalled serving on Wichita's "special police force," a volunteer squad of some forty citizens organized by Marshal Smith shortly after the hod carrier's murder. Wyatt's police duty in 1874 seems to have consisted only of a few months' service as an "extra policeman." However, on April 21, 1875, Wyatt was appointed full time to the small force at $60 a month. And, interestingly, prostitutes with the last name Earp suddenly stopped receiving fines.

Many stories exist pertaining to Wyatt's time as a Wichita peace officer, mostly told by folks other than Wyatt. Jimmy Cairns, who was appointed a policeman at the same time as Wyatt, recalled that rowdy cowboys twice threatened to take over the town, or at least its business district, and that each time, Wyatt played a prominent part in forcing the punchers to back down. "Wyatt was a well-built man, about six feet tall and blond," remembered Cairns. "There wasn't a bad man in the whole West that he was afraid of and some of them came pretty mean. He was always cool and collected in the face of danger and never let a threat of any kind bother him."

During the cattle season, the officers were sometimes on duty twenty-four hours straight, recalled Cairns, "especially when things were pretty hot and we never knew at what minute hell might break loose from the element that caused plenty of trouble in those days." Wyatt and Cairns would try to get some shut-eye on the benches lining the boardwalks. "After a few hours, the one on guard would wake the other and snatch a couple of hours sleep himself on the hard wooden bench. And this would be after having spent the day at work. At times we went for several days at a stretch with this our only rest."

A city ordinance prohibited guns in town, but this law was routinely ignored by the Texans, adding an element of danger to any attempt at an arrest or discipline. But keeping the peace in Wichita could also be downright comical, like the time in September 1875, when "a soiled dove got her guzzle full of whisky . . . and with a fast team drove single handed up and down Main Street, swearing and howling like a wolf." A policeman, perhaps Wyatt, was finally able to get the joyriding woman stopped, and she was hauled off to jail and charged with loose and lascivious behavior.

From time to time, Wyatt's performance of his duties earned a mention in Wichita's two newspapers. On December 8, Wyatt found a drunk passed out near the Arkansas River bridge. He shook the stranger awake and walked him to the jail, where he searched the man and found a thick roll of greenbacks amounting to $500. Wyatt secured the man's money, which was returned to him the next morning after he'd faced the police judge and paid a fine for drunkenness. The *Wichita Weekly Beacon* boasted that "there are but few other places where that $500 roll would ever been heard from. The integrity of our police force has never been seriously questioned."

Another newspaper mention recorded the only instance of Wyatt Earp shooting at himself. On a Sunday night in early January 1876, Wyatt was sitting with two or three others in the back of the Custom House saloon when his revolver slipped out of its holster. As the heavy gun fell, the revolver's hammer, which was resting on a live cartridge, struck the chair, and the gun discharged. Flame and black powder smoke spewed out of the revolver's muzzle. The lead bullet punched a perfect hole in Wyatt's coat before ricocheting off the wall and passing through the ceiling. Ears ringing, the men with Wyatt scattered, fearing an assassin had fired at them through the window. The *Beacon* called it a narrow escape. Indeed, someone could have been killed, if not seriously wounded.

The incident was also an embarrassing amateur mistake, one that presumably Wyatt didn't make again. Experienced gun handlers knew to rest the hammer of a revolver on an empty chamber, not a live cartridge. Wyatt, years later, would come down hard on others who made similar mistakes with gun safety: "[I]t was only with tyros and would-bes that you heard of accidental discharges or didn't-know-it-was-loaded injuries in the country where carrying a Colt's was a man's prerogative."

WYATT EARP'S CAREER AS A WICHITA POLICEMAN ENDED WITH an assault. It was early April 1876, election time, and the man running for city marshal against Wyatt's current boss said some things involving Wyatt's brothers that did not sit well with the steely-nerved officer. With "fight on the brain," reported the *Beacon*, Wyatt attacked the challenger and was promptly arrested. He received a fine the next day in the amount of $30 and cost, more than half his monthly pay, and was relieved from the police force. "The good order of the city was properly vindicated in the fining and dismissal of Earp," commented the *Beacon*. "It is but justice to Earp to say he has made an excellent officer."

Following the election, a new city council deliberated rehiring Wyatt but ultimately failed to do so. In a way, the council did Wyatt a favor. Wichita's days as a major shipping point for Texas cattle were numbered, due to both the settling of the surrounding country and the shifting west of the "Dead Line." To prevent Texas herds from infecting local cattle with the tick-borne "Spanish Fever," the Kansas Legislature had created a quarantine line that Texas cattle were prohibited from crossing during the warm months. No herds meant no boisterous cowpunchers flooding Wichita's business district.

Also winding down were the town's bagnios. A month after Wyatt's dismissal, the city council passed an ordinance for the "suppression of houses of 'plain sewing.'" Madam Ida May didn't wait around for the city to close her doors. She and her "troupe of demi-mondes" departed for Dodge City, where new-built stockyards awaited the Texas herds—more than two hundred thousand longhorns—that were already snaking their way north.

Dodge City, with a population of just over a thousand, had seen its fair share of rough characters as a rendezvous and shipping point for the buffalo hide trade. Soldiers from Fort Dodge, just five miles away, had also contributed to making the young town a lively place. A journalist who visited Dodge in March 1876, proclaimed that, "Of all the devilish holes on the frontier, Dodge City is the worst. . . . Scarcely a house stands in the town that doesn't have its historic bullet hole in it, and twenty-one distinguished *gentlemen* are buried there who died with their boots on." Another correspondent wrote of the buildings along Front Street, the main business district and facing the railroad tracks, that they "lurch to the west, as if impatient to move on, the effects of the prairie wind."

Wind-blown buildings or not, the remote Ford County seat was about to become the new headquarters for the Texas cattle trade, and city leaders knew it be would be unlike anything the town had ever experienced. At the very least, they would need to add a man or two to their small police force. One of the town's founders later explained that when it came to policing Dodge City, they had to "fight the devil with fire, and, if we put in a tenderfoot for marshal, [the cowboys] would run him out of town. We had to put in men who were good shots and would sure go to the front whenever they were called on." What better man to call upon, then, than a former law officer who'd kept the cowboys and rowdies in line in Wichita?

Dodge City's mayor, apparently learning of Wyatt's availability, immediately wrote Wyatt offering him a position on the town's force, and at a higher salary. Several friends in Dodge also wrote Wyatt, encouraging him to accept the mayor's offer. Wyatt didn't have to think too hard about it. Enforcing the law was something he knew how to do and, at least in the last couple of years, was good at. On May 24, 1876, the *Beacon* published one more news item relating to its fired lawman: "Wyatt Earp has been put on the police force at Dodge City."

––––––––––

WYATT ARRIVED IN DODGE ON MAY 17—ALONE. SALLIE EARP was not with him. In fact, they may have separated some months prior.

Wyatt accepted the appointment of assistant city marshal that afternoon and began work the following day. His superior was thirty-one-year-old Marshal Larry Deger, a rotund man weighing more than three hundred pounds. Deger would eventually top out at 375 and be labeled by one newspaper the fattest man in the West. Fortunately, the marshal was as strong as he was heavy, although he wouldn't win any footraces. He could certainly see the advantages of having a man under him as slim and agile as Wyatt.

Surprisingly, Wyatt's first public notice as a Dodge City peace officer didn't come from running a gang of cowboys out of town, catching a horse thief, or a gunfight. Instead, it was an arrest made by him and Deger at a raucous meeting of the town's Republicans. The purpose of the meeting was to elect delegates to attend statewide conventions in Topeka, Wichita, and Great Bend. One particular attendee, reported the *Dodge City Times*, became "too enthusiastic," drawing the attention of Earp and Deger. As the officers attempted to arrest the man, he "doubled himself up on the ground and gave vent to the most violent contortions, but the muscular marshals were equal to the emergency, and the uncompromising prisoner was dragged to the calaboose on his back, with his shirt pulled over his head, exposing his person to the vulgar gaze of the populace, giving him the appearance of a partly skinned jack rabbit."

Wyatt did, of course, have to deal with the usual lawlessness of a cow town. There were three dance halls and several saloons in Dodge that summer, and, like in Wichita, carousing cowpunchers flush with greenbacks immersed themselves in drinking, gambling, and whoring—and ignoring the ordinance forbidding the carrying of guns and bowie knives in town. Just how well Wyatt and Deger maintained the peace that season is revealed in a letter to an Atchison, Kansas, newspaper, dated November 2, 1876:

> *Dodge has had the benefit of being under a good City Marshal, Larry Deger by name, who has with the aid of Wyatt Earp managed the wild and woolly gentlemen, who talk about being wolves and hard to curry, discreetly, firmly, and humanly; consequently we have no deaths to record from the*

*gay, and festive revolver in the hands of whisky, in fact I think there has
never been a shooting scrape even.*

By the time this high praise appeared in print, if not slightly before,
Wyatt had resigned his post and left town. As he explained later, the cattle season was over, and "all the cattlemen and gamblers had left so that
a two-year-old child could have controlled the situation." The town didn't
need Wyatt, not at present, so he purchased a covered wagon and a stout
team of horses to pull it and, with brother Morgan at his side, headed
north. More than six hundred miles north.

Word of mouth and newspaper reports from late in the summer told
of incredible amounts of gold being mined in the Black Hills. One claim
yielded $2,000 in gold in twenty-four hours. Fifty claims along a creek
paid $100 to $2,000 per day. An estimated ten thousand men, mostly miners, populated the Hills, and the town of Deadwood already boasted
thirty saloons. Houses were springing up everywhere.

When Wyatt drove his team into Deadwood, it was easy to see that
all the good mining claims had been taken up long ago. But he didn't
necessarily come here to dig in the dirt. He did come here to see for himself what all the excitement was about, to take in this booming gold rush
town with its writhing mass of hopefuls, where the constant sound of
hammers mixed with saloon music and sporadic gunfire. "There is not an
hour of the day or night, we might say, but what someone is out with his
gun or revolver firing away at rocks, trees, and other marks which best
suit his taste," complained the editor of Deadwood's *Black Hills Pioneer*.
"It is not alone the case that they do shooting on the back streets, but
there is scarcely a day passes but someone can be seen banging away from
the door of some of our business houses. This should be stopped."

Like the other boomtowns Wyatt had lived in, there was money to be
made off those who'd recently come into money, be they Texas cowpunchers or lucky gold miners. Wyatt had a wagon and a good team. He
struck upon the idea of selling firewood to the folks in town, and he had
plenty of takers. Wyatt hauled into Deadwood four to five loads a day,
two cords to each load. After paying the man who owned the wood and

a helper, Wyatt cleared nearly eighty dollars a day, sometimes considerably more. "I didn't gamble much that winter," Wyatt recalled. "I delivered wood seven days a week and when night came I wanted to sleep. But I was young and tough, so were my horses, and we came through to spring in fine shape physically, with a profit of about five thousand dollars."

With the warm weather, Wyatt decided it was time to move on. Years later, the editor of the *Pioneer* recalled that the wood hauler from Dodge "was very quiet and tame while here and never had any trouble." Morgan Earp hadn't remained in Deadwood through the winter like his brother, but he was apparently in town long enough for the editor to form a rather poor opinion of the younger sibling. Fair or not, the editor characterized Morgan as "a worthless sort of fellow."

As Wyatt was about to leave Deadwood, he was presented with a job offer by the agent for the Cheyenne & Black Hills Stage & Express Co. It seemed as though every other stagecoach on the road between Deadwood and Cheyenne was being held up by bandits—it didn't take a genius to figure out that any stagecoach leaving the Black Hills had a good chance of transporting gold, including on the passengers themselves. The agent asked Wyatt if he would ride shotgun for a particularly large shipment of the yellow metal. Wyatt agreed; it would be a new experience, he'd get a little pay, and free passage to boot. Fortunately, Wyatt didn't have to use the shotgun on the bumpy, three-hundred-mile trip. After spending some time exploring Cheyenne, he started south.

The July 7, 1877, issue of the *Dodge City Times* reported that Wyatt was again in town. The newspaper stated that it wanted Wyatt back on the police force, and it didn't hold back in its praise of the former deputy marshal: "He had a quiet way of taking the most desperate characters into custody, which invariably gave one the impression that the city was able to enforce her mandates and preserve her dignity. It wasn't considered policy to draw a gun on Wyatt unless you got the drop and meant to burn powder without any preliminary talk." That "quiet way" was often a debilitating knock on the head with the big barrel of his revolver.

Despite this fawning, Wyatt wasn't ready to rejoin the force just yet. He did earn another mention in the newspaper later that month, for a run-in with a Black prostitute by the name of Frankie Bell. The muscular, twenty-two-year-old Miss Bell had quite an arrest record, especially in Leavenworth, Kansas, where she'd been part of an all-Black brothel. In one particularly notable appearance before Leavenworth's police judge, the charges against her included drunkenness, disturbing the peace, obscene and indecent language, and "being saucy to his Honor." Frankie Bell received a stiff fine of $35.

Frankie was in Dodge for the 1877 cattle season and somewhere, about July 20, encountered Wyatt. What Wyatt did, if anything, to earn her wrath isn't known, but she proceeded to give him a cursing, the tongue-lashing growing steadily more insulting until Wyatt finally hauled back and slapped her. Poor Frankie was taken to jail for disturbing the peace and made to pay a fine the next morning of $20. Wyatt saw no jail time and received the lowest fine under the law: one dollar.

WYATT MAY NOT HAVE BEEN READY FOR POLICE WORK AGAIN, but he didn't mind taking a job that fall as a bounty hunter for the Atchison, Topeka & Santa Fe Railway—ten dollars a day and expenses was pretty decent pay. At any rate, a couple of no-goods named Dave Rudabaugh and Mike Roark had been identified as the culprits in robberies of railroad construction camps, as well as other misdeeds. The railroad wanted them caught. Wyatt received a tip that the pair had fled to Texas, Fort Griffin to be exact. However, by the time Wyatt rode into town, the outlaws were long gone. In sniffing about Fort Griffin, Wyatt was introduced to a twenty-six-year-old tubercular gambler who it was thought might know where the outlaws were heading: John Henry "Doc" Holliday.

Wyatt Earp would forever remember his first impressions of the Georgia native. His dress suggested a man of intelligence and good breeding. Doc's disease, however, was evident in his haggard and pallid face, and he weighed no more than one hundred and thirty pounds. Yet Doc had a fine nose, neatly trimmed mustache, and expressive mouth. Most striking to Wyatt, though, were the sporting man's large blue eyes.

Holliday didn't have any knowledge of the outlaws' whereabouts, but he told Wyatt to give him a little time to ask around. Consequently, Wyatt spent the next few days in Fort Griffin—and with Doc. Wyatt would say later that his only interest in the gambler with the distinctive southern drawl was whether he could get the information he needed—the two didn't form a fast friendship at Fort Griffin. They got along well, though, and Doc pumped Wyatt for everything he could tell him about Dodge City, and he liked what he heard. It sure seemed as though Dodge could use a dentist, and Doc could sure use some inebriated and naive Texas cowpunchers sitting across from him at a poker table.

Doc eventually came up with a lead about Rudabaugh, and Wyatt left Fort Griffin. Unfortunately for Wyatt, the lead didn't pan out, so he continued to poke around Texas for the wanted men. In January 1878, Wyatt was in Fort Worth, where brother Jim was employed as a bartender. On the night of January 25, Wyatt was visiting Jim where he worked, a popular saloon called the Cattle Exchange, when he got into a fight with another patron, a cattleman whose name was recorded only as Mr. Russell.

The next day, the *Daily Fort Worth Democrat* reported on the "difficulty" between the two men, but the paper had been unable to learn what brought them to blows. It was understood, however, that Wyatt gave Mr. Russell "a first class pounding." Wyatt was subsequently arrested, presumably for the usual "disturbing the peace," and posted bond. Russell, on the other hand, hightailed it out of there, and the Fort Worth police were still trying to track him down when the *Democrat* went to press.

Doc Holliday and Kate Elder had their own bit of trouble in Fort Griffin after Wyatt left them, at least according to a story Wyatt related years later. While playing poker, Doc infuriated a player next to him whom he'd caught cheating. The man drew his revolver and began to point it at Doc, but before he could get a shot off, Doc sank a knife deep into the man's side. If not fatal, the wound was certainly ugly, and the city marshal wasn't about to let Doc go about his business, regardless of the circumstances. He and two policemen kept Doc under guard in the front room of a hotel. Soon, however, angry friends of the wounded man crowded their way into the building, intent on revenge.

It didn't take long for Kate to learn of Doc's predicament. She rushed to the hotel and around the corner to the back of the lot, where there was a shed with a horse tied up inside. Kate led the horse out and then struck a match and set the shed ablaze. She now hurried back to the front door of the hotel and pounded on it, yelling, "Fire, Fire!" The door flew open and the folks inside clambered out, all except Doc's guards. Kate burst in with two revolvers, leveled one at the surprised marshal and tossed the other to Doc. "Come on, Doc," she said, laughing. The two backed out the door, jumped on the stolen horse, and disappeared into the night. They hid out not too far from town, where a friend of Kate's met them the next day with fresh mounts and clothing from Doc's room.

Doc and Kate's Fort Griffin escapade is a hell of a story, and it may even be true. In any event, Doc was ready to check out Dodge City. "[I] enjoyed about as much of this [Texas]," Doc wrote a cousin, "as I could stand."

WYATT RETURNED TO DODGE CITY IN EARLY MAY. HIS QUARRY, Dave Rudabaugh, had been arrested back in January after a bungled train robbery northeast of Dodge, along with several cohorts, and was awaiting trial. And he found Doc and Kate settled in and eager to "welcome" those first Texas herds with their drovers. The *Dodge City Times*, in reporting Wyatt's arrival, commended his previous service as a city peace officer and predicted that he'd be needed as a lawman again for the coming cattle season.

Indeed he would. By June 10, 1878, twenty thousand Texas longhorns were at Dodge waiting to be marketed, with another one hundred sixty thousand on their way north. In another month the town and outskirts would reach a population (largely transient) of some five thousand people: drovers, cattle buyers, gamblers, confidence men, pimps, prostitutes, and thieves. The Mary Magdalenes and gamblers spent their winters in large cities like Kansas City and then made a beeline for Dodge to be open for business when the herds arrived and the cowboys were paid off. "They follow the annual cattle drive like vultures follow an army," wrote one journalist, "and disappear at the end of the cattle driving and shipping

Front Street, Dodge City, 1878. Atchison, Topeka & Santa Fe tracks are in the foreground.

season." For those summer and early fall months, though, Dodge saw what the cowboys affectionately referred to as "red-hot times."

Just days after Wyatt pulled into Dodge, he accepted his old post of assistant city marshal. The job paid $75 a month plus $2 for each conviction at police court that resulted from one of his arrests. The top spot on the force, city marshal, paid $100, but that position had been in upheaval since Wyatt was last in town. Marshal Deger had been removed from office after upsetting the mayor by administering city ordinances a little too even-handedly. Then his replacement, Ed Masterson, older brother of Bat, was mortally wounded in early April while trying to disarm a drunken cowboy. Consequently, the city marshal when Wyatt rejoined the force was twenty-nine-year-old Charles Bassett, a solid officer who'd formerly served as the Ford County sheriff. That summer's city force also included two policemen, making for a total of four officers to keep the Texas cowboys in line.

Of those four lawmen, it's telling that it was Wyatt the editor of the *Ford County Globe* singled out for praise that June: "Wyatt Earp is doing his duty as Ass't Marshal in a very creditable manner.—Adding new laurels to his splendid record every day." Wyatt, wearing a broad-brimmed Stetson, cut a striking figure on Dodge's Front Street. He often performed his duties in his shirtsleeves, choosing not to wear a coat or even a vest, and he frequently didn't even carry a gun. Forgoing a coat made sense in the unbearably warm and sticky summer days in Dodge City, but it also wasn't quite proper in Victorian America for a man to go out in public sans coat and vest. Wyatt didn't care. It was hot. He pinned his scroll badge to his shirt and called it good.

For Dodge City's citizenry, how their police officers dressed mattered little compared to their duty to keep the peace. And despite the *Globe*'s approval of Wyatt's performance, the editor wasn't happy about an outbreak of muggings and the seemingly misguided priorities of Dodge's police force. Just a week after praising Wyatt, he wrote that, "If less protection was given to the pimp, the bawdy house loafer, and the robber, and more protection given to visitors and others engaged in legitimate business, it would be much better for the community."

That same month of June, Doc Holliday posted a notice in the *Dodge City Times* announcing his services as a dentist with an office at the Dodge House, a sixty-room hotel on Front Street with an attached billiard hall/saloon. Doc's open association with Kate Elder, who'd previously plied her trade as a sex worker in Dodge, wasn't a detriment to his business. As a former resident explained, social mores were quite different in boomtowns like Dodge. "The women of the hurdy-gurdys and dance halls were welcomed everywhere, by the male population," he said, "and no man lost social standing by being publicly seen talking to a notorious woman."

Why Doc chose to return to the dentistry profession at a time when he appeared to have completely abandoned it for gambling is hard to say. Perhaps his winnings had fallen off and he needed the money. Or maybe he simply enjoyed fixing people's teeth. Doc wasn't without competition, though. In the very same issue of the *Times*, an itinerant dentist, George

W. Milton, advertised his services as well, and with an office also at the Dodge House. Of all the worries the folks of Dodge City might have had, dental care wasn't one of them.

Doc didn't slow down on his gambling, of course. That was unthinkable. And Dodge offered plenty of saloons and gambling halls where he enjoyed his profession of choice. Bat Masterson, then the twenty-four-year-old Ford County sheriff, later wrote that Doc didn't get into any trouble the entire time he was in Dodge, and as sheriff, Bat would know. However, Doc would claim that he was once falsely accused of burglarizing a Dodge City business. As it turned out, the guilty party was the store's owner. That Masterson perhaps wouldn't remember this minor episode among the shootings and more serious crimes he dealt with in the county is understandable, but the accusation rankled Doc, and he never forgot it.

Bat did remember well the Georgian's appearance, that sallow complexion and those pale blue eyes. "It was easily seen that he was not a well man," Bat recalled, "for he not only looked the part, but he incessantly coughed it as well." And although Doc could be a bit of a grouch, "he was not disliked by those with whom he had become acquainted."

In the early morning hours of July 26, Doc and Bat were engaged in a game of monte in a popular theater and dance hall named the Comique. Bat was dealing. Out on the dance floor, the vaudeville actor and dancer Eddie Foy was calling a square dance, the merry couples sashaying back and forth to the music of a five-string banjo. Suddenly, the sound of shattering glass and gunfire erupted in the hall. The shots came from outside on the street, but they were being directed into the Comique. Women screamed as everyone scattered. Doc and Bat well knew that the theater's thin pine walls wouldn't slow a bullet, and they instantly dropped from their chairs and hugged the floor. Eddie Foy was impressed. "I had thought I was pretty agile myself," he wrote later, "but those fellows had me beaten by seconds at that trick."

More shots rang out in the street, and Wyatt and policeman James Masterson, Bat's younger brother, were in the thick of it. Earlier that evening, Wyatt had had some kind of run-in with a Texas cowboy, and the drover wanted revenge. He and two or three of his pals decided they'd get it once they retrieved their revolvers, just before leaving town for camp.

At about 3 A.M., Wyatt stood in front of the Comique as the cowboys slowly rode toward him. When just twenty steps away, the angry drover jerked his revolver, dug his spurs into the flanks of his horse, and shot point-blank at Wyatt as he raced by. Flame from the burning black powder nearly licked Wyatt's face, but the shot went wide. Now all the cowboys began shooting their revolvers into the Comique, other buildings, and, as they fled, back at the lawmen.

Wyatt instantly ran toward the cowboy who'd tried to kill him, intending to yank him off his mount or, at the least, grab hold of the horse's tail, but Wyatt, even if barefooted, wasn't nearly as fast as a horse. He and Masterson fired at the drovers as they galloped away but didn't see anyone drop. Wyatt now crouched down in the middle of the street, took careful aim, and squeezed the trigger. The bullet struck his man in the arm, ripping a gaping hole in it. The drovers thundered across the bridge spanning the Arkansas River to the south side, and Wyatt and policeman Masterson chased after them in the moonlight. Just a few yards past the bridge, the lawmen found the wounded cowboy on the ground bleeding profusely, his horse standing a few feet away.

Wyatt and Masterson got the drover, a young Texan named George Hoy, back to town, where a doctor treated and bandaged the wound. It didn't heal well, though, and the unbearably hot summer weather didn't help. Eventually, gangrene set in. Twenty-six days after Hoy had been shot, a doctor amputated the cowboy's arm. But the painful surgery was all for naught; the weakened cowboy died within hours. Hoy's death marked the first time Wyatt Earp had killed a man, and yet, by all odds, Hoy should have survived that wound.

AUGUST 1878 CAME, AND WITH IT A STEADY STREAM OF TEXAS herds, filling the air with dust and the stench of manure, and Dodge remained as wild—and dangerous—as ever. A former city attorney who'd seen all that was good and bad in the cow town gave his opinion that,

"There have been Abilenes, Tombstones, Deadwoods, and other frontier towns, but in their best days not a one of them could hold a candle to Dodge City. I believe it was the hardest town that ever existed on the face of the earth."

The cowboys tested Dodge's peace officers almost nightly. Many resented the lawmen for interfering with their fun, confiscating their guns, and not hesitating to throw them in the calaboose for a variety of offenses. About 7 P.M. one evening, a large crowd of cowboys gathered at the corner of the Wright, Beverly & Co. general store on Front Street. Feeling rowdy, and emboldened by liquor, they concluded that taking over the town would be a worthwhile use of their time. The cowboys stepped out into the street and began blazing away with their guns. Then they spotted Wyatt standing quietly in front of the Long Branch saloon, just two doors down from the general store.

Catching Wyatt alone was a golden opportunity. The cowboys pointed their guns at the lawman and closed in around him. Wyatt revealed no emotion as he thought about how the next few seconds were going to play out. He knew he didn't dare reach for his revolver. One of the cowboys said they were going to get him now, and it appeared to Wyatt that they were dead serious.

Inside the Long Branch, Doc Holliday sat at a monte table, his seat facing the front of the saloon where a large window gave him a view of the street. As he watched the dealer, "Cock-Eyed Frank" Loving, manipulate the cards, Doc happened to glance up at the window. Instantly, he saw Wyatt was in trouble. "Have you a six-shooter?" Doc hurriedly said to Loving. The dealer handed his gun to Doc, who also had a revolver of his own. Doc rushed to the front door and out onto the boardwalk, and leveling both guns at the cowboys, shouted, "Throw up your hands!"

Wyatt was as surprised as the cowboys, but he took advantage of their shock to draw his own revolvers. He announced that they were all under arrest, and he and Doc led the chastened drovers to the jail. They went before the police court the next morning, paid their fines, and rode back to their camp.

Neither of Dodge City's two newspapers reported Doc Holliday's heroics. Cowboys shooting up the town and landing in jail was a fairly regular occurrence, and not every violent incident made it into the local news columns. But while what happened that night wasn't preserved for posterity by the press, Wyatt would remember it to the end of his days. As far as he was concerned, Doc Holliday had saved his life. "It was because of this episode," he said, "that I became the friend of Doc Holliday ever after."

FOUR

WHEN DODGE CITY LOST ITS SNAP

Change was his mistress, Chance his counselor.

THEODORE ROBERTS

Front Street, Dodge City
A September Night, 1878

W yatt saw the bright flashes in the darkness, and they came with loud gunshots. He ran toward them, the sickening sound of buzzing bullets filling the air. Wyatt nearly collided with a man whose head and face streamed blood. The bleeding man cried that he'd been shot and begged Wyatt to protect him from a man chasing him. The pursuing man was coming up fast, and he was still firing his revolver. Fearless, Wyatt rushed him, knocked him down, and took the gun away. He then hauled him off to jail and got the story of what the violent episode had been about.

The bleeding man was a fiddler at a dance hall, and the man who'd been trying to send him to hell to join fellow fiddlers was a prosperous Texas cattleman named Rachal. A drunken Rachal became enraged when the fiddler refused to continue playing the cattleman's favorite tune ad nauseum. Rachal pulled his revolver and slammed its barrel on the fiddler's head nearly as many times as the fiddler had played that favorite tune, making several large gashes. So the fiddler wasn't shot, after all, although it no doubt felt like it. Nevertheless, Rachal was guilty of assault and attempted murder.

The cattleman, however, was a big customer of the Wright, Beverly & Co. general store. The store's primary owner, Bob Wright, was a town founder and a heavyweight in Dodge's politics. As soon as he learned Wyatt had arrested his moneyed customer, Wright rushed to the calaboose, arriving just as the lawman was opening the cell door.

"You are not going to lock this man up are you, Wyatt," said Wright. "He is worth a million dollars!"

"I don't care if he *is* worth a million dollars. They all look alike to me."

Wright grew angry and agitated. "If you lock this fellow up," he threatened, "I will see that we get another city marshal."

Wyatt coolly took hold of Wright and shoved him in the cell with Rachal and locked the door. Soon Sheriff Bat Masterson arrived and suggested to Wyatt that it might be wise to release the store owner. Wyatt replied that he would—at 9 A.M. the next morning. And that was the end of it, at least as far as Wyatt was concerned. Not so with Wright and Rachal. Wright figured it'd be easier to get Wyatt killed than it would to get him kicked off the force. Together, Wright and Rachal hatched a plan to bring in a known killer to do the job. They settled upon Clay Allison.

Only a select few men in the West deserved their reputations as deadly gunhands, and Allison was one of them. A thirty-seven-year-old Confederate veteran, he stood five feet nine inches tall with blue eyes and dark, tousled hair and a thick beard. A newspaper described him in 1878 as an attractive man who "carries himself with ease and grace, gentlemanly and courteous in manner." Of course, that happened to be a time when Allison wasn't roaring drunk or suffering from a psychotic episode. Allison's military records reveal that he'd received a blow to the head when he was young that sometimes caused "paroxysmal of a mixed character" and suicidal thoughts.

When Allison arrived in Dodge, Wyatt didn't know his purpose. Then, a short time later, he saw Allison and Rachal in a serious conversation, and that was enough. Because Wyatt was on duty through the night and early morning hours, he generally slept until 1 P.M., but one morning about nine, a fellow officer woke him up. He said that Allison was liquored up and looking for Wyatt. And he was making loud threats. Wyatt calmly got dressed and put on his guns. When he stepped out onto the boardwalk, he saw Sheriff Bat Masterson, and they walked together for a moment.

Wyatt and the five-foot-nine Ford County sheriff had first come to know each other on the buffalo range while working as hide hunters sometime in the early 1870s. It was in Dodge City, however, that the two became close, beyond the usual camaraderie shared by fellow lawmen. And they were alike in that they both exhibited nerve and levelheadedness in tight spots. Bat walked with a slight limp from a bullet wound he'd received two years earlier in Texas. The very same bullet killed a dance hall girl Bat was with at the time, and Bat returned the favor to the jealous man who'd fired it. Bat, however, was in awe of Wyatt. He later wrote that his friend was one of the few men he personally knew whom he considered as "absolutely destitute of physical fear."

Wyatt would need more than fearlessness, though, in dealing with Allison. Bat kept a shotgun in the city attorney's office, which was across the street from the Wright, Beverly general store, and it was decided that Bat would position himself as a lookout from the office door, ready to blast Allison with a load of buckshot if needed.

The city attorney, Edward Colborn, had not yet been to his office, but he observed the inebriated Allison yelling and cursing at everyone within sight and wondered why the man hadn't been arrested. The police officers just stood around, Colborn remembered, and "no one seemed to want to take it up. The calm was strange and seemed to be the forerunner of a storm. No sound could be heard but Allison's voice." But when Colborn got to his office and found Masterson crouched behind the cracked doorway, shotgun at the ready, he realized everything was under control.

It was now time for Wyatt to hunt up Allison, and it didn't take long. The two suddenly came face-to-face at the entrance to a saloon, but despite Allison's previous threats, there was no jerking of guns. Instead, the

Bat Masterson and Wyatt Earp, from a tintype taken at Dodge City circa 1876. Assistant City Marshal Earp wears a "scroll badge" on his shirt.
(PUBLIC DOMAIN IMAGE, AUTHOR'S COLLECTION)

men nodded a greeting and then casually backed up against a wall on the boardwalk, Allison on Wyatt's left.

"So," Allison said, "you're the man that killed my friend Hoy?"

Allison and Hoy weren't friends, but a revenge killing would make a good cover for a paid assassination.

"Yes, I guess I'm the man you're looking for," Wyatt answered.

Wyatt could see Allison slowly moving his right hand toward his revolver, but the lawman already had his own right hand on the butt of his gun, and he was ready to grab Allison's revolver with his left hand the moment the hired killer pulled it.

Across the street, Masterson kept a bead on Allison, although Wyatt and Allison were so close that if Masterson was forced to shoot, some of the shotgun's buckshot was sure to strike Wyatt.

A few seconds passed. The tension seemed to have a sobering effect on the hired gun, as did the realization that his position next to Wyatt was rather precarious; Wyatt clearly had the advantage. Allison needed to put some space between him and the lawman.

"I guess I'll go round the corner," Allison said.

"I guess you'd better," Wyatt replied.

Allison went and mounted his horse, rode out into the street, and asked Wyatt to come to him, saying he wanted to talk. This was a ruse to have Wyatt walk alongside the horse and get shot, and Wyatt knew it.

Stepping to the edge of the boardwalk, Wyatt said, "Go on and make your talk. I can hear you."

Allison looked around the street. He'd expected help from some of Wright's and Rachal's men, but from what he could tell, he was on his own. Just then Wright came out of his store and Allison glared at him. "Well, I don't know about you," he growled at Wright, "there were some promises made this morning but I don't see any sign of them." And with that, Allison wheeled his horse and galloped out of town.

JIM KENEDY WAS TROUBLE. THE TWENTY-THREE-YEAR-OLD SON of a wealthy Texas cattleman, he'd brought one of his father's herds to Dodge City that summer of 1878 and was in no hurry to return home. With plenty of money in his pockets, there was no end to the amusements available to him, especially in the evenings. At the Comique, considered

Dodge's marquee dance hall and theater, the featured performers included musician Dick Brown with his "educated banjo," the song and dance team of Eddie Foy and Jim Thompson, comic actors and clog dancers Billy and Nola Forrest, and a number of attractive young female singers guaranteed to bring in cowboys such as Kenedy.

One of the singers Kenedy saw, either at the Comique or at her other venue, Ham Bell's Varieties, was Fannie Keenan, a "very fine looking" brunette in her late twenties. Before coming to Dodge, Fannie had appeared in theaters and opera houses from Cincinnati to Memphis to St. Louis, and her beautiful singing led some to refer to her as "the Nightingale." Years later, in referring to Fannie's wonderful voice, Wyatt said, "Ask any man who knew Deadwood or Dodge in its prime to tell you how she sang 'Killarney.'" Keenan, however, was Fannie's stage name. Her real name was Dora Hand, and if Jim Kenedy happened to read the *Dodge City Times*, he would've seen that Dora Hand was petitioning for a divorce from her musician husband, who'd abandoned Dora for another woman back in Ohio.

But young Jim Kenedy was likely too busy raising hell to read the newspaper. On July 29, Wyatt arrested him for carrying a concealed weapon. In an era when it wasn't hard to escape one's past (something Wyatt had done more than once), Wyatt probably didn't know the man he was arresting nearly shot a cattleman to death in Ellsworth in 1872 in a heated dispute over a card game. Kenedy was just seventeen years old at the time, and the intervening years had done nothing to curb his impulsive anger. On August 17, Kenedy acted out in the presence of Dodge's mayor, James "Dog" Kelley, which caused the mayor to order Marshal Bassett to haul the Texan off to jail. Exactly what Kenedy had done isn't known, but he was charged with disturbing the peace, "in that he did conduct himself in a rude, riotous, and disorderly manner." Two days later, Kenedy pled guilty before the police judge and was fined $10 plus court costs of $7.50.

Kenedy now had it in for the mayor, but he bided his time. He easily learned the location of the mayor's small, two-room cottage and also the particular room he slept in. Then, at about 4 A.M. on October 4, he rode up to the front of the cottage and let loose with his revolver. Four quick blasts shattered the silence, with two of the .45-caliber bullets from Kenedy's gun smashing through the front door. But the mayor wasn't in the cottage. He'd been ill for a couple of weeks and had sought treatment at Fort Dodge, where the best doctor in the region was on duty. Because Kenedy had been away from Dodge City for a few days, he wasn't aware of Mayor Kelley's absence.

The cottage wasn't empty, however. Two lodgers occupied the home, one in each room. In the front, the mayor's room, slept singer Fannie Garrettson, one of the main attractions at the Comique. In the back room slept her friend Fannie Keenan. The first bullet to penetrate the door struck the floor in the front room, ricocheted up into Garrettson's bedstead and then traveled through the thin plaster and lath wall into the floor in Keenan's room. The second bullet, more elevated than the first, passed dangerously close to Garrettson, ripping through her sheets and heavy comforter before punching though the wall and striking Keenan.

The deadly bullet entered the sleeping woman's body between the fifth and sixth ribs. "Poor Fannie, she never realized what was the matter with her," wrote a grieving Garrettson in a letter the next day. "She never spoke but died unconscious. . . . I think she died happy, as her look was such; but what a horrible death! To go to one's bed well and hearty and not dream of anything and be cut down in such a manner, without a chance to breath [sic] a word."

Because gunfire was frequently heard in Dodge at all times of the day and night, no one thought much of the four gunshots near the mayor's cottage. But soon after Garrettson discovered that her friend had been murdered, someone rushed to Wyatt's place and woke him up. Kenedy's known grudge with the mayor immediately made him a prime suspect. Once dressed, Wyatt saw that the only place on Front Street with a light on was the Long Branch saloon. He stepped inside and there sat Kenedy on a monte table, his legs swinging. Wyatt casually approached the bartender and whispered to him.

"Was he there when the shots were fired?"

"For God's sake don't say anything here," replied the bartender nervously. "Come into the back room and I'll tell you all about it."

The bartender didn't immediately follow Wyatt into the back but waited a few minutes so as not to arouse Kenedy's suspicion. When the bartender did enter the back room, Wyatt repeated his question.

"Kenedy's the man!" the bartender said. "He left here with another man just before the shooting and immediately afterward he came in the back way and took a big drink of whisky."

Wyatt ran back to the barroom but Kenedy was gone. And there was no sign of him on the street, either. Wyatt now found Sheriff Masterson and together they tracked down Kenedy's trail boss, who'd come to Dodge with him from Texas, and placed the man under arrest. As Wyatt remembered it, they then gave the trail boss the "third degree," which quickly elicited a confession that Kenedy was the murderer.

That afternoon, a posse of five lawmen left Dodge in pursuit of Kenedy: Sheriff Masterson, Marshal Bassett, Assistant Marshal Earp, Deputy Sheriff William Duffey, and Bill Tilghman, a future Dodge City marshal. The *Dodge City Times* declared the party "as intrepid a posse as ever pulled a trigger." Whether that posse would bring Kenedy back alive or dead, however, was a question. The heinous murder of the innocent Keenan, regardless of the shooter's intent, broke every moral code. Garrettson wrote in her letter that "the man who perpetrated this deed will never exist for a judge or a jury, as the officers [in the posse] have sworn never to take him alive."

Slowed by a hellacious rainstorm, the posse still managed to get ahead of Kenedy, who was making for his Texas home and his rich papa. At a ranch about thirty-five miles southwest of Dodge the posse waited, their horses unsaddled and grazing loose on the prairie. At about 4 P.M., they sighted a lone rider in the distance, heading toward the ranch. The horses were too scattered to gather quickly, so the possemen positioned themselves behind dirt mounds from a newly dug well. As the rider came closer, Bat Masterson spoke up: "That's Kenedy. I know him by the way he rides; and besides, I know his horse." Bat and Wyatt hurriedly devised a strategy. If Kenedy surrendered, fine. If he tried to flee, Wyatt would shoot his horse and Bat would take out the killer.

When Kenedy approached within a few hundred yards of the well, the officers stood up, leveled their rifles, and shouted for Kenedy to surrender. Kenedy froze. They ordered him to surrender a second time, but the Texan remained motionless. The possemen commanded him to surrender a third time, and at this last order Kenedy swiftly raised his hand as if to strike his horse with a quirt. He didn't get a chance. A fusillade erupted from the posse, creating a cloud of white smoke that temporarily obstructed the officers' view. As the smoke thinned, they saw both Kenedy and his horse sprawled on the prairie. The Texan had an ugly wound in his left shoulder from Bat's rifle, but he was alive. The horse was dead with three bullet holes oozing blood.

The lawmen hired a team and hauled their prisoner to Dodge, where he received desperately needed medical attention. On October 22, 1878, Kenedy was well enough to participate in a preliminary examination hearing before the justice of the peace, and that's when things got strange. The hearing was held in the sheriff's office, which was too small to allow the public to observe. The next thing anyone knew, the judge had acquitted Kenedy due to insufficient evidence, and this after a coroner's jury had named Kenedy as Fannie Keenan's murderer back on the day she was shot. Wyatt always ascribed the shocking outcome to the influence and money of Kenedy's father.

Kenedy did return to Texas, but absent several pieces of shattered bone from his shoulder, the largest being about five inches long. The bones were removed by Fort Dodge doctors in a December operation to allow his wound to fully heal. The following March, Kenedy's father took the time to write the Fort Dodge doctors and let them know that the operation had been a "grand success" and that his son Jim was nearly recovered.

THERE'S A REASON DOC HOLLIDAY DIDN'T HELP HIS FRIEND Wyatt in the Clay Allison trouble or that he didn't join the posse that went after Jim Kenedy: Doc and Kate had moved on from Dodge. The tracks of the Atchison, Topeka & Santa Fe had reached Trinidad, Colorado, in September 1878. Nestled in the Purgatoire Valley at the base of Raton Pass, Trinidad now became the main shipping hub for goods transported by wagons to and from New Mexico over what remained of the Santa Fe Trail.

From eight to twelve railroad cars stuffed with freight arrived at the end of the tracks daily. All US Army goods, horses, and mules destined for various military posts in New Mexico and Arizona were shipped over the rails to Trinidad. In truth, the railroad, like the storied trail it was quickly replacing, was the supply line for the entire Southwest, and it was all flowing through this bustling town near the southern Colorado border. A mirror image of other western hot spots, Trinidad was overflowing with saloons, dance halls, and whiskey shops. It even had a theater called the Comique. A visiting journalist described the place matter-of-factly as having all the "numerous necessary evils you always find in a live, wide-awake get-up town."

And that included gambling. The town's several saloons and billiard halls, the journalist continued, offered ornately carpeted and furnished back rooms where "you can 'fight the tiger' [faro], buck at keno, poke at poker, monte, or any other game you wish." Trinidad, then, was a good place for Doc to try his hand at separating neophytes from their money, especially as the slow months had commenced in Dodge.

Only a smattering of Trinidad newspaper issues survive from Doc and Kate's time there, and the two apparently weren't newsworthy enough to appear in those particular pages. But that doesn't mean they stayed out of trouble. Bat Masterson, who would later serve for a year as Trinidad's city marshal, wrote that Doc hadn't been in town a week when he got into an altercation with "a young sport" named Kid Colton. (Wyatt remembered the name as Dalton.) According to Masterson, Doc shot Kid over something trivial, giving the man a serious wound but one he survived.

Like all places where tempers, whiskey, and guns lived together, shootings were all too common in Trinidad. So much so that the editor of Trinidad's *The Enterprise and Chronicle* published a column in December

1878 calling for order and the strict enforcement of the city's laws. He bemoaned those individuals who aspired "to be considered 'bad men,' who swagger about the streets and saloons glorying in the impunity with which they can insult peaceable citizens." And for those who resorted to gunplay, endangering the lives of innocent bystanders, he demanded that they be made to learn "that here, a 'shooter' has no chance of escaping the penalties of his crimes."

Considering this gun violence Trinidad was experiencing, Doc's shooting scrape with Kid Colton, albeit lacking in details, seems believable. If Masterson didn't get the story from Doc himself, he had plenty of opportunities to hear it later from folks in Trinidad. In any event, the shooting is supposed to have resulted in Doc's hasty departure from the town, which also sounds about right for a man of Doc's proclivities.

The next port of call for Doc and Kate was 130 miles down the Santa Fe Trail at Las Vegas, New Mexico Territory. An important trading center of four thousand people, Las Vegas exhibited an overriding Hispanic influence with its adobe buildings, Catholic churches, foodways, and language—Spanish was more likely to be heard on the streets than English. And the town's predominantly Jewish merchants catered to a steady stream of cowboys, freighters, farmers, immigrants, and travelers bound for Santa Fe. But change was on the doorstep. In a few months, the sound of a locomotive's whistle would be heard in the town for the first time. Progress was calling.

A good part of Las Vegas's appeal for the sickly Doc, though, was the celebrated Montezuma Hot Springs an hour's carriage ride from town. Many considered the hot springs, with its well-appointed hotel and several bathhouses, to be on par with those in Arkansas's Ouachita Mountains. The Montezuma Hot Springs, however, also had the benefit of abundant sunshine and pure, dry air at an elevation of 6,719 feet. Any given day would find a number of health seekers soaking in the springs, clinging to hopes that the mineral water's believed curative powers would rid them of their afflictions. Some of the afflicted miraculously got better, but those who did were likely not true consumptives. A cure for tuberculosis was far in the future.

Although regular stage service was available to Las Vegas, Doc and Kate chose to hire a wagon freighter to haul them to their destination, suggesting that their baggage, and perhaps furnishings, were too substantial for a coach. Where they made their home in Las Vegas is unknown, but what's fairly obvious is that Doc wasn't there to fill cavities. No advertisements for John H. Holliday offering "professional services" as a dentist appear in the town's only newspaper at the time, the *Daily Gazette*. And those who later recalled Doc's presence in town definitely didn't remember him as a tooth doctor. In fact, it was anything but.

Writing in 1881—just two years after Doc arrived in Las Vegas—the editor of the *Las Vegas Daily Optic* claimed that "Doc was always considered a shiftless, bagged-legged character—a killer and professional cutthroat." Kate didn't fare any better, the editor writing that she "surrounded her habiliments with a detestable odor" that would "make her memory immortal." These are undoubtedly exaggerated views, but Doc's documented activities in Las Vegas don't portray him as an ideal citizen, either.

During the six-month period from March to August 1879, Doc was arrested three times, twice for "keeping a gaming table" (monte) and once for carrying a deadly weapon (pistol). Gambling had been outlawed in the Territory in 1861, but in Las Vegas and elsewhere, the gambling law was only loosely observed. In August 1879, the editor of the *Daily Gazette* complained that, "At every term of the District court a large number of indictments for gambling are found, the parties are arrested, many of them to avoid trouble pay fines and are released, so it goes from year to year." For Doc and the other gamblers, the occasional fine ($25 plus costs) wasn't enough to entertain thoughts of closing shop and moving on.

Doc's disease may have gone into remission that spring, for, by all accounts, he was hardly convalescing. At some point, he showed up in the new (and short-lived) settlement of Otero, which had succeeded Trinidad as the next end-of-the-tracks town on the ever-lengthening Santa Fe. Otero was ripe for a monte table—the railroad's construction crews numbered about a thousand men, not to mention the freighters and others whose business took them to the latest jumping-off point. While in

Otero, Doc may or may not have killed a man in self-defense. Probably not. However, from the single surviving issue of Otero's only newspaper, we learn that Doc didn't just gamble on cards. On Saturday night, May 31, 1879, he spent five dollars for a chance to win "a splendid violin." Each person who bought a chance got a turn at throwing the dice, with the highest roll determining the winner. Doc didn't win, but his gamble was most likely a lark. A violin was the last thing he needed.

WITH TREMENDOUS FANFARE, THE FIRST TRAIN ROLLED INTO Las Vegas on the Fourth of July 1879, steam whistle shrieking, engine bell ringing, and black smoke belching from the smokestack. But the railroad had not laid tracks into the town proper; it instead ran the line to a spot just under a mile east of the old plaza, which soon acquired the name New Town or East Las Vegas. The buildings were a mixture of wooden structures disassembled at Otero and transported south to New Town by the railroad, and hastily erected new buildings. Among the new constructions was a building on Center Street, a block from the depot, contracted for by Doc and a partner. John Henry Holliday was now the co-owner of a modest, one-story saloon and dance hall.

On the night of July 19, several saloons and dance halls in New Town, including Doc's, hosted a grand opening of sorts. As reported by the *Daily Gazette*, the event attracted a large crowd of both sexes. "The women who did the dancing were American and Mexican ranging through nearly all grades of good and bad looks," went the *Gazette*'s uncharitable reporting. "The halls were brilliantly lighted, music was furnished by excellent string bands for the dancers, glasses jingled in time with the music, and as was to have been expected, many of the pleasure seekers were more than half seas over before the night turned toward the wee small hours."

It was in those wee small hours, however, that a former army scout named Mike Gordon made the mistake of shooting into Doc's saloon. The trouble started when a drunken Gordon tried to coerce a sometime lover to leave Doc's place and go with him to a larger soiree around the block. She refused, and Gordon, "a bad man when drinking," did not take the rejection well. Standing in the street just to the right of the saloon, he began yelling assorted threats. Then, drawing his revolver, he shouted he would kill someone or be killed himself before sunrise. Gordon pointed his gun at the crowd gathered around the front of the saloon and jerked the trigger. His revolver spit flame, the bullet passing through the pants legs of a Hispano and lodging in the saloon floor near the bartender at the end of the bar.

What happened next was a blur of gunshots, screams, and people running for cover. No one could agree later on just how many more shots were fired, whether it was two or four. But there was no debate on the last shot. That bullet came from the gun of Doc Holliday, and it punched a big hole in Gordon's right breast and exited his back just below the shoulder blade. Gordon turned and stumbled into the darkness, his life's blood gushing from his wound with each heartbeat. About an hour or two later, Gordon was found on the ground some distance away, still alive, but at 6 A.M., he died, fulfilling his own prediction.

Word raced across town of the shooting. Doc headed to the home he shared with Kate, and before long, the police appeared at their door. Unfazed, Kate stepped out in her nightgown holding a revolver and closed the door behind her. She calmly sat down in a chair and told the officers that if there was something inside they wanted, to "come and get it." The policemen declined her invitation.

At the coroner's inquest the following afternoon, witnesses were nonexistent when it came to identifying the man who killed Gordon, or providing much information at all about the shooting. According to the *Gazette*, no one wanted to risk being summoned to testify if the case ended up in criminal court. Nevertheless, it doesn't seem a great many tears were shed for Gordon, who received a pauper's grave. As one longtime Las Vegas resident commented about the frequent shooting deaths in New Town, "In the case of killings, usually the right man got killed, and when that happened, rejoicing took the place of grief and the drinks were freely ordered."

Strangely, no sooner had Doc gotten into the saloon and dance hall business than he was out. That August, he and his partner either sold out or were foreclosed on. Doc didn't stop gambling, though. New Town was still wide open when it came to assorted vices. In fact, several less-than-stellar acquaintances had come down the line from Dodge City and set up shop in New Town, even filling local offices from justice of the peace to town marshal. They were corrupt as hell, of course, and became known as the Dodge City Gang. Their main priority was not law and order but lining their own pockets. Doc seems to have avoided becoming involved in the gang's intrigues, though, and was content running his monte table in what used to be the Holliday saloon.

The next month, another Dodge City "old-timer" arrived in Las Vegas. One day when Doc was walking across the plaza in Old Town, he glanced up to see a tall, slim, well-dressed man looking straight at him. There was no mistaking this gentleman with the impressive physique, piercing blue eyes, and big, drooping mustache. Doc picked up his pace, and upon getting closer, reached out to grasp the hand of a smiling Wyatt Earp.

————————

EARP WOULD LATER SAY THAT IN 1879, "DODGE CITY WAS BEGIN-ning to lose much of the snap which had given it a charm to men of restless blood" and that he was "tired of the trials of a peace officer's life and wanted no more of it." Understandably, having to deal with drunks, ne'er-do-wells, and woman beaters on a daily basis—not to mention cold-blooded killers—could indeed take its toll on most any lawman.

That spring of 1879 saw two typical police actions that happened to find their way into the pages of the *Dodge City Times*. On May 5, three armed Missourians, drunk on "bad whiskey," attempted the old take-over-the-town routine. Wyatt was on duty and quickly grabbed the chief ruffian by his ear and was dragging him to the calaboose when one of his buddies intervened. Fortunately, Bat Masterson happened along as Wyatt was scuffling with the two men. In an instant, Bat slammed the side of his revolver onto the head of one of the Missourians, gaining the man's full cooperation. The two troublemakers were disarmed and placed in jail

Docket, Police Judge, City of Dodge City, Kansas.

The City of Dodge City, Plaintiff,

No. 1430 vs.

Tom. E. Eworr Defendant

In the Police Court,

Before Samuel Marshall Police Judge,

In and for the City of Dodge City, Ford County, State of Kansas.

FINE
COSTS,
JUDGE,
Docket,
Number,
Title,
Complaint,
Warrant,
Subpoena,
Swearing Witness
Trial,
Judgment,
Entering Judgment,
Mittimus,
Commitment,
Ordinance,
Entries,
Filing Papers,
Index,
City Attorney,
City Marshal,

Tom E. Eworr Defendant arrested on the Complaint
of Wyatt Earp charging that on the 6" day of
May A. D. 1879, at the said City of Dodge City, the said Defendant
Tom. E. Eworr did within the Corporate limits of the said
City then and there unlawfully Carry Concealed about his person
a dangerous and deadly weapon To wit a Pistol
Contrary to the provisions of Section 11 of Ordinance
No 16 Relating to Misdemeanors. Now on this 7th
8th day of May 1879 Came this Cause for hearing Case
Called Defendant present in Court and after hearing
the Charges Contained in the Complaint Read defendant
Enter a plea of Guilty whereupon it is by the Court
Considered found ordered and adjudged
That the Defendant Tom. E. Eworr is Guilty as Charged
in the Complaint and that he pay a fine of $3 - and
the Costs of this Prosecution and that he stand committed
until the same is paid
Fine and Costs paid May 6" 1879
Fine paid R. W. Cook City Treasurer May 19" 1879
Received by for E. F. Colborn
Paid Marshal Earp May 6" 1879

WITNESSES,

TOTAL, $1050

Witness my Hand:

Samuel Marshall Police Judge

A page from the Dodge City Police Court docket showing an arrest made by Wyatt Earp on May 6, 1879. Note the $2 fee he received out of the court costs.

for the night. The following evening, however, the hate-filled Missourians came up with a plan to murder Sheriff Masterson. That failed, too, and one of the Missouri boys spent another night in the calaboose.

A little more than two weeks later, on May 21, Wyatt and James Masterson rode north of Dodge to the area of Duck Creek. They held a writ on a horse herder who'd left town without paying for a service of some kind rendered by an unnamed Black man. The two lawmen found their drover, but he was with six companions. If it had been anybody but Wyatt and Masterson, it likely would have been a tense standoff. But as the *Times* reported, the two officers, "showing no signs of 'weakening,' soon obtained satisfaction of the claim, the drover promptly paying the debt when resistance was no longer available."

As for Dodge City's loss of "snap," 1879 was the slowest cattle season on record. Because of a drought that spring and for part of the summer, the Arkansas River turned into a bed of sand, and the grasses on the parched prairie around Dodge made for poor grazing. This led many Texas cattle owners to drive their herds to shipping points farther north, which meant noticeably fewer cowboys on the streets of Dodge. Consequently, the town saw a minor exodus of professional gamblers and prostitutes. The number of Mary Magdalenes dropped from ninety the previous summer to forty-seven. Saloons went from twenty-two to fourteen. One newspaper correspondent noted that only two men had been killed during the summer and joked that Dodge's police force had been forced to target practice on tin oyster cans to keep up on their gun skills.

Regardless of how many cattle cars were loaded at Dodge City, however, the town was indeed changing. That same summer, a $6,000 schoolhouse was going up on the ground that had formerly been Dodge's "Boot Hill," the onetime resting place of some forty men who'd met untimely ends. (Not all were buried with their boots on. Some were found to have been buried with their boots under their heads as pillows.) A Dodge City resident saw the coming school building as "a fitting monument to Western progress and civilization." This dramatic overstatement was typical town boosterism, but even so, the image of a school and its playground was not one normally associated with a town with snap.

Wyatt Earp experienced change as well, but that change wasn't reported in the newspapers. He'd begun living with a woman, a former prostitute, although the couple presented themselves as man and wife. She'd been born twenty-nine years earlier in Iowa and given the name Celia Ann by her parents, Henry and Elizabeth Blaylock. Celia ran away from home as a teenager and ended up for a time in Fort Scott, Kansas, about 1870, where she had her photograph made in J. T. Parker's Palace of Fine Art. It's one of only two portraits of her known.

Celia Ann "Mattie" Blaylock, Wyatt's common-law wife while in Dodge City and Tombstone, photographed in Fort Scott, Kansas, circa 1870.
(PUBLIC DOMAIN IMAGE, AUTHOR'S COLLECTION)

At what point Celia turned to sex work and why remains a question mark. It's not surprising, though, that she would end up in that mecca for prostitutes, Dodge City. And like Kate Elder and any number of young women working in the brothels, she left her birth name behind. She was now Mattie. As for the time and place she first met Wyatt, neither she nor Wyatt left an account. In fact, like his second "wife," Sarah, Wyatt never spoke of Mattie to those later chronicling his life. But when Wyatt departed Dodge City in September, Mattie was at his side. For now, she'd tied her fortunes to this restless man.

Among the clothes, toiletries, food and other items Mattie carefully packed for their overland journey west was a small pocket New Testament. If she opened it, and she likely did, she would have seen an ink inscription signed by the Dodge City law firm of Michael Sutton and Edward Colborn. The inscription read:

> *To Wyatt S. Earp, as a slight recognition of his many Christian virtues, and steady following in the foot steps of the meek and lowly Jesus.*

FIVE

THE NEW EL DORADO

Under certain conditions, gamblers are respectable people.

ROBERT ALPHEUS LEWIS

Mr. Wyatt Earp, who has been on our police force for several months, resigned his position last week and took his departure for Las Vegas, New Mexico." That was the single sentence in the *Ford County Globe* of September 9, 1879, announcing the end of Wyatt's career in Dodge City. The *Dodge City Times* made no mention at all of his resignation. Both papers had previously praised Wyatt for his services as one of the town's lawmen, but neither paper offered a word of thanks to a man who'd never shirked from his duty in one of the more dangerous communities in the West for a peace officer. If not for Wyatt and his fellow lawmen consistently disarming rowdy cowboys, Boot Hill would have been a more expansive affair.

Wyatt would say later that the tantalizing reports of big silver strikes at a place called Tombstone, Arizona, prompted his decision to quit Dodge's police force. "I was young and the urge was upon me for a fortune," he said, "so I was on my way." And yet the *Globe* news item made no mention of Tombstone. It gave Wyatt's destination as Las Vegas, which does make sense. His friend Doc Holliday was in Las Vegas, and so were the shady characters known as the Dodge City Gang. Doc surely wrote Wyatt about rip-roaring New Town and its business prospects, those business prospects being gambling, that is.

In the last year, Wyatt had been dealing cards during his off-duty hours in the Long Branch saloon, with monte and faro his specialty. From Peoria to Wichita to Dodge City, he'd always been around gambling halls and gamblers, and he'd seen it all when it came to the ins and outs of the popular games of chance. Dealing cards suited him. Also, one could learn a lot about a man from across a gaming table, and the additional income on top of Wyatt's city salary didn't hurt, either. Wyatt may have believed a fortune awaited him in Arizona, but the gambling halls of Las Vegas were worth a look, and they were on the way.

Before saying goodbye to Dodge, Wyatt somehow got the idea that the Tombstone country needed a stage line, so he purchased a Concord coach. These quality New Hampshire–made passenger coaches sold for over a thousand dollars new. If it was indeed a true Concord, Wyatt most likely acquired a used one. In addition to the coach, the Earp caravan counted two wagons and a total of sixteen head of horses, with the coach being towed behind one of the wagons. Joining Wyatt and Mattie for the journey were brother Jim; his wife, Bessie; and Bessie's daughter, Hattie. They were looking for a better life, too, and Wyatt's big plans sounded good.

The Earp caravan lumbered west over the old Raton Route of the Santa Fe Trail, now paralleled by the tracks of the Santa Fe Railway. From the top of Raton Pass, they got their first view of New Mexico Territory, the vast, grassy plains below them dotted with volcanic cones and buttes. And the cool, dry air was like a gift from heaven, a marked change from the dreadful heat and humidity of Dodge City.

At Las Vegas came the cheerful reunion between Wyatt and Doc. Kate Elder, though, found nothing cheerful about it. She was jealous of anything or anyone she saw as competition for Doc's attentions. She went into a rage when she once found another woman with Doc. Brandishing a big knife, Kate threatened to "rip her open." Doc's gal never threatened Wyatt, but she didn't like him, and she especially didn't like the strong influence he held over her lover. And Kate blamed Wyatt for all the subsequent troubles she had with Doc. "I loved Doc and thought the world of him," she said decades later, "and he was always kind to me until he got mixed up with the Earps." This reunion, she said, "meant the end of the happiness we had enjoyed." Wyatt's simple take on Doc and Kate's relationship: "they were always a quarrelsome couple."

The Earps made camp on the outskirts of Las Vegas. How long Wyatt took to get an idea for what New Town offered is uncertain. Probably no more than a few days or a week. That would be enough time for Wyatt to do some gambling, feel out the situation with the Dodge City transplants, and talk over future plans with Doc. He could see right away, though, that the place was overloaded with both saloons and gambling dens. Together, New Town and Old Town boasted thirty-five liquor joints, and the population now stood at only five thousand.

Thoughts of Tombstone continued to weigh heavily on Wyatt's mind. Doc had heard the exciting reports about the new discoveries too. Everyone had. Eastbound travelers from Arizona passed through Las Vegas, and they brought with them the latest news of the wealth coming out of the ground. A new Tombstone stamp mill, went one report, was producing $2,500 a day from silver ore. The *Chicago Tribune* had run an entire column that summer on the immense potential of the Tombstone mines. Maybe it was a case of "the grass is always greener," but Wyatt decided that Arizona was the place to be. He convinced Doc to come along as well, although it probably took little convincing.

When the Earp caravan pulled away from Las Vegas, Kate and Doc were riding in Wyatt and Mattie's wagon. Recent reports of marauding Apache Indians led by Victorio, and their skirmishes with pursuing US troops, caused some uneasiness for the travelers, but the fighting was actually more than a hundred miles south of the Earps' route. That route would take them first to the home of Wyatt's older brother and wife, Allie, just outside Prescott, the territorial capital of Arizona. Virgil, thirty-six years old, served as a constable in Prescott, a town of about twenty-five hundred people. Gold and silver mining reigned in the region—even Virgil started to excavate a shaft shortly before his brothers arrived—but what kept the town (and its several saloons) going was the nearby military post of Fort Whipple.

The overland journey to Prescott comprised some three weeks under the open sky, and during the long days when the dust from the horses' hooves proved a constant annoyance, Kate witnessed the friendship between Doc and Wyatt grow even stronger. Upon their arrival at Virgil's place, Allie Earp took an immediate dislike to Doc. "Wyatt kind of casually introduced him to us as a dentist," she recalled years later. "Right away I said, 'How'd you like to yank out a loose tooth of mine?' He gave me a nasty look and said, 'Keep

Virgil Earp. Artwork by John McCormack.
(ORIGINAL SCRATCHBOARD IN AUTHOR'S COLLECTION)

your baby teeth in your mouth where they belong. I've got no use for them.' Wyatt roared like it was a big joke."

Doc and Kate took up residence in the town's one hotel, making it easy for Doc to get his gambling fix. Wyatt, Jim, and their families remained at Virgil's place for about three weeks, during which time a number of serious discussions between the Earp brothers occurred. Wyatt remained fixated on Tombstone, talking about it so much that, in Wyatt's words, Virgil "became imbued with the fever of excitement and so joined my party." But to Allie Earp, who liked their life in Prescott, Virgil's "fever" was nothing more than Wyatt coercing his brother. It was just like Wyatt, she recalled—he "was like his father, old Nicholas Porter. Always thinkin' of himself. Always the big cheese. And bossy as all get out." Nevertheless, Allie agreed to the move.

Once again, the Earp brothers were being drawn together as if by some magnetic force, the center of gravity this time being two hundred and eighty miles south at a young mining camp in the San Pedro River Valley, just a day's ride from the Mexican border.

WHILE ALLIE DID HER BEST TO NARROW DOWN HER AND VIR-gil's possessions in preparation for packing the wagons, Virgil had his own business to attend to. On November 27, 1879, he made an important visit to the office of the US marshal for Arizona Territory, Crawley P. Dake, a fellow Civil War veteran. He informed Marshal Dake of his plans and asked for a commission as deputy US marshal for the county in which Tombstone was located. Virgil was well-liked with a good, solid reputation in Prescott, and he'd been a fine constable. Dake gave him the commission. As a deputy US marshal, Virgil would earn fees for serving warrants, escorting prisoners to jail, and other official duties. It wouldn't amount to a lot, but at least he knew he'd have that income while in Tombstone.

When the Earp caravan started south, Doc and Kate weren't part of it, although Doc promised Wyatt he'd follow along in time. Doc and Kate remained in Prescott, and Kate had more than a little to do with that decision. She held out hope that if enough distance separated Doc and his friend, maybe she could weaken the strange bond that existed between them. Another reason for hanging around in Prescott were the several buildings that made up the west side of the courthouse square: nearly all saloons and gambling halls. It became known as Whiskey Row. "A notable fact," wrote a newspaper correspondent about Prescott, "is that respectable ladies scarcely ever walk the pavement of the west side." With the soldiers from Fort Whipple, area miners, and territorial legislators periodically visiting the capital, Doc didn't lack for customers to lay their money down.

The saloons and gambling dens with their banjos and pianos and other diversions into the late hours also made for a lively place to endure the dreary weeks of winter, at least for Doc and the sporting crowd. But he had pressing business back in Las Vegas, among which were his arrests and fines from the previous year that remained on the books. Doc departed Prescott in late February 1880, and although the trip to New Mexico was considerably quicker than the arduous wagon journey he'd experienced with the Earps, it wasn't necessarily better. The Star Line Mail & Transportation Company—also known as the Star Buckboard line—now operated between Prescott and Santa Fe, but passengers traveling between those two points were forced to endure four days and four nights in an open buckboard, often sharing a small seat with a bulky mail sack. Such an ordeal for someone afflicted with tuberculosis seems crazy, but Doc never let his disease stop him. Fortunately, he was able to jump on a Pullman car at the New Mexico capital and ride in comfort for the final leg of his trip.

At Las Vegas, Doc made at least one court appearance and actually got a gambling charge dismissed. A future dismissal for the charge of carrying a deadly weapon appeared likely as well. Of course, getting right with the district court didn't mean he was now going to stroll about Las Vegas unarmed. No, he was going to carry his deadly weapon, and, coldly indifferent to the consequences, he already knew the person he was going to use it on.

As the story goes, an old grudge existed between Doc and a man he'd known in Dodge City named Charles Wright. Doc learned that Wright was now bartending in a saloon in Old Town, right on the plaza. After getting a meal in New Town, Doc paid ten cents to ride in a hack to the plaza. Upon stepping out, he walked to the saloon, reached for his revolver, cocked it, and burst through the front door. Spotting his man serving some customers from behind the bar, Doc quickly raised his revolver. Wright ducked down as terrified customers scattered, knocking over chairs and tables, whiskey glasses and beer bottles crashing to the floor.

The bartender went for his own gun behind the bar, and when he sprang back up, a barrage of hot lead flew in both directions. Despite the close quarters of the saloon, the two foes nearly emptied their revolvers before Wright suddenly dropped in a lifeless heap. Doc calmly turned around and walked out of the saloon and stepped into another hack to take him back to New Town. Wright was not dead, however. One of

Doc's bullets had grazed the bartender's skin near his spine, which sent a debilitating shock through his body. In a couple of hours, Wright was up and as good as new, although he made sure to make himself scarce until Doc left town.

Miguel Antonio Otero, a future territorial governor of New Mexico, vividly remembered this incident, and he related that the Las Vegas peace officers chose to ignore the shooting. They weren't interested in Holliday or Wright, Otero said, because they "were much too busy looking after their own games."

Doc stayed in Las Vegas for a few more days, and despite the violent tendencies Doc exhibited with Wright, Otero made an effort to get to know the gambler. "I met him quite frequently," Otero recalled, "and found him to be a very likeable fellow."

―――――――

IN EARLY JUNE 1880, THE US CENSUS ENUMERATOR WENT HOUSE to house and door to door in Prescott, Arizona, methodically writing down the names of each resident, their age, occupation, and other statistics. He found Doc Holliday living on Montezuma Street, which, conveniently enough, was less than a half block away from Whiskey Row. As for occupation, Doc stated he was a dentist, which he technically was, but one wonders if the census taker silently chuckled as he wrote the word *dentist* on his form.

Doc was living in a boardinghouse, and one of his fellow tenants was thirty-nine-year-old John J. Gosper, a miner, cattleman, recent divorcé, and secretary of Arizona Territory. An individual not listed as living at the boardinghouse that June, however, was Kate Elder. In fact, Kate Elder is missing completely from the 1880 census for Arizona Territory, and no one of the correct age and birthplace using any of Kate's aliases can be found, either. However, census takers weren't perfect and did occasionally miss people. Or perhaps Doc and Kate had another one of their notorious spats and she left him for a short time, traveling to parts unknown. In any event, she was back with her lover by early September, when they left Prescott together.

This move was prompted by a letter from Wyatt informing Doc that the reports regarding the "new El Dorado" were true, and there was good money to be made as a gambler. This definitely appealed to Doc. Not so much Kate—nothing involving Wyatt did. "If you are going to tie yourself to the Earp brothers," she said to Doc, "go to it. I am going to Globe." They traveled together as far as the small settlement of Gillette, sixty miles down the road from Prescott, and then parted. Doc told Kate he probably wouldn't like it in Tombstone and that he would be in Globe in a few days. In Globe, Kate purchased on time a simple hotel or boarding-house. Doc never showed, but Kate was far from out of Doc's life.

Doc's sojourn in Prescott had lasted less than a year, but he did something during that short period that allows us to look into his eyes today. He visited the photography studio of Daniel F. Mitchell and paid for a portrait. In the resulting photo, the last one known to have been taken of Doc in life, he's standing and staring straight at the camera. On his slim frame he wears a nicely fitted double-breasted coat, topped with a neat cravat with diamond stickpin. His hair is light, as is his mustache, which he wears in a style identical to Wyatt's more famous bristles. Nearly every man wore some kind of mustache or beard during this hirsute era, of course, but one can't help but wonder if Doc was emulating his friend.

The paper photographic print was pasted onto a card measuring roughly four and a quarter by six and a half inches and, in this case, it bore the photographer's imprint on the reverse. This type of photo was known as a cabinet card, and normally a sitter would have more than one made. How many Doc ordered from Mitchell is unknown, but he apparently was happy enough with the way he looked that he mailed one to his aunt Ella McKey in Georgia, a sister of his mother. It was a way of saying that he was doing fine. At the bottom of the card he wrote, "Yours Truly, J. H. Holliday."

As evidenced by this cabinet card, Doc kept in touch with family and friends in Georgia. One of his favorite correspondents was his fetching first cousin, Mattie Holliday, with whom he may or may not have had a romantic relationship. He exchanged letters with Mattie for years, and

Doc Holliday from a photograph made circa 1880 by Prescott, Arizona, photographer Daniel F. Mitchell. (DIGITALLY RESTORED BY TETYANA DYACHENKO, DIGITARTGALLERY.COM, AUTHOR'S COLLECTION)

yet not one single letter, not even a paragraph, written by John Henry Holliday, either to Mattie or anyone else, has survived.

———————

SOUTHERN ARIZONA WAS UNLIKE ANYTHING THE EARPS HAD ever seen. Distant mountains appeared barren and uninviting but the mesas and valleys were covered with native grasses perfect for grazing cattle. Desert shrubs such as creosote bush and tarbush took hold in the rocky, broken country. The painful-looking Spanish dagger (yucca) stood sentinel here and there, and there was far too much cactus.

When the Earp caravan arrived at Tombstone, the mining camp consisted of about fifty houses, some of them tents. Among those fifty were ten saloons, six stores, five boardinghouses, one blacksmith shop, and one newspaper. The population numbered more than two thousand but was growing by about twenty people a day, primarily men. A visitor estimated some three-quarters of the residents were "American" and one-quarter other nationalities. The few Chinese in Tombstone faced not only prejudice but an organized effort to force them to leave town. They stayed.

The din of construction—hammers, handsaws, and the shouts and laughter of workers—couldn't have sounded sweeter to Wyatt. He and the others were witnessing a birth, and the energy in the air was almost palpable. The Earps had come to the right place.

Around circular pits filled with muddy water, skilled Hispanos with *adoberas* (wooden molds) rapidly formed one adobe brick after another, and the adobes were barely dry before they were laid into the rising walls of several new buildings. Lodging was scarce until hotels could be completed. A bed in a room with a half-dozen others cost a dollar a night. One could sleep on a floor for half that price, but one had to supply his own blankets.

Miners made four dollars a day; carpenters, masons, and engineers, six dollars; and laborers around the mines, three dollars. These were good wages; in the states, carpenters and masons generally got no more than $2.50 per day. But everything was expensive. A one-hundred-pound bag of flour that cost less than $3 in Topeka, Kansas, sold for $6 in Tombstone, and the "vilest brain-destroying whiskey" offered in the saloons was served up at .25 cents a drink.

The exploding population, however, made finding a job challenging for newcomers. Tombstone was filled with idle men, observed one correspondent. "As a general thing," he wrote, "men appear to make it a point to come here broke, which is a very poor plan. No man can come here and get work at once, and it is a very poor place to be without money." Another Tombstone visitor commented that the town was "overrun and overdone, but not overrated."

Mines and mining, naturally, were the main subjects of conversation on the streets, and everyone, it seemed, had one or several claims for sale. In fact, within a fifty-mile radius, thousands of claims had already been filed. And each mine had a name, many of them quite colorful: Toughnut, Lucky Cuss, Contention, Grand Central, True Blue, Poodle Dog, and Telephone. One man joked that he could ask a Tombstone citizen his opinion of Garfield or Hancock, that year's presidential candidates, "and he will ask you where it is located, whether it has been developed, and how much it assays."

The most storied name in the area, of course, was Tombstone itself. In 1877, a thirty-year-old prospector named Ed Schieffelin was making preparations for an expedition alone into Apache country when he was given some macabre advice. "If you go," he was told, "we shall have to follow you with your tombstone." Schieffelin avoided death at the hands of the Apaches, however, and discovered exactly what he was looking for: silver ore. He recorded his first mining claim in September 1877 and gave it the name "Tumbstone Mine." (The registrar was apparently a poor speller.) Less than a year later, when a town site was laid out on a ridge known as Goose Flats, the miners voted to give it the name Tombstone.

Many of the town's saloons and gambling halls were located along three blocks of Allen Street, in the center of Tombstone's business section. And once the sun slipped below the horizon, that street turned into something like the busiest carnival midway, and just as noisy. "On any evening of the week," wrote a *Daily Arizona Citizen* correspondent in April 1880, "we can turn out into our streets more white men than any other city, town or village in Arizona." The two dance houses were always packed, and at least four faro games (also called "faro banks"), and several monte games ran day and night, all designed to relieve the miners and workers of their hard-earned money.

Tombstone also had the same problems of any other boomtown: drunkenness, violence, and thieving. "Lots of b-a-d men and women in

Tombstone's bustling Allen Street as it appeared in April 1880.
(PUBLIC DOMAIN IMAGE, AUTHOR'S COLLECTION)

the camp," wrote one visitor. "Good ones in the majority." Just who was good and bad in Tombstone, however, wasn't always easily agreed upon. Sometimes it wasn't a matter of right and wrong; it was a matter of picking a side.

WYATT AND HIS BROTHERS HAD HARDLY UNPACKED THEIR wagons when they started acquiring mining claims, although on a very small scale. Speculating in mines, of course, was just another form of gambling. Over the next eleven months, the Earps, along with a partner or two, acquired nine mining claims. Wyatt named one mine the Long Branch, after a Dodge City saloon he obviously had very good memories of. Another he named for his wife, Mattie Blaylock. The brothers also invested in several town lots.

As for Wyatt's plans for a stage line, he'd learned on the way to Tombstone that not one, but two stage lines ran daily coaches between Tucson and the new mining bonanza. Trying to start a third didn't make much sense. However, Wyatt found a ready buyer for his Concord coach in the owner of one of the stage companies. Wyatt would be seeing a lot more of that coach, though, and quite a few others, for he soon took a job with Wells Fargo & Company as a shotgun messenger, riding guard for shipments of bullion and money transported on those very same stagecoaches.

In early June 1880, on the same day a census taker visited Doc Holliday in Prescott, a census taker also made the rounds in Tombstone. All the Earps were listed together in one household. Allie later explained that when they first arrived in the mining camp, "Every house was taken and as fast as men could haul lumber from the Huachucas [Mountains] and build another one, there was people campin' on the spot in wagons or a tent waitin' to move in." The Earps finally secured a one-room adobe that, Allie remembered, "didn't even have a floor, just hard packed adobe, but it cost forty dollars a month. We fixed up the roof, drove up the wagons on each side, and took the wagon sheets off the bows to stretch out for more rooms."

One of the strange things about the 1880 census record for the Earps is that the occupation given for Virgil and Wyatt is "farmer." Wyatt abhorred farming and hadn't walked behind a plow in years, so it boggles the mind to think that he, as well as his deputy US marshal brother, would identify as farmers—if it was indeed Virgil and Wyatt who provided that information to the enumerator. Whatever the case, it's clear that the Earps had not come to Tombstone to raise crops along the nearby San Pedro.

Jim Earp's occupation is given correctly in the census as saloonkeeper. He worked in Vogan & Flynn's saloon and liquor store on Allen Street. Each of the brothers' spouses are identified as "wife." And they did exactly what wives were expected to do: They prepared meals, laundered clothes, and kept the household tidy and clean. The women did do some sewing to bring in a little extra money. As Allie later explained their situation, rather unhappily, "That was our life: workin' and sittin' home. Good women didn't go anyplace." Good women, wives, not prostitutes. Tombstone was another fresh start—for *all* the Earps, drab as it might be for the females.

In late July, Morgan Earp, now twenty-nine years old, arrived in

Tombstone to join his brothers. Morgan, whom Allie considered "the most good natured and handsomest" of the brothers, had been living the last two years or so in Montana, where he'd taken a wife, Louisa Houston. In September 1879, he'd followed the Earp lawman tradition with an appointment as a policeman in Butte. But it seems once family news of Wyatt's Arizona plans reached Montana, Morgan resigned his position, and he and Louisa packed their belongings and left for Arizona Territory via Temescal, California, the home of parents Nicholas and Virginia Ann. Because Louisa was suffering from an illness, possibly rheumatoid arthritis, Morgan left her in the care of the elder Earps until she was well enough to follow him to Tombstone.

Morgan Earp. Artwork by John McCormack. (ORIGINAL SCRATCHBOARD IN AUTHOR'S COLLECTION)

Morgan showed up in the boomtown shortly after a sensational killing on Allen Street, not far from where Jim was working as a bartender. The unusual cause of the killing was an "odd kind of looking" blue-and-black-checkered shirt just purchased by Tom Waters, a gambler who stood more than six feet tall and, when drinking, was not a pleasant fellow. In the Alhambra Saloon, several of Waters's acquaintances couldn't resist teasing Waters about his new shirt, and the more Waters drank, the angrier he became. Waters began being abusive to those around him, finally saying, "Now if anyone don't like what I've said, let him get up, God damn him. I'm chief. I'm boss. I'll knock the first son of a bitch down that says anything about my shirt again."

Before long, Edward Bradshaw, a friend of Waters, walked into the

Alhambra unaware of the shirt situation. Bradshaw started to compliment Waters on his new shirt when Waters suddenly slammed his big fist into Bradshaw's left eye, the blow knocking the poor man off his feet. Bradshaw, nervously laughing, slowly got up and retreated to the saloon's back room, where he washed the blood off his face. He then left the saloon and walked to his cabin, affixed a bandage to his eye, slipped a revolver into his coat pocket, and started back for Allen Street.

In the meantime, the drunken Waters walked across the street from the Alhambra to the Vogan & Flynn saloon to see, he said, if anyone there didn't like his shirt. This was followed by more ranting and raving until Waters finally returned to the Alhambra. As Waters stood in the saloon's doorway, Bradshaw walked up to him and asked, "Why did you do that?" Waters snapped back, "Because you deserve it," and the gambler again delivered a powerful blow to Bradshaw's head. But this time when Bradshaw stood up, he wasn't laughing. He jerked the gun from his pocket and fired point-blank at his friend's chest. The bullet pierced Waters's heart, and the big man, a surprised look on his face, collapsed to the ground. Not yet satisfied, Bradshaw stood over the prostrate body and very deliberately fired three more shots, the last one into Waters's head. The new shirt was now a bloody mess.

Tombstone's marshal, thirty-one-year-old Fred White, quickly placed Bradshaw under arrest, and following a verdict of murder from a coroner's jury, he was taken to Tucson, the county seat, to await the convening of a grand jury. The lawman who got the job of transporting Bradshaw the seventy-five miles to Tucson was the same man who claimed he wanted no more of a peace officer's life. On July 27, 1880, Wyatt Earp had been appointed deputy sheriff for the Tombstone District, Pima County.

———

THE WAY WYATT EXPLAINED IT LATER, HE ESSENTIALLY HAD NO choice but to resign from Wells Fargo and take the deputy sheriff position due to the fact that Tombstone had become so "unruly." With more men flocking to Tombstone each day, the town was indeed experiencing rising lawlessness: fistfights, killings, and, as a diarist described it, "Too much

loose pistol practice." A town ordinance passed in April 1880 forbid
the carrying of firearms, knives, and
other weapons "concealed about the
person" by anyone except law officers. The ordinance would be revised the following year to ban all
weapons, concealed or not. Nevertheless, like in Dodge City, the ordinance was regularly flaunted.

The announcement of Wyatt's
hiring was heartily welcomed by
the nearly three-month-old *Tombstone Epitaph*, then operating out of
a tent: "The appointment of Wyatt
Earp as Deputy Sheriff, by Sheriff
[Charles] Shibell, is an eminently
proper one. . . . Wyatt has filled

John Philip Clum, Tombstone mayor,
Earp supporter, and owner of the
Tombstone Epitaph.
(PUBLIC DOMAIN IMAGE, AUTHOR'S
COLLECTION)

various positions in which bravery and determination were requisites, and
in every instance proved himself the right man in the right place."

The part owner and editor of the *Epitaph*, twenty-nine-year-old John
Clum, was at one time the Indian agent for the Apaches on the San Carlos Reservation and, previous to getting into the newspaper business, a
practicing attorney. Clum, small of stature but with plenty of spunk,
seems to have taken an instant liking to Wyatt and his brothers. They
were "tall, gaunt, intrepid," he wrote years later. Another plus was the
brothers' political affiliation; they were Republicans. Wyatt had even
served as a Republican delegate from Ford County, Kansas, at the state
convention in Topeka. Clum was Republican as well, and, unsurprisingly,
so was his paper. The *Epitaph*'s editor would become a fast friend of Wyatt's and an ally to the Earp brothers over the coming months.

Although the *Epitaph* was right to praise the selection of Wyatt for
deputy sheriff, Wyatt's acceptance of the position wasn't just about en-

forcing the law. As a man with a badge, he benefited from added respect and prestige beyond that of a sporting man, of which Tombstone had no shortage. As a lawman, even though he was a deputy for the county and not an officer of the township, he could be more attuned to the happenings in Tombstone, the comings and goings of people he should know. Just as his father had done in the small towns they jumped to and from, it was a way of positioning himself within the community. A small step in an attempt to "get ahead," but a step nevertheless.

Morgan took Wyatt's job as shotgun messenger, and now that Wyatt was no longer away from Tombstone on stage runs, he had more time for gambling. An ornate new saloon called the Oriental opened just a few days before Wyatt's appointment as deputy sheriff, and it was immediately deemed the finest in Arizona. Situated on the northeast corner of Fifth and Allen, it boasted an ornately carved bar with gilt highlights and dazzling chandeliers hanging from the ceiling. The gaming or club rooms on the second floor were covered with colorful Brussels carpet, and for those patrons taking a brief rest from faro or monte, the latest magazines and newspapers, as well as writing materials, were conveniently placed close at hand.

Clara Spalding Brown, twenty-six-year-old miner's wife and correspondent of the *San Diego Union*, wrote about the Oriental that, "Every evening music from a piano and a violin attracts a crowd; and the scene is really a gay one—but all for the men. To be sure, there are frequent dances, which I have heard called 'respectable,' but as long as so many members of the demi-monde [prostitutes], who are very numerous and very showy here, patronize them, many honest women will hesitate to attend."

The Oriental would come to be almost a second home for Wyatt— and, by the fall of 1880, a business investment. Wyatt became a partner in Rickabaugh & Company, which held the gambling concession at the Oriental. It was a happy arrangement: Having a law officer on the premises helped keep things orderly, and Wyatt could deal "pasteboard and ivory" (faro) to his heart's content.

BY THE END OF SEPTEMBER, DOC HOLLIDAY HAD FINALLY found his way to Tombstone. At some point, he took a room at the boardinghouse of Camillus and Mary Fly on Fremont Street. Camillus was a professional photographer, and his photo gallery, complete with the "finest sky-light and background scenery outside of San Francisco," stood directly behind the boardinghouse. Kate Elder later said that Doc wrote her frequently, begging her to visit him in Tombstone. She would eventually visit him three times, but she claimed that on the first visit, she found Doc "a very changed man." Maybe so, but a bloody altercation at the Oriental on October 10, 1880, suggests Doc hadn't changed much at all.

The trouble began about midnight on a Sunday night when Doc and a hotheaded gambler named Johnny Tyler got into some kind of argument that sprang from a rivalry between two gambler factions in Tombstone, the Slopers and the Easterners. The Slopers were largely sporting men from west of the Continental Divide, mostly California, and the Easterners were from the opposite side of the line. The argument quickly became heated, so much so that friends and bystanders believed the pistols the two men carried were about to come out. The parties rushed in and disarmed Holliday and Tyler and made sure their guns were placed out of reach behind the bar. At that point, Milt Joyce, a partner in the saloon concession, ordered Tyler to leave, telling him he didn't want any trouble, and Tyler complied.

Joyce now began to berate Doc for causing a disturbance in his saloon, but Doc, in a surly mood, wasn't having it. Finally, Joyce had enough. A former blacksmith, he didn't have any trouble manhandling scrawny Doc Holliday and throwing him out the front door. Just as soon as Joyce returned to the saloon, however, Doc walked back in and demanded his gun from behind the bar. Joyce refused to give it to him, and Doc stormed out.

The music in the saloon started up again, and the patrons went back to their drinks and conversation. It turned out to be the lull before the storm. Doc suddenly burst into the saloon, a double-action revolver in his outstretched hand. Spewing a string of curse words, he rushed Joyce, who was just coming out from behind the bar. Doc fired two quick shots, one hitting Joyce's right hand and the other punching through the bar and putting a hole in the big toe of Joyce's partner, William Parker. Joyce got off a shot with his own revolver but missed, and before Doc could fire a third shot, Joyce was on him. As the two came together, Joyce slammed his revolver into Doc's head, and they both fell to the floor. Several men rushed in to pull the two apart, including Marshal Fred White and a policeman. Doc was bleeding so profusely from a head wound that it was initially thought Joyce had killed him. Other than a large knot on his head and a massive headache, however, Doc would be fine.

Deputy US Marshal Virgil Earp arrested Doc and escorted him from the saloon. The following day, Doc, Joyce, and Parker were all laid up in bed. When Doc was finally able to appear before the justice of the peace, four witnesses curiously failed to appear. A charge of attempted murder was dropped, and Doc pleaded guilty to the lesser charge of assault and battery. He got off with a fine of $20 plus $11.24 in court costs. Milt Joyce, however, came very close to losing his hand. The gunshot wound eventually healed, but the scar was a bitter reminder that Doc Holliday had tried to kill him. And the fact that Holliday and the Earps were tight didn't make Joyce think too kindly of the Earps, either. He was already inclined not to see eye to eye with the brothers. Joyce was a Democrat.

TWENTY-THREE-YEAR-OLD DAVID J. DAVIS, IN DESCRIBING Tombstone in a letter to his hometown newspaper in Tremont, Pennsylvania, cautioned that despite the place's untold mineral wealth and the impressive wages for workingmen, he in no way meant to imply that Tombstone was some kind of paradise. No, he wrote, "it has a dark side."

What exactly that dark side was, Davis didn't say. He could have been referring to any number of things, from Tombstone's saloons and gambling halls to its Mary Magdalenes to the seemingly low value placed upon human life. George Parsons, a Tombstone miner who diligently kept a diary, wrote of a horrific thunderstorm that hit the town in October 1880. Lightning struck and killed a worker at the lumberyard, and when news of the tragedy got out, the main topic of discussion was the possibility that the lightning bolt had been drawn to a huge mineral deposit beneath the surface. "A good vein is all that's wanted," Parsons wrote in disgust. "Human life is a secondary consideration altogether."

Davis may also have been alluding to the crimes that occurred beyond town limits by a semiorganized band of cattle thieves and occasional stage robbers who conducted their operations on both sides of the US-Mexican boundary. Other than those "ranchers" in league with the rustlers, no one's herd was safe, whether along the San Pedro southwest of Tombstone or deep into Sonora, Mexico. And horses and mules were just as vulnerable. After altering brands and earmarks, the thieves fenced the herds through the corrupt ranchers, who then sold the stolen cattle to beef and hide buyers in Tombstone or to stockmen in New Mexico. A good many were also driven to the San Carlos Reservation, where they were purchased as beef rations for the Apaches at five dollars a head.

For a long time, the rustlers little feared molestation from US law officers or Mexican authorities. In fact, a strong suspicion existed that certain lawmen were being paid to look the other way. Several members of this gang had Texas origins, and it was said that at one time they numbered as many as two hundred men. The lawbreakers were widely known as the "Cowboys," a term that was generally an innocuous catchall for the young men who drove cattle to market or worked on ranches. But as Arizona Territory's US attorney explained, "the name has been corrupted in the Territories of New Mexico and Arizona, and in its local significance includes the lawless element that exists upon the border, who subsist by rapine plunder and highway robbery; and whose amusements are drunken orgies, and murder." The *Arizona Weekly Star* went so far as to proclaim the gang "worse than the Apache and should be treated as such."

The Cowboys were a common sight in Tombstone, usually in groups of ten or twelve at a time, where they mostly behaved themselves. They came to town when they had money, which, Virgil Earp told a reporter, they spent

free as water in the saloons, dance houses, or faro banks, and this is one
reason they have so many friends in town. . . . The saloons and gambling
houses, into whose treasuries most of the money is ultimately turned, re-
ceive them cordially and must be called warm friends of the cowboys. A
good many of the merchants fear to express themselves against the criminal
element, because they want to keep the patronage of the cowboys' friends,
and the result is that when any conflict between officers and cattle thieves
or stage robbers occurs, followed up by shootings around town . . . most
of the expression of opinion comes from the desperado class and their
friends, and the men who should speak loudest and most decisively to cor-
rect the condition of affairs are generally the quietest.

Not only did merchants and gambling halls seek the Cowboys' patronage, so did those running for political office. The Cowboys did indeed
vote, and in another reflection of their southern roots, they voted Democrat. There was plenty about the Cowboys, then, for the Earps not to
like. The same, of course, could be said of the Cowboys' feelings toward
the Earp brothers, whom they looked upon as interlopers to some ex-
tent (carpetbaggers would be the comparable southern term), townies
who'd plopped themselves into Tombstone and were making life difficult
for them.

To be sure, the Earp brothers weren't saints themselves, but whenever
a posse was formed to go after stage robbers, murderers, or horse, mule,
and cattle thieves, the Earps were nearly always riding with it.

SIX

A REGULAR SLAUGHTERHOUSE

The hot air and the wild, dreary environment seemed to breed
within bad men a spirit that led to desperate acts and reckless
disregard for human life.

"TOMBSTONE'S TOUGH DAYS," *THE SUN*

Allen Street, Tombstone
12:30 a.m., October 28, 1880

Gunshots. There was no mistaking that sound. Wyatt was in a saloon on Allen Street when he heard them, and because several Cowboys were in town that night, he had a good idea who was pulling the triggers. He immediately rushed out the door and saw muzzle flashes down the street, a block away. Wyatt was unarmed but he raced toward where he'd last seen the flashes. He'd nearly reached a vacant lot when he came upon his brother Morgan and his roommate, Fred Dodge; they shared a small cabin at the back of the lot. Wyatt asked his brother who was doing the shooting. Morgan didn't know, but he said several fellows had run around the corner and into the lot.

Wyatt asked Morgan for his revolver. "No," Morgan said sternly. "Get Fred's." Morgan knew better than to be out that night unheeled, even if it was his brother asking. And Wyatt, deputy sheriff, should have known better than to go out without a weapon.

Fred handed over his revolver to Wyatt, who checked to see that the gun was loaded. "Look out for yourselves, now," Wyatt said before entering the lot. As Wyatt turned the corner, he saw Marshal White standing face-to-face with one of the Cowboys: Curly Bill Brocius.

CURLY BILL'S SOBRIQUET CAME FROM THE THICK, BLACK CURLY hair that flowed from beneath his broad-brimmed hat. Charismatic and a natural leader, he stood about five feet nine inches tall, had a lean, muscular body, a prominent Roman nose, and, according to an English correspondent who briefly knew the Cowboy, "a beautiful set of teeth." It was Curly Bill's eyes, however, that most struck the correspondent. "Their expression is not quick and piercing, but steadfast and calm," he wrote. "Still they never rest for an instant on a single subject."

No one knew much about Curly Bill's past except what he chose to reveal. In 1878, he and a cohort ambushed an army ambulance near El Paso, Texas, believing it carried a large payroll. The bandits shot the ambulance full of holes, mortally wounding one soldier and severely injuring another, but fled when an officer brandishing a carbine jumped from the ambulance and charged them. Curly Bill and his accomplice were subsequently captured and sentenced to five years in the penitentiary. Before they could be delivered to prison, however, the two desperados escaped, with Curly Bill eventually making his way to Arizona.

Doc Holliday didn't think much of the Cowboy leader. He once described Curly Bill as "a most notorious character." But, then again, many people thought the same thing about Doc.

"I AM AN OFFICER," MARSHAL WHITE SHOUTED TO CURLY BILL, "give me your pistol!"

The Cowboy pulled his Colt revolver out of its scabbard, and as soon as the gun cleared the leather, Marshal White grabbed the barrel. Just then, Wyatt came up behind Curly Bill and threw his arms around the Cowboy and looked over his shoulder to make sure there were no other weapons.

"Now, you God damned son of a bitch," White yelled, "give up that weapon!"

With that, White gave the barrel a sharp jerk, and a burst of flame erupted from the muzzle as the gun went off, sending a .45-caliber bullet into White's left groin. "I am shot," White gasped as he fell. Uncertain of who now possessed Curly Bill's Colt revolver, Wyatt slammed the butt of his own pistol into the Cowboy's skull, knocking him down. It was then that Wyatt saw Curly Bill's Colt on the ground and picked it up. Wyatt next grabbed Curly Bill by the collar and ordered him to get up.

"What have I done?" a loopy Curly Bill protested. "I have not done anything to be arrested for."

By this time Morgan and Fred Dodge had come up, as well as several onlookers. "Someone put the fire out in Fred's clothes," Wyatt said. The muzzle flash from Curly Bill's gun had caught the marshal's clothes on fire.

Wyatt hauled Curly Bill off to the town jail and afterward, with the help of brothers Virgil and Morgan, rounded up four of the drunken Cowboys who'd been shooting off their guns. Marshal White was still alive, although in tremendous pain. When a doctor examined the wound, he found that the bullet had entered at a forty-five-degree angle and nearly passed through the man's body. The doctor carefully cut the bullet from White's buttock and was optimistic that Tombstone's marshal would survive. However, the bullet had cut through White's small intestines; he was actually dying.

When word got out the next day that the marshal's wound was fatal, rumblings reached Wyatt about a plan to snatch Curly Bill from jail and hang him. Wyatt took the threat seriously and loaded the Cowboy into a buggy to transport him to Tucson to await trial. For the first few dusty miles of their journey, an armed party that included Virgil and Morgan rode along as an escort.

WYATT AND HIS BROTHERS HAD PLENTY KEEPING THEM BUSY in Tombstone besides Curly Bill and the Cowboys. The Earps and their partners continued to try to make something happen with their mining claims. In November 1880, Wyatt tramped about one of the claims near town, holding a flagpole as he assisted in a survey of the 1st North Extension of the Mountain Maid. Wyatt, Virgil, Jim, and partner Robert J. Winders owned the claim, of which a small portion of its seventeen and a half acres extended into the western city limits of Tombstone. This was a clever move, because it allowed them to build their wood-frame houses on the land without purchasing lots from the Townsite Company. Moreover, the partners were able to count their homes as part of the required five hundred dollars in improvements before receiving a patent for the claim.

Additional improvements on the claim included a shaft twenty-three feet deep, a foundry, and a machine shop. "The four houses were built by the claimants," they attested in their filing, "and shaft sunk by them." An affidavit accompanied the survey bearing the signatures of two witnesses who swore that the improvements made on the property exceeded five hundred dollars in value. One of those signing was none other than Doc Holliday. Two months later, Doc would be a partner with Wyatt and two others in two water rights claims in the Huachuca Mountains southwest of Tombstone. The claims were named, simply, the Wyatt Earp Water Right and the Holliday Water Right.

When it came to politics, things weren't going so well. In the November election for Pima County sheriff, Wyatt had surprisingly declined to endorse his boss, Charles Shibell, and, along with his brothers, thrown his support to his friend Bob Paul. Paul was a Wells Fargo detective and shotgun messenger with previous lawman experience as a sheriff in California—and he was a Republican. Unfortunately for Wyatt, Paul lost, and by just fifty-eight votes. Sheriff Shibell quietly let it be known that Wyatt's services as deputy sheriff were no longer needed. On November 9, Wyatt resigned. Three days later, the *Tombstone Daily Nugget*, the camp's Democratic organ, reported that, "Wyatt Earp's resignation as deputy sheriff was heard of by his many friends with regret. During the time he has held the office he has been active and prompt in the discharge of all duties and every citizen had the consciousness that his life and property were as well protected as they could be by any single officer."

Another political blow came in a special election for city marshal on November 12, 1880. Virgil had tossed his hat into the ring, and as the Town Council had promptly appointed him assistant city marshal following the shooting of Marshal White, he appeared to be the frontrunner. But the Tombstone voters chose Virgil's opponent, a thirty-year-old miner with no lawman experience, 311 to 259. One newspaper suggested that the Earp brothers' switching allegiance to Bob Paul in the county sheriff election ten days earlier had soured folks on the Earps.

Maybe it did, but Wyatt wasn't yet done supporting his friend Paul. After Shibell had been declared the winner, Wyatt and other Republicans immediately suspected voter fraud. They were right. In the San Simon precinct, near the New Mexico line, 103 votes had been cast for Shibell and one for Paul, but Wyatt figured that there weren't more than fifty registered voters in the precinct. Additionally, the San Simon Valley was a known stronghold of the Cowboys. In fact, the election inspector and poll judges were either Cowboys or friendly to the Cowboys. The Cowboys, it seems, not only cast their votes for Shibell, but they cast them multiple times. And that one vote for Paul? Wyatt thought that was "just for ridicule."

Wyatt sent a message to Paul in Tucson to come to Tombstone. When Paul arrived, the first thing out of his mouth was "Wyatt, I've been robbed."

"I know it, Bob," Wyatt replied. "But you can win yet."

Wyatt had a plan. It would require one or more of the Cowboys to testify to the ballot stuffing, but Wyatt was convinced he could persuade them to do that—by using Curly Bill as a bargaining chip. Curly Bill was in jail in Tucson awaiting a hearing on the Marshal White shooting. The Cowboys desperately wanted to see him exonerated and released. As Wyatt recalled later,

I sought several of [Curly Bill's] friends and explained to them that upon the condition that they expose the facts of the fraudulent voting in the San Simon district, my testimony at the trial of Curly Bill, accordingly, would be favorable to him, not that it would have been otherwise under any circumstances, but I here sensed an opportunity to use the treachery of these outlaws against themselves and thus have justice served.

It ended up taking a little more than the promise of Wyatt's testimony, as Paul also agreed to "loan" $250 to one of the Cowboys, money that was needed to pay Curly Bill's Tucson attorney. In the meantime, a rumor spread that if Curly Bill failed to receive an acquittal, the Cowboys would ride to Tucson and remove their friend by force. The *Arizona Daily Star* urged county officials to take the threat seriously. "[N]o one acquainted with our jail will for a moment deny the ability of fifty or even twenty men to force an entrance," the paper stated. It advised the county to place heavy iron bars over the windows and strong iron doors at the two entrances.

For his part, Curly Bill doesn't seem to have had much faith that his friends would either secure him an acquittal or break him out, so he planned his own escape. That plan was foiled, however, when a surprise search at the jail revealed a "small, thin-bladed knife" tucked inside Curly Bill's hat rim, and a small saw, "such as criminals use for cutting iron bars, shackles, etc.," in a cellmate's coat collar.

On December 27, 1880, Curly Bill's case was finally brought before a justice of the peace for a preliminary hearing. Among those who testified were Wyatt, the doctor who treated Marshal White, Morgan Earp, and other eyewitnesses. Wyatt stated that when he examined Curly Bill's Colt following the shooting, he found that only one cartridge of the six in the cylinder had been fired. This suggested that Curly Bill hadn't been one of the rowdies shooting off their revolvers. Wyatt also said that he didn't think Curly Bill was drunk that night. "[I]f he was," Wyatt stated, "I did not notice it."

Curly Bill insisted that his Colt was on half cock when it accidentally discharged. Half cock is a safety position, and at half cock, a pull on the trigger shouldn't allow the revolver to fire. To verify Curly Bill's claim, a gunsmith was asked to examine his Colt, and he testified that it had a defect that indeed allowed it to fire on half cock. According to Wyatt, though, the judge appeared skeptical of the gunsmith's findings, so Wyatt grabbed Curly Bill's revolver and took the judge behind the courtroom building to a corral enclosed by an adobe wall. Wyatt loaded the revolver and then fired five shots by pulling on the trigger while the gun was on half cock.

Wyatt's shooting demonstration and the day's testimony, which even included a deathbed statement from Marshal White, all supported Curly Bill's claim that the gun accidentally discharged when the marshal tried to jerk the revolver out of his hand. Consequently, the judge determined that a murder trial wasn't warranted, and he ordered Curly Bill released from custody.

The *Epitaph* and a good many Tombstone citizens were outraged with the judge's decision. Wyatt must have had mixed feelings about it. The shooting may have been accidental, but Tombstone was better off without the likes of Curly Bill, who now held a grudge. "Regardless of the fact that I had testified in his behalf," Wyatt recalled later, "Curly Bill never forgave me for striking him across the head with my gun."

Curly Bill and his followers quickly made up for lost time. On January 9, 1881, a Sunday, they rode into Charleston, a town of 350 people nine miles southwest of Tombstone on the San Pedro River. As usual when they weren't thieving, the Cowboys had been drinking, and spotting a few horses and buggies with their teams tied up next to a church, they decided to join the congregation and share their version of brotherly love. They hadn't been inside very long, however, before Curly Bill tired of the preacher's sermon and ordered him "to stop his talk or he would shoot an eye out." At that, the preacher and his rattled parishioners bolted from the church. Before the Cowboys left town, they shot out some lights and blazed away at the night sky, much like they'd done in Tombstone before Marshal White was killed.

According to a news report, an unnamed but presumably very brave peace officer arrested Curly Bill and all his cohorts a day or two later. The Cowboys were subsequently fined $50 each, which they reportedly paid. However, Curly Bill's bunch wasn't through hell-raising. On January 18 at Contention, ten miles north of Charleston, they terrorized the small community and robbed a cash drawer of fifty dollars. The Cowboys then exchanged gunfire with several townsfolk before riding away, yelling like demons. From there, Curly Bill's gang appeared in Watervale, two miles from Tombstone. Parading about the tiny hamlet wearing two cartridge belts and brandishing a revolver and a lever-action Henry rifle, Curly Bill supposedly sent messages to certain lawmen informing them of his location and to come and take him. No one took the crazed Cowboy up on his invitation.

An exasperated Contention resident wrote the *Arizona Weekly Star* that, "The terror these men have caused on the traveling public, as well as the residents along the San Pedro, is having a serious influence, and this scab on the body politic, needs a fearless operation to remove it."

WYATT KNEW HE SHOULD NEVER HAVE LET HIS BROTHER VIR-gil borrow his favorite saddle horse, a fine racing animal named Dick Naylor. He'd never let anyone else ride him, but Virgil had already started saddling Dick in the corral that day, and so he'd relented. Wyatt made it clear to his older brother, though, that this was the first and the last time anyone besides himself would be riding that horse.

When Wyatt saw Dick again, it was that afternoon, and clumps of sweaty foam were dripping off the fatigued animal. Virgil had galloped into Tombstone with an undersize nineteen-year-old man riding double behind him, but there was no time for Wyatt to look over his horse or give his brother a cussing. Virgil blurted that the kid was Johnny-Behind-the-Deuce, and he'd shot and killed a stamp mill engineer in an altercation in Charleston. The engineer was very well liked, and Johnny-Behind-the-Deuce, a miner and "petty gambler," not so much. Virgil, still a deputy US marshal, immediately deputized Wyatt. A mob of angry men from Charleston, he said, was close on their heels.

When the mob arrived, its outrage spread through Tombstone like a contagion, and men spilled out of the saloons and gambling halls, also eager to lynch young Johnny. Virgil held his prisoner under guard in Vogan's saloon and deputized more men, all gamblers, including Doc and brothers Morgan and Jim. He also sent for a buggy and a fresh team. No way could they keep Johnny in Tombstone. When the buggy pulled up out front, the lawmen rapidly led Johnny to it. "Stand back there and make a passage," Wyatt said firmly to those clamoring to hang the kid.

Wyatt held a double-barreled shotgun pointed at the crowd as Johnny was loaded into the buggy. Doc stood defiantly next to his friend, and they were backed up by Morgan and Jim and the others recently deputized. Marshal Ben Sippy climbed in the buggy and took a seat on one side of Johnny while the man who'd replaced Wyatt as deputy Pima County sheriff, Johnny Behan, sat on the other side of the prisoner. Virgil occupied a seat in the back, along with Charleston's constable and another guard.

Shouts of "Get him!" and "Go on!" came from the miners.

"Boys, you can't do this," Wyatt barked. "The law will take care of Johnny. Stand back!"

But the mob, in a frenzy now, surged forward waving rifles and shotguns.

Wyatt, Doc, and the others didn't budge as Wyatt yelled, "Of course you can get me, but I'll get the first ten."

The buggy driver flicked the reins, and the vehicle began to move slowly down Allen Street, a mounted escort riding alongside. But the mob pressed dangerously close, the miners continuing to make threats. The buggy halted, and once more, it was a standoff. A gunfight, in fact, seemed so imminent that several onlookers dove for cover. But no miner was willing to give his life in an attempt to take Johnny, especially as it appeared the guards were willing to give theirs to protect him. The mob finally grew silent and begrudgingly watched as the buggy and posse passed out of sight.

Johnny-Behind-the-Deuce, who acquired his sobriquet from "his favorite way at faro," would never again experience the kind of luck he did that day in Tombstone. The *Arizona Weekly Citizen* said Johnny "had about as narrow an escape from death as often falls to the lot of ordinary mortals." There were many, though, who'd wished that the mob had had their way with the murderous kid. Miner George Parsons wrote in his diary that Johnny "should have been killed in his tracks. Too much of this kind of business is going on. I believe in killing such men as one would a wild animal. The law must be carried out by the citizens, or should be, when it fails in its performance as it has lately done."

Just or unjust, the law did prevail that day, and it was largely thanks to the Earp brothers. Decades later, one Tombstone old-timer declared that watching Wyatt hold off the mob was "one of the most stirring pieces of drama [he'd] ever seen on or off the stage."

WYATT AND MATTIE DIDN'T HAVE CHILDREN. THEY NEVER would. Whether they wanted children, or tried, no one knows. Just a few feet from Wyatt and Mattie's house was the home of Andrew S. Neff, a thirty-seven-year-old Civil War veteran, Nebraska homesteader, Tombstone grocery owner, and a partner with Wyatt in some of his mining speculations. Neff lived with his wife, two daughters, and a son. The youngest daughter, eleven-year-old Wynona, often played in the Earps' yard. Decades later, "Nona" said that Wyatt and Mattie loved children and dogs. She fondly described Wyatt as "one of the most tenderhearted men she ever saw," and that he "was almost a father to me, and I loved him and his wife very dearly."

Nona had clear memories of all the Earp brothers, but "Wyatt was the one that always told the rest what to do," she recalled, "and they always obeyed." She also remembered Wyatt's friend, Doc Holliday, who would pat her on the head when visiting. Nona's recollections are significant because they reveal a different side of Wyatt Earp, who was invariably described by acquaintances in the simplest of terms: "quiet in manner," "manly," "serene," "modest," "never excited." Absent Nona's account, one would get the impression that beyond being fearless, Wyatt was emotionless as well. Wyatt, however, like most anyone else, could be warm and affectionate, and even a father figure to a child. And that child would cherish her memories of Wyatt and Mattie, and the love she had for them, for the rest of her life.

Nona Neff's youthful days in Tombstone were taken up with attending

Interior of the Alhambra Saloon, from a wood engraving that appeared in the July 1880 issue of *Arizona Quarterly Illustrated*.
(PUBLIC DOMAIN IMAGE, AUTHOR'S COLLECTION)

public school (180 pupils in 1881) and a life centered mostly on home. To a child, those days were long, and nothing much worthwhile or exciting seemed to happen. Beyond the Neff household, however, things were indeed happening, and quickly. That February, Wyatt's good friend Bat Masterson arrived in Tombstone. Since losing the office of Ford County sheriff in November 1879, Bat had been floating around Colorado, Nebraska, and Kansas. Encouraged by a report from Wyatt on Tombstone's prospects for a gambling man, he'd made the journey to Arizona Territory with the intention of staying through the summer. Wyatt quickly set him up as a faro dealer in the Oriental.

Doc ran a faro table at the Alhambra Saloon, just a couple of doors down Allen Street from the Oriental, so it wasn't at all hard for Bat, the Earps, and Holliday—and a few other Dodge City transplants—to find one another and talk about the mines, new arrivals in town, and local politics. And they were all happy to have their friend John Clum, editor at the *Epitaph*, as Tombstone's new mayor. He'd been elected in early January.

When he wasn't busy at the faro table, Bat's time with his friends in

Tombstone gave him another opportunity to better get to know Doc and his interesting personal history, as well as observe firsthand the curious relationship between Doc and Wyatt. The friends were two very different people. Doc was cultured and well educated. Wyatt's education had been rudimentary at best, which was evident in his poor handwriting and spelling. Both men were said to have quiet manners. That was only true, of course, when Doc wasn't drinking. When he was drinking, and that was more often than not, he could hell-raise with the best of them.

Both Wyatt and Doc were "sporting men," professional gamblers, although for Wyatt, gambling wasn't his sole potential moneymaking endeavor. For Doc, gambling was both profession and pastime. In fact, it was an addiction. Both men enjoyed and were most at home, it seems, in the higher-class gambling establishments with their ornately furnished, smoke-filled rooms, live music, and young courtesans. Unlike Doc, however, Wyatt rarely imbibed.

Wyatt was driven by an ambition to be something more than a gambler and lawman, not just well-off, but to be one of the "movers and shakers" in society, and maybe that was going to be in Tombstone. Wyatt and his brothers were intent on carving out their futures in the young mining town. Doc, on the other hand, didn't seem to have any plans for his future, living one day to the next, ready to play whatever hand fate dealt him. He did partner in those water rights claims in the Huachucas, but that was because his buddy Wyatt was involved.

Doc cared deeply about few things, at least that we know of. His relationship with Kate Elder wasn't always the best. But he did enjoy writing long letters to his cousin Mattie in Georgia, in which he's said to have fully described the places and happenings around him and at least some of his experiences. And then there was the gratifying companionship of Wyatt and his brothers.

"Doc's whole heart and soul was wrapped up in Wyatt Earp," Bat wrote later, "and he was always ready to stake his life in defense of any cause in which Wyatt was interested." From Wyatt's perspective, Doc was like having another sibling. He was family—the only real family Doc now had. As Virgil observed to a reporter, "outside of us boys, I don't

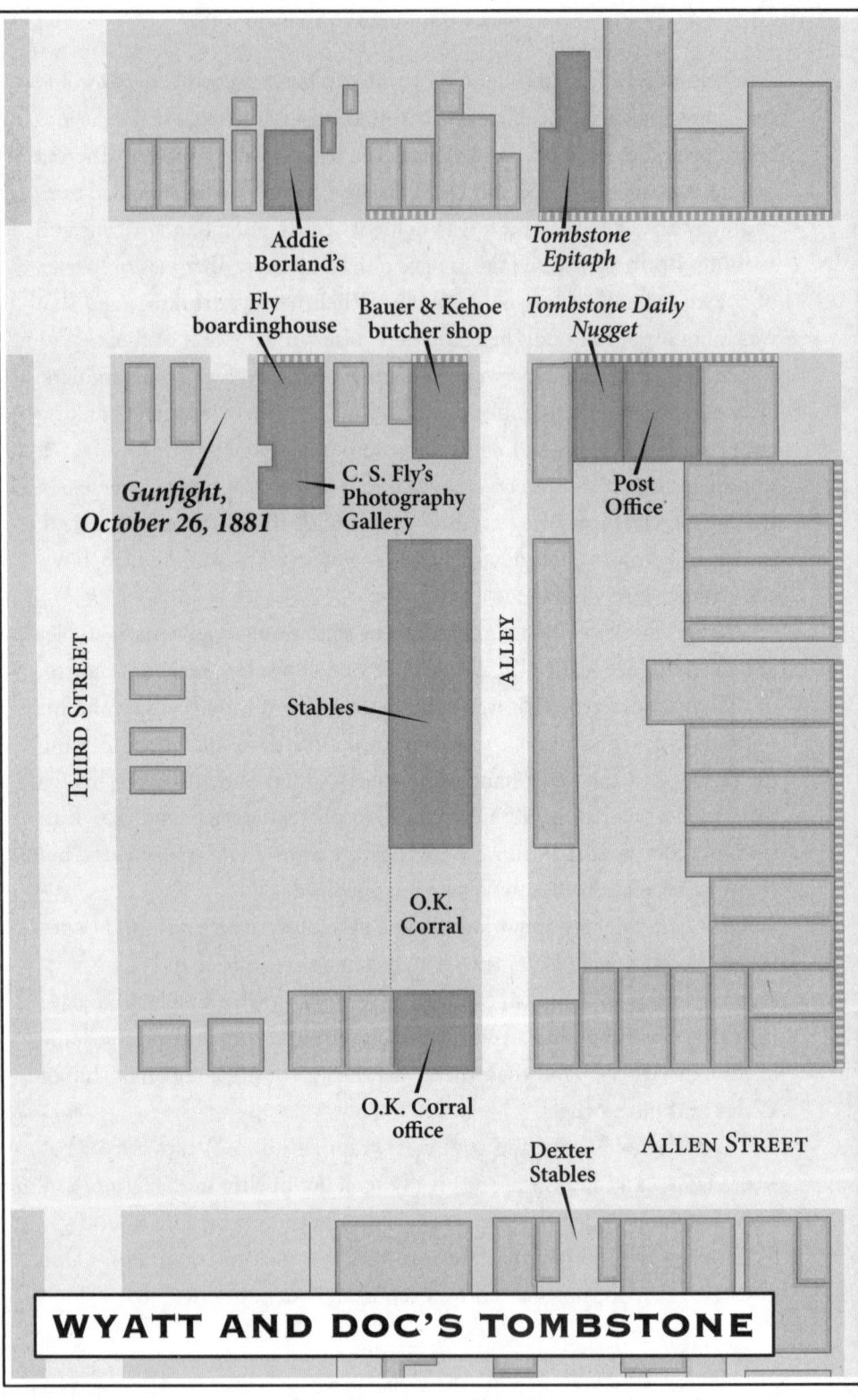

Addie
Borland's

*Tombstone
Epitaph*

Fly
boardinghouse

Bauer & Kehoe
butcher shop

*Tombstone Daily
Nugget*

*Gunfight,
October 26, 1881*

C. S. Fly's
Photography
Gallery

Post
Office

THIRD STREET

ALLEY

Stables

O.K.
Corral

O.K. Corral
office

Dexter
Stables

ALLEN STREET

WYATT AND DOC'S TOMBSTONE

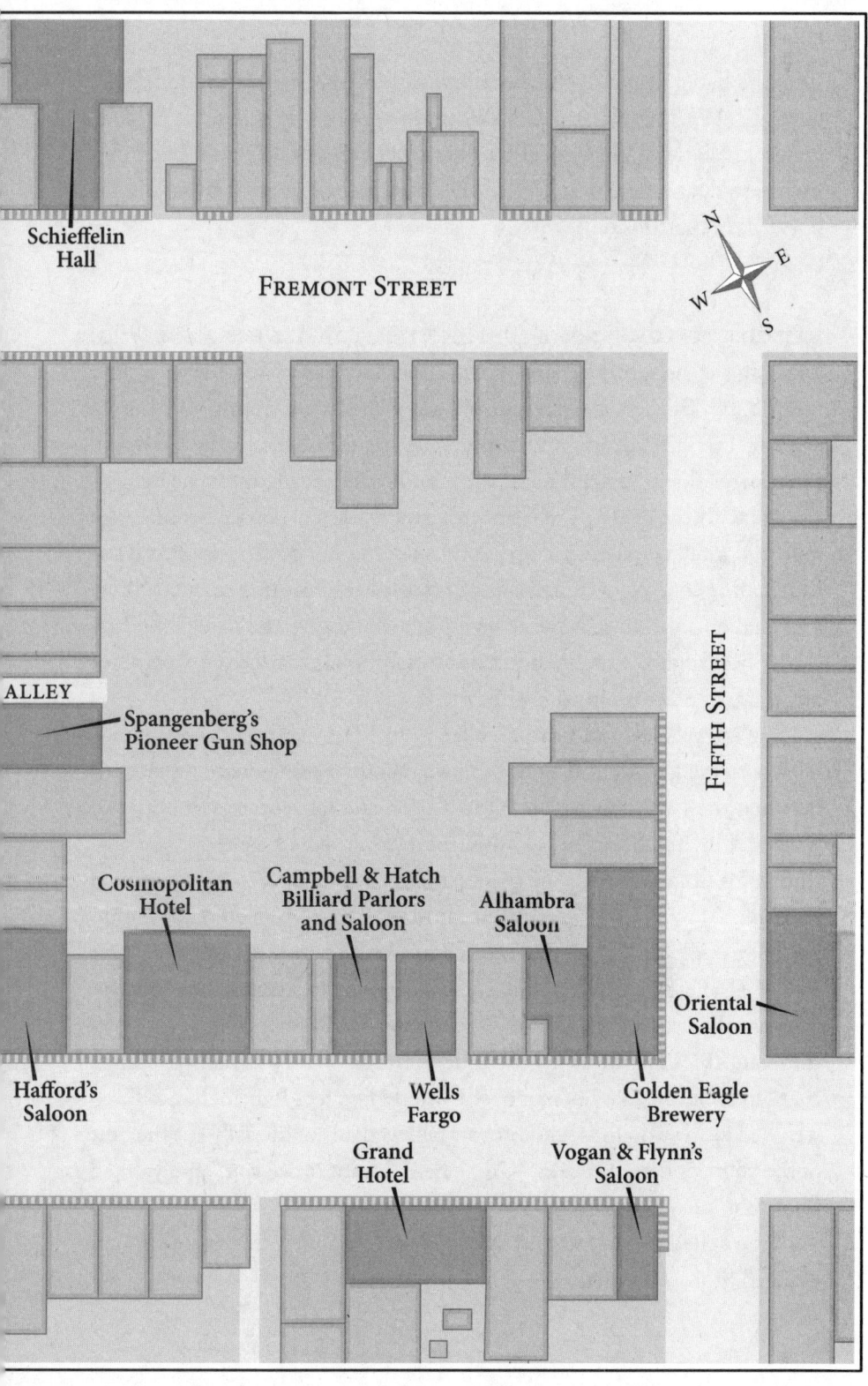

Schieffelin
Hall

FREMONT STREET

N
W · E
S

ALLEY

Spangenberg's
Pioneer Gun Shop

FIFTH STREET

Cosmopolitan
Hotel

Campbell & Hatch
Billiard Parlors
and Saloon

Alhambra
Saloon

Oriental
Saloon

Hafford's
Saloon

Wells
Fargo

Golden Eagle
Brewery

Grand
Hotel

Vogan & Flynn's
Saloon

think he had a friend in the Territory." But no one could say Doc didn't have grit. Wyatt could attest to that, and so could Virgil. "He was a slender, sickly fellow," Virgil recalled, "but whenever a stage was robbed or a row started, and help was needed, Doc was one of the first to saddle his horse and report for duty."

———————

BAT GOT TO TOMBSTONE JUST IN TIME TO WITNESS A KILLING, a killing he thought he'd prevented. The morning of February 25, 1881, saw Charley Storms, a sixty-year-old gambler known from California to Dakota Territory, drunk and belligerent at a faro table in the Oriental. He quarreled with several men near him before getting into a heated exchange with the dealer, Luke Short, a twenty-seven-year-old confidence man and monte dealer who'd recently been run out of Kansas City, Missouri, after conning a Texan out of his bankroll. Storms taunted Short and challenged him to a fight, saying he would give the dealer the first shot. Short replied that he didn't want to fight but that he didn't care for any more of Storms's insults, either.

The angry back and forth escalated until Bat, who was good friends with both men, suspected a gunfight was about to commence and jumped between the two. Storms left Short's table and later ordered a bottle of wine and invited Short to join him for a drink, which he did. Short assumed his difficulty with the gambler had passed, but Storms continued to drink. About 1 P.M., Short went off his shift and stepped outside onto the boardwalk, where he was warned by Bat and Lou Rickabaugh, part owner of the Oriental's gambling concession, to keep an eye out for Storms. The drunk gambler was threatening to kill Short. No sooner had they said this than Storms burst out of the saloon and grabbed Short's coat lapel. Short, like his name, stood only five feet four inches tall and weighed just 120 pounds, and Storms believed he could easily get the best of the younger man. He said, "Come here, I want to see you," and yanked Short out into the street.

"You called me an old gray-bearded son of a bitch this morning!" an enraged Storms shouted.

Short answered that he couldn't remember exactly what he said but that he believed they'd agreed to let it go.

"You called me a son of a bitch and I want to know if you are as good a man as you were then."

Before Short could reply, Storms yelled, "You son of a bitch!" and pulled his revolver—but just a tad too slow. In one swift motion, Short backed away, drew his own pistol, placed the muzzle close to Storm's left breast, and pulled the trigger. A .45-caliber bullet at 1,050 feet per second ripped through the gambler's heart, knocking him on his back. However, pure adrenaline provided a few more seconds of life, and Storms, his head and shoulders up off the ground, steadied his revolver with both hands and squeezed off one errant shot in Short's direction. Short dropped to his knees and pumped two more bullets into the prostrate gambler.

Diarist George Parsons ran out in the street in time to witness Storms shoot. The gambler, Parsons wrote, was "game to the last." At the end of that day's diary entry, Parsons added, "Forgot to say that the faro games went right on as though nothing had happened after [the] body was carried to Storms' room." A coroner's jury held later that day determined that it had been a "justifiable killing." Storms had a reputation for violence, and when word of his demise reached Colorado, a Leadville newspaper sarcastically commented that Storms "died while indulging in his favorite pursuit of seeing another pass from earth to another world."

———

CHARLEY STORMS HAS THE DISTINCTION OF BEING ONE OF THE first people, if not *the* first, to be shot down in the newly formed county of Cochise. Its 6,219 square miles were carved out of the eastern portion of Pima County, and Tombstone was now the county seat. Gone were the dusty, jolting seventy-five-mile trips one way to conduct county business in Tucson. None of this made much difference to poor Charley, naturally, but it made a tremendous difference to Wyatt. A new county required new county officials. "Now the fight begins for offices," George Parsons wrote in his diary, for those offices would be temporarily filled by gubernatorial appointments. And among the appointments the governor would decide was county sheriff.

The office of sheriff was the most lucrative position in county government for one reason: The sheriff had the responsibility of collecting the county taxes. (And in a clear conflict of interest, the sheriff was also the county assessor.) For his efforts, the County Board of Supervisors allowed the sheriff to keep 10 percent of all taxes collected, "a percentage whose exorbitance is without precedent," commented one journalist. Out of these monies the sheriff was to pay his deputies and various office expenses, but that amounted to but a small fraction of the sheriff's overall collection. In silver-rich Cochise County, the sheriff's 10 percent amounted to between thirty and forty thousand dollars. That was an ungodly amount of money for a county sheriff, and Wyatt figured he was just the man for the job. But so did Pima County deputy sheriff Johnny Behan.

The thirty-five-year-old Behan had made Arizona Territory his home for eighteen years, and in that time he'd been many things: freighter, prospector, undersheriff and sheriff of Yavapai County, county recorder, saloon owner, and territorial legislator. In Tombstone, Behan moonlighted as a bartender and was part owner of the Dunbar Bros. & Co. Livery Stable. He was a likable glad-hander and a perpetual office seeker and would be for the rest of his life. Whenever there was an opening, be it through a political appointment or an election, Johnny Behan was Johnny-on-the-spot.

Behan, a divorcé, liked his women young—very young. He'd married his former wife when she was sixteen, and as a regular patron of a Prescott brothel, Johnny became infatuated with a pretty fourteen-year-old prostitute who went by the name Sadie Mansfield. These nighttime visits to the brothel occurred while Behan was still married, but eventually his wife tired of his infidelity, not to mention his abusive behavior, and sued for divorce in 1875. One of the witnesses called at the divorce hearing stated that he'd seen Behan at a popular bagnio on Prescott's Granite Street "at which resided one Sada [Sadie] Mansfield, commonly called Sada, a woman of prostitution and ill-fame, and the said defendant [Behan] did at that time and at the house spoken of, stay all night with and sleep with said Sada Mansfield."

Young Sadie was apparently as taken with Johnny as he was with her, although they would separate and not rekindle a relationship until a few years later. As early as the fall of 1880, however, she was living in Tombstone with Behan and helping to raise his eight-year-old son Albert. Sadie now went by Mrs. Josephine Behan, Josephine being her birth name. Although they were not legally married, Josephine believed they'd eventually wed, and Behan was content using his lover as a pseudobabysitter while he walked Tombstone's streets with an ever-wandering eye.

Johnny Behan and his child bride Victoria. (PUBLIC DOMAIN IMAGE, AUTHOR'S COLLECTION)

BOTH WYATT AND BEHAN WERE AMONG THE APPLICANTS CONsidered for sheriff. Behan indeed had experience as a lawman, but it paled in comparison to Wyatt's. Behan had never dealt with anything like the toughs Wyatt regularly encountered in Wichita and Dodge City. And the medium-size Behan had yet to demonstrate that he possessed one of the more important qualities required of a lawman: nerve. Behan could be everyone's friend, but, according to a Tombstone old-timer, "he was afraid of his own shadow." Politics tended to trump qualifications, however. Behan, a Democrat, had connections in the territorial capital.

Johnny Behan didn't figure Wyatt, a newcomer to Arizona, had much of a chance of getting the position. But the governor, the man making the appointments, was a Republican, so to remove all doubt, Behan met with Wyatt and made him an offer: If Wyatt would give up on the sheriff's appointment, Behan pledged to make Wyatt his undersheriff and split down the middle with him the office's profits. Behan even said he'd hire a clerk to ensure that the monies were divided equally.

Wyatt agreed to the deal, and on February 10, 1881, Behan received the appointment as the first sheriff of Cochise County. But Behan's promise to make Wyatt his undersheriff proved to be pure fool's gold. Instead, he kept Wyatt in the dark for a few weeks and then gave the job to Harry Woods, editor of the *Daily Nugget*, fierce rival of the *Epitaph*. It made perfect sense politically, guaranteeing that at least one newspaper would always take the side of the sheriff in any future dustups.

Sheriff Behan later claimed that he reneged on his promise because Wyatt had interfered in Behan's attempt to serve a

Purported to be a photograph of a young Josephine Sarah Marcus (aka Sadie Mansfield, Mrs. Josephine Behan, Sadie Earp, and Josephine Earp), but provenance is lacking. (PUBLIC DOMAIN IMAGE, AUTHOR'S COLLECTION)

subpoena. Maybe. But there was something else simmering between Wyatt and Behan. Behan wasn't the only spoken-for man in Tombstone with a wandering eye. At some point, Wyatt became aware of the presence in town of Mrs. Josephine Behan, whom Tombstone old-timers recalled as "the belle of the honkytonks, the prettiest dame in three hundred or so of her kind." An affair began. Exactly when is hard to pin down, but probably about the time Josephine realized that Behan had no intention of marrying her. In any event, the tension that developed between Earp and Behan was more than simply competition for a plum office or a promise of patronage; it had a lot to do with a woman as well.

And Doc Holliday only made matters worse. Behan started a quarrel one night at Doc's faro bank, and it became so heated that Doc refused to allow Behan to continue playing, which infuriated Behan even more. "In the quarrel," Doc said later, "I told him in the presence of a crowd that he was gambling with money which I had given his woman. This story got out and caused him trouble. He always hated me after that." Behan well knew, of course, that Doc and Wyatt were close friends.

As for Mrs. Wyatt Earp, Mattie, she would soon be able to add to the list of Wyatt Earp's personal traits: cold and heartless.

———

MARCH DIDN'T COME IN LIKE A LION, BUT IT DID COME IN WITH a bang. Two bangs, actually. About 4 A.M. on March 1, gambler Henry "One-Armed" Kelly got into an argument with fellow sporting man Steve McAllister at the Oriental. Kelly's one arm packed a powerful punch, and he knocked McAllister down—but not out. McAllister drew his pistol and shot Kelly in the left breast, close to his heart. The one-armed man spun around, and McAllister shot once more, hitting Kelly in the loin. Kelly fell to the floor, blood pouring from his wounds. He was still breathing as he was carried away, but his prognosis was grim.

"Oriental a regular slaughter house now," George Parsons wrote in his diary. "Much bad blood today." The shooting of Kelly coming four days after Luke Short killed Charley Storms just steps from the saloon's front door was one too many gunfights for the Oriental's Milt Joyce, whose hand still hurt like hell from when Doc shot it the previous October. Joyce temporarily closed the Oriental's games.

Two more violent deaths shook Tombstone on March 15, but this time, they weren't the result of an argument between drunken, testosterone-fueled gamblers. That night, a Kinnear & Company Concord coach rolled along behind six horses on the road from Contention to Benson. In addition to its six paying passengers, the coach carried a heavy strongbox containing $26,000 in bullion. Seated on the driver's box, twenty-seven-year-old "Bud" Philpott held the lines. Next to him sat the express messenger Bob Paul, whose legal challenge to the Pima County sheriff's election was then being reviewed by the Arizona Supreme Court. Two and a half weeks earlier, another Kinnear coach had been stopped and robbed on this same route, but that coach didn't have a guard. Philpott felt safe with Bob Paul, the equal to the Earps in bravery, at his side. Paul cradled a short double-barreled shotgun across his lap.

A full moon cast a greenish hue upon the landscape, the sharp shadows of the horses and coach upon the ground matching stride for stride their counterparts, a seeming otherworldly companion to the journey. About two miles north of Contention, the coach entered a dry wash some ten feet deep. The sandy bottom offered smooth going for a time until the road left the wash at the opposite bank. Philpott spoke to his team as they started up the slight incline, urging them forward. He was proud of these magnificent animals, and they responded smartly to his voice, pulling the harness tight as they dug their hooves into the rocky soil. The coach swayed on its leather braces, the passengers inside involuntarily leaning one way and the next.

At this moment, Bob Paul saw the figure of a man step out into the road. Three more showed themselves, two on one side and one on the other. The moonlight glinted off the steel barrels of their Winchesters. Paul instantly pulled the hammers of his shotgun to full cock.

"Hold!" shouted the man in the road.

Paul snapped the shotgun to his shoulder, yelling, "By God, I hold for nobody!" and jerked both triggers. The robbers fired their guns at nearly the same instant, the muzzle flashes and blasts from each side making for a kind of fireworks show. And it was a show the horses wanted nothing to do with. The team bolted into a dead run. Paul suddenly saw Philpott falling forward. A single bullet had smashed through the driver's arm and chest, cutting his aorta and punching a hole in his spinal column. Paul reached out to grab him and nearly slipped off the box himself. All Paul could do was watch as Philpott fell between the wheel horses, unfortunately taking the lines with him.

The robbers continued shooting at the coach as it sped away. Frustrated and angry, they rapidly squeezed off nearly twenty shots, apparently wishing to kill as many in the coach as they could. An unlucky passenger riding on top, in the "dickey seat" behind the driver's box, screamed out as a bullet struck him in the back.

Once out of range of the robbers' guns, Paul nearly stood on the brake lever, putting all his weight on it in an effort to slow the runaway team. Only after racing full steam for nearly a mile did the sweat-soaked horses slow to a trot, allowing a passenger to jump from the coach and retrieve the lines. Paul now made sure none of the terrified passengers inside were hurt. The poor man on top was in terrible agony, however, and would soon be dead. Paul got the stage going again, and upon arriving at the railroad depot in Benson, he handed off the lines and rushed straight to the telegraph office.

At about 11 P.M., the shocking news of the attempted robbery and murders reached Tombstone, where it was immediately surmised that the deadly affair was the Cowboys' doing. Within minutes, men on horseback galloped up and down Allen Street, weaving in and out of clusters of miners, drunks, gamblers, and ladies of the night. The news spread from crowd to crowd like a wave, and everything seemed pandemonium as men ran for guns and horses. Wyatt and his brothers, Doc, Bat Masterson, Wells Fargo agent Marshall Williams, Sheriff Johnny Behan, and a few others were soon on their way to the holdup site, a distance of about twenty-one miles, where they met Paul and another posse. The moon had gone down by now, making it impossible to follow any kind of a trail in the darkness, so they waited. When the sky began to glow in the east, the men canvassed the area around the robbers' positions and found numerous spent rifle shell casings, masks, and fake beards made of rope yarn.

More than thirty armed volunteers now waited for their marching orders from Sheriff Behan, but that was far more than was needed to take up the chase of the four robbers. Behan said he only wanted the Earps and Bob Paul. Virgil, of course, wasn't just a posse member; he was serving in his capacity as a deputy US marshal. Marshall Williams also stayed with the Behan group, and Virgil and Wyatt made sure Bat was included in the party as well. The sheriff hadn't named Doc, who was perfectly fine with returning to Tombstone and another game of faro.

The robbers well knew they would be pursued, and they pushed their horses hard, taking the posse on an exhausting zigzag route through the desert country between the Dragoon Mountains and the San Pedro Valley. But the Earps and Masterson were exceptional manhunters. After three days with little rest, the posse discovered one of the robbers' horses at an abandoned ranch on the San Pedro River nearly eighty miles north of Tombstone. Completely used up and covered with saddle sores, the poor animal had been abandoned, which meant the robbers' other horses were probably in the same poor condition. This brought a rush of adrenaline to the weary trackers. After 150 miles in the saddle, they were close.

Continuing a short distance up the San Pedro, they came to the ranch of Hank Redfield. Hank and his brother Len, whose ranch was located four miles distant, were as crooked as the men the posse was chasing. They were not only associates of the Cowboys, they were rustlers themselves. And Cowboys could always count on a warm welcome from the brothers, especially when fleeing the law.

When asked if he'd seen anyone suspicious, Hank lied to the posse, swearing that no riders had passed his ranch in days. That answer didn't make a lot of sense to the Earps and the others, and they proceeded to have a look around the place while Hank fidgeted. Before long, Morgan came upon fresh tracks, and they led in the direction of Len Redfield's place.

There didn't seem to be any activity at brother Len's ranch as the posse approached, but when they got to about a hundred yards from the cabin, a man leaped out the back door and ran like hell toward a large patch of brush on the river. Wyatt and Morgan jumped from their horses and chased after him. Just before the man reached the brush, Wyatt stopped, raised his rifle to his shoulder, and yelled to the suspect to surrender or he would shoot. "He stopped and threw up his hands and came back," Wyatt recalled.

Wyatt recognized the robber as one of four men who, for the last few weeks, had been camping in an abandoned adobe building two and a half miles north of Tombstone, a place known as the Wells. From the very beginning, Wyatt was convinced these men were the culprits. When the first news of the holdup and murders reached Tombstone, Wyatt had quickly ridden to the adobe and found that the men had vanished. Inside the adobe, he discovered part of a pulp novel that had been torn in half, and he'd found pages of that same novel at different points on the robbers' trail. (Cheap paperbacks made handy toilet paper.)

The prisoner's name was Luther "Lew" King, and he'd been armed to the teeth with a rifle, two revolvers, and two heavy cartridge belts. His big pockets were stuffed with more cartridges and other supplies obviously intended for his cohorts. As Wyatt told it years later, "I asked [King] the whereabouts of the other bandits. He inquired whom I meant. I named the other three and he realized that their identity had been discovered. I told him that I would capture all the others and that some of them would turn evidence and that he had the first opportunity." The men Wyatt named were Bill Leonard, Jim Crane, and Harry Head.

Wyatt now left King with Sheriff Behan, saying that he wanted to talk to Bob Paul for a moment before getting King's full confession. Wyatt cautioned Behan not to let King talk to either of the Redfields. Hank, in fact, had just ridden up and dismounted. But Behan unwisely disregarded Wyatt's warning. King conversed briefly with Hank Redfield, after which Hank got back on his horse and rode away. When Wyatt found out, he was less than pleased, and Behan got huffy, reminding Wyatt that *he* was the sheriff of Cochise County.

King admitted that the abandoned horse was his and that the men Wyatt named were indeed his accomplices, although he insisted that he'd merely held the horses during the robbery attempt and hadn't fired a single shot. His companions, he said, were camped about one mile west of Hank Redfield's ranch. King was definitely telling the truth about the camp, except, as Wyatt feared, Hank Redfield got there before they did. All the posse found was an empty camp with its fire still burning.

The posse now split up, with Behan and Marshall Williams taking the prisoner King to Tombstone, where they promised to "secure him properly." The Earps, Paul, and Bat Masterson took up the trail of the remaining three road agents: Leonard, Crane, and Head. But the pursuers were at an extreme disadvantage, as the bandits were riding fresh horses obtained from the Redfields, while the posse was still riding the horses they'd saddled in Tombstone. They were good horses, but their endurance would be sorely tested.

The bandits' trail took the posse past the small town of Tres Alamos, about thirteen miles north of Benson, which had a telegraph office. Virgil Earp rode up in front of the office, dismounted, took a long stretch, and walked inside. He wrote a short note on a piece of paper, handed it to the operator, and instructed him to send it to US Marshal Crawley Dake in Prescott:

Tres Alamos, March 21st, 1881

C. P. Dake, U.S. Marshal:—I left the night the stage was stopped with two of my brothers and Bill Masterson. Have not lost a foot print. Have caught one. Will follow as long as I can find a track.

V. W. Earp
Deputy Marshal

SEVEN

UNHOLY ALLIANCE

"The men known as Cowboys are not really cowboys. . . . The proper name for them is Rustlers. They ran the country down there and so terrorized the country that no man dared say anything against them."

DOC HOLLIDAY

Tombstone
March 24, 1881

Wyatt Earp and Bat Masterson, their clothes dust-covered and sweat-stained, approached the outskirts of Tombstone, and it was an unusual sight to be sure: The two men were on foot. No horseman walks if he doesn't have to, and Wyatt and Bat had to. They'd pushed their mounts to the extreme, to the point that most of the horses' shoes were gone after carrying their riders for days over rock-strewn desert. By the time the posse reached a ranch in the Dragoon Mountains, northeast of Tombstone, Wyatt's and Bat's horses were completely "played out." The two manhunters had no choice but to leave them behind so that the animals could regain their strength. And as no other horses could be had at any price, Wyatt and Bat walked to town—a distance of eighteen hard miles.

Virgil, Morgan, Bob Paul, and others were still on the trail of the Benson stage robbers, but the holdup men were able to steal eight fresh horses, and for the trackers, the pursuit started resembling more a struggle for survival. One night, Paul's exhausted horse lay down and never got up again. Virgil's and Morgan's horses were in nearly as bad a shape, and they were forced to dismount and continue on foot to save their horses from the same sad fate as Paul's. For a stretch of sixty hours, the party went without food and thirty-six hours without water. Finally, after sixteen days and hundreds of miles across a cactus-strewn land-scape, the hunt was abandoned. But even though Lew King's accomplices had escaped, the *Epitaph* praised the efforts of the posse: "The persistent pursuit of the murderers of poor 'Bud' is a credit to each individual member of the party, and will pass into our frontier annals—more especially as regards Paul and the Earp boys, who followed the trail from the night of the murder—as a record of which all and each of them may well feel proud."

The *Epitaph* didn't name the new Cochise County sheriff as one es-pecially worthy of recognition, and for good reason. Upon bringing pris-oner Lew King to Tombstone, Behan placed him under guard in the Dunbar Bros. & Co. Livery Stable building, where he kept an office. The building was hardly the most secure place to confine a suspected murderer, but Tombstone's city jail was in such bad shape—one defense attorney called the jail "uninhabitable"—that there were few other options.

Soon after Wyatt returned to Tombstone, he and Wells Fargo detec-tive Jim Hume went to see the undersheriff, Harry Woods, and strongly encouraged him to not only place an extra guard over the prisoner, but to put him in shackles. A lot of Cowboys were in town, Wyatt said, and it was common knowledge that they were there to break out King. Woods assured the men that he would put the prisoner in irons, but whether he meant it or not isn't known. If Woods did mean it, he was a little slow.

On the evening of March 28, Woods watched as a bill of sale was prepared for King's horse at a desk in the sheriff's office. The prisoner, who was standing in the same room, had decided to sell the animal to John Dunbar, Behan's business partner. Also in the room was Dunbar and another man who was writing up the bill. The entire process was ap-parently so wonderfully fascinating that no one noticed King slowly step to the back of the room, pick up a revolver conveniently left unguarded, and quietly make his way to the back door. Outside, a saddled horse awaited the prisoner, placed there by an accomplice. By the time Woods is said to have realized King was missing and rushed to the backyard, only the stillness of the night greeted him.

"King, the stage robber, escaped tonight early from H. Woods who had been previously notified of an attempt at release to be made," George Parsons wrote in his diary. "Some of our officials should be hanged. They're a bad lot." Parsons wasn't the only one who was angry; there was outrage and disbelief throughout the Territory. Tucson's *Arizona Weekly Citizen* proclaimed that the fiasco was due to "a most flagrant dereliction of duty in a public officer. . . . Utterly disregarding the information that an escape was premeditated, the prisoner was given every opportunity to get away, if not with official connivance, at least by a most simple ruse."

The Earps were furious, too. And then Behan created even more animosity between himself and the brothers when he submitted a $790.84 bill to the county for expenses for the manhunt but purposely left the Earps out, using as an excuse that he hadn't "officially" deputized them. "Everybody but myself and brothers were paid," Virgil explained later, "and we did not get a cent until Wells Fargo found it out and paid us for our time. From that time our troubles commenced."

PRIOR TO KING'S ESCAPE, WELLS FARGO OFFERED A SUBSTAN-
tial reward of $3,600 for the arrest of Cowboys Leonard, Crane, and Head. The company also issued a wanted poster with descriptions of the three men. Of the descriptions, the longest and most detailed was that for Leonard, a thirty-year-old incessant tobacco chewer with long, dark hair that fell to his shoulders in ringlets; dark, boyish mustache; teeth white and straight, dark eyes, effeminate features, weak voice, and "left arm full of scars caused by injecting morphine." What the poster didn't say, but what was the subject of much discussion in Tombstone, was that Leonard and Doc Holliday were friends, and that was a big problem for both Holliday and the Earps.

Doc first met the New York–born Leonard, a jeweler by trade, in Las

Vegas. According to Wyatt, Leonard started out in the thriving New Mexico town with a good reputation. Like Doc, Leonard is said to have suffered from tuberculosis. And also like Doc, he could have the occasional violent outburst and was quick to resort to gunplay in a dispute. In early September 1878, Leonard got into some kind of feud with Las Vegas policeman José Mares. One day, the feud came to a head, and the two searched about town gunning for each other. When they eventually met on the Old Town Plaza, Leonard shot first, striking the policeman in his right arm, causing him to drop his pistol. Mares's friends quickly jumped Leonard and, according to the *Las Vegas Gazette*, "pounded him in a very severe manner."

Leonard was indicted for assault with intent to kill and carrying a deadly weapon. His case dragged on in district court for months, however. Finally, nearly a year later, the case received a continuance because Leonard had "skipped out." Once in Tombstone, the jeweler continued his descent into dissipation. A morphine addict weighing only 120 pounds, he threw his lot in with the Cowboys. Leonard even started, or, rather, squatted on a small ranch just over the line in New Mexico's Animas Valley. Doc was well aware of Leonard's thieving associates, and maybe his nefarious activities as well, but he liked the man's company; Leonard was one of the few people in Tombstone other than the Earps who'd have anything to do with Doc. And not only did Doc occasionally visit Leonard at the Wells, he actually visited him on the day of the Benson stage robbery. Not surprisingly, many people found this highly suspicious.

"Doc was not in the Benson stage holdup," Wyatt wrote emphatically years later. "And he never did such a thing as holdups in his life." But more than a few folks in Tombstone held grudges against Doc, particularly Sheriff Behan, whom Doc had publicly shamed, and Milt Joyce, who had that nasty scar on his hand from Doc's gun. They were quite happy to fan the rumor that the faro dealer was one of the robbers. And Doc didn't do himself any favors when, in early April, he decided to visit the Oriental, where the games in the club room had recently reopened. Doc had to have known that he was unwelcome there, but that didn't stop him. As soon as Joyce spotted Doc, he said in a loud voice, "Well, here comes the stage robber." Joyce then allowed that he would have no road agent in his establishment.

Doc exploded with rage and started to draw his revolver, saying he was going to blast another hole in the saloon owner. Doc didn't get a chance as the fists of both men began to fly. Sheriff Behan stepped between the two and arrested them, although Doc's the one who found himself before a judge facing the more serious charge of threatening a man's life. Doc eventually got off easy, only paying court costs, but, as Wyatt once wrote of his friend, "He was his own worst enemy." The rumor of Doc's involvement in the Benson robbery didn't go away, however, and because of Doc's friendship with Wyatt, some folks would begin to wonder about the Earp brothers as well.

THE GROUNDLESS ACCUSATIONS AGAINST DOC RANKLED WYATT. And he wasn't about to forget Behan's reneging on the promise of the undersheriff position, nor Behan's dirty turn in refusing to include the Earps when seeking compensation for the manhunt from hell. And Wyatt decided to do something about it. That something, Wyatt believed, would exonerate his friend, get even with Johnny Behan, and win for him the coveted Cochise County sheriff's office come election time.

The key to Wyatt's plan was the capture of Leonard, Head, and Crane, which Wyatt thought would make him a hero to the citizens and businessmen of Tombstone, and that meant votes. And once in custody, the murderers of Bud Philpott could put to rest the rumor that Doc Holliday had anything to do with the stage robbery. This all made good sense, but the capture of the stage robbers was going to be tricky, and so was Wyatt's idea on how to do it. He would need to persuade one or more of the Cowboys to turn on their fellow reprobates. It would take a big carrot to tempt a Cowboy to do such a thing, but Wyatt had one: the reward money offered by Wells Fargo. Wyatt, a pretty good judge of character, especially the character of men of a criminal bent, knew there were Cowboys who'd sell their own mother for the right price.

Wyatt was confident he could pull this off, as it hadn't been that long since he'd worked another deal to his advantage with the Cowboys. Because of that deal, Bob Paul was now Pima County's new sheriff, Paul's opponent having finally abandoned his appeal. On the other hand, that same deal helped secure an acquittal for Curly Bill Brocius in the shooting death of Marshal Fred White, with the result being like releasing a caged wolf back out among the sheep. Any bargain with the Cowboys came with a risk of unintended consequences. Wyatt, a gambler at heart, was willing to take that risk.

His best bet among the Cowboys, Wyatt supposed, was Ike Clanton, whom he believed to be, along with Curly Bill, "a sort of chief among the Cowboys." Thirty-four-year-old Ike lived on a ranch on the San Pedro River, near Charleston, with his two brothers, "Fin" and Billy, and father Newman, better known as "Old Man" Clanton. A Tucson newspaper described the brothers as "fine specimens of the frontier cattle man." Billy, about eighteen years old, was "over six feet in height, and built in proportion, while Isaac and Phineas are wiry, determined-looking men, without a pound of surplus flesh." All three Clanton brothers were indeed fine specimens, but rather of the lawbreaker variety.

Wyatt was very familiar with the Clantons. Ike was one of the Cowboys with whom he'd negotiated to obtain the testimony admitting fraudulent voting in the last sheriff's election. And Wyatt had even experienced firsthand the Clantons' penchant for other folks' livestock. Earlier in the year, Wyatt discovered that one of his horses had been stolen. After receiving a tip that the animal had been spotted in Charleston, Wyatt hurried there and found it unattended on one of the streets. He put the horse in a corral until he could obtain the necessary legal papers to recover his property.

Wyatt wired Tombstone for the papers, which entailed a bit of a wait until they could be delivered. In the meantime, young Billy Clanton appeared at the corral and boldly attempted to remove the horse. "I told him that he could not take him out," Wyatt recalled, "that it was my horse." Billy stopped, but he wasn't in a hurry to leave, perhaps thinking that Wyatt was bluffing about the papers. Once the papers arrived that night,

Joseph Isaac
"Ike" Clanton,
a leader of the
Cowboys.
(PUBLIC DOMAIN
IMAGE, AUTHOR'S
COLLECTION)

however, Billy had to let the horse go, but the teenager couldn't help but smart off to Wyatt, asking him if he had any more horses to lose. "I told him I would keep them in the stable after this, and give him no chance to steal them."

The Clantons were tight with two brothers, Frank and Tom McLaury, who operated small ranches southeast and west of Tombstone. Frank, age thirty-two, and Tom, age twenty-seven, had migrated to Arizona from west Texas in 1878. Like the Clantons, the McLaurys appeared to some

Frank McLaury.
(PUBLIC DOMAIN IMAGE, AUTHOR'S
COLLECTION)

Tom McLaury.
(PUBLIC DOMAIN IMAGE, AUTHOR'S
COLLECTION)

folks as hardworking young men just trying to get ahead. "They were both well educated," commented one newspaper, "and Tom, especially, was sober and industrious." But in reality, the McLaury brothers were part of the Cowboy network of friends and accomplices, with their ranches serving as places to hold and fence stolen livestock. An individual close to the events of 1881 offered that the Clantons and McLaurys "were a tough lot of rustlers, who were the main perpetrators of the rascality rife in the region."

The Earps had been in Tombstone just about seven months when they got on the wrong side of the McLaury brothers. In July 1880, Cowboys stole six mules from Camp Rucker, an army post forty miles east of Tombstone. Deputy US Marshal Virgil Earp, brother Wyatt, Wells Fargo agent Marshall Williams, and an army detail of four soldiers traced the mules to the McLaury brothers' place west of Tombstone, near the Mustang Mountains. According to a witness the posse interviewed in

Charleston, the rustlers were altering the army's "U.S." brand by branding over it the letters "D S." "We tracked the mules right up to the ranch," Wyatt recalled. "Also found the branding iron 'D S.'"

Virgil and Wyatt strongly suggested to the lieutenant in charge of the detail that they ride in and recover the stolen mules, by force if necessary. But the lieutenant, wishing to avoid a fight, agreed to give the McLaurys a day to deliver the mules to Charleston, where he would be waiting with his men. It was two days, however, before the McLaurys, Billy Clanton, and another Cowboy rode into Charleston—without the mules. They proceeded to laugh at the lieutenant, admitting that the "deal" was only a ploy to get rid of the Earps. The US Army never saw those mules again.

Frank McLaury wasn't laughing, however, after the lieutenant posted a notice in the *Tombstone Epitaph* offering a reward for the arrest and conviction of the mule thieves and naming him as one of the culprits. A day or two following the notice's appearance, the McLaury brothers and Billy Clanton angrily confronted Virgil Earp in Tombstone and asked if he'd had anything to do with its publication. Virgil told the men no. "If I thought you did," Frank said, "I would make you fight right here." The McLaurys also threatened Wyatt when they ran into him in Charleston a month later. "They tried to pick a fuss out of me," Wyatt remembered, "and told me that if I ever followed them up again as close as I did before, that they would kill me." Virgil and Wyatt chose to let it pass. It wasn't the first time someone had threatened their lives, and usually it was all bluster.

Considering these less than pleasant encounters with the Clantons and McLaurys, it's all the more incredible that when Ike, Frank, and a thirty-year-old Texan named Joe Hill rode into Tombstone on June 2, 1881, Wyatt sought them out for a discreet talk. The four men met in the backyard of the Oriental, and Wyatt quickly got to the point. He said he wanted the glory of capturing the Benson stage robbers. "I told them," Wyatt recalled, "if they would put me on the track of Leonard, Head, and Crane, and tell me where those men were hid, I would give them all the reward and would never let anyone know where I got the information." Ike said later that Wyatt actually promised another thousand dollars of his own money on top of the reward. He wanted to capture those men that bad.

Ike admitted to Wyatt that he wouldn't mind seeing the three robbers done away with, especially Leonard. He explained that, following the bungled stage robbery and murders, he expected Leonard and the others would flee the country and not come back. Ike coveted Leonard's Animas Valley ranch, so Ike right away drove a herd of his cattle from the San Pedro to Leonard's place with the idea of claiming the ranch as his own. But then Ike got a big surprise when Leonard, Head, and Crane showed up. Leonard made it quite clear to Ike that he would either have to buy the ranch or get off. Ike, of course, preferred to get the ranch for free, which would be the case if Leonard was out of the picture.

Ike warned Wyatt that Leonard, Head, and Crane would not be taken alive. They would fight until their last breath. He asked Wyatt to find out if the reward would be good for the robbers dead or alive. Wyatt said he would send a wire to the Wells Fargo headquarters in San Francisco for confirmation and that they would meet again as soon as he heard back.

In the meantime, Ike, Frank McLaury, and Joe Hill decided to hunt up Virgil Earp and see what he had to say about his brother's proposition. It would seem that the proposition was news to Virgil.

"Here are three of you and there is only three of them," Virgil said. "Why don't you capture or kill them? And I would see that you get the reward."

"Jesus Christ!" Ike exclaimed. "I wouldn't last longer than a snowball in hell if I should do that! The rest of the gang would think we killed them for the reward and they would kill us. But, we have agreed to bring them to a certain spot, where you boys can capture them. As soon as Wyatt gets a telegram he is going to send for, in regard to the reward dead or alive, and they will give it, dead or alive, we'll start right after them, to bring them over."

A few days later, Wyatt received the answer to his wire:

San Francisco, June 7, 1881
4 o'clock p.m.

To Marshall Williams.

Yes we will pay rewards for them dead or alive.

L. F. Rowell [Assistant Superintendent, Wells Fargo]

───────────

ON THE MORNING OF JUNE 8, IKE CLANTON NEARLY SPOILED everything when he got into an argument in an Allen Street saloon with a "sporting man" named Denny McCann. McCann slapped Ike in the face, and a furious Ike stormed out of the saloon, saying he was going to get his gun. McCann went to fetch his gun as well. The two met up in front of the Wells Fargo office, and both instantly drew their weapons. Fortunately, Virgil Earp was also there, and at the very real risk of getting shot, he stepped between them. The *Epitaph* reported that Clanton and McCann were "both determined men, and but for the interference of the officer, there would doubtless have been a funeral, perhaps two."

Later that same day, Wyatt showed the Wells Fargo telegram to Ike and Joe Hill. Ike was satisfied. And the Cowboys had already come up with a way to lure the stage robbers to where Wyatt could get them. It called for Joe Hill to ride to the wanted men's New Mexico hideout and tell them that a paymaster was due to be traveling the road south from Tombstone with a large amount of cash intended for miners in Bisbee, Arizona. Hill was to tell the stage robbers that Ike wanted their help to rob the paymaster and to meet him at the McLaury brothers' ranch thirty miles west of Tombstone. That's where Wyatt's posse would be waiting for them.

Joe Hill was instructed to leave right away, and Wyatt and Virgil watched as the Cowboy pulled his pocket watch and chain from his vest and handed it to Virgil, along with two to three hundred dollars that he asked Virgil to keep for him until he returned. Hill then mounted his horse, gently touched his spurs to the animal's flanks, and rode off down Allen Street.

Wyatt likely already had a good idea of the men he wanted as part of his posse to corral the outlaws: certainly Virgil, who'd been appointed Tombstone's acting chief of police on June 6; Morgan; and Doc. It was very important that Doc be there, as his presence at the capture of the robbers would further support his avowal of innocence. Unfortunately, Bat Masterson wasn't available, as he'd gone back to Dodge City in early April and got into a gunfight as soon as he stepped off the train. It seems Dodge City still had a little snap in it.

On June 13, Joe Hill found Leonard and Head at the mining camp of Eureka, New Mexico, one hundred miles east of Tombstone. The problem was that Leonard lay at the bottom of a freshly dug grave, having been shot to death the day previous, and Head was dying with six bullet holes in him. The story Hill got was that the two outlaws had been hired to assassinate the Heslet brothers, Bill and Ike, by a Tombstone businessman who coveted the nearby Heslet ranch. The Heslets, however, learned of the plot and ambushed Leonard and Head. The night before he was killed, Leonard was overheard to say that he "wished someone would shoot him through the heart and put him out of misery, as he had two big holes in his belly that he got the time he tried to rob the stage." Bob Paul's shotgun had done some damage after all.

Hill promptly returned to Tombstone and reported the bad news to the Earps and Ike Clanton and Frank McLaury. It wasn't all bad news for Ike, though. There's no doubt he would like to have gotten the reward money, but there was nothing stopping him now from "jumping" Leonard's ranch. And Leonard's death was definitely good news to the law-abiding folks of southern Arizona. The *Epitaph* ran a lengthy story on the shooting in its edition of June 18 and proclaimed that, "The country is well rid of one of the worst desperadoes that has cursed the world for a long time."

Something else was upsetting Ike, though. Tombstone's Wells Fargo agent Marshall Williams was the one who'd sent the telegram for Wyatt asking about the reward dead or alive and also the one who received the company's answer. Wyatt didn't tell Marshall what was up, but over a few days, Marshall witnessed Wyatt and Ike together a number of times in close conversation. Seeing those two together just once would have been odd, and Williams rightly guessed the two were plotting to nab the stage robbers. Unfortunately, an intoxicated Williams approached Ike sometime later and began mumbling about the reward and Ike aiding Wyatt. Ike couldn't help but conclude that their secret was out.

According to Wyatt, "Clanton, of course, immediately became alarmed, anticipating that the affair would become generally known and that his death would be a certainty because of his betrayal of the rustlers." This was indeed a very real worry. Following stage robber Lew King's escape from Tombstone, he was rumored to have been hanged by his fellow Cowboys somewhere in the Huachuca Mountains. King, it was believed, had made the grave mistake of revealing to the posse the names of his accomplices. A later report said the rumor was false, but, then again, King had vanished off the face of the earth.

But Ike had no doubts that the Cowboys would readily exact vengeance on their enemies, and he received ample proof of this just days after word came of the shooting of Leonard and Head. On June 16, Bill and Ike Heslet were enjoying a game of cards with a friend in a Eureka saloon when Jim Crane and several comrades burst through the front door and shot the threesome to pieces. An eyewitness who viewed the scene once the Cowboys galloped away said he "never saw such a dreadful sight. The place was just running with blood." Three more graves were dug in the mining camp.

Ike Clanton was scared as hell—and furious at Wyatt. He confronted Wyatt and accused him of telling Williams about their deal. Wyatt denied telling anyone, but Ike didn't believe him. Afterward, when the Clantons and McLaurys came to town, "they shunned us," Wyatt recalled, "and Morgan and Virgil Earp and Doc Holliday and myself began to hear their threats against us."

There would be no Wells Fargo reward. There would be no glory for Wyatt. And this rift with the Clantons and McLaurys wasn't going away.

ON THE AFTERNOON OF JUNE 22, WYATT STROLLED ABOUT THE faro and monte tables in the Oriental's second-floor club rooms. Just a week earlier, an *Epitaph* reporter had visited the rooms and wrote glowingly of what he saw: He felt he

> was in a place where taste and culture presides, even though the spot be devoted to Pharo and the four kings. Everything in and about the place has the quiet air of a suite of hotel parlors—the fine Brussels carpets, the lace curtains, fine pictures, and more elegantly upholstered furniture, tables, chairs and sofas being in far better taste than usually displayed in those places. . . . There is nothing loud or flashy.

The gaming tables were quite active for a Wednesday afternoon, with as much as ten thousand dollars spread across the room. But about 3:30 P.M., Wyatt heard a disturbance out on the street. People were shouting. Then some men ran into the club rooms yelling that the Oriental was on fire. Wyatt calmly but quickly told his dealers to gather up their cash and bring it to him. This they did, after which they ran out of the building. Wyatt rushed to the rear of the Oriental, where there was a large safe. Smoke was rapidly seeping inside, and he could hear the crackling of the flames in the adobe structure's ceiling.

As Wyatt cradled the cash in one arm, he attempted to open the safe but accidentally locked it instead. There was no time to work the combination. Wyatt felt his way through the smoke and out the back of the Oriental and headed for a bank a block away, where he handed over the cash for safekeeping. In the meantime, brothers Virgil and Morgan had hurried to the Oriental, which was now almost entirely engulfed in flames. They frantically asked the employees, where was Wyatt? The last they'd seen him, they said, he was taking the cash from the tables to the safe, and no one had seen him since.

Despite the intense heat, Morgan and Virgil ran to the door and shouted for Wyatt. Morgan then got down on his stomach and began to inch himself forward while Virgil held on to his feet, ready to yank him back to safety. Morgan couldn't stand the heat and smoke for long, and the roof and flooring could collapse at any moment. The brothers, coughing and their eyes burning, reluctantly retreated to the street. It was then someone shouted that they saw Wyatt. He was returning from the bank, unaware of the frantic rescue effort on his behalf. "I was very much surprised," Wyatt recalled, "to have Virgil run up to me with tears running down his cheeks and throw his arms around me. Then he explained that they thought me lost in the flames."

The fire started in the Arcade Saloon, three doors away and on the same side of Allen Street, when a barrel of bad whiskey was opened and a bartender stupidly struck a match to light a cigar. The barrel exploded, washing burning liquor over the bar, floor, walls, and ceiling. Amazingly, the three men then in the saloon escaped unhurt except for singed whiskers and mustaches. In four minutes' time, however, the fire had spread to five buildings. Flames jumped from awning to awning, the day's one-hundred-degree temperature contributing to the fire's intensity. In just twenty minutes, the blaze covered four city blocks.

As the flames advanced up and down the streets, a crowd of men, including the Earps, advanced with them, doing everything they could to help people escape and save business records and valuables. A female boardinghouse stood on Sixth Street, and Wyatt heard a woman there shouting for help. He ran over to the burning building and learned that the mother of the woman frantically yelling was ill and unable to flee, and the daughter wouldn't leave without her. "The young woman was rescued without difficulty," Wyatt said, "but it was with great effort that I finally groped my way through the intense heat and succeeded in bringing her mother out of the building."

By 6 P.M., the fire had, thankfully, burned itself out. Herculean efforts in dousing buildings with water, pulling down others, and ripping away the highly flammable cloth awnings had prevented the fire from spreading further. An early estimate placed the loss to businesses at $244,450. Vizina & Cook, the owners of the large adobe structure that housed the Oriental Saloon (known as the Vizina & Cook Block) suffered a loss of

$19,000. They were one of the very few Tombstone firms that had insurance, although their insurance was only in the amount of $14,000. The Oriental's gambling concession, owned by Wyatt and partners under the name Rickabaugh & Company, lost $6,000. They had no insurance.

Incredibly, the last glowing embers had not yet died out before the rebuilding began. The very night of the fire, fresh lumber was being delivered and carpenters beginning work. Several merchants kept the telegraph office busy with wires ordering new stocks of goods to replace those destroyed. "We have not heard of a single case," the *Epitaph* reported, "where a sufferer has thrown up the sponge, to use a sporting phrase, and is going to close out his business."

Virgil Earp performed so well as Tombstone's acting chief of police both during and in the aftermath of the fire that the city council promoted him to chief just days later.

WHAT DOC WAS DOING WHILE THE FIRE RAGED A HALF BLOCK away from his headquarters at the Alhambra Saloon is unknown. What is known is that Doc had his hands full putting out fires of his own. His enemy, Milt Joyce, now chairman of the Cochise County Board of Supervisors, had seen to it that Doc was indicted for their little gunfight back in October 1880. Doc posted bond and the court case dragged on until the fall.

An even bigger problem was Kate, who was back in Tombstone for a visit, apparently because of another one of Doc's letters "begging" her to see him. If Doc did send a letter, he very quickly regretted it. The two began fighting, over what is unrecorded, but it's a good bet the subject of Wyatt and his brothers came up more than once. Kate started drinking, and the more she drank, the angrier she became. And who knows what hurtful things a riled-up Doc said to Kate. In any event, Kate determined to get back at her lover, to make his life miserable, so on July 5, 1881, she found Sheriff Behan and told him she was certain that Doc was one of the Benson stage robbers. She claimed that for a month before the robbery, there was a mask with a rope beard stowed in his trunk.

Behan couldn't find pen and paper fast enough and prepared an affidavit that Kate signed. Affidavit in hand, Behan arrested Doc on the charge of complicity in the murder of Bud Philpott and the attempted stage robbery. Behan found satisfaction in this not just because he disliked Doc, but because he knew the robbery accusation would reflect poorly on Doc's friend: Wyatt Earp. "Whenever [Behan's crowd] would get a chance to shoot anything at me over Holliday's shoulders, they would do it," Wyatt recalled. "So they made Holliday a bad man. An awful bad man, which was wrong."

Decades later, Kate claimed she'd made the shocking accusations against Doc because Virgil and Wyatt were urging Doc to send her away, and she was trying "to block them." Kate made quite a few bizarre (and conflicting) claims in her old age, but the idea that getting Doc arrested and potentially hanged for murder to thwart the Earps is perhaps the strangest. What seems obvious is that after a monster of a lovers' spat, she wanted to hurt Doc, and knowing that the rumors of his involvement in the stagecoach robbery troubled him, she figured that would hurt the most.

Sheriff Behan escorted Doc to the office of Justice of the Peace Wells Spicer, who set bail at $5,000. Doc was released after Wyatt and the proprietors of the Alhambra, John Meagher and Joseph Mellgren, signed off as sureties. Kate remained intoxicated and angry, so much so that Virgil arrested her for being drunk and disorderly and gave her free overnight accommodations in a locked hotel room. After paying a $12.50 fine the next morning, Kate was free, but not satisfied. Virgil arrested her a second time after she was overheard making "threats against life." The identity of the individual she had in her crosshairs isn't known, but Wyatt Earp wouldn't be a bad guess.

The Territory's murder case against Doc came up before Justice Spicer on the morning of July 9, except there was no case. A contrite district attorney reported to Spicer that after questioning the prosecution's witnesses—and that included Kate—"he was personally satisfied that there was not the slightest evidence to show the guilt of the defendant; that the statements of the witnesses did not even amount to a suspicion of the guilt of the defendant." He requested that the case be dismissed, which Spicer was happy to do.

Kate left Tombstone for Globe. In melodramatic fashion, she stated in her memoir that, "It took all the persecution of the Earps and all the law officers aligned with them to make me quit. In doing as I did I was taking a desperate chance, but I lost out." When Kate spoke of losing out, if she was referencing the friendship between Wyatt and Doc, she was correct. Her outrageous behavior hadn't changed a thing between the two men. But she may have meant that she'd lost Doc. "After the stage holdup," she said, "Doc turned against me." And yet that wasn't really true. Despite all the grief she caused, Kate would soon be getting letters from Doc asking her to come see him. And Kate would pack her things and board a stage bound for Tombstone.

EIGHT

BOLD TALK

"The Cowboys as a class are not over brave, though there are some among them who have gone through so much difficulty that they have become desperate and will take desperate chances."

JOSEPH BOWYER, GALEYVILLE, ARIZONA TERRITORY

Peloncillo Mountains
Daybreak, August 13, 1881

Gray-bearded Old Man Clanton with six Cowboys and seventy-five head of stolen Mexican cattle were camped near the head of Guadalupe Canyon, in the far southwest corner of New Mexico's bootheel. One mile to the south stretched an invisible line that was the Mexican border. Clanton had just crawled out of his bedroll and called to the other men to get moving when a hail of bullets ripped into the camp, the echo of the gunfire reverberating between the low hills. Puffs of black powder smoke from as many as fifty guns floated over one of the ridges directly above the camp. Behind those guns were Mexican soldiers, and they weren't there to take prisoners.

In the camp, the buzzing of bullets mixed with the sickening slapping sound of lead smashing into flesh and bone. Several Cowboys were riddled by bullets at the first volley, one of whom never made it out of his bedroll. Just two of the seven Cowboys managed to escape the slaughter, and one of those only by playing dead. Among the killed were Old Man

Clanton and the murderous Jim Crane, who'd brutally gunned down the Heslet brothers at Eureka and was wanted for the killing of stagecoach driver Bud Philpott. In reporting Crane as one of the victims, the *Epitaph* commented that he was "a fugitive from justice, and an outlaw, and the six bullets that struck him were well expended."

The captain commanding the Mexican regulars, Alfredo Carrillo, did not have permission to cross into US territory, but international law was the last thing on Captain Carrillo's mind. This foray was about retribution for robberies and atrocities recently committed by the Cowboys against Mexicans on both sides of the border. A little more than two weeks earlier, on July 26, Cowboys had killed eight Mexican vaqueros and stolen their cattle. The next day, at a place known as Skull Canyon, twenty-five miles north of the Mexican border, a party of six Cowboys under Ike Clanton and Charlie Green surprised a large pack train in charge of thirty Mexican smugglers. Four Mexicans were shot dead in their tracks and the rest fled, leaving behind about two thousand silver pesos, a couple of kegs of mescal, and a small gold bar that was subsequently sold in Tombstone for $800.

News of the "massacre" of Old Man Clanton and his men reached Tombstone three days later, sending the Cowboys and their supporters into a mad frenzy. Within twenty-four hours, a force estimated at two hundred men, including the three Clanton brothers, had galloped away to seek revenge. Many others in Tombstone, however, were secretly rejoicing at the just deserts served upon the Cowboys. "This killing business by the Mexicans, in my mind, was perfectly justifiable," wrote diarist George Parsons. "Am glad they killed [Jim Crane], as for the others—if not guilty of cattle stealing—they had no business to be found in such bad company." A very real concern, though, was that this violence might spawn a war with Mexico. "Serious international complications will arise unless immediate steps are taken to put a stop to the movement on foreign soil," cautioned the *Epitaph*. "Blood will flow like water before another week rolls round."

But the blood didn't flow. The Mexican military immediately beefed up its presence on the border with two hundred regulars plus militia, and nothing more was heard of the revenge raid by the Americans. However, the Cowboys were no less a scourge in the region. Arizona's acting governor was Doc's former boardinghouse neighbor in Prescott, John Gosper, and in a long report to the US secretary of state, Gosper warned that if nothing was done soon to rein in this outlaw element, "The Cowboys will come to control and 'run' that part of our Territory with terror and destruction."

Gosper made his report after visiting Tombstone on September 9 and meeting separately with Sheriff Behan and Virgil Earp, who held the dual positions of deputy US marshal and Tombstone chief of police. Behan was happy to disparage the Earps, confessing to Gosper that there was little he could do to harness the Cowboys, especially as he wasn't getting the full cooperation of the chief of police in bringing the outlaws to justice. When Gosper talked to Virgil, however, he "found precisely the same spirit of complaint existing against Mr. Behan (the sheriff) and his deputies." The acting governor, understandably, didn't know who to believe.

Acting Governor Gosper encountered the same dichotomy with Tombstone's *Nugget* and *Epitaph*. "I found the two daily newspapers published in the city taking sides with the Deputy Marshal and sheriff respectively," he wrote, "each paper backing its special clique and condemning the other." This was true, of course, but it shouldn't have come as a surprise to politician Gosper that a Democratic newspaper and a Republican newspaper would take opposing views.

Gosper seriously mischaracterized the situation with the Cowboys, however, when he lumped the Earps and Behan together as the problem, writing that "the greatest difficulty now in the way, perhaps, of enforcing the law, and bringing to justice these reckless spirits, is the inability or indisposition of the civil officers of that particular county to do their duty." Gosper had to have known that at the very same time he was interviewing Behan and Virgil, Wyatt was in the saddle leading a posse to apprehend the men who'd robbed the Bisbee stage of $2,500 the night before. The robbery and Wyatt's posse were all people were talking about on the streets that day.

Sometime prior to this robbery, Wyatt was appointed a deputy US marshal, just like brother Virgil. And when the news of the holdup reached Tombstone about 9:30 that morning of September 9, he rapidly set about enlisting men to start on the trail of the road agents. Those who started out of town with Wyatt were brother Morgan; Morgan's friend and former roommate, gambler Fred Dodge; and Wells Fargo agent Marshall Williams. Two of Behan's deputies, William Breakenridge and David Neagle, followed a short time later.

The men rendezvoused at the scene of the holdup, about twelve miles from Bisbee. It didn't take long to discover the trail left by the two robbers, which appeared to lead toward Tombstone, but after following the tracks of their horses for a good distance, they lost them where a herd of cattle had trampled across the trail. At this point, Breakenridge and Neagle decided to ride to Bisbee and have a look around. It didn't make any sense that the robbers would go to Tombstone with their booty. Wyatt and his men, however, figured they could pick up the trail again, and by making larger and larger circles, they eventually cut it.

The road agents' trail did indeed turn back toward Bisbee and led Wyatt's posse into the rugged Mule Mountains, where the rough and steep terrain made riding difficult. So difficult, in fact, that one of the robbers had dismounted several times and walked alongside his horse. Wyatt carefully studied this robber's boot tracks and saw that the impression the heels made revealed that each heel had four large screws in it. By this time, the sun was now sinking low in the sky, so the posse made a dry camp and waited until sunrise to take up the trail again, which took them straight into Bisbee.

An observant Wyatt had noticed that two men by the names of Frank Stilwell and Pete Spence had ridden out of Tombstone just before the robbery, and he strongly suspected them as having pulled off the job. Both men were tight with the Cowboys. Stilwell, a handsome young man of twenty-six years, stood five feet nine inches tall and weighed a lean 170 pounds. He was no stranger to violence, having shot two men, one fatally. Stilwell was also no stranger to members of the posse—he was one of Johnny Behan's deputies.

Thirty-year-old Pete Spence (an alias) was a partner with Stilwell in a Bisbee saloon and other ventures. Standing nearly six feet tall, he carried several scars from various shooting scrapes and was wanted in Texas for bank robbery. Spence was known to hate Mexicans and rumor had it that he'd killed more than a few. Judging from the only undisputed photograph of Spence, a prison mug shot, he didn't share Stilwell's good looks.

Once in Bisbee, Wyatt and his men were careful not to alarm Stilwell and Spence. When Wyatt casually encountered Stilwell, he saw that the deputy had new heels on both boots. The man had been smart enough to know that his old boot heels would identify him as one of the robbers, so he'd gone right away to Bisbee's shoemaker and had his boot heels replaced with broader heels. However, Stilwell made a critical mistake: He didn't keep the old heels. After seeing Stilwell, Wyatt made a beeline for the shoemaker and asked for the old heels, and each had those distinctive screws. The shoemaker said it wasn't just Stilwell who'd visited his shop; Spence was with him. The two "were partners and always together," recalled Fred Dodge.

Wyatt and his men found deputies Breakenridge and Neagle and informed them about the robbers' trail leading to Bisbee and about the evidence of the boot heels. Breackenridge and Neagle, meanwhile, had interviewed the passengers in the stagecoach and learned that the shorter robber used certain expressions Stilwell was noted for. Confident that they'd found the holdup men, it was now a matter of taking them into custody and getting them back to Tombstone. Wyatt and Dodge quietly surprised Stilwell and placed him under arrest while Morgan and Neagle took in Spence. The arrests came off without a hitch.

Word of the arrests quickly spread in Bisbee, and a crowd gathered as the manhunters speedily saddled their horses and placed Stilwell and Spence on their own mounts. Some of the prisoners' friends talked loudly of following the posse and ambushing them in the Mule Mountains. That didn't happen, but Stilwell and Spence made their own threats during the ride to Tombstone, swearing to God that they would get Wyatt, Morgan, Dodge, and Williams.

Arraigned before Justice of the Peace Spicer on September 12, bail was set at $7,000 each, $5,000 each on the charge of robbing the US mail and $2,000 each for robbing one of the coach's passengers. In reporting the arrest and arraignment, the *Epitaph* dryly observed that "if it turns out as now anticipated, that the officers of the law are implicated in this nefarious business, it would seem to be in order for Sheriff Behan to appoint another deputy."

Three men immediately stepped forward to post bail for the pair, one of whom was none other than Ike Clanton. Afterward, out on Allen Street in front of the Alhambra, Frank McLaury and Ike motioned to Morgan Earp that they wanted to speak to him. They were with some other Cowboys, and when Morgan approached, a red-faced Frank began giving him hell for arresting their friends. Frank said he was so disgusted with Pete Spence for getting himself arrested by the Earps that he'd never talk to the man again.

"If you ever come after me," Frank said to Morgan, "you will never take me."

Morgan calmly replied that if he ever had reason to come after him, he could be sure that he would be arrested, which only made Frank angrier.

"I have threatened you boys' lives, and a few days ago I had taken it back, but since this arrest, it now goes!"

Morgan, unimpressed by the Cowboy's bold talk, turned and walked away.

News of marauding Apaches under leaders Juh, Naiche, and Geronimo temporarily diverted talk on the streets from the Cowboys and stagecoach robberies. About 10 P.M. on October 4, 1881, a report reached Tombstone of a battle between US cavalry and Apaches near South Pass in the Dragoon Mountains, just twelve miles as the crow flies to the northeast. All through the following morning, men gathered their rifles, revolvers, and ammunition, saddled their best horses, and prepared to ride to the scene of the fight and assist the troopers. At 1 P.M., a party of some twenty heavily armed men loped their horses through town, headed for the Dragoons. This group included Mayor John Clum, Sheriff Behan,

Chief of Police Virgil Earp, Wyatt Earp, and other "prominent citizens," including diarist George Parsons. Just outside Tombstone, the volunteers halted and elected Behan their captain and Virgil first lieutenant.

On the afternoon of the next day, the men arrived at the ranch of brothers Frank and Tom McLaury, southeast of the Dragoons in a broad plain known as the Sulphur Spring Valley. The brothers had lost fourteen head of horses to the Apaches. And it was no surprise that a few Cowboys were lounging at the McLaury place, one of whom, Parsons wrote in his diary, "was Arizona's most famous outlaw at the present time, 'Curly Bill,' with two followers."

George W. Parsons, Tombstone miner, mine agent, and diarist.
(PUBLIC DOMAIN IMAGE, AUTHOR'S COLLECTION)

Curly had been having a typical year. In May, he'd been shot in the neck by a friend and partner during a drunken quarrel. The wound somehow wasn't fatal, much to the disappointment of every law-abiding citizen and legitimate cattleman in southern Arizona. Then, in July, Curly made the newspapers again when another friend, this one a convicted murderer, wrote Curly a cautionary tale the day before meeting his fate on a Tucson scaffold. "Do not be too handy with a pistol," he advised Curly. "Keep cool and never fire at a man unless in actual defense of your life. . . . Words do not hurt, so you must never mind what is said to aggravate you . . . and above all things never hunt a man." Unfortunately, Curly Bill doesn't seem to have benefited from this teachable moment.

What was most curious to Parsons about the Curly Bill encounter was how the Cowboy was greeted by Virgil Earp. Parsons noted Curly Bill's involvement in Marshal White's death and added that "to show you how we do things in Arizona, I will say that our present Marshal [Earp] and said 'C Bill' shook each other warmly by the hand and hobnobbed together some time, when said 'CB' mounted his horse and with his two satellites rode off."

As far as Virgil was concerned, he knew of no outstanding warrants for Curly, and they were out there after Apaches, anyway. And, truth be told, Curly Bill was a likable fellow—when sober. Even lawbreaker hater Parsons couldn't help but be impressed with Curly Bill and his followers' "devil-may-care, braggadocio sort of manner." But Curly Bill and his men were thieves at heart, and sure enough, after the Cowboys had gone, Behan's men discovered a pair of spurs missing. Later that day, the volunteers arrived at the camp of a cavalry detachment on the trail of the raiding Apaches, where they halted for the night. Even in the presence of this force of approximately two hundred troopers and Indian scouts, Behan's volunteers were so worried that the Cowboys might swoop in and drive off their horses that they persuaded the commanding officer to allow them to stake their mounts inside the picket lines.

The Tombstone Apache fighters returned to town the next day, arriving exactly forty-eight hours after they'd left and without having seen a single Apache. It had been another one of those none-too-infrequent endurance rides in a harsh land. "My boots and spurs had not been off in all this time, two days and two nights," wrote Parsons, "and didn't come off easily, and my pants were split all up." In that time, they'd ridden 125 miles. "Distance is nothing in this country," commented Parsons.

———

FRANK STILWELL AND PETE SPENCE SHOULD HAVE PUT A LITtle more distance between themselves and the Earps. Both men had seen their cases dismissed by Justice Spicer after Wyatt and Virgil left town to chase Apaches. The reason behind Spicer's decision was supposedly insufficient evidence. Naturally, this didn't sit well with Wyatt, who was quite confident of these men's guilt and had put considerable effort into their capture. So, claiming to have found additional evidence, Wyatt rearrested Stilwell in Tombstone while brother Virgil found and rearrested Spence.

Expressing concern for the "safety" of the prisoners in the Tombstone jail, Virgil started for Tucson with the prisoners that same day, October 13. In reality, the Earps wanted Stilwell and Spence to face a US commissioner in Tucson on the US mail charges, and they weren't about to take the risk of the men escaping—that is, allowed to escape—from the Tombstone jail. At Tucson, Stilwell and Spence would be held without bail, awaiting a preliminary hearing. This hearing didn't occur until a week later, however, and both men would remain confined for several more days after that. The lengthy jail stay, Wyatt recalled, made Stilwell and Spence "very bitter towards me for causing them so much trouble."

Actually, most all the Cowboys were bitter toward the Earp brothers—and paranoid. Frank McLaury had accosted Virgil on a Tombstone street one day, after news appeared that a vigilante group was being organized to deal with the unchecked outlawry.

"I understand you are raising a vigilance committee to hang us boys," Frank said.

"You boys?" answered Virgil.

"Yes, the McLaurys, and Clantons, and Hicks, and Ringo, and in fact all of us Cowboys."

"Frank, do you remember the time that Curly Bill killed Fred White?"

"Yes."

"Who guarded him that night, and run him to Tucson the next morning to keep the vigilance committee from hanging him?"

"You boys," Frank replied.

"Now do you believe we belong to it?"

"I can't help but believe the man that told me."

"Who told you?"

"Johnny Behan."

Frank's answer gave Virgil pause. Clearly, Behan was stirring up trouble.

"Now, I tell you," Frank continued, "it makes no difference what I do,

I never will surrender my arms to you. I had rather die a fighting man than to be strangled."

It was Frank's typical blowing with an implied threat. All Virgil could say was "All right," and walk away.

In the midst of this growing tension with the Cowboys, Kate Elder returned to Tombstone and Doc's room in the Fly boardinghouse. Kate's Globe boardinghouse had recently been destroyed in a fire, and she'd lost nearly everything. It wasn't all bad, though, she told Doc, because a number of businessmen had offered to back her on a bank loan. Kate urged Doc to return with her to Globe, to get out of Tombstone for good. Doc wasn't persuaded, but he offered that they visit Tucson for a few days. The hearing for Stilwell and Spence was about to take place, and there would be lots of folks in town—and more than a few opportunities to "fight the tiger."

The hearing occurred over two days, October 20 and 21, and each day saw the courtroom packed with spectators. Among those in attendance were Sheriff Behan, Virgil Earp, and Wells Fargo's Tombstone agent Marshall Williams. Before leaving for Tucson, Virgil had sworn in Wyatt to act in his place while he was away. It's not known if Doc and Kate witnessed the hearing, although it was clearly the place to be in Tucson. But so was the city's Congress Hall Saloon, "the favorite resort of the sporting fraternity." It was there, Kate remembered, that Doc lost $75 of her money, all she had left, at a faro bank.

At the conclusion of the second day of the hearing, Behan and Virgil returned to Tombstone. Virgil now made Wyatt a special policeman, "to keep the peace, with power to make arrests." Wyatt, however, was mostly busy at the new Oriental (rebuilt after the fire with just one story), which had opened to much fanfare and the Tombstone Brass Band on October 11. Wyatt and his partners now owned both the saloon and the gambling concessions, and business was booming. The Oriental was seeing from four to five hundred patrons each night. On top of all this, however, Wyatt was again having to deal with an obnoxious Ike Clanton, who was becoming more unhinged by the day.

Clanton found Wyatt one day at the Alhambra Saloon and accused him of telling Doc Holliday about the failed deal to capture stage robbers Leonard, Head, and Crane. Wyatt denied it, of course, but then Ike said that Doc was the one who'd told him. This made no sense to Wyatt, but he assured Ike that once Holliday returned from Tucson, he'd prove that he hadn't breathed a word about the deal to Doc.

Wyatt wanted Doc back in Tombstone, anyway, so he dispatched Morgan to Tucson to retrieve him. On October 22, a Saturday, Morgan easily found Doc and Kate at a faro bank in Congress Hall. Doc warmly greeted Morgan. These two were also close friends, being separated in age by only four months. Kate watched curiously as Morgan pulled Doc aside and had a brief but serious conversation. When Doc returned to Kate, he said Wyatt needed him in Tombstone and that he'd be leaving with Morgan as soon as he escorted her to their hotel.

"I will come after you tomorrow or in a day or two," Doc said.

"No, I am going back with you," Kate protested.

"We are going back on a freight train."

"If you can go on a freight, so can I."

"We are going to Benson on a freight. Then we have to ride on an open buckboard [from there to Tombstone]."

As Kate remembered it, Morgan and Doc "saw that there was no way of getting rid of me, so the three of us went back to Tombstone."

IKE CLANTON WAS ABSENT FROM TOMBSTONE WHEN DOC GOT there, not arriving back in town until the morning of the twenty-fifth. That night, about 1 A.M., Doc entered the Alhambra, where he saw Wyatt eating at the lunch counter and Morgan at the bar. In the lunchroom, however, he spotted a liquored-up Ike Clanton sitting at a table. ("Lunch" at this time did not refer to the noontime meal as it's known today but simply to a small meal or snack.) Wyatt had already informed Doc of Ike's nonsense, so Doc stormed over to Ike's table, accused him of "using his name" and called him a damned son of a bitch and a liar. "Doc's vocabulary of profanity and obscene language was monumental," remembered an eyewitness, "and he worked it proficiently in talking to Ike."

Doc, who'd also had plenty to drink, slid his right hand under his coat on his left side and told Ike to pull his gun and "to go to fighting." Ike insisted he wasn't armed. The two argued loudly until Wyatt called to Morgan at the bar and told him to go into the lunchroom and put a stop to it. Virgil had recently appointed Morgan an additional special policeman and Wyatt, well, he was eating. Morgan went and took Doc by the arm and led him out of the Alhambra. But Ike, smarting under the cursing he'd received from Doc, soon followed them out, and the shouting and threats started up again. "You son of a bitch," Doc said, "if you ain't heeled, go heel yourself!"

Wyatt, having finished his meal, walked to the door of the saloon, but before he could intervene, he saw brother Virgil approaching. Tombstone's chief of police firmly informed Holliday and Clanton that if they didn't stop their quarreling they'd both be arrested. This had the desired effect, but Ike couldn't resist one last taunt as he walked away: He loudly said to Holliday not to shoot him in the back. Before Doc could react, Wyatt led him in the opposite direction.

The excitement seemingly over, Wyatt went into the Golden Eagle Brewery, next door to the Alhambra, where he had a faro game he needed to close. The game still in progress, Wyatt stepped back out after a few minutes and found Ike Clanton on the street waiting for him. Ike asked Wyatt if they could take a walk and discuss some things. Wyatt agreed to a short walk, during which Ike, angry and humiliated over the dressing-down Holliday had given him, felt the need to explain to Wyatt that he hadn't been "fixed just right" for a fight. In the morning, however, it would be different.

The fighting talk had gone on for too long, Ike said, and it was "about time to fetch it to a close." Wyatt responded by saying that he always tried to avoid a fight—"because there was no money in it." Ike began to walk away, turned, and said, "I will be ready for you in the morning." Wyatt didn't reply but headed for the Oriental, just across Fifth Street from the Golden Eagle.

Ike went to the Grand Hotel, a Cowboy hangout kitty-corner from the Alhambra, and retrieved his revolver. From there he wandered over to the Oriental, walking through the doors a short time after Wyatt. He'd already had more than enough to drink, but he ordered another one now. And he wasn't through pestering Wyatt, either. Making sure Wyatt could see his revolver, Ike said, "You must not think I won't be after you all in the morning." As a matter of fact, Ike added, he was ready to fight Doc right then.

Another shooting in town—especially one involving a known friend who had a less-than-stellar reputation—wasn't something Wyatt wanted; it wouldn't do him any good in his bid for county sheriff. So he lied to Ike, saying Doc didn't want to fight. Wyatt well knew that his volatile friend was always ready for a clash, that it took little provocation for him to jerk his revolver and blast away at someone who challenged him. A Dodge City newspaper editor came close to explaining the mentality of men like Doc when he wrote that gamblers "consider it necessary in their business to keep up their fighting reputation, and never take a bluff." The editor added ominously, "On no account should they be allowed to carry deadly weapons."

Thankfully, Wyatt's dealer from the Golden Eagle interrupted Ike's ramblings by bringing in the faro game money, which Wyatt took to the safe and locked away. Wyatt then left the saloon. Outside, he encountered Doc, and they both walked slowly down Allen Street. After about a block, they separated, Doc going to his boardinghouse and Wyatt to his home. What the two discussed before parting, no one knows. The antics of crazy Ike Clanton surely came up, or maybe it was just the usual small talk between friends. It had been a long day for them both.

Ike Clanton, however, wasn't nearly ready to call it quits for the night and wandered over to the Occidental Saloon. Inside, a poker game was being played, and among the men seated at the table were Virgil Earp, Johnny Behan, and Tom McLaury. Ike pulled up a chair and joined the game, making what was already an odd assemblage even odder. Everyone remained civil, however, and they shuffled cards and dealt hands until sunrise. When Virgil finally got up from the table, Ike saw that he'd had a revolver in his lap the entire time.

Ike followed Virgil out of the Occidental and stopped him. He wanted to know if Virgil would take a message to Doc.

What was the message? Virgil asked.

"The damned son of a bitch has got to fight!"

"Ike, I am an officer," Virgil said, "and I don't want to hear you talking that way at all. I am going down home now, to go to bed. I don't want you to raise any disturbance while I am in bed."

Virgil began to walk away.

"You won't carry the message?"

"No, of course I won't."

Virgil started walking again, when Ike said to his back, "You may have to fight before you know it."

Virgil ignored him.

NINE

THIRTY SECONDS

"It is foolish to think that a cow rustler gunman can come up to a city gunman in a gunfight."

KATE ELDER

Tombstone
Wednesday morning, October 26, 1881

The Earps and Doc didn't get much sleep, but Ike didn't get any. With a revolver in his waistband and carrying a Winchester rifle, he paraded around Tombstone, letting anyone know who would listen that he was out for blood. At about 9 A.M., one of Virgil's policemen came to his house and urged the chief to get out of bed. "You better get up," the officer said excitedly, "there is liable to be hell to pay! Clanton is threatening to kill Holliday as soon as he gets up; he says he is counting you fellows in, too." Virgil wasn't too concerned. It would be a while before the men Ike was ranting about would be up and around, and maybe Ike would settle down or go sleep somewhere by then. He told the officer he would get up before long.

About the same time that morning, a barkeeper went to Wyatt's house and woke him up. He reported that he'd seen Ike, armed, down by the telegraph office and that Ike was saying "as soon as those damned Earps make their appearance on the street today, the ball will open; we are here to make a fight. We are looking for the sons of bitches." Wyatt, like Virgil, also didn't feel the situation was worth getting up for, at least not right away, and he went back to sleep for a couple of hours.

Ike soon made his way over to Fly's boardinghouse, where he was greeted by Mary Fly. When Ike asked about Doc, she wisely answered that he wasn't there. A startled Mrs. Fly went to alert Kate, who was then looking at the photographs displayed in the studio gallery. Doc was still asleep, and Kate allowed him to rest a little longer. When she did wake him, she told him first thing that an armed Ike Clanton had been by earlier and was looking for him. "If God lets me live long enough to get my clothes on," Doc said, "he shall see me."

Sometime before noon, Virgil left his house and headed to the business district two blocks away. Nearly everyone in town, it seemed, knew about Ike's threats. Virgil met Jim and Morgan, who repeated to their brother what they'd heard: Ike was threatening to kill them on sight. Virgil told Morgan to come along with him; they'd locate Ike and disarm him before he hurt someone. They encountered Wyatt, who was also on the hunt for Ike, outside the Oriental. After a short exchange, they split up, with Wyatt going west along Allen Street and Virgil and Morgan walking north on Fifth. Virgil and Morgan quickly walked around the block to Fourth Street and turned back south. Halfway down the block, they spotted Ike at an alley entrance.

The police chief walked up behind Ike and grabbed his Winchester with his left hand. Ike let go, half turned his head, and reached for the revolver in his waistband. That's when the Cowboy felt the cold steel of Virgil's six-shooter slam into his skull. The painful blow sent Ike to his knees, and blood began to trickle down the side of his head. Virgil and Morgan took Ike's guns. Looking down at a dazed Ike, Virgil said, "I hear you are hunting for some of us."

Wyatt arrived just in time to see Virgil place Ike under arrest for carrying firearms inside the city limits and then watched as his brothers dragged Ike in the direction of the police court a block away. The judge was absent, however, and Virgil put Ike in Morgan's charge while he went looking for the judge. Not long after, Wyatt entered the courtroom and sat down on a bench. A few other people were seated in the room waiting. Ike Clanton sat facing Wyatt, just eight feet away, holding a bloody handkerchief to his head. A railing separated him from Wyatt. Morgan stood against the wall with Ike's guns.

"I will get even with you for all this," Ike said to Wyatt. "If I had a six-shooter, I would make a fight with all of you."

"You have threatened my life two or three times," Wyatt said angrily, "and I've got the best of evidence to prove it, and I want this thing stopped."

Ike mouthed off again, and Wyatt stepped to the railing, his patience with Ike and his Cowboy pals now fairly used up.

"You are a cattle thieving son of a bitch," Wyatt barked, "and you know that I know you are a cattle thieving son of a bitch. You have threatened my life enough and you have got to fight."

"Fight is my racket," Ike said boastfully, "and all I want is four feet of ground."

Wyatt reminded Ike of the "fight" he'd had with Virgil that ended with him in the police court.

Ike looked over at Morgan. "If you fellows would have been a second later, I would have furnished a coroner's inquest for the town."

Then Ike turned to Wyatt. "You fellows haven't given me any show at all today. You've treated me like a dog."

Suddenly, Morgan held out Ike's rifle. "Here, take this," he said, "you can have all the show you want right now."

This was too much for the few people seated in the courtroom and they jumped up and ran to the door and out onto the street. One of those who ran said it "was the worst scared crowd I ever saw."

Ike started to get up to take the rifle, but one of Sheriff Behan's deputies pushed him back down, saying he wouldn't tolerate any fuss. When those who'd fled didn't hear any gunfire, they slowly began to filter back in.

Disgusted, Wyatt got up and walked out of the courtroom and almost immediately came face-to-face with Tom McLaury, who picked the wrong time to challenge Wyatt.

"If you want to make a fight," McLaury said, "I will make a fight with you anywhere."

"All right," Wyatt replied, "make a fight right here." And he suddenly slapped McLaury across the face with his left hand while drawing his revolver from the large side pocket in his coat with his right. "Jerk your gun and use it!" Wyatt yelled at the stunned Cowboy. When McLaury didn't go for his gun, Wyatt swiftly raised his revolver and hit McLaury twice on the side of the head with it, sending McLaury's hat flying. The Cowboy collapsed to the ground, blood oozing from his left ear. Wyatt left him there and was overheard saying to himself as he walked away, "I could kill the son of a bitch."

From Wichita to Dodge City, Wyatt had found that the quickest way to take the fight out of a man—without killing him—was a sharp blow to the head with the barrel of a heavy revolver. Tom McLaury, confused and trembling, his head throbbing, indeed had lost all interest in fighting—for now.

WHEN THE JUDGE FINALLY APPEARED, HE FINED IKE $25 PLUS costs, making a total of $27.50. Virgil asked Ike where he wanted his firearms left. Ike, just as surly as ever, said, "Anywhere where I can get them, for you hit me over the head with a six-shooter." Virgil said he would leave them at the Grand Hotel bar.

Retrieving his weapons wasn't then a priority for Ike. He first found a doctor, who cleaned his head wound and bandaged it. Hungover, his eyes sunken from no sleep, in need of a shave, and no change of clothes for at least twenty-four hours, Ike Clanton was not the most attractive man in Tombstone that day.

Doc Holliday, on the other hand, wouldn't think of going out without looking his best. Before leaving the boardinghouse, he dressed in a gray suit with a pastel shirt. Snugged around the shirt's stand-up collar was his ever-present cravat with its diamond stickpin. Over the suit he wore a long, gray overcoat that came below his knees, and on his head he placed a broad-brimmed hat. And then there was the silver-headed cane, which, at times, he actually needed. Doc wasn't the same man he was of even a year or two before. His blond hair now had prominent streaks of gray. Doc was only thirty years old, but his disease was taking its toll. So was the liquor he drank to cope with the illness.

When Doc Holliday strolled over to Allen Street, about 2 P.M., the town was fully awake. Many of those, like him, who'd been up all night and into the early morning hours patronizing the saloons and gambling halls, were eating their breakfast. Others were already back at the bars partaking of their favorite booze. Sheriff Behan was at Baron's Barber Shop having a shave.

Doc happened to be near the Grand Hotel when three horsemen came riding up and stopped at a hitching post out front. The riders were Frank McLaury, Billy Clanton, and a cattleman named Frink from the Sulphur Spring Valley. They'd ridden in from Antelope Springs, twelve miles away, and were completely unaware of what had transpired in town over the last several hours. Strangely, Doc stepped up to young Billy and reached out and shook his hand, saying he was pleased to meet him. If there was something about Billy's dress or manner that caught Doc's attention, Doc never said. He didn't shake the hands of Billy's companions, though, and he walked away immediately after.

The two Cowboys and Frink went into the hotel and straight to the bar, where they were joined by an acquaintance named William Allen. As drinks were being poured, Allen quietly motioned Frank aside and asked him if he knew what was going on. When Frank shook his head no, Allen informed him that Wyatt Earp had bloodied his brother. Frank's pleasant demeanor turned to simmering anger: "What did he hit Tom for?" Allen didn't know. "I will get the boys out of town," Frank said. And then, turning to the others, he said, "We won't drink." They left their filled glasses on the bar, walked out and mounted up, and rode down Allen Street.

While Frank and Billy were just getting an inkling of the trouble brewing, the downtown was already buzzing with what someone overheard or saw—or what they thought they heard or saw. A steady stream of concerned citizens approached Virgil on Allen Street with warnings about the Cowboys. "I see two more of them just rode in," one man told him. "Ike Clanton walked up to them and was telling them about you hitting him over the head with a six-shooter." And, the informant added, one of the men that road into town said, "Now is the time to make the fight." The speaker had hardly finished before another man urgently motioned for Virgil to come to him. "For God's sake," the second man said, "hurry down to the gun shop; they are all down there, and Wyatt is all alone. They are liable to kill him before you get there."

This last came across as overly dramatic, and Virgil found it hard to believe. But just to be safe, he walked into the Wells Fargo office and grabbed a short-barreled ten-gauge shotgun that was kept there for his use. He then rushed around the corner to the gun shop, where he saw Wyatt out front. And, instead of being killed, his brother was attempting to move a horse off the sidewalk.

Moments before, Wyatt stood at the entrance of Hafford's Saloon lighting a cigar when he saw the McLaury brothers and Billy Clanton pass by. He followed them and watched as they stopped at Spangenberg's Pioneer Gun Shop a half block away and walked in. Frank McLaury's horse stepped up on the sidewalk and stuck its head in the doorway, and Wyatt went up and grabbed the animal's bridle to remove him when the McLaurys and Clanton appeared at the door. Billy had his hand on the butt of his revolver. Wyatt, choosing to ignore Billy's menacing stance, instructed them that the horse couldn't be on the sidewalk, and Frank backed him off. Ike Clanton came along then, and with nary a word to Wyatt, all the Cowboys reentered the shop. Standing outside, Wyatt and Virgil clearly saw the men putting cartridges in their gun belts and examining various firearms.

The chief of police's movements, especially with a shotgun, drew the stares of numerous townsfolk on the streets, who sensed a train wreck in the making. A group of miners approached Virgil to talk, and not wanting to attract even more attention, Virgil told Wyatt he was going to leave with these men and instructed him to keep the peace until he returned.

After a few minutes, the Cowboys left the gun shop. The bandaged Ike, looking disappointed and sickly, was the only one who appeared to be unarmed. He'd asked the proprietor of the store for a pistol, but the man had knowingly pointed to the Cowboy's bloody bandage and shook his head no.

Wyatt followed the Cowboys back to Allen Street and watched them enter the Dexter Stables. Meanwhile, inside Baron's Barber Shop, Sheriff Behan had a view of Allen Street from the barber's chair and noticed a crowd forming. A man came in and said, "There is to be trouble between the Clanton boys and Earp boys." Behan told the barber to hurry and finish his shave.

Leaving the barbershop, Behan spotted Virgil Earp with the double-barreled shotgun on the street corner, next to Hafford's Saloon, and approached him. The sheriff asked Virgil what all the excitement was about, and Virgil replied that there were a lot of sons of bitches in town looking for a fight. Behan told Virgil he would have to disarm them. But Virgil, his patience running thin like Wyatt's, said he wouldn't. If they were bound and determined to fight, then they could have it. Behan was startled to hear that from the chief of police and strongly argued against any kind of confrontation with the Cowboys. He persuaded Virgil to join him for a drink in the saloon, where they could talk things over.

Virgil leaned the shotgun up against the building and went inside with Behan, but he didn't drink. Virgil asked Behan if he would go with him to disarm the cowboys, but Behan refused, saying that if Virgil was present, the Cowboys wouldn't give up their arms and a gun battle would surely result. "They won't hurt me," Behan said, "and I will go down alone and see if I cannot disarm them." That sounded good to Virgil. All he wanted, he said, was for the Cowboys "to lay off their arms while they remained in town."

Before Virgil left the saloon, a member of Tombstone's newly formed Committee of Safety came in to speak to him and motioned Virgil to the end of the bar. The purpose of the Committee, a group of one to two hundred citizens, was to assist Tombstone's law officers in defending the town from a threat, be it Indians, robbers, or rustlers. The man offered the chief of police twenty-five armed volunteers who could be ready in a minute's notice. Virgil declined, believing he should give Sheriff Behan a chance to follow through with his plan. Outside Hafford's, yet another individual offered Virgil volunteers to deal with the Cowboys, saying he could provide ten good men. Again, Virgil declined the offer.

Wyatt, Morgan, and Doc Holliday now joined Virgil on the street corner. The Cowboys, they learned, had left the Dexter Stables and crossed Allen Street and gone into the O.K. Corral, Frank and Billy leading their horses. With the Cowboys was a twenty-one-year-old man named William Claiborne. Known as "Billy the Kid," Claiborne was friends with the Clantons and McLaurys and, as a local described him, "a stripling belonging to the profession." The Cowboy profession, that is. The Kid was unarmed.

As the Earps and Holliday talked, they were interrupted by a stranger. This man, a locomotive engineer who went by H. F. Sills, was visiting Tombstone for a few days. "Is your name Earp?" he said to Virgil. Virgil said it was. "Are you the marshal?" Virgil answered yes. Sills took Virgil a short distance away from his brothers and then blurted, "I just passed the O.K. Corral and saw four or five men, all armed, and I heard one of them say, 'Be sure and get Earp, the marshal.' The other one replied saying, 'We will kill them all.'"

This information was the tipping point for Virgil. The Cowboys were breaking the law in his town, and he would stand for no more threats. Virgil told Wyatt and Morgan to come along, they were going to disarm and arrest the Clantons and McLaurys.

Doc spoke up, "You're not going to leave me out, are you?"

Wyatt warned Doc it was going to be "a hard game."

"That's the kind I like," Doc replied, smiling.

Virgil stepped over and retrieved his shotgun from against the building. He asked Doc for his cane and handed him the shotgun, telling Doc to hide it inside his long overcoat. Again, people were watching, and it would cause a big stir to see the chief of police walking down the street brandishing a double-barreled shotgun with three grim-faced men marching behind him.

"They have horses," Morgan said to Wyatt, "had we not better get some horses ourselves, so that if they make a running fight we can catch them?"

"No," Wyatt answered, "if they try to make a running fight, we can kill their horses and then capture them."

Fight. That word kept coming up. It seemed inevitable now. Wyatt explained years later that, "It was our intention to disarm them this time, and put them in jail or else make a fight if they wanted it, and we well knew they would fight."

The time was approximately 2:45 P.M., and the afternoon had turned cold and gusty. A winter storm was coming to Tombstone.

———————

THE EARPS AND HOLLIDAY WALKED NORTH FROM HAFFORD'S TO Fremont Street, where they turned the corner and walked west. They moved briskly, four abreast, along the left-hand, or south, side of the road. Halfway down the block was an alley opening. This alley served as a rear entrance to the O.K. Corral stables, and the Cowboys had used it to get to Fremont, where they'd turned left, stopping a short distance away at a small, eighteen-foot-wide vacant lot. On the east side of the lot were Fly's boardinghouse and photo gallery, and on the west stood a small residence. It seems more than a coincidence that the Cowboys had stopped at this particular spot, next to the very place where Doc lived.

The Earps and Holliday spotted the Cowboys as soon as they turned the corner onto Fremont. Doc reached under his coat and pulled back both hammers of the shotgun, and Wyatt removed his revolver from his right coat pocket and held it out of view under his coat.

But Sheriff Behan was with the Cowboys, and he now started on a fast walk toward the Earps. Every few steps, Behan nervously looked back over his shoulder at the Cowboys; he seemed scared. The sheriff met Virgil's party just after they crossed the alley entrance and in front of a small butcher shop. Behan raised his open hands to Virgil.

"For God's sake, boys," Behan said excitedly, "don't go down there or there'll be war!"

"Johnny," Virgil said through gritted teeth, "I am going down to disarm them."

Virgil began to brush past Behan, who blurted, "I have disarmed them all."

The news that Behan had disarmed the Cowboys immediately lessened the uneasiness felt by the Earps and Holliday. Virgil, who'd had his right hand on a revolver sticking in his waistband at his stomach, now pushed the gun around to his left hip and switched Doc's cane to his right hand. Wyatt placed his pistol back in his coat side pocket. In the meantime, the Cowboys had withdrawn into the vacant lot until all that was visible to Virgil was a horse's head.

The Earp brothers and Holliday continued past a flustered Behan and walked another one hundred feet or so until the five Cowboys suddenly came into view, and with that view came an unwanted surprise: The Cowboys were *not* disarmed. Frank McLaury and Billy Clanton rested their hands on revolvers at their sides. The two horses each packed a Winchester rifle in a saddle scabbard, and Tom McLaury's hand gripped the rifle butt sticking out of the scabbard on Billy Clanton's animal.

The two sides stood within a few feet of each other, close enough to easily tell the colors of their eyes. "Boys," Virgil said, "throw up your hands, I want your guns." But the words had barely come out of his mouth when Billy and Frank drew their revolvers, their pistols making the familiar metallic clicks as they pulled the hammers to full cock. Virgil instantly raised his hands and Doc's cane. "Hold!" he shouted. "I don't want that!"

As the two Cowboys brought the barrels of their guns up, Wyatt jerked his revolver from his coat pocket and aimed it at Frank; he believed Frank, a reputed good shot, to be the deadliest threat and meant to take him out first. Wyatt and Billy pulled the triggers of their guns at nearly the same instant, the blasts so close together they sounded like one gunshot. Billy missed Wyatt, but Wyatt sent a lead bullet into Frank's stomach.

These first two shots were followed by the slightest of pauses, as if everyone needed a split second to process that this was really happening, that they were in a fight to the death. Virgil quickly switched the cane to his left hand and jerked out his revolver with his right. Then came more metallic clicks, flame streaking from barrel muzzles, and the sounds of gunshots reverberating off the walls of the buildings on each side.

A panic-stricken Ike Clanton ran up to Wyatt, grabbed his left arm, and yelled, "Don't kill me!"

"The fight has now commenced," Wyatt shouted, "go to fighting or get away!"

Wyatt shoved Ike aside, and the Cowboy ran to the front door of Fly's photo studio and darted inside and out the back. Kid Claiborne also raced for cover in the photo studio.

Billy Clanton's horse became skittish at the first shots, preventing Tom McLaury from sliding the Winchester out of its scabbard. The frightened animal began to move out of the lot with Tom trying to stay with it, clinging to the reins with his left hand and firing his revolver over the animal's back.

"I am shot," Morgan yelled as he dropped to the ground. A bullet had entered at one shoulder and ripped across his back, damaging both shoulder blades and nicking his spine before exiting. But he quickly pulled himself up and continued to shoot, backing into the street until he tripped and fell over a mound of dirt from a recently installed water pipe. A cloud of black powder smoke now stretched across the narrow lot, protected from the wind by the buildings on each side.

Wyatt fired at Tom but missed, his bullet striking the horse in the withers and causing the animal to jump. Doc, the 10-gauge at his shoulder, jerked one of the gun's triggers, sending twelve buckshot into the Cowboy's right side, about five inches below the armpit. Tom clutched his chest and started to run down Fremont, blood filling his lungs. Doc pulled the trigger to the second barrel but couldn't get the gun to go off. He threw the shotgun to the ground and drew a nickel-plated revolver from his pistol pocket. He didn't need to use it on Tom, though, as the Cowboy collapsed near the end of the block.

Even with a bullet in his gut, Frank McLaury was game, firing his revolver as he staggered toward the street with his horse. Frank's first shot punched a hole through Virgil's calf on his right leg, causing him to tumble, but the police chief stood back up and resumed shooting. Another of McLaury's bullets tore out a tiny piece of Wyatt's coat. Frank struggled to get the Winchester out of the scabbard on his horse, but the animal was jumping too much, and, about the middle of the street, the horse got away from him. Swaying as if dizzy, Frank spotted Doc and said, "I've got you now."

"Blaze away!" Doc said in his southern drawl. "You're a daisy if you have."

Both men fired. Frank's bullet cut through the pistol pocket in Doc's coat and slashed the skin on his hip while Doc's hit Frank square in the chest. However, a snap shot from Morgan, who'd raised himself up into a sitting position, sent a bullet crashing into Frank's skull at nearly the same instant. The Cowboy dropped in a heap on the sidewalk.

Poor Billy Clanton never made it out of the vacant lot. With a hole in his chest, just below the left nipple, a second just to the right of his navel, and his right wrist shattered, he slowly slid down against the corner of the house on the west side of the lot, leaving a streak of bright red blood on the wall. Forced to switch his gun to his left hand, he rested the revolver on his leg and got off three quick shots.

Doc fired at Billy twice, apparently missing, but Billy was nearly used up. He fell over onto his back, still grasping his pistol, his fingers struggling to cock it. Camillus Fly came out of the boardinghouse carrying a Henry lever-action rifle and rushed over to Billy. Fly took the pistol out of Billy's hand, who looked at him and gasped, "Give me some more cartridges."

Townspeople now came out of the buildings where they'd sought shelter at the first gunshots. Several gathered around the victims to render what aid they could. Doc saw people around Frank McLaury and, thinking he was still alive, angrily rushed up and said, "The son of a bitch has shot me and I mean to kill him." But what little life was left in Frank's body was quickly fading. He stared blankly at the sky, blood oozing out of the hole in his head. When a bystander asked Frank if he wanted to be moved, his lips quivered, but no words came out.

The street fight, as it was called at the time, had lasted no more than thirty seconds. Some twenty-five to thirty shots had been fired. As the last of the gunsmoke cleared, the Earp brothers and Holliday examined one another, checking on the seriousness of their wounds. They were interrupted by the sound of Sheriff Behan's voice.

"I will have to arrest you."

"No one could arrest me now!" Wyatt barked.

Sylvester Comstock, one of the ever-increasing number of gawkers and the co-owner of the Grand Hotel, spoke up. "There is no hurry in arresting this man," he said. "He done just right in killing them, and the people will uphold him."

"You bet we did right," Wyatt said. "We had to do it. And you threw us, Johnny. You told us they were disarmed."

Behan took offense at this last remark, saying he'd never said the Cowboys were disarmed.

Someone interjected that there was no use arguing about it now.

"I won't be arrested," Wyatt repeated, "but I am here to answer for what I've done. I am not going to leave town."

———

SHORTLY AFTER THE LAST GUNSHOT ECHOED DOWN FREMONT Street, the steam whistle at the Vizina Mine's hoisting works, two blocks away, sounded several short blasts, the signal for the Committee of Safety to gather. As Wyatt remembered it, he was surprised to hear "a commotion, and looking up the street we saw coming, on the run, about seventy-five to one hundred people, all representing the best citizens of Tombstone." These men came toting rifles and wearing belts filled with cartridges, but Virgil and Wyatt assured the Committee members that the trouble was over and that they weren't needed. Wyatt looked to one of the Cowboy bodies and quipped, "We won't have to disarm that party."

Avoiding the crowds of people filling Fremont Street, Doc Holliday went to his room and sat on the side of the bed. Kate asked him if he was hurt. He pulled up his shirt, and Kate saw a bloody streak on his hip. Doc had been lucky. But he had tears in his eyes. Something was hurting him, and it wasn't a physical wound.

"Oh, this is just awful," he said to Kate. "Awful."

TEN

AN EYE FOR AN EYE

*"We went into Tombstone to do our duty as officers. To do that,
we were put in conflict with desperadoes, and it resolved itself
into a question of which side could first drive the other out of
the country, or kill him in it."*

VIRGIL EARP

Tombstone residents awoke on the morning of October 27, 1881, to falling snow, bitter cold, and wind. And they eagerly awaited the morning editions of the *Tombstone Epitaph* and *Daily Nugget* for their reports on the street fight, which was already on the lips of every miner, baker, housewife, butcher, blacksmith, and grocer. The *Epitaph*, under the headline "Yesterday's Tragedy," published a vivid account from an eyewitness who was especially in awe of two men: "Wyatt Earp stood up and fired in rapid succession as cool as a cucumber, and was not hit. Doc Holliday was as calm as if at target practice, and fired rapidly."

If a rare individual existed who hadn't yet formed an opinion on whether the Earps and Holliday were in the right, John Clum of the *Epitaph* did his best to persuade them by reporting that, "The feeling among the best class of our citizens is that the Marshal was entirely justifiable in his efforts to disarm these men, and that being fired upon they had to defend themselves, which they did most bravely." Clum also didn't mind a bit of editorializing, writing that, "If the present lesson is not sufficient to teach the Cowboy element that they cannot come into the streets of Tombstone in broad daylight, armed with six-shooters and Henry rifles, to hunt down their victims, then the citizens will most assuredly take such steps to preserve the peace as will be forever a bar to further raids."

The *Daily Nugget* provided a more detailed, if not entirely accurate, account of the gunfight than the *Epitaph*. But the *Nugget*'s city editor, Richard Rule, had had a firsthand view of the immediate aftermath of the shootout. He was among the men who helped carry the fatally wounded Billy Clanton to a nearby house, remaining with him for the half an hour or so it took Clanton to die. Rule wrote that Billy never uttered "a word of complaint, and just before breathing his last, he said, 'Goodbye, boys; go away and let me die.'"

But Rule was giving Billy a noble death. Another man who was at Billy's side said that the Cowboy writhed in pain, screaming, "They have murdered me! Clear the crowd away from the door and give me air; I have been murdered!" And Billy's last words were not a tearful goodbye to the boys, but "Drive the crowd away!"

Rule also visited the "morgue" (the Dunbar Bros. & Co. Livery Stable) and gave his readers a description of the Cowboys' dead bodies. They lay side by side, he reported, covered with a sheet. Pulling the sheet aside, he saw little blood on their clothing, although his view was presumably limited to the fronts of their bodies. Of the three Cowboys, "only on the face of young Billy Clanton was there any distortion of the features or evidence of pain in dying." Of the McLaury brothers' features, Rule stated that they "looked as calm and placid in death, as if they had died peaceably, surrounded by loving friends and sorrowing relatives." The editor's words made it difficult not to feel some sympathy for the dead Cowboys, and, unlike the rival *Epitaph*, the *Nugget* included no comment on whether the Earps and Holliday were justified in the killings.

Thanks to the wires of the telegraph, news of the gunfight flashed across the country, although the newspapers in faraway states didn't treat it as a top story, with most papers running only one or two paragraphs at most. And the accuracy of the reporting was generally poor. On October 28, just two days after the fight, the *New York Times* ran a short paragraph that was hardly fit to print. It misspelled "Clanton" as "Clandon," which was an easy enough error to make (another newspaper spelled the name "Clarton"), but the *Times* story claimed all four Cowboys had "been parading the town for several days, drinking hard and making themselves obnoxious." It also wrongfully reported that Wyatt was "slightly wounded" and that Ike was wounded in the shoulder when neither were hit. The *Times*'s most egregious error, however, was its reference to Doc as "City Judge Halliday."

Much of the reporting on the street fight ranged from indifferent to morbid. The *Los Angeles Daily Herald* titled its story "Shooting Affray at Tombstone—Three 'Good' Cowboys," a play on the adage popular among most Euro-Americans in the West that the only good Indian was a dead one. The *Oakland Daily Evening Tribune* ran just one sentence, but it was to the point: "Cowboys try to run Tombstone, and get left . . . citizens now determined to exterminate the breed." And according to Sacramento's *The Weekly Bee*, the shootout was "the liveliest street battle that ever occurred in Tombstone." It was indeed "lively," but that characterization would better fit a dance party than a deadly gunfight.

The funeral for the McLaury brothers and Billy Clanton wasn't national news like the gunfight, but it was a local spectacle unlike any other. The bodies were given matching, ornately decorated hardwood caskets featuring glass viewing windows. Prior to the funeral procession, the three caskets were propped up in front of the funeral parlor along with a large sign that read "Murdered in the Streets of Tombstone." Camillus Fly set up his box camera and photographed the caskets, the neatly dressed dead Cowboys clearly visible behind the glass panes, appearing as though they were only sleeping. Although portraits exist of Billy Clanton and Frank and Tom McLaury, it is this photo, taken in death, that would give them immortality.

At 3:30 P.M. on the day after the gunfight, the Tombstone Brass Band led the funeral procession from the undertaking rooms on Allen Street to the cemetery a half mile away. Two horse-drawn creped wagons followed the band, the first holding the casket of Billy Clanton and the second carrying, side by side, the caskets of the McLaury brothers. Then came footmen, numerous horseback riders, and carriages. For three

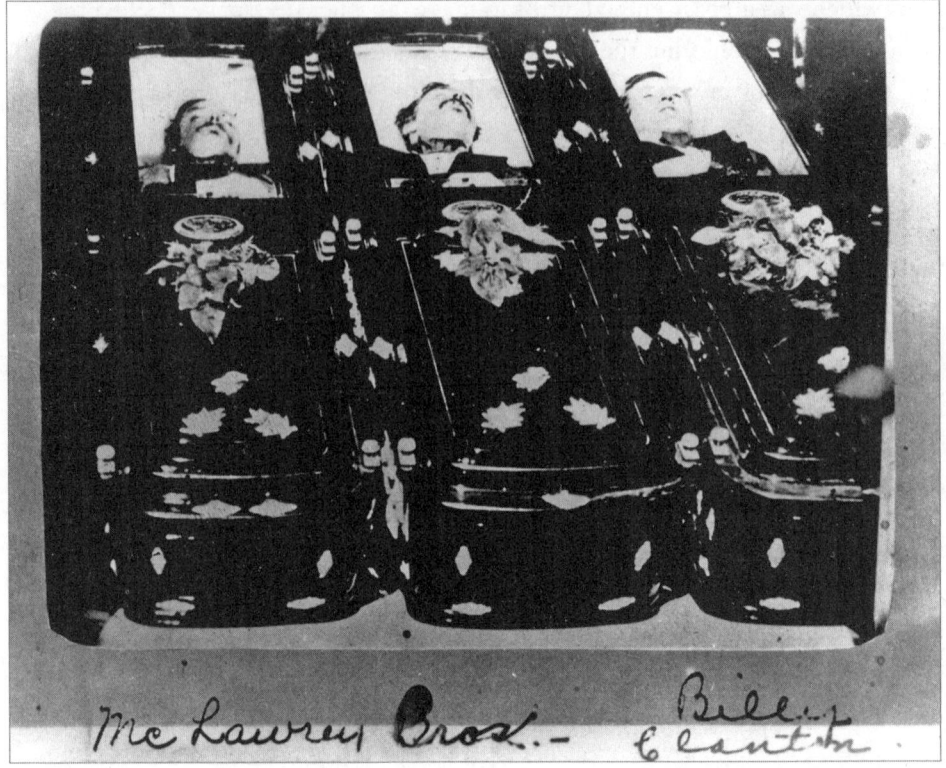

The dead of the Fremont Street fight: Frank McLaury, Tom McLaury, and Billy Clanton.
(COURTESY WILD WEST HISTORY ASSOCIATION)

blocks, the town's sidewalks on each side of the street were packed solid with onlookers.

In a letter to the *San Diego Union*, Clara Spalding Brown found this pretentious display baffling. She wrote that such "a public manifestation of sympathy from so large a portion of residents of the camp seemed reprehensible when it is remembered that the deceased were nothing more or less than thieves." But, she added, the

divided state of society in Tombstone is illustrated by this funeral. While there are many people of the highest order sojourning here, whose voices are always heard on the side of law and order, there yet remains a large element of unscrupulous personages, some outwardly regardless of restraining influences, and others (more than one would suspect) secretly in sympathy with the "cowboys," acting in collusion with them. Even the officers of the law have not escaped the stigma of shielding these outlaws, some of them being believed to have accepted bribes to insure their silence.

But what Clara Brown saw as undeserved sympathy for the dead Cowboys might actually have been a moment of reckoning, a way for the people of Tombstone to express their disapproval of the violence that was haunting the town's streets. Every western boomtown, from Wichita to Dodge City to Deadwood, had gone through its wild adolescence. But at a certain point, the citizens of those communities were more than ready for the rowdy, unruly days to be over.

It was truly a miracle that no innocent bystanders were killed by one of the thirty bullets let loose on Fremont Street. A woman and her two children were sitting in a wagon in front of the post office some fifty yards from the vacant lot when the lead started flying. The children had just been talking to their mother about what they'd do if they saw any Cowboys, and a moment later they got to witness three of them shot to death.

Despite editor John Clum's initial pronouncement that the "best class of citizens" believed the killings to be justified, Clara Brown found no consensus whatsoever. "You may meet one man who will support the Earps," she wrote "and declare that no other course was possible to save their own lives, and the next man is just as likely to assert that there was no occasion whatever for bloodshed, and that this will be a 'warm place' for the Earps hereafter."

———

IKE CLANTON NOW HAD EVEN MORE REASON TO "GET EVEN" with the Earps and Doc Holliday, and he would try to do it, ironically, using the law. He swore out a complaint accusing his enemies of murdering his brother and the McLaurys. Sheriff Behan finally had the pleasure of arresting Wyatt and Doc and bringing them before Justice of the Peace

Wells Spicer. Because Virgil and Morgan were still in bed recovering from their wounds, Behan chose not to serve them with warrants. Virgil, however, was temporarily suspended as chief of police.

Spicer set bail at $10,000 each, an eye-opening sum, but the defendants had no lack of friends and supporters who were willing to guarantee that amount. Among Doc's eight bondsmen were Wyatt, Jim Earp, and Fred Dodge. Wyatt's surety was in the amount of $7,000, the highest by far of any of Doc's bondsmen. Ten bondsmen agreed to back Wyatt's bail, including his brother Jim, his partner Lou Rickabaugh, and Tombstone's most prominent attorney, Thomas Fitch, who guaranteed $10,000. Another bondsman was Albert Bilicke, whose father owned the Cosmopolitan Hotel. It was to this hotel that the Earps and their wives moved a few days after the street fight because of concerns that they weren't safe at their homes on the edge of town.

On October 31, 1881, Justice Spicer took up the case of the *Territory of Arizona v. Morgan Earp et al., Defendants*. This was a preliminary hearing to determine if the evidence warranted a murder trial in front of a grand jury, but it was a most unusual hearing in that it lasted for a full month and saw an incredible thirty witnesses testify. The Earps obtained a crackerjack legal team headed by the well-liked Fitch, a popular lecturer who'd acquired the moniker "the silver-tongued orator of the Pacific." The district attorney was assisted for most of the hearing by thirty-six-year-old Will McLaury, a brother of the dead men and, interestingly enough, a successful Fort Worth, Texas, attorney.

Will McLaury arrived in Tombstone from Texas on November 4 and quickly concluded that his brothers and Billy Clanton were innocent victims of "as cold-blooded and foul a murder as has been recorded." He was incensed to see the killers freely walking the streets, and armed at that. McLaury pressured the district attorney and Judge Spicer to place the defendants back in jail, as the early testimony strongly implied that the gunfight was in reality a grudge killing instead of a legitimate police action. Kid Claiborne, not an unbiased witness, claimed that Billy and Ike Clanton had obeyed Virgil's order to throw up their hands and that Tom McLaury had opened his coat, saying "I haven't got anything, boys, I am disarmed." And a housewife who was in the butcher shop testified that she saw the Earp brothers and Holliday walk by and overheard part of their conversation. One of the Earps, she said, told Doc, "Let them have it!" and Doc had replied, "All right."

Public opinion, a fickle thing, began turning against the Earps and Holliday. The old narrative that the McLaurys and Clantons weren't Cowboys at all but upstanding ranchers was pushed by their friends, and it was also claimed that the victims were actually in the act of leaving town when they were mercilessly gunned down. On November 7, then, Judge Spicer yielded to Will McLaury's wishes and remanded Wyatt and Doc to Sheriff Behan's custody without bail. "The scoundrels are in jail and in beds," McLaury wrote his law partner in Fort Worth, but "this don't bring back my dead brothers."

Because of concerns for Wyatt's and Doc's safety, a strong guard with rifles and shotguns surrounded the "insecure edifice." The *Epitaph* saw great irony in this, stating that if "the sheriff had been as active in preventing prisoners' breaking out, there would have been three more gentlemen for the courts to pass upon at the next term."

FOLLOWING EACH LONG DAY OF TESTIMONY IN THE COURT-room, editors and typesetters at the *Epitaph* and *Nugget* scurried to get the testimony in their columns for the next day's edition. So not only did Judge Spicer hear the witness testimony, but the people of *Tombstone* were able to read it for themselves. Revealed to the world, or southern Arizona, at least, was the betrayal Ike so wanted to keep secret—his agreement to lure the Benson stage robbers to a place where Wyatt could capture them—as well as his paranoia and threats that led to the deaths of his brother and the McLaurys.

Much of the eyewitness testimony was contradictory on a number of points. What exactly did Sheriff Behan say to Virgil Earp when he tried to stop him? What were Virgil's words to the Cowboys in the vacant lot? Did the Cowboys throw up their hands or did they go for their guns? Who was armed and who wasn't? Who fired the first shots? How many shots were fired? Witnesses gave varying answers to all these questions. But then again, no one had a perfect, unobstructed view of the street fight from beginning to end, not even the participants themselves. Perhaps the most truthful answer, and the one that explains why the testimony is often impossible to rectify, came from Mrs. Addie V. Borland, a thirty-six-year-old dressmaker whose house sat across the street from the vacant lot. When asked how many shots were fired, she replied, "I could not tell; all was confusion, and I could not tell." Yes, confusion. All was confusion.

Unlike Mrs. Borland, some of the witnesses held clear biases against the Earps and Holliday, none more so than Ike Clanton and Johnny Behan. Ike not only suffered from amnesia when certain questions were raised, but he had an incredibly inventive imagination as well. He testified that Wyatt wanted to kill the Benson stage robbers because Wyatt and Morgan had taken the money that was in the coach's strongbox and given it to Doc and Bill Leonard. Because Leonard, Head, and Crane were supposedly privy to this, Wyatt "would have to kill them or else leave the country." Ike failed to explain how Wyatt and Morgan pulled off the cunning theft when no one had touched the strongbox between Tombstone and Benson, least of all the robbers who attempted to stop the stage and failed.

Sheriff Behan had plenty of reasons to want to see Wyatt put away for a long time, if not hanged. The same with Doc. But Wyatt's attentions to the now former "Mrs." Josephine Behan, who'd departed Tombstone for San Francisco that summer, were, of course, a sore point. And Behan assumed he would face Wyatt in the November 1882 election for county sheriff. Behan had had the upper hand in getting the gubernatorial appointment because of his political connections in Prescott, but anything could happen come election time. The sheriff's serious miscues preceding the gunfight, his known associations with some of the Cowboys, and the little matter of one of his deputies getting arrested for stage robbery were nothing less than a nightmare for his image.

In his testimony, Behan, like Ike, suffered from bouts of amnesia and strayed far from the truth in some of his answers. Attorney Thomas Fitch quizzed Behan about a visit he'd made to the wounded Virgil Earp the night of the gunfight. Fitch asked Behan if he remembered telling Virgil that he heard him say, "Boys, throw up your hands, I have come to disarm you." Behan answered that he "supposed" he told Virgil that. Fitch further asked if Behan did not say to Virgil, "I am your friend, and you did perfectly right." Behan wouldn't admit that he did, but another man present in the room with Behan and Virgil that night, the recently appointed assistant district attorney Winfield S. Williams, subsequently testified that he heard Sheriff Behan say exactly those words. In a way, Behan ended up being a better witness for the defense than he was for the prosecution.

On November 16, Wyatt gave his account of the street fight and the circumstances that led up to it, and in an unusual twist, he read from a prepared statement, the only witness to do so. No doubt assisted in its preparation by famed orator Fitch, Wyatt's statement was thorough and convincing. Toward the end of his account, Wyatt said,

> When I went as deputy marshal to help disarm them and arrest them, I went as part of my duty and under the direction of my brother the marshal. I did not intend to fight unless it became necessary in self-defense, and in the performance of official duty. When Billy Clanton and Frank McLaury drew their pistols, I knew it was a fight for life, and I drew and fired in defense of my own life, and the lives of my brothers and Doc Holliday.

As part of this prepared statement, Wyatt submitted two extraordinary documents. These were letters from Dodge City and Wichita bearing the signatures of dozens of prominent citizens and officials. The Dodge City letter read, in part, that "as Marshal of our city [Wyatt Earp] was ever vigilant in the discharge of his duties, and while kind and courteous to all, he was brave, unflinching, and on all occasions proved himself the right man in the right place." As for the charges against him in Tombstone, the Dodge citizens proclaimed that "from our knowledge of him we do not believe that he would wantonly take the life of his fellow man, and that if he was implicated, he only took the life in the discharge of his sacred trust to the people." The Wichita letter equally attested to Wyatt's character and integrity and concluded with "no fault was ever found with him as an officer or as a man."

Wyatt could not have had two more ringing endorsements. The prosecution objected to the introduction of the documents but were overruled, and the letters were filed as Exhibit A and Exhibit B. The Kansas letters were duly published in the *Epitaph* as well, which undoubtedly gave Tombstone residents additional knowledge of Wyatt's history as a lawman that many were learning for the first time.

Virgil provided testimony on November 19 and 22, and it was as complete and eminently believable as Wyatt's. H. F. Sills, the locomotive engineer who'd warned Virgil that the Cowboys were threatening to "kill them all," followed Virgil on the witness stand. Sills's account coming on the heels of the testimony of Wyatt and Virgil made for three solid blows to the prosecution and its witnesses. It became rather obvious that the actions of the Earps and Holliday that day were not "the gratification of revenge on their part," that the street fight was anything but murder. Justice Spicer now granted the defense's request that Wyatt and Doc be again released on bail, which was set at $10,000 each. Mine owners and businessmen E. B. Gage and James Vizina immediately stepped forward to cover the amount.

Doc was never called as a witness, although he was present and seen busily taking notes during the hearing. Judge Spicer heard the last of the witnesses on November 28, and two days later he presented a lengthy decision—it filled nearly three columns in the *Epitaph*. Spicer did not find "sufficient cause" to believe that Wyatt and Doc were guilty of the charge of murder. He did believe, however, considering Wyatt's and Doc's runins with Ike previous to the street fight, that Virgil made a poor decision in recruiting his brother and Doc to help disarm the Cowboys. Nevertheless, Spicer continued, Virgil's unwise decision was not criminal. "In fact, as the result plainly proves," the judge explained, "he needed the assistance and support of staunch and true friends, upon whose courage, coolness, and fidelity he could depend in case of an emergency." Spicer ordered Wyatt and Doc released.

San Diego Union correspondent Clara Spalding Brown observed that the Cowboys accepted Spicer's decision "with a very bad grace, and a smoldering fire exists, which is liable to burst forth at some unexpected moment. If the Earps were not men of great courage, they would hardly dare remain in Tombstone."

EVEN THOUGH DOC DIDN'T HAVE A GOOD RELATIONSHIP WITH his father and apparently hadn't been in touch with him since leaving Texas, he was concerned about what his father in Valdosta might have read about the street fight and his arrest for murder. One day, then, Henry Holliday received a letter from Tombstone bearing the signatures of several of the town's citizens vouching for Doc's innocence. Henry also was sent a copy of the *Epitaph* containing Judge Spicer's decision exonerating the Earps and Doc. It's not known if Doc sent a letter of his own to his father, but at least Henry knew that his son wasn't a cold-blooded murderer.

Just two days after Spicer rendered his decision, Doc was arrested yet again, this time for firing a pistol within the city limits. Perhaps Doc got caught up in celebrating his exoneration. If so, he was celebrating without Kate—she was gone. While Doc and Wyatt were in jail, Kate had twice welcomed to her room a handsome thirty-one-year old man by the name of John Ringo, although most people called him Johnny. Johnny Ringo, along with Curly Bill and Ike Clanton, was a Cowboy leader, taking part in many a raid into Mexico, stealing cattle and sheep and relieving smugglers of their goods. Ringo wasn't known as a killer, but he did gain a reputation as a brazen rustler.

Johnny stood six feet tall, sported gray-blue eyes, and had light brown hair and a bushy mustache of the same color. Kate recalled that Johnny "always looked neat and clean and well dressed, [which] showed he took good care of himself," and "his attitude toward women was that of a gentleman." Kate claimed that she never knew Johnny to drink, but a friend of Johnny's described him as a heavy drinker, and when he was drinking, Johnny could be trouble. This friend also found Johnny mysterious, reserved, and morose. Kate, too, sensed a sorrow in Johnny. She said that sometimes she "noticed something wistful about him, like as if his thoughts were way off on something sad."

Kate never forgot her last visit with Johnny. "Mrs. Holliday," Johnny said, "I came here to give you good advice: If I were you, I would leave

Johnny Ringo.
(COURTESY WILD WEST HISTORY ASSOCIATION)

Tombstone, if you stay here, they will get Doc. They are watching to get him in your apartment and they may get you, too."

Kate explained that she was broke—Doc had gambled away all she had.

"If you haven't enough money, here is fifty dollars," Johnny said. "That will get you to Globe."

Kate left for Globe that night. "Every time I think of John Ringo," Kate said years later, "my eyes will fill with tears."

Ringo wasn't wrong about the danger Doc faced. The Cowboys, in fact, were said to have prepared a "death list" that included the Earps, Holliday, their attorney Tom Fitch, Judge Spicer, and Mayor Clum. And some of these individuals received threatening letters. The letter sent to Judge Spicer strongly advised him to seek a "more genial clime . . . as you are liable to get a hole through your coat at any moment." Also worrying were rumors that the Cowboys were planning to conduct a raid on Tombstone, hitting the Oriental and also robbing the bank, the post office, and the Wells Fargo office.

The raids never materialized, but the first attempt by the Cowboys to scratch a name off their death list occurred on the night of December 14 when several assassins attacked the Benson stage four miles from Tombstone. The man they were after was John Clum, a passenger in the coach. The Cowboys fired some twenty-five shots from both sides of the road, but instead of forcing the coach to halt, the gunfire frightened the team, and the stage raced ahead. After a half mile, one of the horses dropped from a bullet wound received during the attack and the coach stopped. Fearing the Cowboys might try again, Clum left the coach and footed it several miles, eventually borrowing a horse and riding alone to Benson.

Strong evidence pointed to the attack being an assassination attempt that was intended to look like a holdup. For one thing, the stage contained no bullion and no registered mail, generally a good source of money and valuables. A coach containing such Wells Fargo "treasure" had departed Tombstone that morning at 10 A.M., and if the gunmen were indeed road agents, that's the coach they would have hit, "as it is a well-known fact," commented the *Daily Arizona Citizen*, "that none are better posted as to when treasure is placed upon a coach then those persons who rob them." Additionally, no rifle shell casings were found at the scene of the attack, which meant the shots fired came from revolvers. Stage robbers who knew their business used rifles.

The morning following the attack on the coach, the Earps' and Doc's loyal antagonist, Milt Joyce, was having a conversation with Virgil in the Oriental. Virgil had recovered well enough from the painful wound he received in the street fight that he was able to get out and about. At some point during their talk, Joyce flippantly remarked that he'd been expecting something like the attack on the coach ever since Wyatt and Doc had gotten out of jail. Maybe he was joking, but if so, it was a poor one, and Virgil immediately slapped Joyce's face. Joyce staggered, and when he caught his balance, he saw that several of Virgil's friends had stepped forward and did not look pleased. Joyce made his way to the Oriental's door, saying as he exited, "Your favorite method is to shoot a man in the back, but if you must murder me, you will be compelled to shoot me in front."

VIRGIL EARP WAS WELL AWARE OF THE THREATS AGAINST HIM and his brothers and Doc, but he wasn't going to stay cooped up in the Cosmopolitan Hotel like a scared child. On the night of December 28, he was in the Oriental with Wyatt. Among the crowd of patrons was Frank Stilwell, whom the Earps and Holliday had inadvertently helped get out of the Tucson jail. Stilwell had planned to call the McLaury brothers as witnesses for his trial on the charge of robbing the US mail from the Bisbee stage. Because of the deaths of the McLaurys, however, Stilwell was granted bail.

About 11:30 P.M., Virgil told Wyatt he was going to bed. Frank Stilwell, seated nearby and close enough to hear, got up and left the Oriental ahead of Virgil. As Virgil stepped out of the saloon, he saw Frank run into an adobe building under construction on the opposite corner. It was odd, but Virgil didn't give it much thought.

Streetlights cast a bright glow on the intersection of Fifth and Allen Streets, and the six-foot-tall Virgil was easily identifiable as he walked across Fifth. He'd nearly reached the west side of the street when four loud blasts, close together, erupted from inside the unfinished adobe. Virgil involuntarily stiffened as a load of buckshot slammed into his left side and back. The lead pellets shattered the bone in his arm and caused other near-fatal damage. One pellet entered above his groin and exited near his spine and another tore through his liver.

Virgil stumbled, but he somehow stayed on his feet. He immediately did an about-face and went back to the Oriental. Ashen-faced and in obvious pain, he told Wyatt he'd been shot and then slunk to the floor. Wyatt yelled for help, and he and several men quickly carried Virgil to the Cosmopolitan. On the way, Wyatt asked his brother if he'd seen who'd shot him. Virgil said he knew one of them, but he refused to give Wyatt the man's name. "I want him myself," Virgil said, "when I get well."

Wyatt and the others laid Virgil on a table in the Cosmopolitan. Someone rushed to Virgil's room and knocked on the door for Allie. She hurried to her husband just in time to see Dr. George Goodfellow cutting away Virgil's bloody shirt. "I almost fainted," Allie recalled. "A load of buckshot had hit him in the side, scallin' a little off the backbone. And then I saw his left arm. It was the worst. A load of slugs had hit him in the elbow. It was awful lookin'."

A strong guard was placed at the hotel, and when George Parsons came to deliver medical supplies requested by Dr. Goodfellow, he nearly didn't get past it. When Parsons did finally get to Virgil's room, he expressed to the suffering lawman how sorry he was. "It's hell, isn't it!" Virgil exclaimed. Then Virgil turned to Allie, who could barely contain herself. "Never mind," Virgil said to her. "I've got one good arm left to hug you with."

Virgil underwent surgery on his arm the next day, and doctors removed his elbow joint and the bone to halfway up his shoulder, leaving his arm a limp appendage and unusable for the rest of his life. One of the two doctors performing the surgery estimated there were four chances in five their patient would die, but Virgil Earp was one tough man—and lucky. Besides the buckshot that struck him, nineteen pellets hit the Golden Eagle Brewery, three breaking through a glass window and passing just over the heads of some faro players. The shooters had tried awfully hard to reduce the number of Earp brothers.

Immediately after the gunshots echoed down Allen and Fifth Streets, three men were seen running into the darkness at the edge of town. At the rear of the unfinished building that had concealed the gunmen, a hat was found. It belonged to Ike Clanton. For a man who was believed to be a leader of the Cowboys, he was seeming more and more like a complete idiot. Other suspects included Curly Bill, Will McLaury, and, of course, Frank Stilwell. McLaury, however, reportedly left Tombstone for Texas two days before the shooting.

On December 29, the same day as Virgil's surgery, Wyatt sent a telegram to US Marshal Crawley Dake in Prescott:

Virgil Earp was shot by a concealed assassin last night. The wound is considered fatal. Telegraph me appointment with power to appoint deputies. Local authorities have done nothing. The lives of other citizens have been threatened.

Wyatt Earp

On Virgil's condition, Wyatt was simply repeating the grim prognosis the doctors had given him. The key phrase in this telegram, however, was Wyatt's request for an appointment "with power to appoint deputies." Wyatt was determined to go after the Cowboys, to make them pay, but he was greatly outnumbered. Morgan and Doc would ride to hell and back for him, but they wouldn't be enough. Wyatt needed an actual posse composed of men with grit, men he could trust. Marshal Dake, who held a high opinion of all the Earps and their efforts to combat the outlawry in Cochise County, immediately sent Wyatt his authorization, telling him to "spare no expense in discovering the perpetrators of the deed."

IN EARLY JANUARY 1882, WYATT SOLD HIS INTEREST IN THE ORI-ental's operations to his partners. He may very well have been in financial straits—retaining lawyers for the thirty days of the Spicer hearing must have come at a substantial cost—but now he could devote his full attention to recruiting men for his posse and to plotting his strategy. Before he could make his first significant move, however, Doc nearly started another gunfight in the middle of Tombstone.

According to the *Daily Nugget*, bad blood had developed between Doc and Johnny Ringo. The *Nugget* didn't state the source of their feud, but it's not hard to guess. Ringo had given Kate money to leave town, and just as Sheriff Behan had been humiliated by Doc giving his Sadie money, Doc didn't like Ringo having this over him, let alone Ringo's attentions to Kate. On the afternoon of January 17, as Doc was walking along a crowded Allen Street, Ringo approached him in front of the Occidental Saloon.

"Holliday, you have been talking about me," Ringo said loudly.

"I don't know that I have been taking about you," Doc replied, "but if I have, it still goes."

Both men had their hands on guns in their coat pockets, and the hatred the two men had for each other in this moment was unmistakable—and scary. Those close by nervously began to step away. Fortunately, the police chief saw the commotion and rushed in and grabbed Ringo by the arm and pulled him back. Doc, still full of fight, yelled at the chief to turn Ringo loose. Wyatt, who stood nearby with brother Morgan, firmly took hold of Doc's arm and led him away, saying, "Come on, enough of this." Doc and Ringo were arrested and fined $32 each for carrying concealed weapons. The police chief also arrested Wyatt on the same charge, but as Wyatt was a lawman entitled to carry a weapon, his charge was dismissed.

The Allen Street altercation became the greatest gunfight that never was. But the tension and fear of onlookers that day had been very real, mostly because of Doc's supposed fatalism. A Tombstone resident described Doc at this time as a very hard character who "carries his death warrant with him at all times. He is dying of consumption, and he is correspondingly reckless."

Seven days later, on the afternoon of January 23, 1882, Wyatt Earp and eight men of his posse mounted their horses and rode east on Allen Street on their way out of town. The throngs of people on the sidewalks suddenly grew silent, staring in awe as the posse members rode past—they made for a truly impressive and fearsome sight. According to one report, each posse member was armed with a shotgun, a Winchester rifle, two revolvers, and at least one hundred rounds of ammunition. Wyatt and his men were ready for war, but no one knew where they were headed, which became the subject of much chattering among the townspeople as the posse disappeared down the street.

————

THE MEN RIDING WITH WYATT WERE FRIEND DOC; BROTHERS Morgan and Warren; Texas Jack Vermillion; Sherman McMaster; Jack

Johnson; Origen C. Smith; and Daniel G. Tipton. Warren, twenty-six years old, was the youngest of the Earp brothers and, some say, the most volatile. He'd joined his brothers in Tombstone early in 1881 and was promptly arrested and fined $25 for discharging firearms within the town limits. He was in California when the street fight occurred, or he surely would have made that determined walk with Doc and his brothers.

Warren Earp.
(COURTESY TRUE WEST ARCHIVES)

Texas Jack, a thirty-six-year-old Civil War veteran (122nd Ohio Volunteer Infantry) was a carpenter. Twenty-eight-year-old McMaster was a former Texas Ranger as well as a former lawbreaking associate of the Cowboys, which meant he brought with him an intimate knowledge of the prey Wyatt was after. In fact, Wyatt had been using McMaster as a spy among the Cowboys for some time. Jack Johnson, an alias, was thirty-four, and Wyatt would recall years later that Johnson was a bookkeeper. Maybe, but Johnson was far more familiar with a revolver than a pencil, having been involved in shooting scrapes from Missouri to Colorado before landing in Tombstone.

Daniel G. Tipton, thirty-seven, served in the Union navy during the Civil War. He gave his occupation as miner when registering to vote in Cochise County. So, too, did Origen C. "Charlie" Smith, also thirty-seven. Smith had known Jim Earp in Fort Worth, where he'd survived a couple of shooting scrapes. Both men were known gamblers, but who wasn't in Tombstone? As members of Deputy US Marshal Earp's posse, each man received $5 a day, a horse, saddle, bridle, firearms, and rations. They probably didn't wear badges, but they were official deputy US marshals nonetheless. Leaning toward the melodramatic, the *Daily Nugget* characterized the Earp posse "as desperate men who will each fight to their death."

Wyatt led his posse toward the San Pedro. He held arrest warrants for Ike and Fin Clanton and Pony Diehl, the latter a Cowboy whom Wyatt suspected of having a connection to the Bisbee stage robbery. The warrants, however, were issued as a result of charges accusing the three men of participating in the attempted murder of Virgil Earp.

On the night of January 25, the Earp posse, bolstered by the addition of about twenty-two armed men from Tombstone, rode into Charleston, Arizona, and essentially took over the town. Earp's men stopped and questioned individuals on the roads going in and out of Charleston and even went door to door looking for the suspects. Unfortunately, the Cowboys had been warned before the posse arrived, supposedly by Johnny Ringo. And the nighttime raid left many locals none too pleased. One Charleston resident wrote a letter to Sheriff Behan that was published in the *Nugget*. It strongly condemned Earp and his men for being heavy-handed and "nearly paralyzing the business of our place." Tellingly, Behan was missing in action when it came to these law enforcement activities in his county.

Wyatt's posse returned to Tombstone without making any arrests. However, they succeeded in unnerving Ike and Fin Clanton. With assurances that they'd be protected from Earp and his men, the Clantons surrendered to a different posse and appeared before Judge William Stilwell in Tombstone on January 30, 1882, when they were quickly released on bail. Three days later, the brothers stood trial. Ike's hat was produced as evidence, and Sherman McMaster testified that he'd had a conversation with Ike in Charleston the night Virgil was ambushed and Ike had said he "would have to go back and do the job over." That would seem to be fairly incriminating evidence—until the defense produced seven witnesses who swore that Ike and Fin were in Charleston at the time of the shooting. Judge Stilwell discharged the prisoners.

THE DAY BEFORE THE CLANTONS' TRIAL, WYATT AND VIRGIL penned a letter of resignation to US Marshal Crawley Dake, citing "much harsh criticism in relation to our operations, and such a persistent effort having been made to misrepresent and misinterpret our acts." In other words, the Earps were fed up. The night before, at a meeting of some of the town's citizens with Marshal Dake, one man commented that it was a problem that his deputies seemed to have "private wrongs to avenge" and that Dake should appoint men who weren't part of either faction. Another said it was hard to tell just how many deputy marshals there were. No one at the meeting had a word of praise for the Earps. No one mentioned their many miles in the saddle pursuing stage robbers and murderers. No one said a thing about the serious wounds received by Virgil and Morgan while attempting to enforce the law, let alone Virgil's maiming in a hideous assassination attempt.

Dake did appoint a deputy US marshal for Cochise County, but at the same time, he did not accept the Earps' resignation. The Earps, as Dake well knew, were the only men willing to go head-to-head with the Cowboys, who were not simply a problem for Cochise County but for the entire territory. The "Cowboys are a great obstacle to the material development of Arizona," explained a British author in *The Graphic*. "Many capitalists in the Eastern states would invest in that region, and thus open it up, were it not for their dread of the Cowboys. They are afraid, naturally, to trust their money and themselves in a country where 'hard cases' are so plentiful." As far as Dake and most other territorial officials were concerned, if the Earps had private wrongs to avenge, so be it. They were after the same hard cases the territory wanted rid of.

But Wyatt was willing to attempt a truce, at least, with the Clantons. He knew that unless he actually caught Ike in the act of committing a crime, the Cowboy would always have an endless supply of alibis to prove he was somewhere else when another bullet took out another Earp—or Doc. According to a report in the *Nugget*, Wyatt sent a message to Ike through a friend, likely McMaster, that he wished to meet and see if they could put this thing to rest. Ike had other plans, however, and "most emphatically declined to hold any communication whatever with Earp."

Ike's other plans were revealed on February 9 when he filed a complaint in Contention with a justice of the peace sympathetic to the Cowboys. That complaint accused Wyatt, Virgil, Morgan, and Doc of murdering Billy Clanton and the McLaurys. It was the same case from three months before all over again. Sheriff Behan didn't bother with Virgil, who remained bedridden, but he took the others into custody. The filing of a writ of habeas corpus by the men's lawyer failed to resolve the matter, and a hearing was set for February 14 in Contention. Wyatt promised Behan that he, Morgan, and Doc would meet him that morning for the journey. But Wyatt couldn't help but suspect something was afoot. "This was all planned for the purpose of having us murdered by the rustlers on the road between Tombstone and Contention," Wyatt would claim later.

On the morning of the fourteenth, Wyatt and Behan got into a heated argument over Wyatt's insistence that he and Doc retain their weapons during the ride to Contention. Wyatt won. A dozen supporters "armed to the teeth" accompanied the Earps and Holliday, and even their lawyer and his sixteen-year-old daughter each had their own Winchester at the ready. Upon arriving safely at the Contention courtroom, the Earp party leaned their rifles against the wall, after which the lawyer announced to the justice, "Your Honor, we have come here for law, but we will fight—if we have to." He then argued that it made little sense to hold the hearing in Contention when Tombstone, the county seat, was but a few miles away. The wide-eyed justice willingly agreed and ordered the case transferred to the county seat.

Ike Clanton gleefully wrote a fellow Cowboy that same day that, "I have got the Earps all in jail and am not going to unhitch. I have got them on the hip and am going to throw them good." But Ike was being his typical blowhard self. Following considerable legal wrangling the next day in Tombstone, the Earps and Holliday were ordered discharged. The entire episode had been a legal farce. Ike was furious, of course, about being abruptly unhitched, and many Tombstone residents feared the worst that night with the Earps and Holliday headquartered in the Cosmopolitan and lots of Cowboys at the Grand Hotel, each separated by just a hundred feet.

"A bad time is expected again in town at any time," George Parsons gloomily wrote in his diary. "Earps on one side of street with their friends and Ike Clanton and Ringo with theirs on the other side—watching each other. Blood will surely come. Hope no innocents will be killed."

———

WYATT HAD A BAD FEELING. IT WAS SATURDAY, MARCH 18, AND he'd seen some men in town he didn't trust, primarily Frank Stilwell and Johnny Ringo. He'd also spotted two "half breeds" whom he'd found highly suspicious. When Wyatt ran into Briggs Goodrich, an attorney for Johnny Ringo, he asked him point-blank if he believed his brothers and Doc were in any danger. The attorney acknowledged that he did, that "they were liable to get it in the neck [at] any time." As far as Ringo was concerned, though, Goodrich had a message. Ringo wanted Wyatt to know that if there was a fight, he wouldn't be a part of it, that "he was going to take care of himself & everybody else could do the same."

A play was scheduled that night at Schieffelin Hall titled "Stolen Kisses," a comedy, and Morgan Earp had a ticket. The appeal for Morgan was a vivacious young actress named Lottie Wade, who was described as having a "remarkably trim and elegant figure and pretty face." Before the performance, Wyatt found Morgan and told him he had good information that an attempt on their lives was imminent. He urged his brother to go to the hotel and go to bed. "He said 'No,'" Wyatt remembered, "that he wanted to see the play and so he went." So did Doc and Daniel Tipton. Attorney Goodrich attended the play as well and he, too, warned Doc and Morgan to be on the lookout.

Once the cast of "Stolen Kisses" took their final bow, Morgan and Tipton walked one block to Allen Street and were met by Wyatt in front of the Campbell & Hatch Billiard Parlors and Saloon about 11 P.M. Wyatt hadn't been able to shake a premonition that something was going to happen, and instead of going to bed, he'd waited up for Morgan. Wyatt now strongly suggested to his brother that they both go to the Cosmopolitan and get some sleep, but Morgan said he wanted to play one game of pool and then he would go with Wyatt. Morgan, Wyatt, and Tipton all went inside and were soon followed by Bob Hatch, the co-owner.

Hatch was quite fond of the younger Earp, and Morgan challenged him to a game.

Morgan and Hatch picked a pool table at the rear of the room, about four or five feet from the back door, which had a glass window in its upper half. This rear door opened onto an empty lot. Wyatt and Tipton found seats and observed the two friends play. But Morgan didn't stop after one game like he'd promised. He and Hatch started a second game. Morgan stood at the end of the table, his back to the rear door, and was watching Hatch line up his pool cue at the corner pocket when two loud gunshots, nearly simultaneous, came from the rear door, two lightning-like flashes visible through the glass.

Morgan instantly collapsed to the floor. Bits of plaster rained down upon Wyatt from a bullet that hit the wall some eight inches above his head and ricocheted into the ceiling. Everyone in the room either ducked to the floor or ran—except Wyatt. He pulled his revolver and fired three or four quick shots at the door and then rushed to his brother's side. Wyatt dragged Morgan away from the back door and stopped near the entrance to a small card room. He asked his brother if he was badly hurt and Morgan said he wasn't, that he believed he would recover. Then Morgan asked Wyatt to straighten his legs, and Wyatt told him his legs were perfectly straight. "Well," Morgan said, "if that is the case, I am gone, my back is broken."

Morgan asked Wyatt to remove his shoes, which he did. The card room contained a chaise lounge, and with the assistance of others, Wyatt attempted to stand Morgan up to take him in, but Morgan, wincing in pain, said, "Don't, boys, don't. I can't stand it." They instead carried him to the lounge and placed him on it. Morgan, growing pale, looked at Hatch and said, "I have played my last game of pool."

Two doctors quickly arrived and confirmed that Morgan's wound was fatal. The bullet not only cut into his spinal column, it also passed through his kidney and liver, and he was hemorrhaging internally. After exiting Morgan's body, the same bullet actually struck a man standing at the front of the saloon, inflicting an ugly wound in his thigh.

Wyatt asked the doctors to give his brother something for the pain, which was increasing. Word of the shooting had been sent to brothers Virgil, Jim, and Warren, and they were on their way, along with wives Allie and Bessie. Wyatt was seen whispering something to his brother. "I then told Morgan that I would get even," Wyatt remembered. "He said that was all he asked but for me to be careful."

Angrier at himself than his brother, Wyatt said, "Morgan, if you had taken my advice this never would have happened!"

"Yes, Wyatt, you are right," Morgan replied, "you are always right."

ELEVEN

ABOVE THE LAW

"I there and then made a vow that I would kill each and every one of those bandits, that they would prove no more alibis on me."

WYATT EARP

Railroad depot, Contention
March 19, 1882

A train waited on the tracks, steam hissing from the engine at its head. A group of men, including Wyatt, slid the casket containing Morgan's body from a wagon and then carried it to one of the train's boxcars. Wyatt was sending his brother's remains to Colton, California, where parents Nicholas and Virginia Ann now lived. Morgan's wife, Louisa, was there, too, having departed Tombstone just the month previous, little knowing she would never see her husband alive again. Jim Earp would also make the rail journey and see to it that his brother's body was delivered safely.

After bidding goodbye to Jim, Wyatt started back on the road to Tombstone. There was much to be done, and the first order of business was getting Virgil and Allie out of Arizona. The Cowboys might very well make another attempt on Virgil's life. Upon arriving in town, then, Wyatt went straight to the Cosmopolitan and sat down next to Virgil's bed.

"Now, Virgil," Wyatt said, "I want you to go home. I am going to get those men who killed Morgan, and I can't look after you and them, too. So you go home."

From long experience, Virgil knew there was no use arguing with Wyatt, but his brother's thinking also made sense, so he agreed that he and Allie would make the trip to Colton. Virgil was still very weak, however, and he would need assistance getting on and off the cars. And he and Allie would also require protection until safely out of range of the Cowboys, at least as far as Benson. The following day, then, Wyatt and his posse—Doc, Warren, Texas Jack, Sherman McMaster, and Jack Johnson—rode alongside a buggy carrying Virgil and Allie to the Contention depot. The men bristled with hardware: rifles, short-barreled shotguns, and revolvers. Virgil, his left arm in a sling, wore a pistol on his side—he only needed one hand to pull a trigger. Allie was elated. "I thanked God I was takin' Virge away livin' and breathin' beside me," she remembered.

Somewhere along the nine miles between Tombstone and Contention, they met a man carrying a message for Wyatt: Frank Stilwell, Ike Clanton, and others were in Tucson watching the trains going through, apparently hoping to surprise Virgil and kill him. Wyatt, just like his enemies, now had his own "death list," and Frank Stilwell was at the top. Moments after Morgan was shot, Stilwell was recognized as one of the three to five men seen running from the alley behind the billiard parlors.

And Stilwell's guilt was confirmed by Pete Spence's wife, Marietta, in shocking testimony given at the coroner's inquest. In addition to her husband, Marietta identified Morgan's murderers as Stilwell, a man called "Indian Charley," another with the last name Freeze or Frees, and an unnamed Indian. Although Marietta didn't name Curly Bill or Johnny Ringo, Wyatt was convinced they were also involved, and he would go with his gut over any testimony. Ultimately, if a man was a known Cowboy, then he was an enemy—and he was liable to get shot.

Wyatt's original plan was to escort his brother and sister-in-law only as far as Benson, but the message about Ike and Stilwell changed everything. Wyatt and his men would see them all the way to Tucson. Arriving at Contention, they helped Virgil and Allie board the train and then stabled the horses. All the posse got on the train except for Texas Jack, who would wait at Contention and look after the horses and buggy until Wyatt's return.

The Earp party's train pulled into Tucson at dusk. Doc got off carrying a shotgun in each hand and deposited the weapons at the railroad office. Wyatt escorted Virgil and Allie to Porter's Hotel for a quick dinner. At Porter's, Wyatt met John W. Evans, a deputy US marshal for Pima County. Evans warned Wyatt to be on his guard, as he'd seen Stilwell and Ike at the depot, although they'd since disappeared. Evans added that he was pretty sure Stilwell was armed, as he'd seen the telltale bulge in his coat. Wyatt walked out in front of the hotel and looked around but didn't spot either man.

Back at the depot platform, the train newsboy excitedly shared with the baggage checker what he'd learned in one of the cars on the way to Tucson. "I guess there will be hell here tonight," he said. When the checker asked what he meant, he answered that the Earps and Holliday were aboard and that they'd told him they were stopping here because "the man who killed Morgan Earp was in Tucson."

When Virgil and Allie exited the hotel, Doc told McMaster to fetch the shotguns from the office. Doc placed one of them under an Ulster coat draped over his shoulder. Wyatt took the other one, and they then walked Virgil and Allie to their sleeper car. Wyatt accompanied Virgil and Allie inside to their berth and said goodbye. He then walked through a few cars toward the front of the train, making doubly sure no Cowboys were on board.

It was getting dark and hard to see, but before stepping out onto the platform, Wyatt observed a train of flat cars on the next track over. He slowly glanced to his right, following the line of cars with his eyes, until he suddenly spotted several armed men lying on one of them, their guns pointed directly at him. Wyatt instantly leaned back inside the train door and started to lift his shotgun to his left shoulder, but being right-handed, it wasn't particularly easy. At the same time, the Cowboys, realizing they'd been discovered, got down from the car and ran toward the front of the train. Wyatt jumped down on the opposite side of the train and also raced toward the front. He saw two of the men, about fifty feet apart, cross the tracks in front of the engine and over to his side.

Wyatt ran up to the closest man and pointed his shotgun at him. He couldn't make out who the man was, and the darkness wasn't helping. Wyatt asked him to identify himself but the man was so terrified he couldn't speak. However, Wyatt could see that the man was wearing a new suit of clothes. "This suit of clothes probably saved his life," Wyatt recalled, "as I failed to recognize him. I had no desire to harm an innocent person, so I told him he had better get away from there, and so he did not tarry."

The second man didn't stop but was walking fast down the tracks. Wyatt ran up to within ten feet of him and yelled "Halt!" The man spun around, leaped toward Wyatt, and grabbed the shotgun near its muzzle. Wyatt was close enough to see he was looking into the eyes of Frank Stilwell. He jerked one of the triggers, sending a load of buckshot into Frank's stomach and making a mess of his internal organs. "As he started to fall," Wyatt remembered, "I fired the other barrel and his career was ended."

Doc and the rest of the posse were close behind and ran up to see Wyatt standing over Stilwell. Despite Wyatt's recollections, Frank was likely still alive and gasping on the ground, as Wyatt's second shot struck Frank's left leg, pulverizing the bone. The posse members fired several more shots into the man's writhing body, one of which, a rifle ball, entered below his armpit and ripped through Stilwell's lungs as it passed through the upper part of his torso. When the body was discovered the next morning, it was found to have "an expression of pain or fear on the face." One man who saw the corpse wrote that Stilwell was "shot all over, the worst shot-up man I ever saw."

The locomotive's bell rang and the train jolted forward. As Virgil and Allie's sleeper car passed, Wyatt jogged alongside the train and held up his hand next to their window.

"It's all right, Virge!" he shouted. "We got one! One for Morg!"

Wyatt could scratch Stilwell off his "list." And it was something of a belated birthday gift. He'd turned thirty-four the day previous.

———————

ON MONDAY, MARCH 20, 1882, GEORGE PARSONS WROTE IN HIS diary of the news of "Frank Stilwell's body being found riddled with bullets and buckshot. A quick vengeance, and a bad character sent to Hell, where he will be the chief attraction until a few more accompany him." Clara Brown, reporting for the *San Diego Union*, was sympathetic toward the Earps, and as for Stilwell, she commented that although the Cowboy was "only twenty-seven years of age, his career was not a beneficial one to this country, and his removal is no loss, however unlawful."

In Tucson, however, Stilwell's murder was another story, at least according to the columns of the *Arizona Daily Star*, which strongly condemned both the killing and the Earp brothers. "If one-twentieth part of what is said of their record is true, they are certainly no desirable acquisition to any community," the paper stated about the Earps. "They are a roving band; their path is strewn with blood." This was the same newspaper, incidentally, that described the Clantons as "fine specimens of the frontier cattle man."

Wyatt and his men rode back into Tombstone late in the afternoon of Tuesday, March 21. After stabling their horses, they walked to the Cosmopolitan, where Wyatt talked over with Mattie the arrangements for her and Jim's wife, Bessie, to depart for Colton to join the rest of the family. Wyatt's bloody revenge campaign had just begun, and he didn't know when he'd be back in Tombstone. The wives would be better off in California for the time being, and three days later, Mattie and Bessie left Tombstone. Wyatt's lover, the former "Mrs. Behan," had returned to Tombstone in February and now went back to using the name Sadie Mansfield, the name she was using when she first met Behan in Prescott. Sadie, who'd also apparently returned to her previous occupation of prostitute, wasn't leaving town anytime soon.

While Wyatt was at the Cosmopolitan, Sheriff Behan received a telegram from Pima County sheriff Bob Paul in Tucson asking him to arrest

Wyatt, Doc, and the others in his posse for the murder of Stilwell. Behan went to the hotel that evening and was in the office when Wyatt and his men passed through.

"Wyatt, I want to see you," Behan said.

"You can't see me," Wyatt replied as he continued toward the front door, "you have seen me once too often."

Wyatt and his men retrieved their horses at the stable and rode out of town unmolested. Behan was humiliated, and it must have brought back the bad memory of Virgil brushing past him to disarm the Clantons and McLaurys. And once again, the sheriff demonstrated his propensity to lie by claiming that the Earp party drew their guns and that he was "forcibly resisted." Bystanders said nothing of the sort occurred. In fact, they said the word *arrest* was never used by Behan. But even if Behan had told Wyatt he was under arrest, the result would have been the same. Nothing was going to stop him from inflicting his wrath on the men who'd killed Morgan and maimed Virgil. Not Sheriff Behan. Not the law.

The next day, at a woodcutting camp in the Dragoon Mountains operated by Pete Spence, a teamster named Theodore Judah observed a group of horseback riders crest a hill and head straight for the camp. In the lead was Wyatt, and following him, riding mostly in pairs, were Doc, Warren, Texas Jack Vermillion, Sherman McMaster, Jack Johnson, Charlie Smith, and Daniel Tipton, eight men total. They rode into the camp but didn't see Judah at first, as he was resting in the shade. Then Judah spoke up, asking the possemen if they'd seen any mules. Wyatt and the others wheeled about and rode in close to Judah, and Wyatt asked where Spence was. Judah replied that Pete was in Tombstone to answer to an assault charge. "You are a friend of Pete Spence, I believe, and Frank Stilwell, too," Wyatt said. Judah answered that he was.

Wyatt next asked Judah about Indian Charley and an individual named Hank Swilling. Swilling, also known as "Apache Hank," was the unnamed American Indian or "half breed" believed to have been another one of Morgan's assassins. Wyatt later understood that Swilling was the man in the new suit he'd let get away the night he killed Stilwell. But Swilling wasn't there, either. As for Indian Charley, who also was known by the name Florentino Sáiz, Judah said he was out looking for some lost mules and pointed to where he'd gone.

Wyatt led the posse out of the camp, and in but a few minutes' time, they surprised Indian Charley, who was searching for the mules on foot. Charley had no trouble making out Wyatt Earp, and he started to run toward a stand of trees. A woodcutter on a hill some two thousand yards away heard a shot and looked around to see the terrified man running and zigzagging, puffs of smoke coming from the muzzles of the posse's rifles and revolvers as a flurry of gunshots reached his ears. Charley fell to the ground, his hat rolling in the dirt.

Wyatt and the others got off their horses and gathered around the dead man to examine their handiwork. Charley had been struck four times, but it was a bullet in his right temple that had finished him. Wyatt told his men to mount up, and they slowly rode away, with Charley, in Wyatt's words, "left stretched in his tracks." When the news of Charley's demise reached Tombstone, George Parsons remarked in his diary, "More killing by the Earp party. Hope they'll keep it up."

———

FOR TWO DAYS, SHERIFF BEHAN MADE A SHOW OF ORGANIZING a posse and riding out of Tombstone and then returning the same day empty-handed. And it didn't go unnoticed by locals that Behan was getting a $10 per diem for the posse's horses, as they were rented from the stable Behan co-owned. More eyebrow-raising, however, was the fact that Behan's posse contained a strong contingent of Cowboys, including Ike and Fin Clanton and Johnny Ringo.

Sheriff Bob Paul, who'd come down from Tucson, refused to ride with Behan's posse, believing that if the Earp party and Behan's posse did meet, no one would be trying to make an arrest, to bring them in peacefully—it would be a bloodbath. Besides, Paul had been assured by people close to Wyatt that his friend would either surrender to him in Tucson in a few days or leave the Territory. "If the truth were known," George Parsons wrote in his diary, "[Paul] would be glad to see the Earp party get away with all of these murderous outfits."

The killings of Stilwell and Indian Charley, and the rumored movements of Wyatt's posse, generated sensational headlines in the nation's press, primarily in the West. Newspapers began using the term "Earp vendetta," and it stuck. Neighboring California was especially interested in what was happening in and around Tombstone, as strong business ties existed between the two, and many Arizona citizens had California connections. Wells Fargo, based out of San Francisco, did a heavy business in the region, and the company not only had been appreciative of the Earps' service as shotgun messengers, but it held a great deal of gratitude for their efforts in going after stage robbers.

On March 23, as everyone wondered when the next sighting of the Earp posse would occur and what bloody violence would come with it, San Francisco's *The Daily Examiner* ran a lengthy interview with Wells Fargo officials, who strongly supported the Earps. They denied reports that Wyatt was a "professional gambler" (he was, of course) and pointed to the endorsements he'd received from Dodge City and Wichita during the Spicer hearing attesting to his sterling reputation as a lawman and citizen. And the *Examiner* dutifully printed the names of several of the prominent signers of those documents. The slanderous accusation that Wyatt and "his brothers were ever concerned in any of the stage robberies is pronounced by the officials of Wells Fargo to be absolutely untrue."

The Wells Fargo officials also offered a double-edged endorsement of Doc Holliday, stating that Doc, "although a man of dissipated habits and a gambler, has never been a thief and was never in any way connected with the attempted stage robbery when Philpott, the stage driver, was killed." The claim that Doc was involved was put forth by the Cowboys, Wells Fargo asserted, to cast aspersions on the Earp brothers and their supporters.

As San Franciscans read about Wyatt and Doc, two posses were in the field looking for them, one headed by Sheriff Behan and the other of doubtful legality composed of Cowboys from around Charleston. The latter included Curly Bill Brocius. "Sheriff Behan has turned all of the cowboys loose against the Earps," George Parsons wrote in his diary, "and with this lawless element is trying to do his worst."

WYATT NEEDED AN INFUSION OF CASH. HE'D DISPATCHED TWO meñ, Charlie Smith and Daniel Tipton, to go into Tombstone and request $1,000 from friend and supporter E. B. Gage, the same man who'd come up with half the bond for Wyatt and Doc during the Spicer hearing. Once they'd secured the funds from Gage, they were to rejoin Wyatt's posse at a remote but well-known spring at the southern end of the Whetstone Mountains. Wyatt planned to rest up there with his men for a few days.

About 3 P.M. on March 24, the Earp posse neared the spring, located in a deep hollow or depression and surrounded by desert willow trees that thrived on the spring water, giving the spot the air of an oasis. The spring was fairly hidden from view for a rider on horseback until almost at the hollow's edge. The day had turned warm but Wyatt, in the lead, wore a coat with a gun belt strapped around it. Because Wyatt had loosened the belt a few times during the ride, his holstered revolver had worked its way around to his back. On the left side of his mount, a saddle scabbard held a Winchester repeater. A shotgun hung in a scabbard on the right, and looped over the saddle horn was a web cartridge belt stuffed with shotgun shells.

Some fifty feet from where the trail dropped down to the spring, Wyatt said, "Hold!"; turning to look back at his men, he cautioned, "There is something wrong here." Doc and the others looked puzzled, but, as Wyatt explained years later, he'd "received a subconscious warning, an invisible influence (call it what you may) that had shielded me and guided me through perilous situations in other months past." Wyatt and his men slowed their horses but continued forward, all their senses on edge. Wyatt pulled his shotgun from the scabbard.

Nine men suddenly rose from the ground several yards away and opened fire, the muzzles of their guns spitting flame. "Curly Bill!" shouted McMaster, who instantly wheeled his horse around and raced off. His panic infected the others, and they spurred their horses after him. Wyatt sprang from his horse to return fire and was stunned when he looked around and saw his men abandoning him. Curly Bill worked his Winchester's lever action as fast as it would let him, firing shot after shot at Wyatt, but this kind of shooting didn't allow for anything like a steady aim, and Curly's shots went wide. Wyatt snapped his shotgun to his shoulder, put the front bead on Curly, and let loose both barrels. The Cowboy let out a ghastly shriek and collapsed, his chest perforated by numerous heavy buckshot.

Curly Bill's men ran for the cover of the nearby willows. Wyatt wished he hadn't jerked both triggers of his shotgun, for he could've easily gotten Pony Diehl, whom he saw scrambling away with the others. However, the shotgun blast had spooked Wyatt's horse, causing the "spirited animal" to jump and rear. Wyatt tried to grab at the belt of shotgun shells but couldn't get it over the saddle horn. Then he tried drawing his Winchester from its scabbard, but his horse spooked each time he reached for it.

All the while, the Cowboys kept up a steady fire from the willows, their bullets slicing through the air around Wyatt, buzzing like bees. He tried to keep his horse between him and the Cowboys as he struggled to reach the revolver at his back. Once he got it, he opened up on the gunmen, which frightened his horse even more. The situation far too hot for Wyatt alone, he started backing his skittish horse away. After going about seventy-five yards, he managed to get his horse to settle down somewhat. At the same time, Wyatt heard a sound to his left and saw Texas Jack struggling to pull a rifle from underneath his dead horse, shot by the Cowboys.

As bullets kicked up dirt around them, Wyatt yelled to Texas Jack to leave the gun and go; the rifle was too far under his horse. Texas Jack asked Wyatt if he was coming, too. When Wyatt answered yes, Texas Jack scampered away in the direction of the rest of the posse. Wyatt now stuck his foot in his saddle's stirrup, but as he attempted to pull himself up, he couldn't lift his leg over the horse—his loose gun belt had slipped down over his hip. Wyatt fell back on his butt. Cussing up a storm, he jumped back up and struggled to pull the belt above his hip. As he did so, a bullet knocked away the horn of his saddle. Finally, with the belt in its proper place, Wyatt mounted his horse, which, incredibly, had not been hit.

"Regardless of the excitement and danger," Wyatt recalled about the fight, "my temper had risen a little and I was pretty well provoked at the horse and belt and all the other interferences at my attempts at action and I determined that I would not run one step, so I walked my horse down the road for at least two hundred yards before I could gain cover."

When he reached his posse, Doc rushed up to him and gently took hold of his arm.

"I'll help you from your horse, Wyatt," Doc said. "You must be shot to pieces."

"No," Wyatt said to the men staring at him in disbelief. "I'm not touched."

Wyatt couldn't say the same for his coat, the skirts of which were riddled with holes, several from a load of buckshot. A bullet had also struck the heel of one of his boots, causing a severe bruise.

Doc and the others, their courage having returned, proposed making a charge against the Cowboys, but Wyatt wasn't interested. The ground all around the spring was level, no cover, and the Cowboys would surely kill one or more of them in such a foolhardy attempt. Besides, he was pretty disgusted with his men for running off and leaving him. He'd killed Curly Bill. That was victory enough for the day. Another one for Morg.

"If you fellows are hungry for a fight," Wyatt said, "you can go on and get your fill." Wyatt turned his horse in the opposite direction and touched its flanks with his spurs. His men followed after him, Texas Jack riding double.

"That was the closest call I ever had," Wyatt would say later, "and how I came out alive is more than I can ever guess."

———

EARP POSSE SIGHTINGS—AND FALSE SIGHTINGS—TOOK UP space in newspapers from Arizona to California. "There are fresh rumors almost every hour of the day," commented the *Nugget*, and at present their precise whereabouts is yet a matter of speculation." The day after the fight with Curly Bill, however, the Earp posse appeared at the Southern

Pacific's Dragoon Summit station, some twenty-two miles north of Tombstone. At 1 p.m., as the eastbound train slowed and came to a stop at the depot, the sight of the heavily armed men standing on the siding caused a stir among the passengers. Once the train stopped, the passengers became even more uneasy as Earp, Doc, and the others boarded the train and walked slowly up and down the cars, clearly looking for someone.

Exactly who they were looking for wasn't known at the time. One story said that Wyatt had been tipped off that "Apache Hank" Swilling would be on the train. Another claimed that Wyatt was expecting to meet brother Virgil and their father, Nicholas, from California. Still another had it that Wyatt was looking for a "friendly messenger" with money, which he desperately needed. This last was correct, but Wyatt was either too early or the messenger was late. Daniel Tipton, carrying the $1,000 from E. B. Gage, was on the eastbound train the next morning.

Soon the locomotive's engineer let out a blast of the steam whistle, and, without saying a word, Wyatt and his men stepped off the train, saddled up, and rode north. The next afternoon, March 27, they tied up at the headquarters of the Sierra Bonita Ranch in the Sulphur Valley, about twenty miles northwest of Willcox. The sprawling ranch of approximately four hundred square miles was owned by fifty-three-year-old Henry C. Hooker, widely known as the cattle king of Arizona. Scattered over different parts of his ranch were four thousand head of blooded cattle, worth three to three and three-quarter cents per pound on the hoof, and 350 horses. Of course, the king's domain was a favorite target of rustlers, and thus Hooker was a strong backer of Wyatt Earp, who fondly remembered the cattle baron as "a fine man."

Following a warm greeting between the two, Wyatt told Hooker that he'd no longer have to worry about Curly Bill, news that pleased Hooker to no end. "You are doing good work and keep right on," he said to Wyatt, "and when you get through, I have money to pardon you out." Indeed, the cattle baron had a good deal of influence in the Territory, and he wasn't the only one with influence who was rooting for Earp's posse. Wells Fargo was firmly in Wyatt's corner as well.

Wyatt said he needed a horse to replace Texas Jack's, and Hooker ordered his men to drive several into a large corral. After selecting a handsome animal, Wyatt asked the price, but Hooker wouldn't take any money, saying it was a gift. Next Hooker counted out $1,000 and offered the stack of greenbacks to Wyatt. When Wyatt looked puzzled, Hooker explained that the Stockraisers' Protective Association had a standing reward of $1,000 for Curly Bill. Wyatt thanked Hooker, but he couldn't accept it. He hadn't killed one of his brother's murderers for a reward.

After getting a good meal and restocking supplies, the Earp posse left the Sierra Bonita headquarters that evening at 7 P.M. Before they left, however, Daniel Tipton finally caught up to them with the money from Gage. Tipton had ridden the morning train to Willcox, where he'd acquired a horse and hurried north to the Sierra Bonita. The Earp posse now rode north for a few miles and made camp for the night.

Henry Hooker received more visitors early the following day, but they weren't nearly as welcome as Wyatt and his men. The visitors were Sheriff Behan and his posse of fourteen men. And Behan got straight to business, asking Hooker if he knew the whereabouts of Wyatt, Doc, and the others. Hooker replied that he didn't, but if he did, Behan would be the last man he'd tell.

"You must be upholding murderers and outlaws, then," Behan said with a sneer.

"No, sir, I am not," Hooker snapped. "I know the Earps and know you, and I know they have always treated me like gentlemen. Damn such laws, and damn you, and damn your posse." Hooker then looked at Behan's men and saw Johnny Ringo and Fin Clanton and added, "They are a set of horse thieves and outlaws."

"Damn the son of a bitch!" interjected one of Behan's men. "He knows where they are, and let us make him tell."

Hooker's foreman, Billy Whelan, suddenly appeared with a Winchester rifle and pointed the gun straight at the threatening Cowboy.

"You can't come here into a gentleman's yard and call him a son of a bitch!" Whelan shouted. "Now you skin it back! Skin it back! If you are looking for a fight and come here to talk that way, you can get it before you find the Earps. You can get it right here!"

A disgusted Hooker shook his head, looked Behan in the eye, and said, "These are a pretty set of fellows you have got with you, a set of horse thieves and cutthroats. Sheriff, every man you have looking for the Earps has stolen cattle and horses from me."

Behan and his undersheriff, Harry Woods, attempted to differentiate themselves from the thugs in the posse, but it only made them look like fools. "They are not our associates," they said. "They are only here on this occasion with us."

"Well, they are not your associates," Hooker said, "I will set an extra table for you and set them by themselves."

Following breakfast, Behan hunted up Billy Whelan in the stable. The sheriff pulled a diamond stud from his pocket and handed it to the foreman. "Take this," Behan said. "It cost a hundred dollars, but don't say anything about what occurred here."

Failing to discover the Earp party's trail, and with Hooker being uncooperative in that regard, Behan decided he would need some real trackers if he was to find Wyatt and his men. He knew that Fort Grant, twenty-five miles away, was home to a unit of Apache scouts, justly famed as among the world's best trackers. So Behan and Woods left the rest of the posse to continue the search around Hooker's place while they rode to the fort. Once at the military post, they met with Major James Biddle, offering $500 for the use of a few of his Native trackers. But unfortunately for Behan, he let slip a little too much information about his visit with the cattle king.

"Hooker said he didn't know and would not tell you if he did? Hooker said that, did he? Well, if he did, you can't get any scouts here."

———————

BEHAN AND WOODS RETURNED TO THE SIERRA BONITA HEAD-quarters following their dismal failure at Fort Grant. Their men hadn't discovered any sign of the Earp party, so Behan led the posse north to the Eureka Springs station, twelve miles away, where they spent the night. They didn't know it, but they actually weren't far at all from the Earp party. Wyatt and his men chuckled among themselves as they passed around a pair of binoculars and watched Behan's posse ride by in the distance.

Earp and his men went back to Hooker's place. Both Wyatt and the cattleman knew Behan would eventually show up there again, and Hooker suggested that Wyatt fight it out with Behan's posse from his adobe ranch house. The house, a U-shaped structure surrounding a plaza, resembled a small fortress, its thick walls made up of two rows of adobe bricks. Hooker said that when the Behan posse rode up, Wyatt and his men could easily make quick work of them.

Wyatt wasn't about to do that, however. Hooker had a wife and three children living with him, and Wyatt didn't want to put them in any danger. Instead, Wyatt pointed to a prominence about a mile to the west and told Hooker he and his men would camp there as long as the sheriff's posse was roaming about. And Wyatt had a message for Behan. He told Hooker to let the sheriff know of his camping place and that they'd be waiting for him.

Behan reappeared at the headquarters the next day, March 29. Hooker pointed to where the sheriff could find the Earp party.

"They told me to tell you to come out and get them," Hooker said.

Behan asked how Wyatt and his men were armed, and Hooker listed off the weapons: Each man had a Winchester, two revolvers, and three men carried double-barreled shotguns with twenty-one balls to the barrel. Then Hooker handed Behan his field glasses.

"By the way," he said, "you can see some of them up there now."

Behan made the wise decision to return to Tombstone, where he reportedly submitted a bill for expenses to the Cochise County Board of Supervisors in the amount of $8,000. George Parsons predicted such an outcome nearly a week earlier when he wrote in his diary, "Mileage still counting for our rascally sheriff. He organizes posses, goes to within a mile of his prey and then returns. He's a good one."

Wyatt, Doc, and the others remained at Hooker's headquarters for a few days, resting men and horses and discussing their next move. During this time, a former stage driver named Lewis Cooley arrived to deliver $1,000 from Wells Fargo. This and the money from E. B. Gage would help a great deal. Wyatt had originally let Sheriff Bob Paul know that he and his men would either surrender to him in Tucson or leave the Territory. He likely never intended to surrender, however, but saying he would turn himself in or vacate the Territory allowed Paul an excuse not to get involved in Behan's controversial manhunt.

No—Wyatt, Doc, and the rest of the posse would leave the Territory for a short spell and allow their powerful friends to hopefully straighten out the serious matter of the arrest warrants for the Stilwell killing. They were deputy US marshals, after all. But Wyatt's plan was definitely to return to Arizona. The brothers, too. As Jim Earp told a *Los Angeles Daily Times* reporter, they had "too much property in Tombstone to leave it." And Wyatt still had a strong desire to run for Cochise County sheriff in November. He was convinced Behan didn't stand a chance of being re-elected.

Before leaving Arizona, however, Wyatt would make one last attempt to wrap up unfinished business. Rumor had it that Johnny Ringo was in Charleston, and that's where Wyatt took his men first. When they arrived on the San Pedro, however, he was told that Ringo had departed for the San Simon Valley. The Earp posse then headed for Tombstone, setting up a discreet camp not far from the town. Wyatt hoped to locate (and kill) Pete Spence and "Apache Hank" Swilling. He soon learned, however, that Swilling was in the county jail serving a twenty-day sentence following a saloon fight in Charleston. As for Spence, he'd been placed on trial for the murder of Morgan but was discharged for want of evidence on April 4. After that, Pete wisely made himself scarce, eventually riding south to Sonora.

There remained one other individual in Tombstone Wyatt was interested in seeing, however, and that was twenty-one-year-old Sadie Mansfield. He wasn't about to leave town without visiting his lover. When or how many times they rendezvoused isn't known, but there's a clue. In its issue of April 11, the *Epitaph* stated that it was "reported on the streets this afternoon, for a fact, that members of the Earp party were in town last night spending several hours here. It is hardly probable that such was the case. However, improbable things are always coming to pass."

THE IMPROBABLE APPEARED ON THE STREETS OF SILVER CITY, New Mexico, 130 miles northeast of Tombstone, at about 10 P.M. on April 15, 1882. Eight men "well mounted and armed to the teeth" rode up to the Elephant Corral stables and put up their horses. The men were Wyatt, Doc, Warren, Sherman McMaster, Texas Jack Vermillion, Jack Johnson, Daniel Tipton, and Charlie Smith. They were hesitant to give their real names—when asked, one of the posse said his name was John Smith and another gave his as Bill Snooks—which made the stables' owner suspicious.

Why the posse would land in Silver City, a mining town nearly forty miles north of a rail line that could whisk them away to safety, isn't clear, but the answer may be that virtually no one in Silver City knew who they were. The men needed to sell their horses and saddles before jumping on a train, and if they'd done that at any point along the line in Arizona, they would have been recognized and their presence and the particular train they boarded immediately wired to the authorities and the press. Also, some member of the group apparently had a friend in Silver City, for they reportedly spent the night at a private residence. The Silver City newspaper, which didn't carry the news of the Earp party's presence until a week later, stated that "as they had not registered at any hotel, it was not known they were in town until after their departure."

The next morning, a Sunday, Wyatt attempted to negotiate the sale of their horses to the Elephant Corral's owner, but he was too leery of these intimidating strangers, especially once they offered the horses at a price far below their real worth. And it didn't help that the men seemed anxious to leave town. Wyatt finally sold six of the horses to a man who was planning to open a livery stable but found no takers for the saddles and remaining two horses. They left them with a ranchman.

When the stagecoach for Deming, New Mexico, pulled out of Silver City, the Earp posse was on it—all except Charlie Smith, who would go back to Tombstone. At Deming, forty-five miles to the southeast, they boarded a Santa Fe train, their destination Albuquerque. Seated in a well-appointed smoking car, the clacking sound of the tracks beneath them, must have seemed strange to these weatherworn men who'd spent the last twenty-six days in the saddle, riding across miles of desert and mountains, and sleeping under the stars. And incredibly, one of the men who participated in this strength-sapping manhunt suffered from a debilitating disease. Doc Holliday may have appeared thin and sickly, but no man could ever question his toughness. Nor his loyalty. He'd backed his friend Wyatt's hand all the way.

On this same day, April 16, the people of Council Bluffs, Iowa, opened their daily paper to find a long column headlined "An Arizona Vendetta." It offered a blood and thunder review of the Earp and Clanton feud, the street fight ("the short-triggered revolvers cracked like a blazing pack of fire-crackers"), and Wyatt's revenge tour. The story concluded with a prediction: "Tomorrow, or the next day, or the next, the wires will bring news of another murder. The Clantons will have been killed, or another of the Earps sent to his last reckoning, and the vendetta will continue until one side or the other is removed from the face of the earth." In reality, however, the Earp vendetta ride was over. Only in legend would it continue to thrive.

A bigger story at the time than the Earp vendetta was the April 3 assassination of the outlaw Jesse James in St. Joseph, Missouri, which captured the imaginations of people around the world. The *Albuquerque Morning Journal* of April 16 noted that it had received a photograph of the dead desperado, "taken after his murder by the officers of the law." The assassins, Bob and Charley Ford, weren't actually law officers but gang members, although they were colluding with Missouri's governor to bring about their leader's demise. Nevertheless, the *Journal* offered the opinion that, "There is no law in heaven or on earth that will justify an officer of the law in murdering a man, no matter what may be the magnitude of his crimes."

It was a sentiment shared by many. For now, though, Wyatt Earp only had to worry about the law on Earth.

TWELVE

YES, WE ARE FRIENDS

I'll camp upon creation's edge
A wanderer to the last.

AMELIA JOSEPHINE BURR

Office of the Albuquerque Evening Review
Morning, April 17, 1882

T he reporter at the front desk in the *Review* office was stunned.
Standing before him was Wyatt Earp, all six feet of him. He could
hardly believe he was looking at the famed Dodge City and Arizona lawman and, more recently, headline-grabbing vendetta rider. And Wyatt
was there with a request. He asked that the presence of himself and his
men in Albuquerque not be reported in the paper for the time being. They
had come to Albuquerque, he said, to escape persecution while waiting
for Arizona's governor, Frederick Tritle, to hopefully obtain their pardons
from the president. If the whereabouts of he and his men were known,
Wyatt believed it might "bring a party of Cowboy avengers down upon
them." To back his claim about the possible pardons, Wyatt produced
"several convincing documents."

The *Review* agreed to honor Wyatt's request. He next visited the office of the city's other newspaper, the *Albuquerque Morning Journal*, and
they also promised to hold the story. Wyatt and his men remained in

Albuquerque for approximately two weeks. During that time, Wyatt sought the help of Wells Fargo, the Santa Fe railroad, and even New Mexico's territorial governor. What he asked of them is unknown, but it may have been nothing more than protection from any Arizona authorities intent on serving those warrants. It was also in Albuquerque that the strength of Wyatt and Doc's friendship would be tested, the only such instance that's recorded.

According to a story in the *Review*, published a short time after the Earp party left Albuquerque, Wyatt and Doc quarreled, which prompted the two to later go their separate ways. The paper didn't state what the quarrel was about, but the fact that it was mentioned would suggest it was a significant occurrence. The *Daily Nugget* offered its take, stating that "Doc Holliday became intoxicated and indiscreet in his remarks, which offended Wyatt and caused the party to break up." However, the *Nugget*, which didn't provide a source for its information, was more than four hundred miles away. And Wyatt was well used to Doc's drunken spells and occasional outlandish talk.

Another version of the quarrel is found in a letter written some fifty-eight years after the fact by an individual who acquired the story second-hand. According to this letter, Wyatt and Doc were eating at an establishment run by a man known as Fat Charlie when "Holliday said something about Earp being a Jew boy. Something like Wyatt are you becoming a damn Jew boy? Earp became angry and left. Charlie said that Holliday knew he had said it wrong, he never saw them together again."

While in Albuquerque, Wyatt lodged with prominent Jewish merchant Henry Jaffa, and if this story is indeed true, Doc may have been referring to Wyatt's friendship with this businessman. Jaffa is supposed to have given Wyatt a coat from his store to replace the one the Cowboys shot up in the fight with Curly Bill. However, another intriguing possibility is that Doc was referring to Wyatt's lover, Sadie Mansfield. Sadie was Jewish. Probably few people knew this, but Wyatt certainly did, and he may have told Doc.

Whatever it was that caused the falling-out between Wyatt and Doc, it's important to remember that these two friends had spent more time

Atchison, Topeka & Santa Fe depot, Albuquerque, from a carte de visite circa 1881.
(ORIGINAL CARTE DE VISITE IN AUTHOR'S COLLECTION)

together in the last month than in all of the last five years. Even the best of friends can get on each other's nerves after a certain amount of time in close contact. And this particular time was stressful, as Wyatt wasn't yet sure where they would go or what the future held. However, one quarrel generally doesn't end a deep friendship, and Doc brushed this spat aside when asked about it a few weeks later. "We had a little misunderstanding," Doc told a reporter, "but it didn't amount to much."

When the *Review* did publish its story about the Earp posse's sojourn in the city, it claimed that at least fifty people knew their identities while they were in town. One of those was a Frank McLain, whom Wyatt described as a friend. He must have been a pretty good friend, as he met the Earp posse at the train station when they pulled in, and Wyatt borrowed $2,000 from him before departing Albuquerque.

The *Review* seemed to be impressed with Wyatt, Doc, and the rest of the posse, writing that during their stay, they "deported themselves very sensibly, performing no acts of rowdyism, and [in] this way gained not a few friends for their side of the fight."

About May 1, 1882, the posse members boarded a Santa Fe train and rode it as far as Trinidad, Colorado. Here they were the guests of their friend Bat Masterson, who'd recently been appointed the city marshal. A Trinidad newspaper reported that a "few easily frightened people fear trouble from the number of 'hard men' in town, but they needn't be afraid of the Earp boys, who are among the best in the West."

At Trinidad, Wyatt took the money he received from Gage, $1,000, and the $2,000 he borrowed from McLain and divided it among the posse members. They'd certainly earned it. Wyatt, Warren, Texas Jack, and Daniel Tipton then left Trinidad for Gunnison, a budding mining town on Colorado's western slope. Doc promised to follow in time, but he was enjoying getting reacquainted with Trinidad's gambling establishments.

After a week or so, Doc moved on to what he hoped were greener pastures in South Pueblo, a rowdy burg of twenty-five hundred people eighty-five miles to the north and just across the Arkansas River from Pueblo proper.

Not only was the place generously supplied with gambling dens and brothels, but a former Tombstone resident had just opened a club room there. Considering himself far from the reach of the Cowboys, Doc didn't try to hide his identity. One night at a variety theater, a man named Perry Mallon introduced himself to Doc and said he wanted to do Doc a favor. Mallon, a medium-size man in his late twenties with a short, reddish mustache and thin beard, and "small, ferrety eyes," told Doc that he'd just arrived on the train with the brother of Frank Stilwell. The brother threatened to shoot Doc on sight.

Doc detected something a little off with Mallon. After another encounter with the man in a saloon, Doc learned that Mallon was claiming to be a ranchman and was borrowing money and not repaying it. It was when Mallon pulled down his clothes and proudly pointed to a scar from

Rare image of Union Avenue, South Pueblo, at the time Doc met the "crank" Perry Mallon. The large cottonwood in the street was known as the "Big Tree," and was cut down by order of the city council in 1883.
(ORIGINAL CABINET CARD IN THE AUTHOR'S COLLECTION)

a bullet that appeared to be anything but a bullet wound, however, that Doc became convinced Mallon was an outright "crank." Doc soon put the man out of his mind, though, as he left for Denver on May 14 to attend the Denver Jockey Club spring meets and bet on the horses.

In downtown Denver the following evening, about 8:30 P.M., Doc was walking toward his hotel when he was suddenly staring at the muzzles of two revolvers pointing at him. "Throw up your hands!" said a shadowy figure. "Doc Holliday, I have you now!" The man holding the revolvers kept the guns on Doc as two deputy sheriffs came up and the three escorted their prisoner to the sheriff's office. In the light of the office, Doc recognized the man with the revolvers as crazy Perry Mallon.

Unfortunately, Doc was the only one who knew Mallon was a nut, at least in the beginning.

The following day, Denver newspapers carried the story of Holliday's capture by Mallon, who claimed to be a Los Angeles sheriff who'd been trailing Holliday for years after Holliday murdered his partner. The story was a fantasy, of course, but the fact remained that very real warrants did exist for Holliday, as well as for the Earps, and quickly the telegraph wires between Arizona and Denver were humming. In fact, Mallon sent a telegram to Sheriff Behan the night of the arrest requesting a $500 reward, money Behan apparently offered out of his own pocket.

Behan telegraphed Governor Tritle the next day and asked for a requisition on Colorado's governor, Frederick Pitkin, for Holliday and the Earps—initial reports stated that the Earp brothers had also been arrested in Denver. The Cochise County sheriff began making preparations to leave for Denver immediately. He desperately wanted to be the man to bring the Earps and Holliday back to Arizona to face justice—yet again. The previous March, Behan had told Henry C. Hooker, the cattle king, "If I can catch the Earp party, it will help me in the next election." And for Behan, keeping the sheriff's job was much more than pride or a dedication to serving the people. It was about money. For his one term in office, he earned an incredible $40,000. Of course, that thing of Wyatt moving in on Sadie Mansfield drove Behan as well.

But, in a shock to Behan, Governor Tritle, then in Tucson, appointed Sheriff Bob Paul as the special agent to bring Holliday back to Arizona. Because of Paul's known friendship with the Earps, Tritle's decision received much criticism, but Behan only had himself to blame. The Territory had nothing in its treasury earmarked for extraditing suspects, so the funds would likely come from Pima County (Stilwell was killed in the Pima County seat of Tucson). The chairman of the Pima County Board of Supervisors had already gotten a taste of how Behan operated, as the Cochise County sheriff had submitted a bill to Pima County for $2,000 for chasing the Earp posse. No, if Pima County was footing the bill, they wanted their own man, Paul.

Sheriff Paul started for Denver while the requisition was sent from

Tucson to Prescott for the territorial seal, after which it would be mailed to the Colorado governor. The requisition, dated May 16, was for the return of Doc Holliday, Wyatt Earp, Warren Earp, Sherman McMaster, and John (Jack) Johnson. Meanwhile, many friends of Doc and Wyatt came to Doc's support. Bat Masterson, who'd joined Doc on the trip to the races, told a reporter for the *Denver Tribune* that Doc was a deputy US marshal and that the Cowboys wanted to assassinate him like they did Morgan Earp. Bat even worried that Doc would be taken from the jail and murdered. Within hours of Doc's arrest, Bat and an attorney sought a writ of habeas corpus, which was just the beginning of the legal wrangling.

On the afternoon of May 17, South Pueblo's city marshal appeared at the Denver jail with a warrant for Doc's arrest, charging him with robbing a mark of $150 in a confidence game. By law, local charges took precedence over charges beyond state lines. It was a smart move, orchestrated by Bat, to keep Doc from being sent to Arizona right away, but it didn't get him out of the Denver jail. And Sheriff Paul, whose train pulled into Denver on May 19, made it clear he would fulfill his duty, friends or not.

Even before the Arizona requisition arrived on Pitkin's desk, Doc's allies pressured the Colorado governor to return it. Yet the governor had few options if he was to strictly abide by the law. Fortunately for Pitkin, the Arizona officials gave him an easy out. To be valid, the requisition needed the Arizona governor's certification, contained in a separate document. Once Pitkin had the requisition in hand, it was found to lack this all-important certification. Based on that fact, and the Pueblo arrest warrant, Pitkin declined to honor Tritle's request.

The Arizona press was outraged, and the requisition fiasco filled newspaper columns for weeks. The *Arizona Daily Star* mockingly described the territorial library as containing "the revised statues, an old spelling book, a primer, and a tome of enormous volume known to the world as 'Tritle on Defective Requisitions.'" Tritle wasn't alone; Pitkin also got hammered in the papers.

Finally released from the Denver jail, Doc was escorted to South Pueblo to answer to the larceny charge. The proceeding went smoothly as planned: Doc posted bond in the amount of $300 and his case was scheduled for the district court's July term. Sheriff Paul returned to Arizona with no prisoner, while Perry Mallon was exposed as a "petty swindler." But Doc and the Earps were not out of danger; far from it. On June 9, Arizona sent a second requisition to Colorado, and according to Wyatt, this one was "flawless." And even though the posse members named in the requisition weren't then in custody, Pitkin had the authority to issue a warrant for their arrest, allowing Colorado law officers to go after the fugitives.

Bat Masterson wrote Wyatt in Gunnison and told him they would need to use their "last resort" on Pitkin, the one card that remained up their sleeve. That last resort was Irish-born George W. Crummey. Crummey had run a gambling house in St. Paul, Minnesota, for years, and he'd received temporary fame in 1880 when he won $12,000 playing faro in Chicago, starting with only $100. He was an investor in Colorado's San Juan mining district, and one of his partners was Pitkin. Crummey was also a friend of Wyatt's.

Wyatt contacted Crummey regarding their predicament with the Arizona requisition, and Crummey immediately boarded a train for Denver. When he arrived at the governor's office, he found Pitkin going over the requisition, trying to find some irregularity, but it was hopeless. Territorial officials had made certain this time that they'd crossed every "t" and dotted every "i."

"Governor, can you drive a four-in-hand?" Crummey asked, referring to a carriage pulled by four horses and driven by one person.

Pitkin answered that he could.

"Well, then," Crummey said as he pointed to the papers, "drive a four-in-hand through that."

Pitkin returned the requisition to Arizona, but not because he'd found anything wrong with it. The reason he offered for refusing this time was that he didn't believe it possible for Arizona's special agent "to deliver the parties named in safety at Tucson." Unlike the first requisition, which the press devoted considerable ink to, no one seemed to know that Arizona sent a second one. It seems not a word about it appeared in newspapers in either Arizona or Colorado. And that was perfectly fine with both governors; they very much wanted the story to go away.

———————

AN UNNAMED REPORTER FOR THE GUNNISON *DAILY NEWS-Democrat* lucked into a pretty good scoop when a businessman pointed out a tall, well-dressed, pleasant-looking man and told him it was Wyatt Earp. Earp was leaning against a counter and tapping his boot with a cane. Sitting nearby was brother Warren. The reporter figured he had nothing to lose and boldly approached each brother separately and actually got both of them to talk for his paper. Surprisingly, the usually quiet older Earp had a lot to say.

Wyatt talked freely about the troubles with the Cowboys, the street fight, Stilwell, and the killing of Curly Bill. Six of the Cowboy gang, Wyatt said, had "gone under." "I promised my brother to get even," Wyatt continued, "and I've kept my word so far. When they shot him he said the only thing he regretted was that he wouldn't have a chance to get even. I told him I'd attend to it for him."

The reporter asked Wyatt what he intended to do now.

"I shall stay here for awhile. My lawyers will have a petition for a pardon drawn up. Everybody in Tombstone knows we did nothing but our duty. Anyway, I'd do it over again under like circumstances, and all the best people there will sign the petition. Governor Pitkin knows the facts pretty well and will sign it, too. We look for a pardon in a few weeks, and when it comes I'll go back; but if no pardon is made, I'll go back anyway and stand trial. I'd go now but I know we would have no show. They'd shoot us in the back, as they did my brother."

Wyatt told the reporter that he was going to run for Cochise County sheriff in the fall. "Behan knows he can't get it again," Wyatt said, "and that's what makes him so hot towards me."

It was quite a piece for the *Daily News-Democrat*, and two weeks later, the reporter got an even better one when yet another businessman directed the reporter's attention across the street, saying, "Do you see that man yonder? That's Doc Holliday, of Arizona." The man he motioned toward was dressed in a black, close-fitting suit and wore the latest style of bowler hat. He had gray hair, a heavy sandy mustache, and piercing dark blue eyes—and he was infamous. Holliday's Denver arrest had generated sensational stories across the country. The *Cincinnati Enquirer* topped them all, describing Doc as a devil incarnate who'd killed no less than fifty men. Yes, this was a much bigger scoop than Wyatt Earp.

A passing sporting gent introduced the reporter to Holliday, and the two shook hands. The reporter, apparently a clairvoyant as well, noted Doc's strong, friendly grip and wrote that it conveyed to him "here is a man who once a friend, is always a friend; once an enemy, is always an enemy."

Doc was initially hesitant to talk to the newspaperman, saying he wasn't traveling about the country seeking notoriety. But the reporter persisted, and, much like Wyatt, Doc soon opened up, providing a brief overview of his life and travels.

"You are acquainted with the Earps, I believe?" said the reporter.

"Yes, we are friends."

"You had some trouble in Arizona with the Cowboys, didn't you?"

"Well, yes," Doc drawled. "You might call it trouble. . . . One day six of the Cowboys came into town and proposed to run it. The Earps were informed of their doings, and they invited me to go over where the Cowboys were. One of the Earps said, 'Throw up your hands, we have come to disarm you.' Instead of putting up their paws, they put up their revolvers and began firing. Three of them were killed on the spot and two of the Earps wounded. I received a slight wound on the hip, which caused me some inconvenience for a few days."

The reporter mentioned the possibility of Perry Mallon having to answer for his shenanigans to a Denver judge and if Doc would do anything at his trial.

"No, that is not my way of doing. I avoid trouble. My father taught me when young to attend to my own business and let other people do the same."

Surely the dead from the street fight and Wyatt's vendetta wished Doc had more closely adhered to his father's teachings. In any event, the reporter's published interview with Holliday, appearing on June 18, carried the headline, "Man of Sand, 'Doc' Holliday of Arizona Caught on the Wing by a Reporter, and Pumped."

WITH ITS SALOONS BY THE DOZEN, SIX DANCE HALLS, THREE breweries, and a population of five thousand, Gunnison was a honey hole for professional gamblers such as Wyatt and Doc. Wyatt ran a popular faro game in back of the Biebel saloon. One of the town's police officers that summer, Judd Riley, clearly remembered the Earps and Holliday. They were well heeled, he said, and went everywhere armed. Wyatt "always wore two guns high up under his arms, but he never used them here." Like lots of other people who had memories of Wyatt, Riley recalled him as "quiet in manner and never created a bit of trouble here." The former Tombstone lawman told the officers on the Gunnison police force that they could call on him anytime if they needed help. "Doc Holliday was the only one of the gang that seemed to drink much," Riley added, "and the minute he got hilarious [out of control], the others promptly took him in charge and he just disappeared."

The Earps and Doc didn't remain in Gunnison for long. Doc made his way to the Colorado silver mining town of Leadville, touted as "the liveliest, biggest, richest mining camp in the world." Sometime in July 1882, Wyatt and Warren started for San Francisco, where Virgil had opened a gambling hall.

Also that July, the body of a man was found seated on the ground with his back against a tree in the Chiricahua Mountains, forty miles northeast of Tombstone. The man was Johnny Ringo. A gaping hole entered his right temple, and blood and brains were matted in his hair on the top of his head where the bullet had exited. Johnny's right hand gripped a revolver with an empty shell casing in one chamber. It appeared an obvious suicide, especially as the *Epitaph* reported Johnny "was subject to frequent fits of melancholy and had an abnormal fear of being killed."

But there were some odd things about Johnny's body. Part of his scalp appeared to have been cut off with a knife, and his cartridge belt was upside down. Even stranger, Johnny wasn't wearing boots. Instead, wrapped around his stocking feet were pieces of cloth torn from his undershirt. Virgil Earp gave his opinion on Johnny's demise to a newspaper that August. He said it was common in Arizona for stage robbers and outlaws to make it appear that they were wearing moccasins so that their crimes would be blamed on the Apaches. Virgil thought that Johnny was "trying the Indian dodge when someone killed him."

Virgil was far from the only one who didn't buy the suicide theory, believing someone besides Johnny himself had ended the rustler's life. In 1890, the *Tombstone Prospector* claimed that, "There is more than one man living in Cochise County who knows who did it, but with them the mystery is a secret."

Decades later, one man did confess to killing Johnny Ringo, and in considerable detail: Wyatt Earp. Wyatt did indeed want Johnny dead, but his known movements that July argue against his being able to pull off the killing. If Wyatt didn't kill Ringo, that leaves another mystery: Why did he claim he did? "It is highly improbable that Wyatt deliberately lied," observed southwestern writer Eugene Manlove Rhodes regarding certain problems with Wyatt's recollections, "lying is the coward's vice—and Wyatt was a brave man. But he might easily get mixed."

———

THE SAN FRANCISCO POLICE RAIDED ALL THE FARO GAMES IN the city on August 1, 1882, and one of the worst hit was Virgil's, who ran games on Geary Street and another on Morton. The police confiscated his faro layouts, $1,422 in cash, and ran in fifteen players. News of the raid caused one California newspaper to comment that it didn't help the Earps' claim that their fights in Arizona were a result of efforts to preserve law and order. "They are evidently a hard party," stated the paper, "and no benefit to any community."

Gambling wasn't the only appeal San Francisco held for Wyatt. It was also where Sadie Mansfield now lived. San Francisco was Sadie's former home, and she'd gone back there from Tombstone sometime late in the summer of 1882. Whether Wyatt and Sadie stayed in touch after he fled to Colorado isn't known, but they did find each other in San Francisco and renewed their intimate relationship. As for poor Mattie Earp, who'd been staying with Wyatt's parents in Colton, Wyatt made no attempt to see her.

Mattie returned to Arizona sometime that August, out of Wyatt's life forever. Unfortunately, Mattie couldn't get Wyatt out of hers so easily. She soon returned to prostitution and battled depression and alcoholism for the rest of her years, which were few. In 1888, Mattie committed suicide through an overdose of laudanum. Sometime before her death, she said that Wyatt had "wrecked her life by deserting her and she didn't want to live." Mattie's few possessions were shipped to her family in Iowa. Among the items found inside her trunk was the New Testament given to Wyatt by the Dodge City law firm, the one with the inscription attesting to his "many Christian virtues." When Wyatt sent Mattie off to Colton prior to the vendetta ride, he apparently figured that where he was going, he didn't need a bible.

DESPITE ALL THE TALK OF PARDONS, THEY WOULD NEVER COME; receiving a pardon for murdering suspects hardly stood a chance to begin with. Wyatt didn't run for Cochise County sheriff in the November 1882 election, nor would he ever return to Tombstone. He was right about Behan, though. The sheriff's prospects in the election were so bad that Behan didn't even bother to run.

Wyatt was back in Colorado by the spring of 1883, and Sadie was with him. Like Wyatt's previous women, she took the last name Earp, although they never legally married. They landed in Silverton, where Wyatt ran the club rooms in the Arlington Saloon and Gambling Hall. Trouble in Dodge City, however, soon interrupted Wyatt's focus on pasteboard and ivory. In April, following a heated city election, Dodge's new city council passed two ordinances aimed at eliminating prostitution. The problem arose when the ordinances weren't enforced equally. Luke Short, who'd migrated from Tombstone to Dodge, co-owned the Long Branch saloon and gambling hall, and three of his "singers" were promptly arrested. Yet the "singers" in the saloon of his competitor next door were ignored by the police. The neighboring saloon hadn't been doing nearly as well as the Long Branch, and its owner just happened to be a good friend and backer of the new mayor in the election.

An enraged Luke Short wasn't going to stand for it, but the mayor decided Dodge could do without Short, and the saloon owner soon found himself arrested and illegally forced on a train out of town. Even more, he was told not to come back. The aggrieved Short fired off a lengthy complaint to the Kansas governor, but a rumor also took hold that Short was calling in the big guns—literally. Bat Masterson, Wyatt Earp, and others of Short's sporting friends and gunhands were supposedly on their way to Dodge to assist Short in his planned return.

On May 13, Wyatt sent a letter to the *Denver Republican* strongly denying this rumor. He claimed he wasn't aware that such a plan was afoot, nor did he have any intention of participating if there was a plan. "It has and always shall be my wish to promote law and order," he wrote, "and it has only been in the performance of my duty as an officer of the law that trouble has fallen to my lot."

Eighteen days after Wyatt penned his carefully worded letter, he stepped off the train in Dodge City. The *Ford County Globe* calmly noted his arrival: "Wyatt is looking well and glad to get back to his old haunts, where he is well and favorably known." He got a different reception, however, from the district attorney. As Wyatt walked from the station followed by several well-armed hard cases from Colorado, the district attorney said, "My God, Wyatt, who are those people you've got with you?"

"Oh, they're just some bushwhackers I've brought over from Colorado to straighten you people out."

"In whose interest?"

"Luke Short's and Bat Masterson's."

Luke's gang, dubbed the Dodge City Peace Commission, included two former members of the Earps' vendetta posse: Texas Jack Vermillion and Daniel Tipton. And according to several newspapers, Doc Holliday of Leadville was there, too—it would take an army to keep Doc from

The Dodge City Peace Commission. Seated, left to right: Charles E. Bassett, Wyatt Earp, M.F. "Frank" McLain (also McLean), and Neil Brown. Standing, left to right: William H. Harris, Luke Short, Bat Masterson, and W. F. Petillion. Although Doc Holliday is not pictured, several newspapers reported him as one of Wyatt's gunhands. (PUBLIC DOMAIN IMAGE, AUTHOR'S COLLECTION)

backing his friend Wyatt. Consequently, with such a menacing lineup led by Wyatt, it didn't take long to bring about a change of heart with the city leaders. The gunplay between the two factions that so many sensational news reports predicted never happened. And the city even let slide its ordinance forbidding the carrying of concealed weapons—at least while the Peace Commission was in town.

Luke Short returned to the Long Branch and the gambling and "singing" resumed as usual. After a few days, the shootists left for their respective homes, but not before some of them—including Wyatt, Bat, and Luke—posed for a group photograph, which soon appeared as an engraving in the *National Police Gazette*. The *Gazette* described the men in the picture as "A Group of Prominent Frontiersmen Who Restored Quiet in a Troubled Community."

Sometime while Wyatt and Doc were in Dodge, or perhaps on their way back to Colorado, the two made a visit to Garden City, Kansas, fifty-two miles to the west. Wyatt's half-brother, Newton, was Garden City's marshal. Newton's daughter, Alice, then seven years old, remembered two men riding up to their house and dismounting. One she recognized as her uncle Wyatt, the other she hadn't seen before. Wyatt barely nodded at the child as he walked in the house with Newton, but the other man, Doc, asked to sit with her on the porch, and Alice thought that would be fine.

Doc and Alice chatted a long time, and, though a child, she felt he was truly interested in what she had to say. At some point, Doc excused himself and walked off toward downtown. He was gone but a short time, and when he returned, Alice saw he was carrying a colorful rag doll. Doc gave the doll to Alice with his compliments. After Wyatt and Doc rode away, Newton told his daughter that the man who'd been so kind to her was the "notorious" Doc Holliday.

———

MISSING FROM DOC'S LIFE NOW WAS KATE ELDER. SHE DIDN'T follow him to Colorado. If he had other female companions in Leadville or elsewhere, there's no record of it. A writer who saw Doc dealing cards in Leadville in the spring of 1883 described him as "a thin, spare looking man; his iron gray hair is always well combed and oiled; his boots usually wear an immaculate polish; his beautiful scarf, with an elegant diamond pin in the center, looks well on his glossy shirt front, and he prides himself on always keeping scrupulously neat and clean." However, one of Doc's Leadville friends pointed out that the sharp-looking gambler didn't overdo it. He came across as "neither a lady's man nor a dandy."

But Doc was also visibly ill, and the thin, cold air at Leadville's elevation of 10,158 feet wasn't necessarily helping his constitution. In addition to self-medicating with whiskey and snake oil tonics, he began taking laudanum, which he got at no charge from a local druggist who took pity on him. The famous Earp posse member who'd ridden across southeastern Arizona now looked frail. Always a slim man, his weight dropped to less than 125 pounds. Due to his weakened immune system, Doc came down with pneumonia again and again. He worked for a while at the Monarch Saloon, where the going rate for faro dealers was $6 a day. But he lost that job before the year was out, presumably because his drinking and frequent sick spells made him unreliable.

Doc continued to faithfully write his favorite cousin, Mattie, in Georgia, but he got a shock when he learned she'd entered a convent in Savannah. As of October 1883, she was Sister Mary Melanie. If Doc did have romantic feelings for his cousin, he already knew that they would never be together, but this news must have been a blow to his psyche nevertheless. And although Doc acquired friends in Leadville—he even helped organize a club of independent voters—he didn't have his adopted brothers, the Earps, to socialize with and to look after him when needed.

And someone definitely needed to be looking after Doc. An old Sloper rival from Tombstone, gambler Johnny Tyler, had also established himself in Leadville, and Johnny still held a grudge against Doc from the time they butted heads in the Oriental. On July 21, 1884, Tyler and several cronies accosted Doc at a saloon and gambling hall he frequented called Hyman's Place. Tyler hurled a string of expletives at Doc and told him to draw. Doc said he had no gun, but he wasn't going to back down, either. Friends of both parties finally intervened.

Doc still worried about being extradited to Arizona, and he believed if he killed someone in Colorado, he'd surely be sent there, and the Cowboys would be waiting for him. "I am afraid to defend myself," Doc told a reporter, "and these cowards kick me because they know I am down. I haven't a cent, have few friends, and they will murder me yet before they are done."

Compounding Doc's problem with the Tyler bunch was that he owed money to one of them, Billy Allen. Allen, a stout man of 170 pounds, was a bartender at the Monarch and also a special policeman. Doc had promised to repay the money, $5, in a few days or a week, but after three weeks passed, Allen began to angrily badger Doc for it. On Friday, August 15, Allen confronted Doc at the Monarch and said, "Holliday, I'll give you 'till Tuesday to pay this money, and if you don't pay it, I'll lick you, you son of a bitch!" Allen told another individual that if Doc didn't pay by noon on Tuesday, he'd knock him down and "kick his damned brains out."

Doc didn't have the money. He'd already pawned the little jewelry he owned, and he was unable to obtain a loan. It's a mystery how he even paid for his meals. On the Tuesday deadline, Doc slept until 3 P.M. As soon as he dressed, he went to Hyman's Place, where some of his friends warned that Allen was looking for him, and he had a gun. They persuaded Doc to go back to his room, which he did. A couple of hours later, Doc sent a friend to Hyman's with his revolver and told him to place it behind the end of the bar—the police, expecting trouble, had taken to searching Doc for weapons. Doc then went to Hyman's and stood by a cigar case near the bar.

Allen was at work at the Monarch, two doors from Hyman's, when he saw Doc walk by. As Allen slipped on his coat to go demand his money, one of the saloon's owners pleaded, "For God's sake, don't go into Hyman's, as Holliday is in there." Allen ignored him and stormed out. Doc discreetly retrieved his revolver from behind the bar and fixed his eyes on the saloon's front door, and in the Old West tradition of get-them-before-they-can-get-you, he shot at Allen just as soon as the big man got three feet inside.

Doc's bullet slammed into a glass in the door. A panic-stricken Allen turned to flee but slipped and fell. Doc leaned over the cigar case and fired again, flame and smoke streaming from the muzzle of his revolver. The lead bullet tore a hole in Allen's right arm as he was lifting himself up. Allen screamed in pain, blood spurting from his arm and splattering on the floor. He made a leap for the entrance and stumbled outside. Doc started to fire a third time but the bartender grabbed him. A police officer rushed inside and secured the revolver. "I want you to protect me," Doc said to the officer, and Doc was quickly escorted to the city jail.

Interviewed from his cell a few minutes later, Doc told a reporter that, "It was not about the $5. That was taken as a pretext. It is the old trouble,

Leadville street scene, from a circa 1881 cabinet card. The office of the *Leadville Democrat* is on the left. (ORIGINAL CABINET CARD IN THE AUTHOR'S COLLECTION)

and Allen was picked out as the man to kill me." Doc believed Johnny Tyler was behind it. As Doc put it, Allen was "a tool of the gang," something Allen strongly denied. Fortunately for Doc, Allen's wound wasn't fatal, although the bullet did nick a main artery. Doc was charged with assault with intent to kill.

Doc remained behind bars until September 6, when he was released on $5,000 bail. A real concern existed that because of Doc's fragile health, he might die if he was forced to remain behind bars until his trial date, but sureties were eventually found. Things now seemed to settle down for Doc, and although there was no love lost between him and Tyler, they stayed clear of each other. A Leadville newsman later said that "the local bad men shied away from [Doc] for good after he spoiled Billy Allen's pistol arm." When Doc finally faced a jury of his peers in March 1885, he was acquitted.

It's uncertain if Allen ever got his $5. Doc, however, had a very direct way of collecting from those in his debt, if a June 1885 story published in an Aspen newspaper is to be believed. A sporting man named Curley

Mac owed Doc $50, and one night at a Leadville faro bank, Mac won $150. Doc happened to be standing behind Mac watching him play, and once Mac started to collect his winnings, Doc stepped to where Mac could see him and pulled a nickel-plated revolver from his waistband. Doc pointed the gun's muzzle at Mac, saying, "I'd like that fifty tonight, Curley." Mac, trembling, told Doc he could have it all, but Doc took only what he was owed and shoved the rest back at Mac.

Doc appears to have worn out his welcome in Leadville about this time. Or, in the words of a Leadville newspaper, he'd reached "the end of his string." He apparently used that $50 from Curley Mac to help him get to Butte, Montana, more than seven hundred miles away. The mining town was the latest El Dorado, with a population of eighteen thousand, fifteen gambling halls, four variety theaters, four to five thousand miners making $4.50 a day, and an unlimited supply of prostitutes. The *New York World* proclaimed Butte the "wickedest city on earth." Exactly Doc's kind of town.

By July 13, Doc had checked into Butte's Revere House. "Doc is well known throughout the country," announced Butte's *Daily Town Talk*, "and is a hale fellow well met." However, a Leadville resident who visited Butte in November wasn't quite as cheery when it came to Doc. He reported that the sporting man's "habits are unchanged," and that his "existence is as precarious as ever." It was only a matter of time before Doc made trouble for himself, and that happened in January 1886, when a drunken Doc used the persuasive powers of his revolver to force a man to dance his best quickstep. A Butte newspaper called it "a cowardly attack on an innocent and inoffensive person."

The following month, the grand jury indicted Doc on the charge of "drawing and exhibiting a deadly weapon," and a warrant was issued for his arrest. When a deputy sheriff went to make the arrest, he found Doc sick in bed. A doctor caring for Doc advised the deputy that it would be dangerous to move the patient to the county jail. Doc had been in bed for two days, he said, and was quite weak. Doc looked and sounded pretty sick to the deputy, so he allowed him to remain in his room. Two days later, the dangerously ill patient was seen boarding a morning train out of town. The Butte *Semi-Weekly Miner* reported that "Doc Holliday has come to the conclusion that this is not a good country for shooting men."

WYATT AND SADIE CHECKED INTO DENVER'S BRUNSWICK HOTEL in early June 1886. The couple then lived in Trinidad but made occasional visits to the Colorado capital. And they were delighted to learn that among the Brunswick's guests was a Tombstone friend and his wife: Thomas Fitch, the "silver-tongued orator" who'd served as Wyatt's and Doc's counsel at the Spicer hearing. The Earps and Fitches were sitting in the hotel's lobby one day when Wyatt let out a gasp of surprise—and there wasn't much that surprised Wyatt. Sadie looked up and saw Doc Holliday coming toward them. It was startling to see how much thinner and delicate he was, but the famed sporting man was as well dressed as ever.

"I have never seen a man exhibit more pleasure at meeting a mere friend than did Doc," Sadie recalled. Wyatt and Doc moved a short distance away and sat down.

"When I heard you were in Denver, Wyatt, I wanted to see you once more," Doc said, "for I can't last much longer. You can see that."

Doc struggled to talk at times because of his coughing, but Wyatt listened patiently. The two had much to catch up on, and they sat conversing for a good long spell.

"Isn't it strange," Wyatt said to Doc, "that if it were not for you, I wouldn't be alive today, yet you must go first."

Doc and Wyatt walked back to where Sadie and the Fitches were sitting and they chatted a bit longer. Then the two stepped away again, and Doc gave Wyatt a hug.

"Goodbye, old friend," Doc said. "It will be a long time before we meet again."

Doc turned and Wyatt watched as his friend walked across the lobby, weaving as he fought to keep his balance. When Wyatt came back to Sadie and the Fitches, Sadie saw tears in his eyes.

Sadie recalled that Wyatt was "deeply affected by this parting from the man who, like an ailing child, had clung to him as though to derive strength from him."

DOC LIVED IN DENVER FOR MUCH OF THE SUMMER. BUT IN early August, the Denver police made a sweep to arrest vagrants, and in that category they placed "tinhorn gamblers, confidence men, and other worthless characters." On the night of August 3, 1886, Doc and two other men were standing on Sixteenth Street when the police threw them into a paddy wagon and hauled them to jail. The *Rocky Mountain News* applauded the arrests and encouraged the police to keep it up so that "Denver may be rid of a good many worthless beings. There are lots of them left."

But Denver was more interested in getting Doc out of town than it was in seeing him go through the court system on a vagrancy charge. He was taken to the train station and advised not to come back. Doc traveled the rails to a place where he still had friends, Leadville, and he somehow survived the mountain town's insufferable winter months.

In May 1887, as large piles of snow slowly melted in the shade of Leadville's buildings, Doc boarded the Kit Carson stage for Glenwood Springs. A booming town on the line of the rapidly approaching Denver & Rio Grande Railroad, Glenwood Springs was famed for its healthful hot springs. If the bubbling mineral water baths and vapors couldn't stave off his disease, perhaps they could at least provide some relief for that damned cough and allow him to breathe.

Doc took up residence in Hotel Glenwood, a new three-and-a-half-story brick edifice on Eighth Street, and eked out a living for a while dealing faro in the town's saloons. His spirits were likely lifted, though, by the news of Ike Clanton's death on June 1. Ike was wanted for cattle rustling and made the mistake of showing up at a remote cabin in Arizona's White Mountains that was being visited by two lawmen on his trail. Ike had had success running away from danger in the past, but not this time. A bullet knocked him out of his saddle as he attempted to flee.

Doc's nemesis received a lonely, unmarked grave not far from where he fell.

By about mid-September, Doc worsened to the point that he couldn't get out of bed. For the next several weeks, he wasted away, eventually becoming delirious. Although only thirty-six, his sunken face, gray hair, and emaciated body made him look like an elderly man. Doc's friends in Leadville, learning that he was destitute and dying, took up a collection and sent the money express to the Hotel Glenwood, but he would never know of their gift. Death took him at 10 A.M. on November 8.

Twenty-four hours before he died, Doc slipped into a coma. But before his consumption silenced Doc forever, those tending to him heard him say, in his low voice, "This is funny."

IMMORTALITY

For truly, when a man shall end,
He lives in memory of his friend.

AUSTIN DOBSON

Linwood Cemetery, Glenwood Springs
4 p.m., November 8, 1887

Reverend Walter S. Rudolph, a Presbyterian minister, gave the funeral address near the freshly dug grave for John Henry Holliday. Despite the short notice, a large crowd of Doc's friends from town had gathered at the hilltop graveyard overlooking Glenwood Springs to pay their final respects. Because Doc died indigent, no stone carver's headstone would mark his grave. His personal possessions, gathered in a small leather trunk, were shipped to his family in Georgia. It wasn't much: a few clothes, toiletries, "gaming devices," a straight razor, small knife, and his signature gold stickpin—missing its diamond. None of Doc's guns made it to Georgia. He'd probably pawned or sold them long ago.

By the time Doc's friends made their way down the steep hill, the news of his passing was already flashing over the telegraph wires. The story of his death published by the *Denver Republican* was picked up by papers in New York City, Washington, DC, Kansas City, and San Francisco. Ironically, in the city he was run out of as a "worthless character" and a vagrant the year before, he was now found to have "many excellent qualities." Doc's "coolness and courage, his affable ways and fund of interesting experiences, won him many admirers. He was a strong friend, a cool and determined enemy, and a man of quite strong character."

In tracing Doc's career, the stories of his death invariably noted that he'd been a member of the "Earp gang," or that he'd participated in "Earp's war." Unquestionably, Doc's association with Wyatt and his brothers during the tumultuous Tombstone days was considered the seminal chapter in his short career. And maybe Doc would have agreed. That time had certainly changed his life, and not necessarily for the better. And yet, it had all been made possible because he saved a man from certain death one night in Dodge City.

When and how Wyatt learned of his friend's death is unknown. Nor is anything known of his reaction to it. Wyatt and Sadie were then living in San Diego, where Wyatt ran gambling halls, raced trotting horses, refereed boxing matches, and invested in real estate. By all accounts, it was one of the more prosperous periods of his life. But those periods never lasted. In the decades that followed, Wyatt and Sadie bounced all over the West, always looking to make a fortune. If there was a "rush," Wyatt did his best to get there among the first, just like he'd done in Tombstone, Silverton, and other boomtowns. He even ran a saloon in Nome, Alaska, during the Klondike Gold Rush.

Wyatt outlived Doc Holliday by more than forty years. Another lifetime, really, but whenever Wyatt made the newspapers, and for whatever reason, his Arizona career always garnered a mention to remind readers of his singular claim to fame—or, more often than not, infamy. In fact, the entire country was reminded in 1896 when Wyatt made a highly controversial decision as referee for a heavyweight championship boxing match between Bob Fitzsimmons and Tom Sharkey. Tens of thousands of dollars rested on the fight's outcome, and when Wyatt called it because of a low blow by Fitzsimmons that hardly anyone saw, many concluded the fight was fixed.

Much of the outrage over the bout was directed at Wyatt, and the press devoured his past in a feeding frenzy. "His remarkable career is being told and retold throughout every hamlet, village and city through this United States," reported the *San Francisco Call*, a paper that came down on the side of the fight being a put-up job, "and the exchanges reaching the City bring new recitals daily of his man-killing deeds."

The *New York Journal* published author Alfred Henry Lewis's highly fictionalized (and defamatory) summary of Wyatt's Tombstone days, an account that was copied by

Wyatt Earp in 1887, six years after the Fremont Street fight. (COURTESY TRUE WEST ARCHIVES)

numerous other newspapers. Lewis wrote that the Earp brothers "had treated themselves to many a killing. But there was no money in murder; nothing but relaxation. So they devoted themselves to holding up the stage." These holdups were planned in cahoots with the Wells Fargo agent, Lewis declared, and the shotgun messenger on the stage was always an Earp. The robberies, "a family affair," netted the boys $25,000 each time, and the brothers made even more money by joining the posse and "chasing themselves."

It was just this kind of salacious hack writing that infuriated Wyatt. But whether he liked it or not, Tombstone had come to define him, just as it did Doc. Word for word of Lewis's caricature of the Earps again made the rounds of the press in 1900 when Warren Earp was shot and killed in a drunken saloon squabble in Willcox, Arizona. And this time, Lewis's words traveled far beyond the United States. In introducing Lewis's account, the *Western Grazier* of Wilcannia, Australia, identified Wyatt as the man who "robbed" Fitzsimmons and "a product of the frontier gambler and a gunfighter. There is not a drop of respectable blood in his veins."

Fortunately for Wyatt, an old friend soon came to his rescue and helped to greatly rehabilitate his public image. In 1907, Bat Masterson, now a journalist as well as a deputy US marshal for the Southern District of New York, accepted an assignment from *Human Life* magazine to write several biographical sketches for a series titled "Famous Gun Fighters of the Western Frontier." (Ironically, the editor who gave Bat the assignment was Alfred Henry Lewis, a friend of Bat's.) Naturally, Bat chose Wyatt Earp as the subject of one of his articles, and he portrayed his friend as a hero who never strayed from the side of law and order. "Much has been written about Wyatt Earp," he asserted, "that is the veriest rot."

Bat briefly covered Wyatt's days in Kansas with most of his article being devoted to the troubles with the Cowboys in Arizona. He gave a thrilling account of the famed street fight, the attempted assassination of Virgil and the murder of Morgan, the killing of Frank Stilwell, and the subsequent vendetta ride. And he offered not a single criticism of Wyatt's choices and actions. In his description of the street fight, he embellished the courage and skill of the Earps and Holliday by writing that their opponents used their horses as breastworks while the Earps and Holliday were exposed in the open, which was only partially true.

The article concluded with a stirring testament to Wyatt the man and a condemnation of his critics:

> *Wyatt Earp, like many more men of his character who lived in the West in its early days, has excited, by his display of great courage and nerve under trying conditions, the envy and hatred of those small-minded creatures with which the world seems to be abundantly peopled, and whose sole delight in life seems to be in fly-specking the reputations of real men. I have known him since the early seventies and have always found him a quiet, unassuming man, not given to brag or bluster, but at all times and under all circumstances a loyal friend and an equally dangerous enemy.*

Another gunfighter for Bat's series was one he also knew: Doc Holliday. And whereas Wyatt seemingly had no flaws, Doc's were numerous. He didn't possess the leadership qualities of such men as Wyatt, Bat wrote, and he was "selfish and had a perverse nature—traits not calculated to make a man popular in the early days on the frontier." Doc couldn't stay out of trouble for very long, with one scrape following another, but "the strange part of it is," Bat wrote, "he was more often in the right than in the wrong." According to Bat, Doc had few real friends in the West. "While I assisted him substantially on several occasions, it was not because I liked him any too well," Bat admitted, "but on account of my friendship for Wyatt Earp, who did."

Bat's article was the first to reveal just how strong a friendship existed between Doc and Wyatt. After Dodge City, Bat wrote, the two were "always fast friends ever afterwards." But Bat went further, comparing Doc and Wyatt's friendship to one from Greek legend that is among the greatest stories of friendship and sacrifice of all time. "Damon did no more for Pythias," wrote Bat, "than Holliday did for Wyatt Earp."

WYATT'S FIRST MAJOR BIOGRAPHER, STUART LAKE, CLAIMED that Bat once said, "The real story of the Old West can never be told unless Wyatt Earp will tell what he knows; and Wyatt will not talk." If Bat really did say that, it wasn't entirely true. Wyatt did talk. He gave interviews to a number of newspapermen and others over the years. And he did tell what he knew. But by the 1920s, he'd become hesitant, or at least more discriminating. For one, Wyatt had found that some journalists took shocking liberties with what he told them. "After Holliday died, I gave a San Francisco newspaper reporter a short sketch of his life," Wyatt recalled. "Apparently the reporter was not satisfied. The sketch appeared in print with a lot of things added that never existed outside the reporter's imagination, and the account repeatedly has been picked up and further manhandled."

Wyatt was also working with John Flood on his own book, so he wanted to save his story for its hoped-for publication. Yet another reason for not talking was that Wyatt had been betrayed by two writers. Walter Noble Burns, author of the bestselling *The Saga of Billy the Kid*, had gotten Wyatt to talk to him and provide a good deal of historical information based on Burns's assertion that he was writing a biography of Doc Holliday. But Burns wasn't writing Holliday's biography. He was telling the story of the Earps and the Cowboys, of Curly Bill, the street fight, and the vendetta ride.

When Wyatt got wind of Burns's trickery, he contacted his publisher, Doubleday, Page & Company, and protested the book's publication: "The story of Wyatt Earp, or any portion of it, if it is to be written, must be written, only, by Wyatt Earp." The publisher offered Earp a thousand dollars and 25 percent of possible motion picture proceeds, but Wyatt wanted half of the proceeds from all sources and also errors in Burns's manuscript corrected. Doubleday refused and went ahead with publication, claiming the book, titled *Tombstone*, was really a history of the town.

And in an effort to prevent a possible lawsuit from Wyatt, Burns committed yet another slimy move when he crafted a section at the beginning of his book titled "Sources." Burns emphasized all the printed records he consulted so as to make it appear he didn't use anything obtained from Wyatt. But the greater affront was that Burns purposely left Wyatt's name off the list of individuals whom he'd either interviewed or who had sent him information.

The other betrayer was William Breakenridge, former deputy of Johnny Behan. Breakenridge published his reminiscences in 1928 as *Helldorado: The True Story of Tombstone*. In it, he presented the Earps as no better than the Cowboys while Johnny Behan was "a brave and fearless officer, who could see some good in even the worst of men." Like Burns, Breakenridge had visited Wyatt, professed to be a friend, and pumped him for information. "If there ever was a mean contemptible person, he certainly is one," Wyatt wrote Lake about Breakenridge. "Just imagine a man to come to you for favors, which he has done, and then to be so treacherous."

In *Helldorado*, Breakenridge repeated a silly tale that Wyatt wore a steel vest when he killed Curly Bill. And Breakenridge didn't actually believe Wyatt had killed the notorious Cowboy. He included stories of individuals who claimed they saw Curly alive after the fight, stories that are reminiscent of those told by people who said they saw Billy the Kid, Jesse James, and Butch Cassidy alive following their deaths.

Breakenridge wasn't the first to question Curly's death, however. The *Daily Nugget* refused to believe the claims of the Earp posse and offered $1,000 for conclusive evidence that Curly was deceased. Not to be outdone, the rival *Epitaph* offered $2,000 if Curly would come to their office and prove that he was alive, the money to go to Curly's charity of choice— the *Epitaph* jokingly recommended the Stockraisers' Protective Association. Curly failed to make an appearance, and the *Epitaph* proclaimed the Cowboy was "as dead as two loads of buckshot can make him."

What seemed to upset Wyatt most about Breakenridge's book, though, was that the author sided with the accusations of the Cowboy supporters that the McLaurys and Clantons were unarmed and holding up their hands when the street fight broke out. "All of which is very interesting," Wyatt bitingly wrote Stuart Lake, "and probably explains how Virgil Earp, Morgan Earp, and Doc Holliday were wounded during the fight."

One story Breakenridge neglected to include in his book was the time the citizens of Galeyville gave him three hours to get out of town. Breakenridge, then Behan's deputy, had tipped off a Cowboy with a stolen horse that the animal's owner was on his way to retrieve his property. The Cowboy jumped on the horse and galloped away. This shenanigan was too much for the folks of Galeyville, and Breakenridge left as instructed.

BY EARLY 1927, JOHN FLOOD HAD COMPLETED HIS MANUSCRIPT of Wyatt's life, and it was unpublishable. Even coming with an endorsement from movie star William S. Hart, no one wanted it. Flood was a former mining engineer turned Los Angeles realtor. That he wasn't a writer was painfully obvious to the editors who rejected his manuscript. The response of Ann Johnston of the Bobbs-Merrill Company was typical. She didn't feel that the story Flood presented was as fascinating as those of Wild Bill and Billy the Kid, but the real problem was the writing. It was "stilted and florid and diffuse. It would be far more effective if it were simple, direct, straightforward. A lot of the stuff ought to be cut out altogether and the rest boiled down. Then there *might* be a story."

Then, in December 1927, Wyatt received a letter from journalist and magazine writer Stuart N. Lake proposing they collaborate on Wyatt's biography. The thirty-eight-year-old Lake had never written a book, but his writings had been published in such national periodicals as the *Saturday Evening Post* and *The Outlook*. And Lake had worked with Bat Masterson when both were employed by the New York *Morning Telegraph*.

Wyatt agreed, and Lake, by his own account, spent weeks at Wyatt and Sadie's modest Los Angeles bungalow. "I was pumping, pumping, pumping for names and incidents and sidelights," Lake recalled, "all of which Wyatt could supply but none of which he handed out in any sort of narrative form." Wyatt was then eighty years old.

"He and I got on beautifully," Lake remembered about Wyatt. "He talked freely to me, that is, answered my questions fully and freely, but it just wasn't in the nature of the man to speak at any length. He was delightfully laconic, or exasperatingly so." In other words, Lake had his work cut out for him.

Unlike John Flood, Lake didn't stop with what Wyatt told him. Lake deeply researched the people and places connected with Wyatt's life, writing countless letters to Tombstone and Kansas old-timers seeking their recollections of Wyatt, his brothers, and Doc Holliday. He received especially good responses from Tombstone's first mayor and founder of the *Epitaph*, John Clum, and the diarist George W. Parsons, both of whom now resided in Los Angeles. And then, on January 13, 1929, Wyatt Earp died.

Wyatt's Los Angeles funeral occurred three days later, and among his pallbearers were film stars William S. Hart and Tom Mix, and several old Tombstone friends, including Clum and Parsons. One former Tombstone resident at the funeral was Mrs. Roma Thorndyke, and she was in tears. She told a reporter for the *Los Angeles Times* of her memory of October 26, 1881, "the day Wyatt shot it out with the Clantons." Roma was just seven years old, and as soon as she heard the shots, she ran out on the street to see. She didn't see much, though, as little Roma was quickly grabbed and brought into a store and thrown flat on the floor.

Lake started writing Wyatt's biography shortly after his death, and by September 1930, Lake's manuscript totaled a massive 634 pages. This was far too long, and his publisher, Houghton Mifflin, instructed him to cut it down. But length wasn't the only problem. His editor, Ira Rich Kent, wrote Lake that there was "altogether too much personal animus in the book, too much adverse criticism—amounting now and then almost to insult and abuse—of men who were on the other side." That is, the Cowboys.

Lake's Wyatt could do no wrong, much like Bat's portrayal in *Human Life* magazine, and even after Lake revised and cut, the publisher's outside readers were troubled by how Wyatt was presented "in such a uniformly glowing light." The chapters on the street fight and its aftermath, they felt, "has the air of being presented not quite ingenuously—that is, it evidently still seems a bit too much like a brief for the defense."

Kent found something else curious about Lake's treatment: the long quotes from Wyatt. "Did he really talk in this rather literary and polysyllabic style," Kent asked, "or have you perhaps unconsciously smoothed out his speech to an undue degree?" It wasn't an unconscious act. Lake admitted later that Wyatt didn't dictate anything to him. He'd used the long quotes to make his book appear authentic. Still, Lake opted to keep the quotes and confided to a fellow author that, "I've often wondered if I did not overdo in this respect."

Wyatt's wife was given the opportunity to review Lake's finished manuscript. (By this time, Sadie was signing her correspondence "Josephine Earp.") She wrote editor Kent that it impressed her "more as that of the blood and thunder type than a biography." What she'd pushed Lake for was a "nice, clean story." Sadie was a lot like the indomitable Libbie Custer, who worked tirelessly to protect the image of her husband, George Armstrong Custer, following his spectacular defeat at the Little Big Horn. "Mr. Earp was not a bad man," she insisted. "He never shot unless he had to."

Lake's *Wyatt Earp: Frontier Marshal*, appeared in September 1931. It was still parts blood and thunder and hero-worshipping, but no one could say it wasn't clean. There was no embezzling of tax money in Missouri, no horse stealing in Indian Territory, no arrests for keeping a house of ill fame in Illinois, and no living out of wedlock. Lake did briefly go into the rivalry between Wyatt and Sheriff Behan over a woman, but she's nameless in his narrative, and he also ignored Wyatt's then significant other, Mattie Earp.

Many of the seamier aspects of Wyatt's early years Lake knew

The 1931 first edition, first printing of Lake's Earp biography.
(AUTHOR'S COLLECTION)

nothing about, but he certainly was aware of Mattie, and he'd been informed of Sadie's promiscuous past as well. The easier, and diplomatic, path for Lake was to avoid the delicate subject of Mattie and Sadie altogether. So while Lake did tell the story Wyatt wanted told, achieving, in the eyes of most readers, the vindication Wyatt had been hell-bent on getting, the biography wasn't anywhere close to the *whole* story.

Wyatt Earp: Frontier Marshal was a popular and critical success. Notices and reviews appeared in newspapers nationwide, and the book was serialized by the *Saturday Evening Post*, one of the most widely read periodicals of its day. Lake's book went through multiple printings and made Wyatt Earp a bona fide Old West legend, a lawman's lawman, and a pop culture icon. It also elevated the story of the bond between Wyatt and Doc so that their friendship became the stuff of legend as well. There were some, though, who refused to buy into Lake's myth building. Author

Frank Waters, who'd interviewed Virgil's wife, Allie, for a book of his own, blasted Lake's work as "a piece of fiction." Even more, it was a "disgraceful indictment of the thousands of true Arizona pioneers whose lives and written protests refute every discolored incident in it."

One of those true pioneers was perpetual Earp hater Kate Elder, who at the time of *Frontier Marshal*'s release was a new resident at the Home for Aged and Infirm Arizona Pioneers in Prescott. Kate's whereabouts after Doc left Arizona aren't certain. She claimed that Doc sent for her in Glenwood Springs and that she nursed him until he died, which appears to have been nothing more than a fantasy. She was known at the Pioneers Home as Mary K. Cummings, for she'd married a prospector and blacksmith named George Cummings in Aspen, Colorado, in 1890. They'd moved to Arizona six years later, but her husband had a drinking problem, which she'd had enough of with Doc, and she soon left him.

Kate seems to have gotten the idea that her story might be worth something and twice enlisted the help of writers to get it published. "I am the only one alive now," she avowed, "that can tell the truth about the Earp brothers and Doc Holliday." Unfortunately, Kate wasn't very careful with that truth, and she couldn't stand the fact that Wyatt had received a hagiographic biography, which she called "the wildest and most improbable dime novel ever published." Kate's recollections, which failed to interest a national periodical, do offer rare glimpses into Doc's life available nowhere else, but they're also a minefield of errors and fabrications. She died at the Pioneers Home on November 2, 1940. Only a handful of people knew she was Doc Holliday's Big Nose Kate.

Sadie Earp also got the bug to publish her story. She shared in the proceeds of *Frontier Marshal* with Lake, and duly impressed with the money coming in—she got a whopping $3,750 from a movie deal with Fox—she thought she could make even more with a book on her life. Sadie convinced two distant cousins of Wyatt's, Mabel Earp Cason and Vinnolia Earp Ackerman, to help write it. Sadie visited Tombstone in 1937, and when quizzed by a reporter about her Tombstone experiences, she said he would have to wait until the book she was writing came out.

"I will tell all that there is to tell in the book," she said.

The cousins spent four years working with Sadie, but when they sent the manuscript to Houghton Mifflin, who'd expressed an interest in it, the publisher wanted to know why the Tombstone portion of her story was virtually nonexistent. It wasn't that the cousins hadn't tried. When it came to Tombstone and how she met Wyatt, Sadie was a lot like the way Bat described Wyatt: She would not talk. The cousins soon realized that Sadie was guarding secrets from the past, both hers and Wyatt's, and that they would never get the complete story. Mrs. Wyatt Earp, as she was nearly always referred to now, died December 19, 1944, believing her secrets had been well kept, just as Wyatt and Kate believed they'd taken theirs to the grave, too.

Believed to be a photograph of Doc's paramour, Big Nose Kate (aka Mária Horony, Kate Elder, and Mary Cummings), taken late in life.
(COURTESY *TRUE WEST* ARCHIVES)

AFTER MORE THAN 140 YEARS—AND THOUSANDS OF BOOKS, AR-ticles, films, TV shows, documentaries, and podcasts—Wyatt has returned to being the divisive figure that he sometimes was in territorial Arizona. And it's just as hard now to get at the heart of the relationship between Wyatt and Doc as it was then. Neither spoke at length about it, only to say that they were friends. But, truly, they didn't need to. Just as in the old maxim, "actions speak louder than words," the essence of their friendship is revealed in what they did for each other, that in the toughest of moments, they were side by side. When one or the other needed help, whatever that help was, and no matter how dangerous, they didn't hesitate. Wyatt and Doc were friends but acted like brothers.

When Sadie was working on her life's story, she told the cousins that she and Wyatt had visited Doc one last time when he was dying in Glenwood Springs. There's no evidence of such a visit, no reports in the local newspaper of the presence of the famed Wyatt Earp in town. It may never have happened.

Even so, it's the ending we want.

ACKNOWLEDGMENTS

In August 1930, Houghton Mifflin editor Ira Rich Kent wrote to author Stuart Lake to tell him that his Wyatt Earp manuscript was far too long. "You have evidently found it difficult to leave out anything," Kent wrote. "Good writing means leaving out a lot."

All nonfiction book authors face Stuart Lake's dilemma: what to leave out. In the lives of Wyatt and Doc, I encountered a good many interesting details, incidents, and connections that would've easily made this a bigger book, but not really a better one. Always, my goal is to provide a lean, fast-paced narrative that's impeccably accurate, compelling, and a pleasure to read. One thing I would never think of leaving out of a book, though, is the names of those individuals who generously assisted me in this effort.

Fellow authors, historians, and researchers who gave of their time to talk to me, answer emails, or otherwise provide assistance include Roy B. Young, Gary L. Roberts, Bob Boze Bell, Casey Tefertiller, John Boessenecker, Victoria Wilcox, Kevin Mulkins, William B. Shillingberg, Mike O'Keefe, Ron Hansen, Garth Gould, Tom Gaumer, Jeremy Rowe, Mark Boardman, Sherry Monahan, Robert Ray, Craig Fouts, Mackenzie

Holian, John Ulrich, and Jeff Morey. I literally peppered my friend Roy Young with emails from the beginning days of my research to the writing of these acknowledgments. He never failed to respond quickly with the information I needed. And if he didn't have what I needed, he knew where I could get it. I also want to make special mention of Doc Holliday biographer Gary Roberts, who gave his blessing to my use of "Brothers of the Gun" for the title of this book. Gary used that evocative phrase as the title of an article he wrote on Wyatt and Doc that first appeared in *Wild West* in 2012.

I'm also extremely grateful to the librarians, archivists, and curators who provided access to important manuscript materials and historic images. They are, in no particular order, Perri Pyle and Jennifer Merry of the Arizona Historical Society; Cathy Smith of the Haley Memorial Library and Research Center; Jazmin Rew-Pinchem and Sarah Francis of the Huntington Library; Dena Hunt and Rick Hendricks of the New Mexico State Records Center and Archives; Melissa Murphy, Baker Library, Harvard University; Connie Penick, Ford County Historical Society; Patricia Ballesteros of the University of Arizona Libraries Special Collections; Adrienne Sockwell of the Ransom Center; Natasha Khandekar, curator of the William I. Koch collection; Heather McClure at the Fray Angélico Chávez History Library; Mary C. Haegert at Houghton Library; Curtis B. Leslie of Tombstone State Historic Park; Kelsey Berryhill, State Historical Society of Iowa; the staff of the State Historical Society of Missouri; the staff of the Circuit Court Clerk office, Barton County, Missouri; and the most capable librarians in the interlibrary loan department of the Pikes Peak Library District.

During one of my research trips to Tombstone, Arizona, friends Greg and Marty Scott hosted me at their charming cottage in Elgin, Arizona. In Missouri, my mom, Venita Gardner, provided a comfy room from which I made research excursions to Columbia, Jeff City, and Lamar. When I wasn't ensconced in the archives, I enjoyed some excellent trap shooting and turkey hunting courtesy of Curly Gardner, David Greenwood, Ivan Greenwood, Teri Gardner, Scott Gardner, and David Wayne

Gardner. And I mustn't forget Kurt House of Three Rivers, Texas, who provided an exceptional deer and hog hunt for my son, Vance, and I.

It takes an entire team, of course, to turn a manuscript into a finished book and present it to the world. At Dutton, then, I owe hearty thanks to David Howe, my editor; Erica Rose, production editor; Daniel Brount, designer; Hannah Poole, publicist; and Diamond Bridges, marketer. And I'm grateful to Dutton vice president and publisher, John Parsley, for his faith in this book and dedication to publishing nonfiction. I also mustn't forget Brent Howard, former editor at Dutton, who acquired this book.

Laurie McGee, freelance copyeditor, saved me yet again with this book, the fifth one she's scrutinized for me. Thank you, Laurie!

I'm deeply indebted as well to my literary agent and friend Jim Donovan of Dallas, Texas. This is our fifth book together, and I'm excited for the sixth (spoiler alert: Jesse and Frank James's experiences as bushwhackers in the Civil War, also for Dutton).

To my old compadres Andy Morris, Rex Rideout, and Ron Kil, I hope you enjoy this book as much as you have those that came before. Know that your friendship and keen interest in my work is duly appreciated.

I always save my family for last, and for good reason. I can't imagine how I could have researched and written this book without their love and support. Nearly every author makes a similar statement, I know, but it's absolutely true. Thank you Katie, Christiana (and husband, Eric), and Vance.

Mark Lee Gardner
Ute Pass, Colorado

RESOURCES

MANUSCRIPTS AND VISUAL RESOURCES

American Heritage Center, University of Wyoming
Owen Wister Papers: Journal, 1894, and "Frontier Notes," 1894

Arizona Historical Society, Tucson, Arizona
Glenn Boyer Research Collection, MS 0087
Mabel Earp Cason Papers, MS 138
Earp Family Papers, MS 238
Josephine Sarah Marcus Earp Papers, MS 0952
Wynona Leaona Neff Hixenbaugh Biography File, MS 1475
John B. Wright Papers, MS 1123

Baker Library, Harvard Business School, Boston, Massachusetts
R.G. Dun & Co. credit report volumes

Barton County Historical Society, Lamar, Missouri
Wyatt Earp deed records (photocopies)
Wyatt Earp and Arella Sutherland Marriage Record (photocopy)

Bureau of Land Management
General Land Office Records

Center for Southwest Research, University Libraries, University of New Mexico, Albuquerque, New Mexico
Frank Waters Papers

Circuit Court's Office, Barton County Courthouse, Lamar, Missouri
State of Missouri ex rel. vs. Wyatt S. Earp et al., Petition & Affidavit, March 14, 1871
James Cromwell vs. Wyatt S. Earp, James Maupin, N. P. Earp, and J. D. Earp, Petition, March 31, 1871

Denver Public Library, Western History Collection, Denver, Colorado
Karen Holliday Tanner and John D. Tanner Jr. Papers, WH2486

Fray Angélico Chávez History Library, Santa Fe, New Mexico
Otero Optic, June 5, 1879

Ford County Historical Society, Dodge City, Kansas
Dodge City Police Docket, 1878–1882
"Wyatt Earp" by John Henry Flood Jr., typescript

The Haley Memorial Library and Research Center, Midland, Texas
Recollections of Mary Cowperthwaite Fulton Holliday Concerning John Henry Holliday, D.D.S., typescript
Mrs. John H. Holliday (Kate Elder) memoir

History Colorado, Denver
Fred M. Mazzulla Collection

Houghton Library, Harvard University, Cambridge, Massachusetts
Houghton Mifflin Company correspondence and records, MS Am 1925

The Huntington Library, San Marino, California
Stuart N. Lake Papers

L. Tom Perry Special Collections, Harold B. Lee Library, Brigham Young University, Provo, Utah
Eugene Manlove Rhodes papers

Missouri State Archives, Jefferson City
Barton County Circuit Court Records (microfilm)

New Mexico State Records Center and Archives, Santa Fe
San Miguel County District Court Records

RESOURCES

State Historical Society of Iowa, Des Moines
Diary of Mrs. James Rousseau, 1864

State Historical Society of Missouri, Columbia
Barton County Circuit Court Records, U.S. WPA-HRS, Missouri, microfilm rolls 106 and 107
Wyatt Earp Vertical File

Tombstone Courthouse State Historic Park, Tombstone, Arizona
Josephine Earp Collection

University of Arizona Libraries Special Collections, Tucson, Arizona
Cowboy Depredations in Arizona, Microfilm 2061
Correspondence of Crawley P. Dake, AZ 165 (microfilm)
Glenn Boyer Wyatt Earp Collection, MS 752
Walter Noble Burns Papers, AZ 291

PRIVATE COLLECTIONS
Kevin Mulkins, Tucson, Arizona
Roy B. Young, Apache, Oklahoma
William I. Koch, Palm Beach, Florida

PUBLISHED MATERIAL

Government Documents
Journals of the Twelfth Legislative Assembly of the Territory of Arizona. Lincoln, NE: Journal Company, 1883.
Revised Statutes and Laws of the Territory of New Mexico in Force at the Close of the Session of the Legislative Assembly Ending February 2, 1865. St. Louis, MO: R. P. Studley & Co., 1865.

Maps
"The Streets of Tombstone, Territory of Arizona, on October 26, 1881," by Gary S. McClelland. Glendale, AZ: W.A.I. Productions, 1998.
"Tombstone, Arizona Territory, Circa 1881–82," by John D. Gilchriese. Self-published, 1975.

Books and Articles
Ackerman, Rita K. W. O. K. Corral Postscript: The Death of Ike Clanton. Honolulu, HI: Talei Publishers, Inc., 2006.
Bailey, Lynn R. Henry Clay Hooker and the Sierra Bonita. Tucson, AZ: Westernlore Press, 1998.

————, ed. *A Tenderfoot in Tombstone: The Private Journal of George Whitwell Parsons: The Turbulent Years, 1880-82.* Tucson, AZ: Westernlore Press, 1996.

————. *Tombstone from a Woman's Point of View: The Correspondence of Clara Spalding Brown, July 7, 1880, to November 14, 1882.* Tucson, AZ: Westernlore Press, 1998.

Bailey, Lynn R., ed., and Don Chaput. *Cochise County Stalwarts: A Who's Who of the Territorial Years.* 2 vols. Tucson: Westernlore Press, 2000.

Barra, Allen. *Inventing Wyatt Earp: His Life and Many Legends.* New York: Carroll & Graff Publishers, Inc., 1998.

Bartholomew, Ed. *Wyatt Earp, 1848 to 1880: The Untold Story.* Toyahvale, TX: Frontier Book Company, 1963.

————. *Wyatt Earp, 1879–1882: The Man & the Myth.* Toyahvale, TX: Frontier Book Company, 1964.

Bell, Bob Boze. *The Illustrated Life and Times of Doc Holliday, Third Edition.* Cave Creek, AZ: Two Roads West, 2019.

————. *The Illustrated Life and Times of Wyatt Earp.* Peoria, AZ: Tri-Star—Boze Publications, Inc., 2008.

Bishop, William Henry. *Old Mexico and Her Lost Provinces: A Journey in Mexico, Southern California, and Arizona by Way of Cuba.* New York: Harper & Brothers, 1883.

Breakenridge, William M. *Helldorado: Bringing the Law to the Mesquite.* Boston: Houghton Mifflin Company, 1928.

Boessenecker, John. *Ride the Devil's Herd: Wyatt Earp's Epic Battle Against the West's Biggest Outlaw Gang.* Toronto, Canada: Hanover Square Press, 2020.

————. *When Law Was in the Saddle: The Frontier Life of Bob Paul.* Norman: University of Oklahoma Press, 2012.

Bork, A. W., and Glenn G. Boyer, eds. "The O.K. Corral Fight at Tombstone: A Footnote by Kate Elder." *Arizona and the West* 19 (Spring 1977): 65–84.

Boyer, Glenn G. *Suppressed Murder of Wyatt Earp.* San Antonio, TX: Historical Research Associates, 1997.

Brand, Peter. "Holliday in Montana." *Wild West* 29 (Oct. 2016): 28–33.

————. "Josephine 'Sadie' Earp's Sordid Secrets and Lies." *Wild West History Association Journal* 16 (March 2023): 10–34.

————. *The Life and Crimes of Perry Mallon.* Meadowbank, Australia: published by the author, 2006.

————. "Trauma and Tragedy: The Life of Victoria Behan, 'A Good, True Woman.'" *Wild West History Association Journal* 17 (June 2024): 25–35.

————. *Wyatt Earp's Vendetta Posse Rider: The Story of Texas Jack Vermillion.* Meadowbank, Australia: Published by the author, 2012.

Burns, Walter Noble. *Tombstone: An Iliad of the Southwest.* Garden City, Doubleday, Page & Company, 1927.

Burrows, Jack. *John Ringo: The Gunfighter Who Never Was.* Tucson: The University of Arizona Press, 1987.

Carmony, Neil B., ed. *Apache Days and Tombstone Nights: John Clum's Autobiography, 1877–1887.* Silver City, NM: High-Lonesome Books, 1977.

———. *Next Stop: Tombstone, George Hand's Contention City Diary, 1882.* Tucson, AZ: Trail to Yesterday Books, 1995.

Cataldo, Nicholas R. "Father of the 'Fighting Earps.'" *Wild West* 29 (Oct. 2016): 52–57.

———. "The Rousseau Diary and the Earp Wagon Train to San Bernardino, 1864." *Overland Journal* 33 (Fall 2015): 114–28.

Chaput, Don. *The Earp Papers: In a Brother's Image.* Encampment, WY: Affiliated Writers of America, 1994.

———. *Virgil Earp: Western Peace Officer.* Encampment, WY: Affiliated Writers of America, 1994.

Chaput, Don and David D. de Hass. *The Earps Invade Southern California, Bootlegging Los Angeles, Santa Monica, and the Old Soldiers' Home.* Denton, TX: University of North Texas Press, 2020.

Chesley, Hervey E. *Adventuring with the Old-Timers.* Midland, TX: Nita Stewart Haley Memorial Library, 1979.

Cox, William R. *Luke Short and His Era.* Garden City, NY: Doubleday & Company, 1961.

Courtney, Brad. "Doc Holliday Before He Went to Tombstone." *True West* 71 (July–August 2024): 20–27.

Cunningham, Gary L. "Gambling in the Kansas Cattle Towns: A Prominent and Somewhat Honorable Profession." *Kansas History* 5 (Spring 1982): 2–22.

DeArment, Robert K. *Bat Masterson: The Man and the Legend.* Norman: University of Oklahoma Press, 1979.

Derham, Richard. "Dave Rudabaugh: A Myth Deconstructed, Part One." *Wild West History Association Journal* 16 (June 2023): 10–21.

Devere, Jeanne. "The Tombstone Bonanza, 1878–1886." *Arizoniana* 1 (1960): 16–20.

Dworkin, Mark J. *American Mythmaker: Walter Noble Burns and the Legends of Billy the Kid, Wyatt Earp, and Joaquín Murrieta.* Norman: University of Oklahoma Press, 2015.

———. "Henry Jaffa and Wyatt Earp: Wyatt Earp's Jewish Connection, A Portrait of Henry Jaffa, Albuquerque's First Mayor." *Western Outlaw-Lawman History Association Journal* 13 (Fall 2004): 25–37.

Dykstra, Robert R. *The Cattle Towns.* New York: Alfred A. Knopf, 1968.

Earp, Wyatt S. *Wyatt Earp.* Sierra Vista, AZ: Yoma V. Bissette, 1981.

Elwood, Nelson D. *Proceedings of the Grand Royal Arch Chapter of the State of Illinois at their Ninth Annual Grand Convocation.* Chicago: Steam Presses of Chas. Scott & Co., 1858.

Fattig, Timothy W. *Wyatt Earp: The Biography*. Honolulu, HI: Talei Publishers, Inc., 2002.

Foy, Eddie, and Alvin F. Harlow. *Clowning Through Life*. New York: E. P. Dutton & Company, 1928.

Galesburg, Monmouth, Knoxville and Abingdon Directories. Chicago: Henry N. McEvoy, 1857.

Gatto, Steve. *Curly Bill: Tombstone's Most Famous Outlaw*. Lansing, MI: Protar House, 2003.

Guinn, Jeff. *The Last Gunfight: The Real Story of the Shootout at the O.K. Corral—And How It Changed the American West*. New York: Simon & Schuster, 2011.

The History of Marion County, Iowa, Containing a History of the County, Its Cities, Towns, &c. Des Moines: Union Historical Company, 1881.

Hooker, Forrestine. *An Arizona Vendetta: The Truth About Wyatt Earp*. Edited by Don Taylor. Old West Research & Publishing, 2011.

Hornung, Chuck. *Wyatt Earp's Cow-boy Campaign: The Bloody Restoration of Law and Order Along the Mexican Border, 1882*. Jefferson, NC: McFarland & Company, Inc., 2016.

———, and Gary L. Roberts. "The Split: Did Doc & Wyatt Split because of a Racial Slur?" *True West* 48 (Nov./Dec. 2001): 58–61.

Hussey, Tacitus. "History of Steamboating on the Des Moines River, From 1837 to 1862." *Annals of Iowa* 4 (April 1900): 323–382.

Hutton, Paul Andrew. "Showdown at the Hollywood Corral: Wyatt Earp and the Movies." *Montana, the Magazine of Western History* 45 (Summer 1995): 2–31.

Irvine, Mrs. William, comp. *Data on the Earp Family*. 6 mimeographed installments. Milwaukie, OR: Mrs. William Irvine, 1958.

Isenberg, Andrew C. *Wyatt Earp: A Vigilante Life*. New York: Hill and Wang, 2013.

Johnson, Paul Lee. *The McLaurys in Tombstone, Arizona: An O.K. Corral Obituary*. Denton, TX: University of North Texas Press, 2012.

Keeler, B. C. *Where to Go to Become Rich: Farmers', Miners' and Tourists' Guide to Kansas, New Mexico, Arizona and Colorado*. Chicago: Belford, Clarke & Co., 1880.

Kühn, Berndt. *Chronicles of War: Apache & Yavapai Resistance in the Southwestern United States and Northern Mexico, 1821–1937*. Tucson: The Arizona Historical Society, 2014.

Lake, Carolyn, ed. *Under Cover for Wells Fargo: The Unvarnished Recollections of Fred Dodge*. Boston: Houghton Mifflin Company, 1969.

Lake, Stuart N. *Wyatt Earp, Frontier Marshal*. New York: Houghton Mifflin Company, 1931.

Leonard, Carol, and Isidor Wallimann. "Prostitution and Changing Morality in the Frontier Cattle Towns of Kansas." *Kansas History* 2 (Spring 1979): 34–53.

McArdle, Pete. "Grave Doubts: Where Is Wyatt Earp's First Wife Buried? Part One." *Wild West History Association Journal* 6 (April 2013): 44–59.

———. "Grave Doubts: Where Is Wyatt Earp's First Wife Buried? Part Two." *Wild West History Association Journal* 6 (August 2013): 47–58.

———. "Grave Doubts: Where Is Wyatt Earp's First Wife Buried? Part Three." *Wild West History Association Journal* 6 (Oct. 2013): 69–82.

———. "Grave Doubts: Where Is Wyatt Earp's First Wife Buried? Part Four." *Wild West History Association Journal* 6 (Dec. 2013): 60–74.

The Manners That Win, Compiled from the Latest Authorities. Minneapolis, MN: Buckeye Publishing Co., 1879.

Masterson W. B. (Bat). "Famous Gun Fighters of the Western Frontier, Second Article, Wyatt Earp." *Human Life* 4 (Feb. 1907): 9–10, 22.

Meyers, E. C. (Ted). *Mattie: Wyatt Earp's Secret Second Wife.* Blaine, WA: Hancock House Publishers, 2010.

Michelson, Charles. "Stage Robbers of the West." *Munsey's Magazine* 25 (July, 1901): 448–459.

Mihaljevich, Mike. "Eddie Foy: Clowning Through Lies?" *Wild West History Association Journal* 15 (March 2022): 66–71.

Miller, Nyle H., and Joseph W. Snell. *Why the West Was Wild: A Contemporary Look at the Antics of Some Highly Publicized Cowtown Personalities.* Topeka, KS: Kansas State Historical Society, 1963.

Molony, Janelle. "1864: More than Massacres." *The Annals of Wyoming* 93 (Autumn 2021): 30–47.

Monahan, Sherry. *Mrs. Earp: The Wives and Lovers of the Earp Brothers.* Guilford, CT: TwoDot, 2013.

Montana, Sybil. *Wyatt Earp's Missouri Legend, Including other Family History.* Springfield, MO: Sybil Montana, 2000.

Morey, Jeff. "Blaze Away! Doc Holliday vs. Everyone." *True West* 48 (Dec. 2001): 34–40.

Myers, John Myers. *Doc Holliday.* Boston: Little, Brown and Company, 1955.

Myers, Roger. "Between Wichita and Dodge: The Travels and Friends of Kate Elder." *Quarterly of the National Association for Outlaw and Lawman History* 31 (April–June 2007): 22–27.

Neider, Charles, ed. *The Autobiography of Mark Twain.* New York: Harper & Brothers, 1959.

Otero, Miguel Antonio. *My Life on the Frontier, 1864–1882.* New York: The Press of the Pioneers, 1935.

Palenske, Garner A. *Wyatt Earp in San Diego, Life After Tombstone.* Santa Ana, CA: Graphic Publishers, 2011.

Parsons, Chuck. *Clay Allison: Portrait of a Shootist.* Seagraves, TX: Pioneer Book Publishers, 1983.

The Past and Present of Warren County, Illinois. Chicago, IL: H. F. Kett & Co., 1877.

Pendleton, Albert S. Jr., and Susan McKey Thomas. "Doc Holliday's Georgia Background." *The Journal of Arizona History* 14 (Autumn 1973): 185–204.

———. *In Search of the Hollidays: The Story of Doc Holliday and His Holliday and McKey Families.* Valdosta, GA: Lowndes County Historical Society, 2008.

Portrait and Biographical Album of Warren County, Illinois. Chicago, IL: Chapman Brothers, 1886.

Reidhead, S. J. *Travesty: Frank Waters' Earp Agenda Exposed.* Roswell, NM: Jinglebob Press, 2005.

———, ed. *A Church for Helldorado: The 1882 Tombstone Diary of Endicott Peabody & the Building of St. Paul's Episcopal Church.* Roswell, NM: Jinglebob Press, 2006.

Roberts, Gary L. "Brothers of the Gun, Wyatt and Doc." *Wild West* 25 (Dec. 2012): 28–35.

———. *Doc Holliday: The Life and Legend.* New York: John Wiley & Sons, Inc., 2006.

Rogers, W. Lane, ed. *When All Roads Led to Tombstone: A Memoir by John Plesent Gray.* Boise, ID: Tamarack Books, 1998.

Root, O. E. *Root's Peoria City Directory, For 1870–71.* Peoria, IL: N. C. Nason, 1870.

———. *Root's Peoria City Directory, For 1872–73.* Peoria, IL: N. C. Nason, 1872.

Scott, Kim Allen. "Erroneous Ellsworth: Letters Help Prove That the Wyatt Earp–Ben Thompson Showdown Is a Tall Tale." *True West* 66 (Feb. 2019): 32–37.

The Seventeenth Annual Announcement of the Pennsylvania College of Dental Surgery. Philadelphia: W. B. Selheimer, 1872.

Shillingberg, Wm. B. *Dodge City: The Early Years, 1872–1886.* Norman: The Arthur H. Clark Company, 2009.

———. *Tombstone, A.T.: A History of Early Mining, Milling, and Mayhem.* Spokane, WA: The Arthur H. Clark Company, 1999.

———. *Wyatt Earp & the "Buntline Special" Myth.* Tucson, AZ: Blaine Publishing Company, 1976.

Silva, Lee A. *Wyatt Earp: A Biography of the Legend, Volume 1: The Cowtown Years.* Santa Ana, CA: Graphic Publishers, 2002.

Silva, Lee A., and Susan Leiser Silva. *Wyatt Earp: A Biography of the Legend, Volume II, Part 1: Tombstone Before the Earps.* Santa Ana, CA: Graphic Publishers, 2010.

Sitnina, Anastasia. "Becoming Doc: John Henry Holliday and His Classmates at the Pennsylvania College of Dental Surgery." *Wild West History Association Journal* 15 (Dec. 2022): 50–62.

"A Smoking Gun." *True West* 48 (July 2001): 42–43.

Souvenir History of Pella, Iowa. Pella, Iowa: The Booster Press, 1922.

Stephens, John Richard, ed. *Wyatt Earp Speaks! My Side of the O.K. Corral Shootout, Plus Interviews with Doc Holliday.* Cambria, CA: Fern Canyon Press, 1998.

Streeter, Floyd Benjamin. *Prairie Trails & Cow Towns: The Opening of the Old West,* NY: The Devin Adair Company, 1963.

Tanner, Karen Holliday. *Doc Holliday: A Family Portrait.* Norman: University of Oklahoma Press, 1998.

Taylor, Don. *The United States of America v. The "Cowboys."* Tombstone, AZ: Old West Research & Publishing, 2006.

Tefertiller, Casey. *Wyatt Earp: The Life Behind the Legend.* New York: John Wiley & Sons, Inc., 1997.

Traywick, Ben T. *Wyatt Earp: Angel of Death.* Honolulu, HI: Talei Publishers, Inc., 2007.

———, ed. *"Death's Doings in Tombstone."* Tombstone, AZ: Red Marie's Books, 2002.

——— *Historical Documents and Photographs of Tombstone.* Tombstone, AZ: Red Marie's Bookstore, 1994.

Turner, Alford E., ed. *The Earps Talk.* College Station, TX: Creative Publishing Company, 1980.

———, ed. *The O.K. Corral Inquest.* College Station, TX: Creative Publishing Company, 1981.

Twain, Mark. *Mark Twain's Autobiography.* 2 vols. New York: Harper & Brothers, 1924.

Urban, William. "The Birthplace of Wyatt Earp." *Western Illinois Regional Studies* 12 (Spring 1989): 20–43.

———. "Nicholas Earp's Iowa Land," published online at https://department.monm.edu/history/urban/wyatt_earp/nicholas_earp_iowa_lands.htm.

———. "Wyatt Earp's Father." *True West* 36 (May 1989): 30–39.

———. "Wyatt Earp was Born Here: Monmouth and the Earps, 1845–1859." *Western Illinois Regional Studies* 3 (Fall 1980): 154–167.

———. "The People Versus Nicholas P. Earp." *Illinois Historical Journal* 90 (Autumn 1997): 173–190.

Vestal, Stanley. *Dodge City: Queen of the Cowtowns.* London: Peter Nevill, 1955.

Walling, Emma, compiler. *John "Doc" Holliday, Colorado Trials and Triumphs.* Snow mass, CO: published by the author, n.d.

Waters, Frank. *The Colorado.* New York: Rinehart & Company, 1946.

———. *The Earp Brothers of Tombstone: The Story of Mrs. Virgil Earp.* New York: Clarkson N. Potter, Inc., 1960.

Wilcox, Victoria. *The World of Doc Holliday, History and Historic Images.* Guilford, CT: Twodot, 2021.

Wise, John S. *Recollections of Thirteen Presidents*. New York: Doubleday, Page & Co., 1906.

Wood, L. Curtise. *Dynamics of Faith: Wichita 1870–1897*. Wichita, KA: The Center for Management Development, College of Business Administration, Wichita State University, 1969.

Wright, Robert M. *Dodge City, the Cowboy Capital and the Great Southwest in the Days of the Wild Indian, the Buffalo, the Cowboy, Dance Halls, Gambling Halls and Bad Men*. Wichita, KS: Wichita Eagle Press, 1913.

Young, Roy B. *Cochise County Cowboy War: A Cast of Characters*. Apache, OK: Young & Sons Enterprises, 1999.

——."George Hearst—Wyatt Earp: Another 'Wyatt Whopper'?" *Wild West History Association Journal* 16 (March 2023): 39–73.

——. *Newton Jasper Earp: Mystery Brother of the Famous "Fighting Earps."* Apache, OK: Young & Sons Enterprises, 2022.

——. *Pete Spence: "Audacious Artist in Crime."* Apache, OK: Young & Sons Enterprises, 2000.

——. "Who Killed Morgan Earp? 'The Atrocious Assassins.'" *Wild West History Association Journal* 13 (Dec. 2020): 7–44.

——. Gary L. Roberts, and Casey Tefertiller, eds. *A Wyatt Earp Anthology: Long May His Story Be Told*. Denton, TX: University of North Texas Press, 2019.

NEWSPAPERS

The Alton Weekly Courier (IL)

Albuquerque Evening Review (NM)

Albuquerque Morning Journal (NM)

The Anaconda Standard (MT)

Arizona Daily Star (Tucson)

The Arizona Republican (Phoenix)

The Arizona Silver Belt (Globe, AZ)

Arizona Weekly Enterprise (Florence, AZ)

Arizona Weekly Star (Tucson)

The Aspen Daily Times (CO)

The Atchison Daily Champion (KS)

The Atchison Weekly Champion (KS)

The Atlanta Constitution (GA)

Augusta Advance (KS)

The Avalanche (Carbondale, CO)

The Biblical Recorder (Raleigh, NC)

The Black Hills Daily Pioneer (Deadwood, SD)

The Black Hills Pioneer (Deadwood, SD)
Black Hills Weekly Times (Deadwood, SD)
The Boliver Free Press (MO)
The Boston Globe (MA)
The Brooklyn Daily Times (NY)
The Buffalo Commercial (NY)
Burlington Hawk-Eye (IA)
The Butte Daily Miner (MT)
Carbonate Chronicle (Leadville, CO)
Cheyenne Daily Leader (WY)
The Cheyenne Daily News (WY)
Chicago Tribune (IL)
The Chronicle and Constitutionalist (Augusta, GA)
Cincinnati Enquirer (OH)
Colorado Daily Chieftain (Pueblo)
Colorado Weekly Chieftain (Pueblo)
The Commonwealth (Topeka, KS)
The Constitutionalist (Augusta, GA)
Daily Arizona Citizen (Tucson)
Daily Arkansas Gazette (Little Rock)
Daily Democratic Statesman (Austin, TX)
Daily Evening Bulletin (San Francisco)
The Daily Examiner (San Francisco)
Daily Fort Worth Democrat (TX)
The Daily Gate City (Keokuk, IA)
Daily Gazette (Las Vegas, NM)
The Daily Mail (Wellington, KS)
The Daily Miner (Butte, MT)
Daily National Democrat (Peoria, IL)
The Daily Nebraska State Journal (Lincoln)
Daily News-Democrat (Gunnison, CO)
The Daily Nonpareil (Council Bluffs, IA)
Daily Rocky Mountain News (Denver, CO)
Daily Times (Denver, CO)
The Daily Town Talk (Butte, MT)
Dallas Daily Commercial (TX)
The Dallas Daily Herald (TX)
The Dallas Weekly Herald (TX)
The Deadwood Daily Pioneer (SD)
The Denver Republican (CO)

Denver Tribune (CO)

Denver Tribune-Republican (CO)

Dodge City Times (KS)

El Paso Times (TX)

Ellis County Star (Hays City, KS)

Ellsworth Reporter (KS)

The Enterprise and Chronicle (Trinidad and El Moro, CO)

The Evening Express (Los Angeles)

The Examiner (San Francisco)

Field and Farm (Denver, CO)

Ford County Globe (Dodge City, KS)

The Galveston Daily News (TX)

The Graphic: An Illustrated Weekly Newspaper (London, England)

The Great Bend Register (KS)

The Hutchinson Examiner (KS)

Kansas City Daily Journal (MO)

The Kansas City Evening Star (MO)

The Kansas City Star (MO)

The Kansas City Times (MO)

Las Vegas Daily Gazette (NM)

Las Vegas Daily Optic (NM)

Las Vegas Gazette (NM)

The Leadville Democrat (CO)

Leadville Evening Chronicle (CO)

The Leadville Herald (CO)

Leavenworth Daily Commercial (KS)

The Leavenworth Daily Times (KS)

The Leavenworth Weekly Times (KS)

The Leeds Mercury (Leeds, England)

Los Angeles Daily Herald (CA)

Los Angeles Daily Times (CA)

Los Angeles Times (CA)

The Missouri Republican (St. Louis)

National Police Gazette (NY)

The Nebraska Republican (Omaha, NE)

New Oregon Plain Dealer (IA)

The New York Times (NY)

New York Tribune (NY)

Oakland Daily Evening Tribune (CA)

The Omaha Daily Bee (NE)

Peoria Daily Transcript (IL)

The Phoenix Herald (AZ)

The Pioche Weekly Record (NV)

Rocky Mountain News (CO)

Sacramento Daily Record-Union (CA)

The St. Johns Herald (St. Johns, AZ)

St. Louis Globe-Democrat (MO)

St. Louis Post-Dispatch (MO)

The Salt Lake Herald (UT)

San Bernardino Daily Sun (CA)

The San Francisco Call (CA)

Savanah Morning News; later *The Morning News* (Savannah, GA)

Semi-Weekly Miner (Butte, MT)

Silver World (Lake City, CO)

The Solid Muldoon (Ouray, CO)

South-West Missourian (Lamar, MO)

The Stockton Daily Evening Mail (CA)

The Sumner County Press (Wellington, KS)

The Sun (Baltimore, MD)

The Sun (NY)

The Sun (San Diego, CA)

The Sunday Chronicle (San Francisco, CA)

Tombstone Daily Nugget (AZ)

Tombstone Epitaph (AZ)

Tombstone Weekly Epitaph (AZ)

Topeka Daily Blade (KS)

The Topeka Daily Capital (KS)

Topeka Weekly Blade (KS)

Tri-Weekly Herald (Marshall, TX)

Ute Chief (Glenwood Springs, CO)

The Valdosta Times (GA)

The Vallejo Evening Chronicle (Vallejo, CA)

The Van Buren Press (Van Buren, AR)

The Washington Post (Washington, DC)

The Weekly Arizona Miner (Prescott)

The Weekly Bee (Sacramento, CA)

Weekly New Mexican (Santa Fe)

The Weekly Ottumwa Courier (IA)

Weekly Rocky Mountain News (CO)

West Schuylkill Press (Tremont, PA)

The Western Grazier (Wilcannia New South Wales, Australia)
The Wichita Daily Beacon (KS)
The Wichita Eagle (KS)
The Wichita Herald (KS)
The Wichita Weekly Beacon (KS)

NOTES

ABBREVIATIONS

AHS: Arizona Historical Society, Tucson, Arizona
UA: University of Arizona Libraries Special Collections, Tucson, Arizona

ONE: THE WAY WEST

1 **"And the world began":** Charles Badger Clark Jr., "The Westerner," *Sun and Saddle Leather* (Boston: Richard G. Badger, 1915), 55.

2 **"I am getting tired of it all":** Wyatt Earp to Walter Noble Burns, Vidal, CA, March 15, 1927, Walter Noble Burns Papers, box 3, folder 2, UA.

2 **"nasty and ugly article":** Josephine Earp to William S. Hart, Vidal, CA, March 22, 1922, folder 1, Earp Family Papers, MS 238, AHS. The offending article was "Lurid Trails Are Left by Olden-Day Bandits," *Los Angeles Times*, March 12, 1922.

2 **came to the old lawman's defense:** "Bill Hart Sets Us Right About Bandit Story," *Los Angeles Times*, March 16, 1922.

2 **"It does beat the band":** Wyatt Earp to William S. Hart, Los Angeles, CA, Nov. 18, 1924, folder 1, Earp Family Papers.

3 **"first and only authentic story":** John Flood notes, group 3, box 1, Josephine Earp Collection, Tombstone Courthouse State Historic Park, Tombstone, AZ.

3 **truth, correctness, and vindication:** John Henry Flood Jr., "Wyatt Earp," undated typescript, ii, Ford County Historical Society, Dodge City, Kansas.

3 **soldiering south of the Rio Grande:** For Nicholas Earp's brief military career, see William Urban, "Wyatt Earp's Father," *True West* 36 (May 1989): 32; and William

Urban, "Wyatt Earp Was Born Here: Monmouth and the Earps. 1845–1859," *Western Illinois Regional Studies* 3 (Fall 1980): 158–9. Nicholas Earp mentioned the kick to the groin in his 1877 pension application. See Mrs. William Irvine, comp., *Data on the Earp Family*, installment for July 30, 1958, 37.

3 **sold the house for $300:** Urban, "Wyatt Earp Was Born," 165 n. 24.

4 **"considerable pecuniary means":** "The Pilgrim Hollanders in Iowa," *The Biblical Recorder* (Raleigh, NC), August 19, 1848. See also "Interesting Dutch Colony," *The Sun* (Baltimore, MD), Feb. 22, 1848.

4 **coopering and farming:** 1850 US census for Lake Prairie Township, Marion County, Illinois.

4 **flatboat captain:** Earp's employer was the Pella firm of Bousquet, Wolters & Smeenk. Reminiscence of P.H. Bousquet in Tacitus Hussey, "History of Steamboating on the Des Moines River, From 1837 to 1862," *Annals of Iowa* 4 (April 1900): 348–49.

4 **"love for the soil":** As quoted in Stuart N. Lake, *Wyatt Earp, Frontier Marshal* (New York: Houghton Mifflin Company, 1931), 7. In a 2013 biography of Wyatt Earp, the author writes that the Earps were "either tenant farmers or squatters" in Iowa. He somehow missed or ignored the valuation placed upon Nicholas Earp's Iowa real estate in the 1850 US census for Marion County. See Andrew C. Isenberg, *Wyatt Earp: A Vigilante Life* (New York: Hill and Wang, 2013), 23.

4 **"Even the most thoughtful":** *The History of Marion County, Iowa, Containing a History of the County, Its Cities, Towns, &c.* (Des Moines: Union Historical Company, 1881), 321.

4 **160 acres of bounty land:** Military Warrant 15806, available online at https://glorecords.blm.gov/details/patent/default.aspx?accession=1097-289&docClass=MW&sid=4veurjol.wtb.

4 **Date of his trip is uncertain:** Nicholas Earp's obituary states he first went to California in 1849. He told the San Bernardino Society of California Pioneers it was 1851. And Wyatt Earp biographer Stuart Lake offers us "the early fifties." *San Bernardino Daily Sun*, Feb. 15, 1907; Nicholas R. Cataldo, "Father of the 'Fighting Earps,'" *Wild West* 29 (Oct. 2016): 54; and Lake, *Wyatt Earp*, 8–9.

4 **sold his Iowa land:** William Urban, "Nicholas Earp's Iowa Land," published online at https://department.monm.edu/history/urban/wyatt_earp/nicholas_earp_iowa_lands.htm.

5 **purchased three lots in town:** William Urban, "The Birthplace of Wyatt Earp," *Western Illinois Regional Studies* 12 (Spring 1989): 41 n. 18.

5 **ran for the office of constable:** William Urban, "The People Versus Nicholas P. Earp," *Illinois Historical Journal* 90 (Autumn 1997): 181–82; and *Galesburg, Monmouth, Knoxville and Abingdon Directories* (Chicago: Henry N. McEvoy, 1857), 108.

5 **doing a "small business":** Illinois, Vol. 220, p. 110, R.G. Dun & Co. credit report volumes, Baker Library, Harvard Business School, Boston, MA.

5 **Warren chapter of Masons:** Nelson D. Elwood, *Proceedings of the Grand Royal Arch Chapter of the State of Illinois at Their Ninth Annual Grand Convocation* (Chicago: Steam Presses of Chas. Scott & Co., 1858), 67.

5 **charged with selling liquor:** Urban, "The People Versus Nicholas P. Earp," 183.

5 **"The roudyism, and drunkenness":** *Monmouth Review*, Feb. 12, 1858, as quoted in Ibid., 175.

5 **"not worth anything":** Illinois, Vol. 220, p. 110, R.G. Dun & Co. credit report volumes.

5 **returned to Pella, Iowa:** Urban, "Nicholas Earp's Iowa Land." It's uncertain if Newton Earp, then age 22, was still part of the Earp household in Monmouth in 1859.

6 **Nicholas helped to recruit:** Nicholas Earp obituary, *San Bernardino Daily Sun*, Feb. 15, 1907; Flood, "Wyatt Earp," 11; and Lake, *Wyatt Earp*, 9.

6 **Pella's town marshal:** *Souvenir History of Pella, Iowa* (Pella, IA: The Booster Press, 1922), 243.

6 **an acre field:** Flood, "Wyatt Earp," 9. Stuart Lake quotes Wyatt as saying that the cornfield spanned eighty acres (equaling more than sixty football fields), which is extremely far-fetched.

6 **"I gained my lifelong sympathy":** As quoted in Lake, *Wyatt Earp*, 9.

6 **Wyatt started for Ottumwa:** Wyatt Earp narrative as given to John Flood, typescript, Josephine Earp Collection, group 3, box 1 (hereafter cited as Wyatt Earp narrative); Flood, "Wyatt Earp," 13–18; and Lake, *Wyatt Earp*, 9–10. The unvarnished, just-the-facts narrative presented in the typescript pages in the Josephine Earp Collection are undoubtedly the closest to Wyatt Earp's actual recollections. Earp's attempt to join the army is embellished considerably in Flood's "Wyatt Earp," and it differs in some details with Lake. In "Wyatt Earp," Flood has Wyatt boarding a train at Pella, but the Des Moines Valley Railroad didn't reach Pella until December 1864. The closest railhead between Pella and Ottumwa in 1862 was at Eddyville. See the advertisement for the Keokuk, Ft. Des Moines, and Minnesota Rail Road in *The Daily Gate City* (Keokuk, IA), Feb. 10, 1862.

7 **Republican John C. Fremont:** A letter from Monmouth published in *The Alton Weekly Courier* (IL), Oct. 1, 1856, makes prominent mention of Nicholas Earp's switch from the Democrats to Fremont.

7 **"It was begun with":** "Speech of Hon. Thomas M. Seymour," *New Oregon Plain Dealer* (IA), Jan. 15, 1864.

7 **an ingrained racist bias:** Flood, "Wyatt Earp," 20.

8 **A scuffle broke out:** "A Rebellion by the Copperheads of Marion County," *The Weekly Ottumwa Courier* (IA), Jan. 7, 1864; and *The History of Marion County, Iowa*, 422.

8 **Nicholas resigned:** *Souvenir History of Pella*, 243.

8 **horse-drawn carriage:** Wyatt Earp narrative.

8 **"It was a cumbersome weapon":** As quoted in Lake, *Wyatt Earp*, 11.

9 **some forty wagons:** The exact size of the Pella train varies depending on the source. Wyatt said there were forty or fifty wagons, with emigrants numbering 125 men, plus wives and children. A grandson of one of the emigrants said that the wagon train initially counted thirty people. Scholar Janelle Molony writes that the train had twenty wagons "by mid-June." See Nicholas R. Cataldo, "The Rousseau Diary and the Earp Wagon Train to San Bernardino, 1864," *Overland Journal* 33 (Fall 2015): 117; and Janelle Molony, "1864: More than Massacres," *The Annals of Wyoming* 93 (Autumn 2021): 41 n. 61.

9 **more than five thousand teams:** *The Nebraska Republican* (Omaha), June 3, 1864.

9 **"Every man was for his gun":** Diary of Mrs. James Rousseau, typescript, July 12, 1864, State Historical Society of Iowa, Des Moines.

9 **shouted at Wyatt and Jim:** Wyatt Earp narrative.

10 **"We are in the most dangerous part":** Rousseau diary, July 14, 1864.

10 **Because of Wyatt:** Wyatt Earp narrative.

10 **"we commenced popping away":** Abstract of letter of Nicholas Earp, April 1865, in Don Chaput, *The Earp Papers: In a Brother's Image* (Encampment, WY: Affiliated Writers of America, 1994), 16.

10 **killing one of the attackers:** Wyatt Earp narrative. Neither Nicholas Earp nor Sarah Rousseau mention the death of a warrior. However, Nicholas believed that he may have wounded one or, rather, a white man who was riding with the warriors. Nicholas said the white man fell to one side of his horse after he shot at him. However, the man regained his saddle and raced away. Wyatt, remembering decades later, likely imagined the man had been killed. See Ibid.

10 **"kill every Indian":** Rousseau diary, July 20, 1864.

11 **lieutenant from Griffin:** Holliday recounted his Mexican War service in "Campaign Reminiscences," *The Morning News* (Savannah, GA), April 22, 1885. See also Albert S. Pendleton and Susan McKey Thomas, *In Search of the Hollidays: The Story of Doc Holliday and His Holliday and McKey Families* (Valdosta, GA: Lowndes County Historical Society, 2008), 6.

11 **peddler's license:** "Description of Pedlers Licensed," *The Constitutionalist* (Augusta, GA), May 14, 1840.

11 **Holliday family trait:** "Recollections of Mary Cowperthwaite Fulton Holliday Concerning John Henry Holliday, D.D.S.," collected and transcribed by Carl B. Olson, 1835–1940, typescript, Karen Holliday Tanner Collection, The Haley Memorial Library and Research Center, Midland, Texas. Hereafter cited as Recollections of Mary Holliday.

11 **"no means":** Georgia, Vol. 19, p. 187, R.G. Dun & Co. credit report volumes.

11 **Francisco Hidalgo:** Pendleton and Thomas, *In Search of the Hollidays*, 6–8; and 1850 US census for District No. 68, Pike County, Georgia.

12 **born with a cleft palate:** Recollections of Mary Holliday.

12 **pioneer in the use of anesthesia:** "Death of Dr. Crawford W. Long," *The Chronicle and Constitutionalist* (Augusta, GA), June 18, 1878; and M. Madden, "Crawford Long." New Georgia Encyclopedia, last modified Oct. 31, 2018, https://www.georgiaencyclo pedia.org/articles/science-medicine/crawford-long-1815-1878/.

12 **mild speech impediment:** Recollections of Mary Holliday.

12 **"quiet, well-mannered child":** Ibid.

12 **he owned six:** Henry B. Holliday is enumerated as a slave owner in the 1850 US Slave Schedule for District No. 68, Pike County, Georgia, and the 1860 US Slave Schedule for District No. 1001, Spaulding County, Georgia.

12 **owned thirteen:** John Stiles Holliday in the 1860 US Slave Schedule for Fayette County, Georgia.

12 **"I was not aware":** Charles Neider, ed. *The Autobiography of Mark Twain* (New York: Harper & Brothers, 1959), 6.

12 **"Slavery was at the bottom":** John S. Wise, *Recollections of Thirteen Presidents* (New York: Doubleday, Page & Co., 1906), 70.

13 **"a good blood-letting":** Ibid., 72.

13 **"Chronic Diarrhea":** Surgeon's report for Henry Holliday as quoted in Pendleton and Thomas, *In Search of the Hollidays*, 9.

13 **"deeply anxious":** Facsimile of Alice Jane Holliday 1866 obituary as reproduced in Ibid., 12.

NOTES

14 **twelve-month mourning period:** *The Manners That Win, Compiled from the Latest Authorities* (Minneapolis, MN: Buckeye Publishing Co., 1879), 249.

14 **"mischievous but not mean":** "'Doc' Holliday," *The Morning News* (Savannah, GA), Jan. 23, 1896.

14 **take up dentistry:** Recollections of Mary Holliday.

14 **$100 per course:** *The Seventeenth Annual Announcement of the Pennsylvania College of Dental Surgery* (Philadelphia: W. B. Selheimer, 1872), 10. See also Anastasia Sitnina, "Becoming Doc: John Henry Holliday and his Classmates at the Pennsylvania College of Dental Surgery," *Wild West History Association Journal* 15 (Dec. 2022): 50–53.

14 **"Diseases of the Teeth":** Ibid., 13.

14 **carte de visite photograph:** The original carte de visite sold at auction in 2019 for $50,000. See https://auctions.oldwestevents.com/lots/view/1-1JFMK8/the-famous -signed-dental-school-cdv-of-doc-holliday. It's currently part of the collections of William I. Koch, Palm Beach, Florida.

15 **By the summer of 1872:** Holliday biographers Gary Roberts and Victoria Wilcox believe that John Henry Holliday made a quick trip to St. Louis in the spring of 1872, where he practiced dentistry for two or three months in the office of a fellow dental school graduate. However, the only evidence suggesting such a scenario are the recollections of Doc Holliday's lover, Big Nose Kate (aka Mary K. Cummings, Kate Elder, Kate Fisher, and Mária Horony), who claimed to have first met (and married!) Holliday in St. Louis. While Kate's recollections can be an important source when used with caution, they are filled with errors, fabrications, and rants against Wyatt Earp. To date, no contemporary evidence has surfaced documenting Holliday's presence in St. Louis in 1872. See Gary L. Roberts, *Doc Holliday: The Life and Legend* (New York: John Wiley & Sons, Inc., 2006), 51–53; Victoria Wilcox, *The World of Doc Holliday* (Guilford, CT: Twodot, 2021), 22 and 28–29; Mary K. Cummings Recollections, typescript by Anton Mazzonovich, Kevin Mulkins collection, Tucson, Arizona (hereafter cited as Mary K. Cummings Recollections); and A. W. Bork and Glenn G. Boyer, eds., "The O.K. Corral Fight at Tombstone: A Footnote by Kate Elder," *Arizona and the West* 19 (Spring 1977): 65–84.

15 **dentist Arthur C. Ford:** "Card" of Arthur C. Ford, D.D.S. *The Atlanta Constitution*, July 26, 1872.

15 **John Stiles confirmed:** Recollections of Mary Holliday.

15 **A macabre joke:** *The Atlanta Constitution*, Nov. 27, 1872.

16 **his son to try Texas:** Recollections of Mary Holliday.

16 **The most well-known version:** W. B. "Bat" Masterson, "Famous Gun Fighters of the Western Frontier," *The Washington Post* (Washington, DC), May 5, 1907. Hereafter cited as Masterson, *Doc Holliday*.

17 **slightly different versions:** See Pendleton and Thomas, *In Search of the Hollidays*, 33–34; and Roberts, *Doc Holliday*, 65–67. An obituary for Holliday published in Butte, Montana, in 1887, stated that when Doc was eighteen, "he shot one of his father's Negroes in a quarrel. For this he had to leave home, and was next heard of as a student of dental surgery." While this statement differs significantly from the other known versions of the incident, it tells us that it was somewhat common knowledge that Doc was involved in some kind of shooting involving one or more African Americans before he left Georgia. *Semi-Weekly Miner* (Butte, MT), Nov. 23, 1887.

17 **fired over the heads:** Lillian McKay account as reported in J. F. DeLacy to Robert N. Mullin, Havana, Florida, Jan. 9, 1949, box 10, folder 48, Stuart N. Lake Papers, The Huntington Library, San Marino, CA.

TWO: THE PEORIA BUMMER AND THE DISSIPATED DENTIST

18 **Arella Sutherland:** There is much confusion on the correct spelling of Miss Sutherland's first name. It appears in the 1850, 1860, and 1870 US censuses as Aurilla, Arella, and Rilla. The 1870 Barton County marriage record looks to read Urilla. I've chosen to use Arella, which is a form of the name Aurelia and is said to mean "angel."

18 **"loyal to the young love":** Lake, *Wyatt Earp*, 29.

18 **Wyatt was tightlipped:** When Stuart Lake began research for his Wyatt Earp biography, Wyatt wrote his first cousin, George W. Earp, and instructed him to say nothing to Lake about the Earp family's time in Lamar. Glenn G. Boyer, *Suppressed Murder of Wyatt Earp* (San Antonio, TX: Historical Research Associates, 1997), 123 n. 25.

19 **owned a piece of land:** Pete McArdle, "Grave Doubts: Where Is Wyatt Earp's First Wife Buried? Part One," *Wild West History Association Journal* 6 (April 2013): 49.

19 **bakery and small grocery:** "A Look Around Town," *South-West Missourian* (Lamar), Feb. 24, 1870. Nicholas Earp's occupation is given as grocer in the 1870 US census for the Lamar Township.

19 **appointed Wyatt Earp:** Barton County Court Records, Vol. A, 1866–1871, microfilm US WPA-HRS, Missouri, roll 106, State Historical Society of Missouri, Columbia.

20 **"law-breakers had better look out":** *South-West Missourian* (Lamar), March 3, 1870.

20 **in a beautiful country:** "Description of Barton County," South-West Missourian (Lamar), May 12, 1870.

20 **levied upon circuses:** A copy of this ordinance, marked "Exhibit B," is found in State of Missouri ex rel. v. Wyatt S. Earp et al., Petition & Affidavit, March 14, 1871, Circuit Court's Office, Barton County Courthouse, Lamar, Missouri.

20 **bought a house:** Wyatt Earp deed record dated Aug. 29, 1870, photocopy on display at the Barton County Historical Society, Lamar, Missouri.

20 **Wyatt won with 137 votes:** *South-West Missourian* (Lamar), Nov. 17, 1870.

20 **Arella Earp died:** Josephine Earp, in her quasi-autobiography, stated that Wyatt's first wife died following childbirth, and that "her death and that of their child [was] no doubt due to the effects of typhus." Josephine (Sadie) Earp, "She Married Wyatt Earp," typescript, box 1, folder 5, Glenn Boyer Wyatt Earp Collection, MS 752, UA. No obituary for Arella is found in the *South-West Missourian* or any other newspaper, which is puzzling. Earp family tradition is quite strong that she died before Wyatt abandoned Lamar, but historian Pete McArdle, noting the lack of documentation (including the absence of a contemporary tombstone), offers the possibility that Arella may not have died in Lamar, nor in 1870. Pete McArdle, "Grave Doubts: Where Is Wyatt Earp's First Wife Buried? Part Three," *Wild West History Association Journal* 6 (Oct. 2013): 71. For Earp family recollections of Arella's death, see Everett M. Earp comments to Lake, box 3, folder 34, Stuart N. Lake Papers; Everett M. Earp letter, Nov. 4, 1946, quoted in Irvine, comp., *Data on the Earp Family*, installment for Jan. 15,

1959, 75; and George W. Earp letter, n.d., quoted in *Data on the Earp Family*, installment for Jan. 15, 1958, 97.

20 **Sold his house:** Earp deed record dated Nov. 7, 1870, photocopy on display at the Barton County Historical Society.

20 **filed for a judgment:** State of Missouri ex rel. v. Wyatt S. Earp. Wyatt was also hit with a lawsuit brought by James Cromwell, a farmer, who claimed Wyatt, as constable, pocketed part of a judgment Cromwell had been ordered to pay. See James Cromwell v. Wyatt S. Earp, James Maupin, N. P. Earp, and J. D. Earp, Petition, March 31, 1871, Circuit Court's Office, Barton County Courthouse.

21 **lawsuits against him:** See Judgment in James Montgomery v. Nicholas P. Earp, Book B, 151, and Judgment in Derrick A. January, James F. Johnson, Howard J. Brother, and Leslie A. Moffet v. Nicholas P. Earp, Book B, 170–71, both in Barton County Circuit Court records (microfilm), Missouri State Archives, Jefferson City, Missouri.

22 **the sheriff sold their home:** "Sheriff's Sale," *South-West Missourian* (Lamar), Sept. 21, 1871.

22 **grave in the town cemetery:** Arella Earp is believed to have been buried in what is now known as East Side Cemetery, which was the only cemetery in Lamar in 1870. Everett M. Earp made a crude monument with a cross and placed it on her supposed grave sometime prior to his death in 1956, although he probably didn't know the grave's actual location. Based on local fantasy, a modern stone for Wyatt's wife was placed in the Howell Cemetery, south of Milford, Missouri (more than ten miles from Lamar), in 1994. "Grave of Wyatt Earp's first wife," Information Form, Historical Sites Survey, recorded by Mrs. Ed McKee, Aug. 1, 1960, Wyatt Earp Vertical File, State Historical Society of Missouri, Columbia; and McArdle, "Grave Doubts: Where Is Wyatt Earp's First Wife Buried? Part Three," 71.

22 **court documents disclose:** These documents from the US Court of the Western District of Arkansas are available online through Ancestry.com under Fort Smith, Arkansas, US, Criminal Case Files, 1866–1900. They are excerpted in Ed Bartholomew, *Wyatt Earp, 1848 to 1880: The Untold Story* (Toyahvale, TX: Frontier Book Company, 1963), 33–41; and Roy B. Young, "Wyatt Earp, Outlaw of the Cherokee Nation," in Roy B. Young, Gary L. Roberts, and Casey Tefertiller, eds., *A Wyatt Earp Anthology: Long May His Story Be Told* (Denton, TX: University of North Texas Press, 2019), 103–6.

23 **three prisoners escape:** "Come to Grief," *South-West Missourian* (Lamar), June 16, 1870.

23 **an abandoned building:** This building seems to have been a stone house formerly occupied by a dry goods firm. The house "fell in" on November 16, 1869. *The Boliver Free Press* (MO), Dec. 2, 1869.

23 **"it is apparent":** "Jail Delivery," *The Van Buren Press* (Van Buren, AR), May 9, 1871. See also "State News," *Daily Arkansas Gazette* (Little Rock), May 14, 1871.

24 **"one old fellow":** Wyatt Earp as quoted in "Frontier Tales," *Field and Farm* (Denver, CO), June 23, 1894.

25 **"[B]uyers of hides":** As quoted in Lake, *Wyatt Earp*, 35.

25 **$2,500 the first winter:** Bat Masterson's brother Tom stated in 1934 that, "Bat and Wyatt first came together on the Salt Fork of the Arkansas, west of here, in 1872, when they were both hunting buffaloes there." "Ellsworth's Ship Prompts Brothers of Bat Masterson to Recall Exploits of Wyatt Earp," *The Kansas City Star* (MO), Jan. 21, 1934.

26 **steady job as a bartender:** O. E. Root, *Root's Peoria City Directory, for 1870-71* (Peoria, IL: N. C. Nason, 1870), 72.

26 **five million gallons:** *Chicago Tribune*, March 20, 1873.

26 **"root and branch":** "Energetic Raids," *The Missouri Republican* (St. Louis), Jan. 20, 1872.

26 **A January 13 report:** "Raid on Houses of Prostitution," *Chicago Tribune*, Jan. 15, 1872.

26 **Peoria Daily Transcript tells us:** Feb. 27, 1872, issue, as quoted in Young, "Wyatt Earp, Outlaw of the Cherokee Nation," 108. The original police complaints are reproduced in E. C. (Ted) Meyers, *Mattie: Wyatt Earp's Secret Second Wife* (Blaine, WA: Hancock House Publishers, 2010), 237–8.

26 **"keeping and being found":** As quoted in Ibid., 109.

26 **same dwelling as Madam Haspel:** O. E. Root, *Root's Peoria City Directory, For 1872–73* (Peoria, IL: N. C. Nason, 1872), 81 and 104. Haspel's name is spelled Haspill in the directory.

26 **the 1870 US census:** In the fifty-two pages of the 1870 census comprising Peoria's Fourth Ward, four brothels operated, totaling just twelve prostitutes. A brothel in the Sixth Ward employed eleven prostitutes.

27 **"that hotbed of iniquity":** *Peoria Daily Transcript*, May 11, 1872, as quoted in Young, "Wyatt Earp, Outlaw of the Cherokee Nation," 109.

27 **"They were the quietest set":** *Daily National Democrat* (Peoria, IL), Sept. 10, 1872, as quoted in Roger Jay, "The Peoria Bummer: Wyatt Earp's Lost Year," in *A Wyatt Earp Anthology*, 119.

27 **daughter of Jane Haspel:** Jay, "The Peoria Bummer," 119–20.

27 **"People very seldom":** Deposition of Louis V. Leese, John B. Wright Papers, MS 1123, AHS.

28 **recommended by an Atlanta:** Recollections of Mary Holliday.

28 **best set of teeth:** "The Fair," *The Dallas Daily Herald*, Oct. 4, 1873.

28 **"a typical frontier town":** Masterson, Doc Holliday.

28 **town was overly blessed:** "Can anyone tell how many keno saloons, gambling hells, and bar rooms Dallas boasts of? Is one hundred and fifty a small estimate?" *The Dallas Daily Herald*, Dec. 31, 1874.

28 **"I attended the Methodist Church":** As quoted in "A Man of Sand," *Daily News-Democrat* (Gunnison, CO), June 18, 1882.

28 **"hectic Georgian":** Masterson, Doc Holliday.

29 **"betting at a Keno Bank":** The State of Texas v. Dr. Holliday, No. 2236, Dallas County, Court Minutes, photocopy in Karen Holliday Tanner and John D. Tanner, Jr. Papers, WH2486, Western History Collection, The Denver Public Library.

29 **put out his dentist sign:** John Flood notes, Josephine Earp Collection, group 3, box 1.

29 **two dentists already served:** Roberts, *Doc Holliday*, 72.

29 **"The cheerful note":** *The Dallas Weekly Herald*, Jan. 2, 1875.

30 **appeared before a judge:** The State of Texas v. J. H. Holliday, No. 2643, Dallas County, Court Minutes, photocopy in Tanner Papers.

30 **arrested twice:** Roberts, *Doc Holliday*, 432 n. 72; Karen Holliday Tanner, *Doc Holliday: A Family Portrait* (Norman: University of Oklahoma Press, 1998), 96–97; and Shackelford County, Minutes of the District Court, photocopies in Tanner Papers.

30 **grand jury indicted:** "State News," *The Galveston Daily News*, July 1, 1875.

30 **"beautiful, progressive"**: "To the Rocky Mountains," *New York Tribune*, June 10, 1875.

31 **"[I]t is almost impossible"**: "Case's Council," *Daily Rocky Mountain News* (Denver, CO), January 30, 1874.

31 **employment as a dealer:** Holliday told a reporter for the *Denver Republican* that he was "dealing for Charley Foster, in Babbitt's house, where Ed. Chase is now located." However, the reporter garbled what Doc said. John A. Babb's Canterbury was at 357 Blake, which is where Chase was operating at the time of Holliday's interview. "Awful Arizona," *The Denver Republican*, May 22, 1882, as reprinted in Emma Walling, compiler, *John "Doc" Holliday, Colorado Trials and Triumphs* (Snowmass, CO: published by the author, n.d.), 13.

31 **the Canterbury:** Babb opened the Canterbury for business on March 4, 1874, stating that it would be "kept in first-class order." The *Daily Times* (Denver, CO) described his saloon a year later as "a dive on Blake Street." See *Daily Rocky Mountain News* (Denver, CO), March 4, 1874; and "Lost His Money," *Daily Times* (Denver, CO), April 8, 1875.

31 **frequently in court:** "Waiter Girls," *Daily Rocky Mountain News* (Denver, CO), April 19, 1874; "Couldn't Get a License," *Daily Times* (Denver, CO), March 5, 1875, and "Arrests," *Daily Times*, May 10, 1875.

31 **license was revoked:** *Daily Times* (Denver, CO), February 11, 1875.

31 **"Imagine, if you can":** "The Hoodlums of Denver," *Weekly Rocky Mountain News*, Feb. 24, 1875.

32 **alias: Tom Mackey:** *The Denver Republican*, Dec. 25, 1887, as reprinted in Walling, *John "Doc" Holliday*, 52. The name T. S. McKey appears in two lists of uncalled for letters at the Denver post office in 1876, and some historians have assumed that this was Doc using his alias. I find this to be wishful thinking. "Advertised Letters," *Daily Rocky Mountain News* (Denver, CO), Sept. 29, 1876, and "Advertised Letters," *Weekly Rocky Mountain News* (Denver, CO), Dec. 6, 1876.

32 **knife to Ryan's neck:** In an 1886 interview, Bat Masterson claimed that Doc actually killed Ryan. Masterson would revise his story in 1907 to say that Doc "stabbed Bud Ryan in a frightful manner." Wyatt Earp, in a 1926 interview with John Flood, said that Doc cut Ryan in the face, but one has to consider that Wyatt may have gotten his information from reading Masterson's tales. Finally, Doc's former lover, Kate Elder, stated that, "He did not cut up anyone in Denver with a knife." "Doc Holliday's Career," *The Boston Globe*, Aug. 4, 1886; Masterson, Doc Holliday; John Flood interview notes with Wyatt Earp, Sept. 15, 1926, reproduced in *Wyatt Earp, Tombstone, & the West from the Collections of John D. Gilchriese, Auction 10A, Part 1* (San Francisco: John's Western Gallery, 2004), 71; and Mary K. Cummings Recollections.

32 **Neither the names:** Bud (also Budd) Ryan was a real person, and indeed a gambler, but his first appearance in the Denver newspapers doesn't come until 1880. "A Raid on the Dens," *Rocky Mountain News* (Denver, CO), Jan. 23, 1880.

32 **Doc Holliday lore:** See Lake, *Wyatt Earp*, 196; Roberts, *Doc Holliday*, 77; and Tanner, *Doc Holliday*, 261 n. 9.

32 **legal in Wyoming:** "The Gambling License Law," *Cheyenne Daily Leader*, Sept. 2, 1875.

32 **gone bankrupt:** "A Business Failure," *Daily Rocky Mountain News* (Denver, CO), July 21, 1875.

32 **the Bella Union:** "A Card to the Public," *The Cheyenne Daily News*, Nov. 29, 1875.

32 **didn't mention Cheyenne:** Kate Elder stated that Doc was never in Wyoming. Mary K. Cummings Recollections.

32 **briefly visiting his aunt:** Recollections of Mary Holliday.

32 **three counts of gambling:** Roberts, *Doc Holliday*, 81 and 434 n. 92.

32 **"The recent enforcement":** *The Dallas Daily Herald*, Jan. 27, 1877.

33 **occurred on June 30:** *Tri-Weekly Herald* (Marshall, TX), July 12, 1877. The *Tri-Weekly Herald*'s account was reprinted from the *Dallas Mail*.

33 **the first reports:** See Ibid., and *The Dallas Weekly Herald*, July 7, 1877; and the *Daily Democratic Statesman* (Austin, TX), July 7, 1877. Other Holliday biographers have written that Henry Kahn was a fellow gambler, but the fullest account of the shooting, that appearing in the *Tri-Weekly Herald*, states that Kahn was the saloon's owner.

33 **Holliday, traveled to Texas:** Recollections of Mary Holliday; and Daily *Fort Worth Democrat*, July 21, 1877.

33 **"he was not one":** John Jacobs as quoted in Roberts, *Doc Holliday*, 83.

33 **arrested again in Dallas:** Ibid., 82 and 435 n. 99.

33 **116-pound prostitute:** Mary K. Cummings Recollections.

33 **Mária Izabella Magdolna Horony:** Baptismal record, "Slovakia Church and Synagogue Books, 1592–1935," FamilySearch (https://www.familysearch.org/ark:/61903/1:1:QVN8-2YG2 : Wed Nov 29 15:18:40 UTC 2023), entry for Mária Izabella Magdolna Horony and Mihály Horony, 09 Nov 1849.

34 **moved with her family:** "New York Passenger Lists, 1820–1891," database with images, FamilySearch (https://familysearch.org/ark:/61903/1:1:QV33-7XY9 : 20 February 2021), Victor Horony, 1860; citing Immigration, New York City, New York, United States, NARA microfilm publication M237 (Washington, D.C.: National Archives and Records Administration, n.d.), FHL microfilm 175, 561; and "New York Passenger Lists, 1820–1891," Family Search (https://www.familysearch.org/ark:/61903/1:1:QV33-75QH: Sun Dec 03 08:28:33 UTC 2023), Entry for Marie Horony, 1860.

34 **died just seven weeks:** Dr. Horony obituary, *Burlington Hawk-Eye* (IA), May 6, 1865.

34 **administrators mismanaged:** Anne E. Collier, "Big Nose Kate and Mary Katherine Cummings: Same Person, Different Lives," in *A Wyatt Earp Anthology*, 346–47; and "Tax Sale for Delinquent City Taxes for 1868," *Daily Davenport Democrat* (IA), Jan. 22, 1869.

34 **the name Kate Fisher:** In her recollections, Kate claimed to have married a Silas Melvin, presumably in St. Louis, and that her husband and a young son were deceased. No scholar has been able to confirm this. See Bork and Boyer, "The O.K. Corral Fight at Tombstone," 68 and 72.

34 **prostitution in Wichita:** Collier, "Big Nose Kate and Mary Katherine Cummings," 357 n. 35; and Roger Myers, "Between Wichita and Dodge: The Travels and Friends of Kate Elder," *Quarterly of the National Association for Outlaw and Lawman History* 31 (April–June 2007): 24.

34 **assault and battery:** *The Great Bend Register* (KS), Nov. 19, 1874.

34 **one of seven women:** 1875 Kansas state census, Dodge Township, Ford County, 5.

34 **Italian word for brothel:** I must credit my friend, novelist and screenwriter Ron Hansen, for providing me with this intriguing possibility.

35 **an unequal relationship:** Gary L. Cunningham, "Gambling in the Kansas Cattle Towns: A Prominent and Somewhat Honorable Profession," *Kansas History* 5 (Spring 1982): 18.

35 **"very pretty mustache"**: Bork and Boyer, "The O.K. Corral Fight at Tombstone," 83.

35 **"a mean disposition"**: Masterson, Doc Holliday.

35 **a couple of outlaws**: The outlaws were Dave Rudabaugh and Mike Roark. See Wyatt Earp narrative; and Richard Derham, "Dave Rudabaugh: A Myth Deconstructed, Part One," *Wild West History Association Journal* 16 (June 2023): 14–15.

36 **"Your best bet"**: As quoted in Lake, *Wyatt Earp*, 192.

THREE: IN THE GODLESS HOLES

37 **Charley Sanders:** My description of the shooting of Charley Sanders comes from contemporary newspaper reports, as well as later reminiscences. His surname also appears as Saunders and Green. See "A Fatal and Disgraceful Affair," *The Wichita Eagle*, May 28, 1875; June 4, 1874; and July 16, 1874; "Colored Man Shot," *Western Home Journal* (Lawrence, KS), June 4, 1874; *The Head Light* (Thayer, KS), June 3, 1874; Maurice Benfer, "Early Day Law Enforcement Problems in Wichita," *The Wichita Eagle Sunday Magazine*, Jan. 27, 1929; and Wyatt Earp narrative.

38 **"They're not after you"**: Wyatt Earp narrative.

38 **surrender of gunman Ben Thompson:** Wyatt Earp narrative; Wyatt Earp to Stuart Lake, Los Angeles, CA, Nov. 30, 1928, box 3, folder 39, Stuart N. Lake Papers; and Josephine Earp to unidentified writer, Oakland, CA, Dec. 8, 1932, Josephine Sarah Marcus Earp Papers, MS 0952, AHS. There's been considerable debate over Wyatt Earp's exact involvement, if any, in the arrest of Thompson. Wyatt never wavered from his insistence that he arrested the famed gunfighter, but there's very little evidence beyond Wyatt's word. For a sampling of the debate, see Gary Roberts, "Did Wyatt Earp Arrest Ben Thompson in Ellsworth in 1873?" available online at https://web.ar chive.org/web/20160305005353/http://home.earthlink.net/~knuthco1/benthompson /garyroberts.htm; Roger Myers, "Did Wyatt Earp Arrest Ben Thompson?" available online at https://web.archive.org/web/20070930084424/http://www.larned.net/rog myers/ben_earp.htm; and Kim Allen Scott, "Erroneous Ellsworth: Letters Help Prove That the Wyatt Earp–Ben Thompson Showdown Is a Tall Tale," *True West* 66 (Feb. 2019): 32–37.

38 **harassing his wife:** Benfer, "Early Day Law Enforcement Problems in Wichita." These are the recollections of James Cairns, who served on the Wichita police force with Wyatt.

39 **"Drunken roughs"**: *The Wichita Eagle*, June 4, 1874.

39 **"else our streets will flow"**: Ibid., May 28, 1874.

39 **odd theory that small men:** David D. Leahy to John Madden, Wichita, KS, Nov. 11, 1928, photocopy in Glenn Boyer Research Collection, MS 0087, AHS.

39 **appointment to the police:** Wyatt Earp narrative; and Floyd Benjamin Streeter, *Prairie Trails & Cow Towns: The Opening of the Old West* (New York, NY: The Devin Adair Company, 1963), 151.

39 **"noticed that I had only one gun"**: Wyatt Earp narrative.

40 **numbered 48,137:** "Wichita Cattle Trade for 1874," *The Wichita Eagle*, Dec. 3, 1874.

40 **"Wichita is a godless hole":** *The Wichita Eagle*, July 15, 1875.

40 **"Every other door opened"**: Ibid., Dec. 2, 1875.

40 **Madam Ida May's brothel:** Roger Jay, "Wyatt Earp, Wichita Policeman, Part One," in *A Wyatt Earp Anthology*, 153.

40 **Wyatt's wife Sarah:** Sherry Monahan, *Mrs. Earp: The Wives and Lovers of the Earp Brothers* (Guilford, CT: TwoDot, 2013), 13–14.

41 **thirty "soiled doves":** *The Wichita Weekly Beacon*, June 10, 1874.

41 **"a bawdy house":** As quoted in Nyle H. Miller and Joseph W. Snell, *Why the West Was Wild: A Contemporary Look at the Antics of Some Highly Publicized Cowtown Personalities* (Topeka, KS: Kansas State Historical Society, 1963), 146.

41 **pseudotaxes:** Carol Leonard and Isidor Wallimann, "Prostitution and Changing Morality in the Frontier Cattle Towns of Kansas," *Kansas History* (Spring 1979): 39–41.

41 **"Kate Earb":** Collier, "Big Nose Kate and Mary Katherine Cummings," 348; and Bartholomew, *Wyatt Earp, 1848 to 1880*, 96.

41 **a bartender in Dagner's saloon:** "Wyatt Earp," *The Wichita Daily Beacon*, Dec. 4, 1896; and Leahy to John Madden, Nov. 11, 1928. Leahy names the saloon as Pryor's.

42 **"special police force":** Jay, "Wyatt Earp, Wichita Policeman, Part One," 152; and *The Wichita Eagle*, July 9 and 16, 1874.

42 **an "extra policeman":** "Wichita as a Frontier Town Was Never 'Wild,'" *The Wichita Eagle*, Aug. 25, 1935.

42 **Wyatt was appointed full time:** *The Wichita Weekly Beacon*, April 28, 1875; and Miller and Snell, *Why the West Was Wild*, 147–8.

42 **stopped receiving fines:** Jay, "Wyatt Earp, Wichita Policeman, Part One," 153.

42 **"Wyatt was a well-built man":** As quoted in Benfer, "Early Day Law Enforcement Problems in Wichita."

43 **"a soiled dove":** *The Wichita Weekly Beacon*, Sept. 15, 1875.

43 **"there are but few":** Ibid., Dec. 15, 1875.

43 **a narrow escape:** *The Wichita Weekly Beacon*, Jan. 12, 1876.

44 **"it was only with tyros":** As quoted in Lake, *Wyatt Earp*, 43.

44 **"fight on the brain":** *The Wichita Weekly Beacon*, April 5, 1876.

44 **of the "Dead Line":** Robert R. Dykstra, *The Cattle Towns* (New York: Alfred A. Knopf, 1968), 17–18 and 60–61; and "The Shipment of Texas Cattle," *Ellsworth Reporter* (KS), April 6, 1876.

44 **"suppression of houses":** *The Wichita Eagle*, May 11, 1876.

44 **"troupe of demi-mondes":** "Echoes from the Frontiers," *The Leavenworth Daily Times* (KS), May 28, 1876; and *The Hutchinson Examiner* (KS), June 1, 1876.

45 **"Of all the devilish holes":** "That Excursion," *Topeka Daily Blade*, March 17, 1876.

45 **"lurch to the west":** "The Cattle Drives of 1878," *The New York Times*, June 17, 1878.

45 **"fight the devil":** Robert M. Wright, *Dodge City, the Cowboy Capital and the Great Southwest in the Days of the Wild Indian, the Buffalo, the Cowboy, Dance Halls, Gambling Halls and Bad Men* (Wichita, KS: Wichita Eagle Press, 1913), 173.

45 **Dodge City's mayor:** Wyatt Earp narrative; and *The Wichita Eagle*, May 16, 1878.

45 **they may have separated:** Monahan, *Mrs. Earp*, 14–15.

46 **fattest man in the West:** *The Daily Mail* (Wellington, KS), Dec. 7, 1889.

46 **the town's Republicans:** "Our Dodge City Letter," *Ellis County Star* (Hays City, KS), July 27, 1876.

46 **"too enthusiastic":** *Dodge City Times*, as quoted in the *Topeka Weekly Blade*, July 27, 1876.

46 **"Dodge has had the benefit"**: "Along the A,T & SFRR," *The Atchison Weekly Champion* (KS), Nov. 11, 1876.

47 **"all the cattlemen"**: Wyatt Earp narrative.

47 **$2,000 in gold**: "The Golden Hills," *The Leavenworth Weekly Times*, Aug. 31, 1876.

47 **"There is not an hour"**: *The Black Hills Pioneer*, Aug. 26, 1876.

47 **selling firewood**: Lake, *Wyatt Earp*, 156–7; "Wyatt Earp, the Referee," *The Deadwood Daily Pioneer* (SD), Dec. 8, 1896; and "Wyatt Earp," *The Wichita Daily Beacon*, Dec. 4, 1896. Some authors have questioned whether Wyatt actually spent time in Deadwood. The story in the *Pioneer* should end any debate, as the editor writes that "Billy Day, John Steinmetz, Frank Meihls and other old-timers remember him [Wyatt]— especially Meihls."

48 **"I didn't gamble much"**: As quoted in Lake, *Wyatt Earp*, 157.

48 **"was very quiet and tame"**: "Wyatt Earp, the Referee."

48 **a job offer**: Wyatt Earp narrative. Wyatt said the shipment he was hired to guard consisted of gold dust.

49 **all-Black brothel**: 1875 Kansas State census, City of Leavenworth, Leavenworth County, p. 13.

49 **"being saucy to his Honor"**: "Police Pickings," *The Leavenworth Daily Times* (KS) Aug. 13, 1875.

49 **hauled back and slapped her**: *Dodge City Times*, July 21, 1877.

49 **bounty hunter for the Atchison**: Wyatt Earp narrative; and Lake, *Wyatt Earp*, 191.

49 **introduced to a twenty-six-year-old**: Lake, *Wyatt Earp*, 192; and Flood interview with Earp, Sept. 15, 1926, reproduced in *Wyatt Earp, Tombstone, & the West from the Collections of John D. Gilchriese*, 71.

49 **his first impressions**: Lake, *Wyatt Earp*, 194.

50 **Doc pumped Wyatt**: "How Wyatt Earp Routed a Gang of Arizona Outlaws," *The Examiner* (San Francisco, CA), Aug. 2, 1896.

50 **"disturbing the peace"**: "Punching," *Daily Fort Worth Democrat*, Jan. 26, 1878.

50 **a story Wyatt related years later**: "How Wyatt Earp Routed a Gang of Arizona Outlaws."

51 **"[I] enjoyed about as much"**: As quoted in Tanner, *Doc Holliday*, 115.

51 **His quarry, Dave Rudabaugh**: "The Train Robbers," *The Atchison Daily Champion* (KS), Feb. 2, 1878; and Derham, "Dave Rudabaugh," 15–16.

51 **reporting Wyatt's arrival**: *Dodge City Times*, May 11, 1878.

51 **of some five thousand people**: "The Cattle Drives of 1878."

51 **"They follow the annual"**: "Dodge," *Colorado Daily Chieftain* (Pueblo), June 1, 1878.

52 **"red-hot times"**: "The Cattle Drives of 1878."

52 **The job paid $75**: *Dodge City Times*, June 8, 1878; and Dodge City Police Docket, 1878–1882, Ford County Historical Society, available online at https://scholars.fhsu.edu/dodgecity/#.

53 **"Wyatt Earp is doing his"**: *Ford County Globe* (Dodge City, KS), June 18, 1878.

53 **in his shirtsleeves**: Wyatt exhibited the same irregular dress in Tombstone. See William J. Hunsaker, San Francisco, CA, Oct. 2, 1928, box 5, folder 4, Stuart N. Lake Papers.

53 **"If less protection was given"**: Ibid., June 26, 1878.

53 **services as a dentist**: *Dodge City Times*, June 8, 1878.

53　"**The women of the hurdy-gurdys**": "Dodge City When It Was Wicked," *St. Louis Post-Dispatch*, March 3, 1896.

54　**falsely accused of burglarizing:** "He Started Many Graveyards," *The Sun* (NY), June 7, 1886.

54　"**It was easily seen**": Masterson, Doc Holliday.

54　**morning hours of July 26:** The sources I used for my narrative of this incident, which vary considerably in details, are "Bullets in the Air," *Dodge City Times*, July 27, 1878; "Lively Scene at a Variety Performance," *National Police Gazette* (NY), Aug. 10, 1878; Wyatt Earp narrative; "Wyatt Earp's Tribute to Bat Masterson," *The Examiner* (San Francisco), Aug. 16, 1896; W. B. (Bat) Masterson, "Famous Gun Fighters of the Western Frontier, Second Article, Wyatt Earp," *Human Life* 4 (Feb. 1907): 9; and Eddie Foy and Alvin F. Harlow, *Clowning Through Life* (New York: E. P. Dutton & Company, 1928), 112–14.

55　**cowboy died within hours:** "Death from a Pistol Shot," *Dodge City Times*, Aug. 24, 1878.

56　"**There have been Abilenes**": The city attorney was Edward Fenton Colborn. He's quoted in "Dodge City When It Was Wicked."

56　"**Have you a six-shooter?**": Wyatt Earp narrative.

57　"**It was because of this**": Ibid.

FOUR: WHEN DODGE CITY LOST ITS SNAP

58　"**Change was his mistress**": Theodore Roberts, "The Vagrant's Epitaph," *Scribner's Magazine* 36 (Aug. 1904): 204.

58　**Wyatt saw the bright flashes:** What follows is a highly debated episode in the life of Wyatt Earp: his encounter with gunman Clay Allison. The exact date remains a matter of conjecture as well. I've based my narrative largely on two accounts left by Earp, the Wyatt Earp narrative and "Wyatt Earp's Tribute to Bat Masterson," and the recollections of city attorney Edward Fenton Colborn as quoted in "Dodge City When It Was Wicked." A lengthy discussion of Earp's encounter with Allison, including a number of different versions of the standoff, can be found in Lee A. Silva, *Wyatt Earp: A Biography of the Legend, Volume 1: The Cowtown Years* (Santa Ana, CA: Graphic Publishers, 2002), 547–86.

59　**shoved him in the cell with Rachal:** Curiously, neither the name Rachal nor Robert Wright are found in the Dodge City police docket. Did Wright use his influence to keep charges from being filed?

59　**They settled upon Clay Allison:** A story circulated later that Wright offered "one thousand dollars to anyone putting Wyatt Earp out of business." Samuel J. Crumbine as quoted in S. J. Reidhead, *Travesty: Frank Waters' Earp Agenda Exposed* (Roswell, NM: Jinglebob Press, 2005), 71 n. 198.

59　"**carries himself with ease**": *The Wichita Herald*, Dec. 28, 1878.

59　"**paroxysmal of a mixed character**": As quoted in Chuck Parsons, *Clay Allison: Portrait of a Shootist* (Seagraves, TX: Pioneer Book Publishers, 1983), 3.

60　**on the buffalo range:** "Ellsworth's Ship Prompts Brothers of Bat Masterson to Recall Exploits of Wyatt Earp."

60　**killed a dance hall girl:** Kate Elder stated that the gunfight between Bat Masterson and Sergeant Melvin King started because King accused Bat of cheating him at poker.

Mollie Brennan jumped between the two just as King fired the first shot. Other versions of the incident, including one by Bat's brother Tom, cite jealousy as the cause of the gunplay. Mary K. Cummings Recollections; "Ellsworth's Ship Prompts Brothers of Bat Masterson to Recall Exploits of Wyatt Earp"; and Bob Boze Bell, "Lay Lady Gay," *True West* (Nov. 2021), available online https://truewestmagazine.com/article/lay-lady-gay/.

60 **"absolutely destitute of physical fear":** Masterson, "Wyatt Earp," *Human Life*, 9.

62 **Jim Kenedy:** A fine biographical sketch is Chuck Parsons, "James W. Kenedy: Cattleman, Texas Ranger, Gambler and 'Fiend in Human Form,'" in *A Wyatt Earp Anthology*, 208–20.

62 **At the Comique:** "The Comique," *Ford County Globe* (Dodge City, KS), July 16, 1878, and "Comique," July 30, 1878.

63 **"very fine looking" brunette:** *Topeka Weekly Blade*, Oct. 10, 1878.

63 **"Ask any man who knew":** "Wyatt Earp's Tribute to Bat Masterson." See also Tom Masterson as quoted in "Ellsworth's Ship Prompts Brothers of Bat Masterson to Recall Exploits of Wyatt Earp."

63 **petitioning for a divorce:** *Ford County Globe* (Dodge City, KS), Sept. 24, 1878.

63 **carrying a concealed weapon:** Dodge City Police Docket, 1878–1882, p. 24.

63 **order Marshal Bassett:** *Topeka Weekly Blade*, Oct. 10, 1878; and "Wyatt Earp's Tribute to Bat Masterson."

63 **"in that he did conduct himself":** Dodge City Police Docket, 1878–1882, p. 39.

64 **Four quick blasts:** Fannie Garrettson to Messrs. Eshers, Dodge City, Oct. 5, 1878, as quoted in Miller and Snell, *Why the West Was Wild*, 362. Other contemporary accounts of the shooting I consulted are "Midnight Assassin," *Ford County Globe* (Dodge City, KS), Oct. 8, 1878; "Another Victim," *Dodge City Times*, Oct. 5, 1878; and *Topeka Weekly Blade*, Oct. 10, 1878. An account of the shooting and its aftermath by Bat Masterson's brother Tom is in "Ellsworth's Ship Prompts Brothers of Bat Masterson to Recall Exploits of Wyatt Earp."

64 **"Poor Fannie, she never realized":** Garrettson to Eshers, Oct. 5, 1878.

64 **"Was he there when the shots":** "Wyatt Earp's Tribute to Bat Masterson."

65 **"as intrepid a posse":** "The Capture of Jim Kennedy," *Dodge City Times*, Oct. 12, 1878.

65 **"That's Kenedy, I know him":** "Wyatt Earp's Tribute to Bat Masterson."

66 **the judge had acquitted Kenedy:** *Dodge City Times*, Oct. 26, 1878; and "Free as Air," *Ford County Globe* (Dodge City, KS), Oct. 29, 1878.

66 **coroner's jury had named Kenedy:** "Midnight Assassin."

66 **several pieces of shattered bone:** "Surgical Operation," *Ford County Globe* (Dodge City, KS), Dec. 17, 1878; and *Dodge City Times*, Dec. 21, 1878.

66 **a "grand success":** *Ford County Globe* (Dodge City, KS), March 25, 1879.

67 **eight to twelve railroad cars:** "Railroad Notes," *Weekly New Mexican*, Nov. 9, 1878.

67 **"numerous necessary evils":** Taine, "Trinidad—Man About Town, by Daylight and Lamplight," *Colorado Daily Chieftain* (Pueblo), Nov. 1, 1878. Kate would say that Trinidad was only an unintended layover because Doc was too sick to travel farther. Bork and Boyer, "The O.K. Corral Fight at Tombstone," 76.

67 **"a young sport" named Kid Colton:** Masterson, Doc Holliday; and Flood interview with Earp, Sept. 15, 1926, reproduced in *Wyatt Earp, Tombstone, & the West from the Collections of John D. Gilchriese*, 71.

68 **"to be considered 'bad men'"**: "Wanted—Good Order," *The Enterprise and Chronicle* (Trinidad and El Moro, CO), Dec. 14, 1878.

68 **Montezuma Hot Springs:** See "Las Vegas," *Colorado Daily Chieftain* (Pueblo), Aug. 4, 1878; "The Hot Springs of Las Vegas," *Colorado Weekly Chieftain*, July 18, 1878; and "Life at Las Vegas," *St. Louis Globe-Democrat*, Sept. 25, 1879.

69 **hire a wagon freighter:** Bork and Boyer, "The O.K. Corral Fight at Tombstone," 76.

69 **wasn't there to fill cavities:** A dental chair and drill stamped with the name of John H. Holliday and Las Vegas, N.M., popped up in a 2013 auction of Old West artifacts in Harrisburg, Pennsylvania. The chair and drill were among thousands of artifacts obtained with Harrisburg city funds for a planned Wild West museum that became the subject of much controversy. The auction itself was notorious for the number of fakes and items of questionable authenticity that were offered. I believe the chair and drill to be spurious. And beware, it's not the only "Doc Holliday dental chair" floating around out there! See Wilcox, *The World of Doc Holliday*, 101–2; and Meghan Saar, "Dibs on Doc," *True West* (Oct. 2013), available online at https://truewestmagazine .com/article/dibs-on-doc/.

69 **"Doc was always considered":** "Holliday's Holliday," *Las Vegas Daily Optic* (NM), July 20, 1881.

69 **During the six-month period:** Many authors and historians have written that Doc was a participant in the "Royal Gorge War," in which the Atchison, Topeka & Santa Fe contested with the Denver & Rio Grande for the right of way through the famed Arkansas River canyon. In March 1879, the Santa Fe enlisted Sheriff Bat Masterson to recruit an armed party of men in Dodge City to seize and hold the gorge. Doc is supposed to have been a member of the "posse." However, there are several problems with this scenario. First, the only historical reference to Doc being involved comes from vaudevillian Eddie Foy, who wrote in his 1928 autobiography that Doc tried to get him to join Masterson's fighters. We now know, however, that Foy created a number of fictions about his western experiences. A second red flag is that Bat Masterson, the man who supposedly recruited Doc, makes no mention of this episode in his biographical sketch of Holliday. Additionally, there are no contemporary references to Doc being a member of Masterson's fighters, nor is there even a contemporary reference to Doc being in Dodge City at the time Masterson was recruiting. For Foy's fibs, see Mike Mihaljevich, "Eddie Foy: Clowning Through Lies?," *Wild West History Association Journal* 15 (March 2022): 66–71; and "When Eddie Foy Played in Dodge City," *The Topeka Daily Capital*, March 29, 1908. In the *Capital* story, Foy claimed to have knocked out with his fist, on separate occasions, both Doc Holliday and Ben Thompson and relieved them of their weapons. Tellingly, these sensational takedowns didn't make it into his book, *Clowning Through Life*.

69 **arrested three times:** The Territory of New Mexico v. John Holliday, Case No. 931, March 8, 1879; The Territory of New Mexico v. John Holliday, Case No. 990, Aug. 12, 1879; and The Territory of New Mexico v. John Holliday, Case No. 996, Aug. 13, 1879; San Miguel County District Court Records, New Mexico State Records Center and Archives, Santa Fe.

69 **Gambling had been outlawed:** *Revised Statutes and Laws of the Territory of New Mexico in Force at the Close of the Session of the Legislative Assembly Ending February 2, 1865* (St. Louis, MO: R. P. Studley & Co., 1865), 398–402.

69 **"At every term of the District":** *Las Vegas Daily Gazette* (NM), Aug. 8, 1879.

70　killed a man in self-defense: John Myers Myers, *Doc Holliday* (Boston: Little, Brown and Company, 1955), 112.

70　"a splendid violin": *Otero Optic* (NM), June 5, 1879, original issue at the Fray Angélico Chávez History Library, Santa Fe, New Mexico. Doc Holliday biographers have assumed that Doc opened a dental office in Otero, based primarily on a notice in this same newspaper issue that a Dr. Washington had "purchased a half interest in the room occupied by Holliday & Fagaly." Fagaly, however, also appears in the newspaper as a partner in Fraley & Fagaly, butchers "with the choicest meats in Otero." I've not seen any primary evidence that Doc Holliday practiced dentistry in Otero.

70　a building on Center Street: The building contractor charged Doc $372.50. Claim of W. G. Ward against "Mr. Hollyday commonly called Doc Holyday," Oct. 7, 1879, photocopy in Tanner Papers. See also Tanner, *Doc Holliday*, 133; and Roberts, *Doc Holliday*, 441 n. 65.

70　"The women who did the dancing": "Mike Gordon Crosses the Range," *Las Vegas Gazette* (NM), July 26, 1879.

70　shooting into Doc's saloon: The most detailed account of this incident is "Mike Gordon Crosses the Range." See also *Thirty-Four*, Las Cruces, NM, July 30, 1879; and "Life at Las Vegas," *St. Louis Globe-Democrat*, Sept. 25, 1879. Bat Masterson, who was not present, provided two versions of the killing: "Doc Holliday's Career," *The Boston Globe*, Aug. 4, 1886; and Masterson, Doc Holliday.

71　"come and get it": As quoted in Bork and Boyer, "The O.K. Corral Fight at Tombstone," 76 n. 9. In her account, Kate doesn't say what brought the police to their door, but she does indicate that this happened in Las Vegas, and the Gordon shooting would seem to be the best candidate.

71　man who killed Gordon: A short time after Doc was no longer a fixture in Las Vegas, New Mexico, two of the town's newspapers didn't hesitate to name him as Gordon's killer. See "Holliday's Holliday," *Las Vegas Daily Optic* (NM), July 20, 1881; and *Las Vegas Daily Gazette* (NM), Dec. 3, 1881.

71　"In the case of killings": Miguel Antonio Otero, *My Life on the Frontier, 1864–1882* (New York: The Press of the Pioneers, 1935), 184.

72　either sold out or: Roberts, *Doc Holliday*, 113.

72　Dodge City Gang: Otero, *My Life on the Frontier*, 182; and "Thugs," *Las Vegas Daily Gazette* (NM), Aug. 24, 1879.

72　the plaza in Old Town: Mary K. Cummings Recollections; and Bork and Boyer, "The O.K. Corral Fight at Tombstone," 76. Wyatt had arrived in Las Vegas by September 23. "Las Vegas Correspondent," *Ford County Globe* (Dodge City, KS), Sept. 30, 1879.

72　three armed Missourians: "Unruly Missourians," *Dodge City Times*, May 10, 1879. The two men arrested were Henry Kaufman and Tom E. Ewen. They were charged and found guilty of carrying a concealed weapon. Dodge City Police Docket, 1878–1882, 81–82.

74　"showing no signs of 'weakening'": *Dodge City Times*, May 24, 1879.

74　turned into a bed of sand: "Kansas Letters," *The Kansas City Times* (MO), Aug. 22, 1879.

74　dropped from ninety: "The Land of Peat," *The Kansas City Times* (MO), Dec. 19, 1878, and "Dodge City, Kas.," *The Kansas City Times* (MO), Aug. 28, 1879.

74 **boots under their heads:** "Boot Hill," *Ford County Globe* (Dodge City, KS), Feb. 4, 1879.

74 **"a fitting monument":** "Dodge City, Kas.," *The Kansas City Times* (MO), Nov. 23, 1879.

75 **given the name Celia Ann:** Monahan, *Mrs. Earp*, 18.

75 **ran away from home:** O.H. Marquis to Merritt L. Beeson, Feb. 7, 1950, as quoted in Glenn G. Boyer, *Suppressed Murder of Wyatt Earp*, 21–23.

76 **"To Wyatt S. Earp":** This bible is now part of the collections of the AHS.

FIVE: THE NEW EL DORADO

77 **"Under certain conditions":** Deposition of Robert Alpheus Lewis, John B. Wright Papers, MS 1123, AHS.

77 **"I was young":** Wyatt Earp narrative.

78 **Wyatt had been dealing cards:** Lake, *Wyatt Earp*, 227.

78 **purchased a Concord coach:** Wyatt Earp narrative. Earp gives two different accounts of how he acquired the coach. In one version, he purchased it before leaving for Arizona. In another, he says he traded one of his wagons for a Concord coach while in Prescott. I believe it's more likely that he acquired the coach in Dodge City. In addition to his narrative, Wyatt would also refer to his idea for an Arizona stage line in his 1926 testimony given for the Carlotta Crabtree trial. See John Richard Stephens, ed., *Wyatt Earp Speaks! My Side of the O.K. Corral Shootout, Plus Interviews with Doc Holliday* (Cambria, CA: Fern Canyon Press, 1998), 195.

78 **"rip her open":** Bork and Boyer, "The O.K. Corral Fight at Tombstone," 76 n. 9.

79 **"I loved Doc":** Mary K. Cummings Recollections.

79 **"they were always a quarrelsome":** "How Wyatt Earp Routed a Gang of Arizona Outlaws."

79 **Tombstone stamp mill:** *St. Louis Globe-Democrat*, July 17, 1879.

79 **an entire column:** *Chicago Tribune*, July 18, 1879.

79 **Virgil started to excavate:** "Mining Notes," *Arizona Daily Star* (Tucson), Sept. 2, 1879.

80 **friendship between Doc and Wyatt:** Mary K. Cummings Recollections.

80 **"Wyatt kind of casually":** As quoted in Frank Waters, *The Earp Brothers of Tombstone: The Story of Mrs. Virgil Earp* (New York: Clarkson N. Potter, Inc., 1960), 43.

80 **Doc and Kate took up residence:** Mary K. Cummings to Lillie Raffert, Pioneer Home, Prescott, AZ, March 18, 1940, folder 1, box 1, Glenn Boyer Wyatt Earp Collection, MS 752, UA.

80 **"became imbued with the fever":** Wyatt Earp narrative.

80 **"was like his father":** Reidhead, *Travesty*, 214.

81 **Dake gave him the commission:** Don Chaput, *Virgil Earp: Western Peace Officer* (Encampment, WY: Affiliated Writers of America, 1994), 52. The Nov. 14, 1879, issue of the *Weekly Arizona Miner* (Prescott) reported that Virgil was about to leave for Tombstone.

81 **Doc and Kate remained in Prescott:** Mary K. Cummings to Lillie Raffert, March 18, 1940.

81 **west side of the courthouse:** "The Land of the Cactus," *Silver World* (Lake City, CO), April 26, 1879.

81 **"A notable fact":** Ibid.

81 **his arrests and fines:** Roberts, *Doc Holliday*, 119; Tanner, *Doc Holliday*, 139; and "District Court," *Las Vegas Daily Gazette* (NM), March 3, 1880.

82 **The Star Line Mail:** Star Line Mail & Transportation Co. ad in *Las Vegas Daily Gazette* (NM), Nov. 15, 1879; "A Letter from Arizona," *The Wichita Weekly Beacon*, Dec. 1, 1880; and "From New Mexico to Arizona," *The Weekly Arizona Miner* (Prescott), Aug. 8, 1879.

82 **at least one court appearance:** Roberts, *Doc Holliday*, 119.

82 **As the story goes:** The only known account of this incident is found in Otero, *My Life on the Frontier*, 217–18.

83 **"I met him quite frequently":** Ibid., 218.

83 **on Montezuma Street:** 1880 US census for Prescott, Yavapai County, Arizona.

83 **stated he was a dentist:** Prescott already had a well-established dentist, E. P. Ryder, who advertised regularly in *The Weekly Arizona Miner.*

84 **"If you are going to tie":** Bork and Boyer, "The O.K. Corral Fight at Tombstone," 77.

84 **Kate purchased on time:** Mary K. Cummings to Lillie Raffert, March 18, 1940.

84 **mailed one to his aunt Ella:** Pendleton and Thomas, *In Search of the Hollidays*, 54. The original cabinet card is now part of the collections of William I. Koch.

84 **exchanged letters with Mattie:** Roberts, *Doc Holliday*, 399–400; and Doc Holliday obituary, *Ute Chief* (Glenwood Springs, CO), Nov. 12, 1887, as reprinted in Walling, *John "Doc" Holliday*, 49–50.

86 **consisted of about fifty houses:** *The Weekly Arizona Miner* (Prescott), Oct. 3, 1879.

86 **twenty people a day:** "Tombstone News," *The Pioche Weekly Record* (NV), July 3, 1880.

86 **three-quarters of the residents:** "Tombstone Letter," *The Pioche Weekly Record* (NV), Aug. 7, 1880.

86 **The few Chinese:** Wm. B. Shillingberg, *Tombstone, A.T.: A History of Early Mining, Milling, and Mayhem* (Spokane, WA: The Arthur H. Clark Company, 1999), 130–32; and "Tombstone," *Tombstone Epitaph*, Aug. 8, 1880.

86 **Hispanos with adoberas:** "Our Tombstone Letter," *Daily Arizona Citizen* (Tucson), April 29, 1880.

86 **A bed in a room:** "Letter from Arizona," *The Sumner County Press* (Wellington, KS), July 29, 1880.

86 **Miners made four dollars:** "Tombstone News," *The Pioche Weekly Record* (NV), July 3, 1880; and "Southeastern Arizona," *Sacramento Daily Record-Union*, July 2, 1880.

86 **"vilest brain-destroying whiskey":** "Tombstone's Tough Days," *The Sun* (NY), March 5, 1899.

86 **"As a general thing":** "A Letter from Arizona," *West Schuylkill Press* (Tremont, PA), July 3, 1880. One report from August stated that half the population was out of employment. "Tombstone," *Tombstone Epitaph*, Aug. 8, 1880.

87 **thousands of claims:** The *Colorado Daily Chieftain* (Pueblo), Dec. 21, 1880, reported that thirty thousand claims had been filed in Pima County alone.

87 **"and he will ask you":** "Letter from Arizona," *The Sumner County Press* (Wellington, KS), July 29, 1880. There actually were two mines in the Tombstone District named for Garfield, at least according to an 1881 "Map of the Tombstone Mining District," published by Kelleher, Peel & Ingoldsby, original in the Library of Congress. Available online at https://www.loc.gov/resource/g4333c.ct003583/?r=0.332,0.702,0.057,0.036,0.

87 **"If you go"**: As quoted in "The New El Dorado, Tombstone in Arizona," *The Leeds Mercury* (Leeds, England), May 22, 1880. Other early versions of the name's origins are found in "Letter from Arizona," *The Sumner County Press* (Wellington, KS), July 29, 1880; B. C. Keeler, *Where to Go to Become Rich: Farmers', Miners' and Tourists Guide' to Kansas, New Mexico, Arizona and Colorado* (Chicago: Belford, Clarke & Co., 1880), 111; and William Henry Bishop, *Old Mexico and Her Lost Provinces: A Journey in Mexico, Southern California, and Arizona by Way of Cuba* (New York: Harper & Brothers, 1883), 486.

87 **the name "Tumbstone Mine"**: Jeanne Devere, "The Tombstone Bonanza, 1878–1886," *Arizoniana* 1 (1960): 17.

87 **"On any evening"**: "Our Tombstone Letter," *Daily Arizona Citizen* (Tucson), April 29, 1880.

87 **at least four faro games**: "Tombstone News," *The Pioche Weekly Record* (NV), July 3, 1880.

88 **nine mining claims**: "Mining Notice," *Arizona Weekly Star* (Tucson), April 20, 1880; and "Mining Locations and Property Transfers," *Arizona Daily Star*, June 2, 1880. A list of the Earps' mining claims is found in Alford E. Turner, ed., *The Earps Talk* (College Station, TX: Creative Publishing Company, 1980), 92 n. 4.

88 **found a ready buyer**: Stephens, ed. *Wyatt Earp Speaks!*, 195. Wyatt sold his coach to J. D. Kennear, owner of one of the stage lines. Kinnear did indeed run Concord coaches. See *Arizona Daily Star* (Tucson), Dec. 19, 1879.

89 **a shotgun messenger**: Wyatt Earp narrative; and Robert J. Chandler, "Wells Fargo and the Earp Brothers: Cash Books Talk," in *A Wyatt Earp Anthology*, 315.

89 **Earps were listed together**: 1880 US census for Tombstone, Pima County, Arizona.

89 **"Every house was taken"**: Reidhead, *Travesty*, 164.

89 **the occupation given for**: Interestingly, Morgan Earp is also found in the 1880 census with his occupation listed as farmer. Although he's said to have homesteaded for a short time in Montana, Morgan's last job before being enumerated was as a policeman in Butte, Montana. 1880 US census for Temescal, San Bernardino County, California.

89 **Vogan & Flynn's saloon**: Roy B. Young, *Cochise County Cowboy War: A Cast of Characters* (Apache, OK: Young & Sons Enterprises, 1999), 39.

89 **"That was our life"**: Reidhead, *Travesty*, 166.

90 **"the most good natured"**: Ibid., 310.

90 **a wife, Louisa Houston**: Monahan, *Mrs. Earp*, 87.

90 **policeman in Butte**: *The Daily Miner* (Butte, MT), Sept. 16, 1879.

90 **"odd kind of looking"**: "Tombstone Letter," *The Pioche Weekly Record* (NV), Aug. 7, 1880. The letter referred to in the title was written at Tombstone on July 23, the day after the killing. My narrative that follows is based on this letter and the account of the shooting that appeared in the *Tombstone Epitaph*, July 23, 1880, under the title "A Fatal Garment."

91 **he was taken to Tucson**: Wyatt Earp narrative; and *Arizona Daily Star* (Tucson), July 27, and July 30, 1880.

91 **had become so "unruly"**: Wyatt Earp narrative.

91 **"Too much loose pistol practice"**: Lynn R. Bailey, ed. *A Tenderfoot in Tombstone: The Private Journal of George Whitwell Parsons: The Turbulent Years, 1880–82* (Tucson, AZ: Westernlore Press, 1996), 66.

92 **"concealed about the person"**: This was Tombstone's Ordinance No. 9. See "Carrying Concealed Weapons," *Tombstone Epitaph*, Aug. 14, 1880; "A Needed Ordinance," *Arizona Daily Star* (Tucson), Nov. 2, 1880; and *Tombstone Epitaph*, April 19, 1881.

92 **"The appointment of Wyatt"**: "Good Appointment," July 29, 1880.

92 **"tall, gaunt, intrepid"**: Neil B. Carmony, ed. *Apache Days and Tombstone Nights: John Clum's Autobiography, 1877–1887* (Silver City, NM: High-Lonesome Books, 1977), 31.

92 **served as a Republican delegate**: "Republican County Convention," *Ford County Globe* (Dodge City, KS), Aug. 13, 1878.

93 **the finest in Arizona**: *Tombstone Epitaph*, July 22 and Aug. 8, 1880.

93 **"Every evening music"**: Lynn R. Bailey, ed. *Tombstone from a Woman's Point of View: The Correspondence of Clara Spalding Brown, July 7, 1880, to November 14, 1882* (Tucson, AZ: Westernlore Press, 1998), 22.

93 **a business investment**: Wyatt Earp narrative.

93 **"pasteboard and ivory"**: Earp testimony, Stephens, ed. *Wyatt Earp Speaks!*, 195.

94 **By the end of September**: Doc registered to vote in the Tombstone precinct of Pima County on Sept. 27, 1880. Great Register for Pima County, 1880.

94 **"finest sky-light and background scenery"**: *Tombstone Epitaph*, May 11, 1881. Fly operated under the name C. S. Fly.

94 **"a very changed man"**: Mary K. Cummings Recollections; and Mary K. Cummings to Lillie Raffert, March 18, 1940.

94 **The trouble began**: The two sources for Doc's row in the Oriental are *Tombstone Daily Nugget*, Oct. 12, 1880; and *Tombstone Epitaph*, Oct. 12, 1880. For the Slopers and the Easterners, see "At the Bar," *Carbonate Chronicle* (Leadville, CO), April 4, 1885.

95 **He got off with a fine**: Precinct 17 Justice Court Proceedings, Oct. 11, 1881, reproduced in Ben T. Traywick, *Historical Documents and Photographs of Tombstone* (Tombstone, AZ: Red Marie's Bookstore, 1994), 134; Tanner, *Doc Holliday*, 147; and Roberts, *Doc Holliday*, 129.

95 **close to losing his hand**: *Tombstone Epitaph*, Oct. 23, 1880.

95 **"it has a dark side"**: Davis's letter was written from Tombstone on June 12, 1880, and published in the *West Schuylkill Press*, July 3, 1880.

96 **"A good vein is all"**: Bailey, ed. *A Tenderfoot in Tombstone*, 98.

96 **band of cattle thieves**: Wyatt Earp narrative; "Wholesome Truth," *Tombstone Epitaph*, March 18, 1881; John J. Gosper to Crawley P. Dake, Prescott, AZ, Nov. 28, 1881, Correspondence of Crawley P. Dake (microfilm), UA; and William M. Breakenridge, *Helldorado: Bringing the Law to the Mesquite* (Boston: Houghton Mifflin Company, 1928), 103–5.

96 **beef rations for the Apaches**: Letter of W. B. Hicks to Frederick R. Bechdolt published in *Adventure Magazine* 37 (Nov. 1927): 183.

96 **"the name has been corrupted"**: E. B. Pomroy to Wayne MacVeigh, Tucson, AZ, June 23, 1881, Correspondence of Crawley P. Dake (microfilm), UA.

96 **"worse than the Apache"**: "Outlaws," *Arizona Weekly Star* (Tucson), Feb. 17, 1881.

97 **"free as water in the saloons"**: "Virgil W. Earp," *The Daily Examiner* (San Francisco), May 27, 1882.

SIX: A REGULAR SLAUGHTERHOUSE

98 **Gunshots:** My narrative of the shooting of Marshal White is drawn from the Wyatt Earp narrative; the initial news report published in the *Tombstone Epitaph*, Oct. 28, 1880; the news story on Curly Bill's examination before Justice of the Peace Joseph Neugass in the *Daily Arizona Citizen* (Tucson), Dec. 27, 1880; and Carolyn Lake, ed. *Under Cover for Wells Fargo: The Unvarnished Recollections of Fred Dodge* (Boston: Houghton Mifflin Company, 1969). Unless otherwise noted, all quotes are taken from the preceding sources.

99 **"a beautiful set of teeth.":** John Jee, "The Arizona Cow-boys," *The Graphic: An Illustrated Weekly Newspaper* (London, England), Nov. 26, 1881. This lengthy article contains the only eyewitness description of Curly Bill published in his lifetime. Several authors have used a description of Curly Bill that appears in the *Omaha Daily Bee* of Aug. 1, 1883, but that account reads as fiction.

99 **ambushed an army ambulance:** "An Old Offender," *Tombstone Epitaph*, Oct. 31, 1880; and Steve Gatto, *Curly Bill: Tombstone's Most Famous Outlaw* (Lansing, MI: Protar House, 2003), 12. Curly Bill's actual surname is believed to have been Bresnaham.

99 **"a most notorious character":** As quoted in Gatto, *Curly Bill*, 17.

100 **"through White's small intestines":** "The Dead Marshal," *Tombstone Epitaph*, Oct. 31, 1880.

100 **rumblings reached Wyatt:** "Assault to Murder," *Tombstone Epitaph*, Oct. 29, 1880. Also *Tombstone Epitaph*, Oct. 23, 1880.

101 **their mining claims:** See "Claim Sold and Another Bonded," *Arizona Weekly Citizen* (Tucson), Nov. 13, 1880; and Shillingberg, *Tombstone, A.T.*, 170.

101 **he assisted in a survey:** The field notes for this survey are published in facsimile in Roy B. Young, "George Hearst—Wyatt Earp: Another 'Wyatt Whopper'?," *Wild West History Association Journal* 16 (March 2023): 53–62. A copy of the deed of sale for this mining claim is in box 3, folder 42, Stuart N. Lake Papers.

101 **their wood-frame houses:** *Tombstone Epitaph*, Oct. 23, 1880; and Wyatt Earp narrative.

101 **two water rights claims:** "George Hearst—Wyatt Earp," 63–64.

101 **by just fifty-eight votes:** John Boessenecker, *When Law Was in the Saddle: The Frontier Life of Bob Paul* (Norman: University of Oklahoma Press, 2012), 147.

101 **"Wyatt Earp's resignation":** As quoted in Shillingberg, *Tombstone, A.T.*, 163.

102 **chose Virgil's opponent:** *The Weekly Arizona Miner* (Prescott), Nov. 19, 1880.

102 **switching allegiance:** "Never Swap Horses Crossing a Stream," *Arizona Daily Star* (Tucson), Nov. 14, 1880

102 **weren't more than fifty:** Wyatt Earp narrative.

102 **"Wyatt, I've been robbed":** As quoted in Boessenecker, *When Law Was in the Saddle*, 147.

102 **"I sought several of [Curly Bill's] friends":** Wyatt Earp narrative.

103 **agreed to "loan" $250:** Boessenecker, *When Law Was in the Saddle*, 148.

103 **"[N]o one acquainted with our jail":** "Needs Looking After," *Arizona Daily Star* (Tucson), Dec. 7, 1880.

103 **"small, thin-bladed knife":** "Watching for a Chance," *Arizona Daily Star* (Tucson), Dec. 9, 1880.

103 **"[I]f he was," Wyatt stated:** In a complete about-face from his hearing testimony, Wyatt says in his dictated narrative that Curly Bill "had been drinking considerably" and was staggering. Did Wyatt omit Curly Bill's drunkenness in his testimony to help ensure the Cowboy's exoneration?

104 **Wyatt grabbed Curly Bill's revolver:** Wyatt Earp narrative.

104 **"Regardless of the fact":** Ibid.

104 **"to stop his talk":** "Hooked Again," *Arizona Weekly Star* (Tucson), Jan. 20, 1881. This newspaper account places the church four miles from Charleston. Other contemporary accounts place the church in Charleston.

104 **fined $50 each:** *The Evening Express* (Los Angeles), Jan. 22, 1881, reprinting a story from the *Arizona Daily Star* (Tucson).

105 **"The terror these men":** "Tombstone 'Cow-Boys,'" *Arizona Weekly Star* (Tucson), Jan. 27, 1881.

105 **Johnny-Behind-the-Deuce:** There are many versions of the Johnny-Behind-the-Deuce episode, both primary and secondary accounts. Some eyewitnesses, including Wyatt himself, state that Wyatt was largely responsible for holding off the mob in Tombstone, while contemporary newspaper reports fail to mention Wyatt's name whatsoever! I've constructed my narrative, including quotes, from the following sources: "Another Murder," *Arizona Weekly Citizen*, Jan. 15, 1881; "Slaughtered," *Tombstone Epitaph*, Jan. 17, 1881; "The Charleston Homicide," *Arizona Weekly Citizen*, Jan. 22, 1881; Bailey, ed. *A Tenderfoot in Tombstone*, 119–20; George W. Parsons to Stuart Lake, Los Angeles, Oct. 25 and Nov. 6, 1928, box 10, folder 88, Stuart N. Lake Papers; Wyatt Earp narrative; Flood, "Wyatt Earp," 162–74; Lake, ed. *Under Cover for Wells Fargo*, 11–12; Breakenridge, *Helldorado*, 111–12; "Along Highway to Tombstone," *Arizona Daily Star* (Tucson), Feb. 10, 1929; and Frederick R. Bechdolt, *When the West Was Young* (New York: The Century Co., 1922), 90–97.

107 **"one of the most tenderhearted men":** The quotes from Nona Neff Hixenbaugh are from three letters (undated) she wrote to the Arizona Pioneers Historical Society and an interview she gave to the *Tombstone Epitaph* for its May 11, 1944, issue. The letters and a typescript of the *Epitaph* interview are divided between two collections: Wynona Leaona Neff Hixenbaugh Biography File, AHS; and folder 3, Earp Family Papers.

108 **Tombstone's prospects:** Several historians have written that Bat was called to Tombstone to add firepower in a supposed "gambler's war" over the Oriental's lucrative gambling concession. Bat says nothing about the feud in his writings, and the idea that the Earps would need help defending their interests is rather ludicrous. See Roger Jay, "The Gambler's War in Tombstone: Fact or Artifact?" in *A Wyatt Earp Anthology*, 256–85.

108 **staying through the summer:** Miller and Snell, *Why the West Was Wild*, 410.

109 **"Doc's whole heart and soul":** Masterson, Doc Holliday.

109 **"outside of us boys":** As quoted in "Virgil W. Earp," *The Daily Examiner* (San Francisco), May 27, 1882.

112 **conning a Texan:** This episode was a big story in the Kansas City, Missouri, newspapers. See *The Kansas City Times* (MO), Oct. 5, 6, 8, 9, and 12, 1880; *The Kansas City Evening Star* (MO), Oct. 5 and 7, 1880; and the *Kansas City Daily Journal* (MO), Oct. 6, 8, and 9, 1880. It resulted in the chief of police shutting down all the gambling houses.

112 **jumped between the two:** Both Bat and Wyatt recalled Bat jumping between Storms and Short. However, Short, in his testimony for the coroner's inquest, does not mention this. W. B. "Bat" Masterson, "Famous Gun Fighters of the Western Frontier," *The Washington Post*, March 31, 1907; Wyatt Earp narrative; and "Bound to Fight," *The Black Hills Daily Pioneer* (SD), March 13, 1881.

112 **Short, like his name:** "Hurrahs and Homicides," *The Omaha Daily Bee*, March 13, 1887.

112 **"Come here, I want to see you!":** "Charley Storms," *Black Hills Weekly Times* (SD), March 12, 1881.

113 **"You called me a son of a bitch":** "Bound to Fight."

113 **"game to the last":** Bailey, ed. *A Tenderfoot in Tombstone*, 129.

113 **"died while indulging":** "Shot Down," *The Leadville Democrat*, March 2, 1881.

113 **"Now the fight begins":** Bailey, ed. *A Tenderfoot in Tombstone*, 124.

114 **"a percentage whose exorbitance":** Bailey, ed. *Tombstone from a Woman's Point of View*, 39. See also "Tombstone Topics," *Arizona Weekly Citizen*, Aug. 28, 1881; and Breakenridge, *Helldorado*, 102.

114 **by the name Sadie Mansfield:** Sadie Mansfield was born Josephine Sarah Marcus. The most recent scholarship on the woman who would become Wyatt's fourth wife is Peter Brand, "Josephine 'Sadie' Earp's Sordid Secrets and Lies," *Wild West History Association Journal* 16 (March 2023): 10–34. But see also Monahan's very good chapter on Josephine in *Mrs. Earp*.

114 **"at which resided one Sada":** As quoted in Monahan, *Mrs. Earp*, 48.

115 **raise his eight-year-old son:** Mabel Earp Cason to Eleanor B. Sloan, Whitmore, CA, May 20, 1959, Mabel Earp Cason Papers, MS 138, AHS.

115 **"he was afraid of his own shadow":** Sol Israel to Stuart Lake, Los Angeles, Sept. 21, 1928, box 5, folder 15, Stuart N. Lake Papers. Tombstone resident John Pleasant Gray said that "Behan was a good fellow, but it takes more than a good fellow to be a good sheriff." W. Lane Rogers, ed. *When All Roads Led to Tombstone: A Memoir by John Plesent Gray* (Boise, ID: Tamarack Books, 1998), 32.

115 **made him an offer:** Testimony of Wyatt Earp and John H. Behan, Territory of Arizona v. Morgan Earp, et al., Defendants, Doc. No. 94, In Justice Court, Township No. 1, Cochise County, A.T., "Testimony, Earp-Clanton Murder Case," typescript, 120 and 100, respectively, box 2, folder 1, Glenn Boyer Wyatt Earp Collection, MS 752, UA. Hereafter cited as Spicer hearing typescript.

116 **attempt to serve a subpoena:** Ibid., 109–10.

116 **"the belle of the honkytonks":** Stuart Lake to Ira Rich Kent, Feb. 13, 1930, box 7, folder 9, Stuart N. Lake Papers.

117 **a lot to do with a woman:** Ibid.; and Ira Rich Kent to Stuart Lake, Boston, MA, Feb.19, 1930, box 4, folder 47, Stuart N. Lake Papers; and Brand, "Josephine 'Sadie' Earp's Sordid Secrets and Lies," 31.

117 **"In the quarrel":** Holliday interview in "Awful Arizona," *The Denver Republican*, May 22, 1882, as reprinted in Walling, *John "Doc" Holliday*, 11.

117 **Henry "One-Armed" Kelly:** "The Daily Arizona Episode," *The Stockton Daily Evening Mail* (CA), March 2, 1881; and *The Pioche Weekly Record* (NV), March 5, 1881.

117 **prognosis was grim:** At the end of May, Kelly was "still clinging to life with a desperation seldom equaled." *The Daily Nebraska State Journal* (Lincoln), June 1, 1881.

117 **"Oriental a regular slaughter house":** Bailey, ed. *A Tenderfoot in Tombstone*, 130.

118 **another Kinnear coach:** "Road Agents Beginning to Operate in the Tombstone Region," *Black Hills Daily Times*, March 16, 1881, reprinting an article from the *Tombstone Epitaph*.

118 **"Hold!" shouted the man:** My narrative of the Benson stage robbery is derived from "Hold," *Tombstone Epitaph*, March 16, 1881; "The Stage Robbery," *Tombstone Epitaph*, March 17, 1881; "Road Agents at Work," *Arizona Weekly Citizen*, March 20, 1881; "The Cow-Boys at Work," *Arizona Weekly Star* (Tucson), March 17, 1881; "Particulars of the Attempted Stage Robbery Near Benson," *Los Angeles Daily Herald*, March 17, 1881; Bailey, ed. *A Tenderfoot in Tombstone*, 134; "A Stage Coach," *The Arizona Republican* (Phoenix), June 26, 1892; "Wyatt Earp Tells Tales of the Shotgun-Messenger Service," *The Examiner* (San Francisco), Aug. 9, 1896; and Boessenecker, *When Law Was in the Saddle*, 161–62.

119 **on their way to the holdup site:** Not all accounts mention Doc as part of the posse, but the *Tombstone Epitaph* of March 17, 1881, does. The *Arizona Daily Star* of March 26, 1882, in a long article recounting the troubles between the Earps and the Cowboys, also includes Doc as a posse member, and so does Wyatt in "Wyatt Earp Tells Tales of the Shotgun-Messenger Service." And recall what Virgil said about Doc: "[W]henever a stage was robbed or a row started, and help was needed, Doc was one of the first to saddle his horse and report for duty."

119 **masks, and fake beards:** "Letter from Benson," *The Phoenix Herald*, March 19, 1881; "The Vendetti," *Arizona Daily Star* (Tucson), March 26, 1882; and "Wyatt Earp Tells Tales of the Shotgun-Messenger Service."

119 **wanted the Earps and Bob Paul:** "Arizona Affairs," *The Daily Examiner* (San Francisco), May 28, 1882.

120 **an exhausting zigzag route:** "The Stage Robbers," *Arizona Weekly Star* (Tucson), March 24, 1881.

120 **covered with saddle sores:** Walter Noble Burns, *Tombstone: An Iliad of the Southwest* (Garden City: Doubleday, Page & Company, 1927), 167.

120 **Hank lied to the posse:** Lake, *Wyatt Earp*, 257.

120 **"He stopped and threw up his hands":** Wyatt Earp narrative. Walter Noble Burns writes that King was milking a cow at the time he was caught, but as I've found no primary source that states this, I defer to Wyatt. See also Spicer hearing typescript, 123.

121 **part of a pulp novel:** Ibid.

121 **stuffed with more cartridges:** "The Stage Robbers," *Arizona Weekly Star* (Tucson), March 24, 1881.

121 **"I asked [King] the whereabouts":** Wyatt Earp narrative.

121 **Behan got huffy:** Lake, *Wyatt Earp*, 258.

121 **"secure him properly":** "The Stage Robbers," *Arizona Weekly Citizen*, March 27, 1881.

122 **bandits were riding fresh horses:** "Who They Are," *Tombstone Epitaph*, March 24, 1881.

122 **Virgil Earp rode up:** "Hot on Their Trail," *The Weekly Arizona Miner* (Prescott), March 25, 1881. At the same time as Virgil, Bob Paul sent a telegram with an update on the manhunt to the Wells Fargo agent in Tucson. See *Arizona Weekly Citizen*, March 27, 1881.

SEVEN: UNHOLY ALLIANCE

123 **"The men known as Cowboys"**: "Awful Arizona," *The Denver Republican*, May 22, 1882, as reprinted in Walling, *John "Doc" Holliday*, 10.

123 **horses' shoes were gone**: Wyatt Earp narrative.

123 **Wyatt and Bat walked to town**: "Arizona Affairs," *The Daily Examiner* (San Francisco), May 28, 1882.

124 **the party went without food**: "Home Again," *Tombstone Epitaph*, April 2, 1881.

124 **"The persistent pursuit"**: Ibid.

124 **called the jail "uninhabitable"**: At the examination of George Perine for murder in August, 1880, his attorney asked that Perine be "allowed a room in some hotel, under guard, as the town jail was uninhabitable." *Tombstone Epitaph*, Aug. 19, 1880.

124 **put him in shackles**: Wyatt Earp narrative; and "Arizona Affairs," *The Daily Examiner* (San Francisco), May 28, 1882.

124 **a bill of sale**: "Escape of an Arizona Murderer," *The Evening Express* (Los Angeles), April 1, 1881, reprinting a story from the *Tombstone Daily Nugget* of March 29.

125 **"King, the stage robber"**: Bailey, ed. *A Tenderfoot in Tombstone*, 137.

125 **"a most flagrant dereliction"**: *Arizona Weekly Citizen*, April 3, 1881.

125 **"Everybody but myself and brothers"**: "Arizona Affairs," *The Daily Examiner* (San Francisco), May 28, 1882.

125 **"left arm full of scars"**: Wells Fargo wanted poster as reproduced in Boessenecker, *When Law Was in the Saddle*, 167.

126 **a good reputation**: Wyatt Earp to Walter Noble Burns, Vidal, CA, March 15, 1927, Burns Papers, box 3, folder 2, UA.

126 **"pounded him in a very severe manner"**: *Las Vegas Gazette* (NM), Sept. 14, 1878.

126 **Leonard had "skipped out"**: *Daily Gazette* (San Francisco), Aug. 8, 1879, and March 3, 1880.

126 **"Doc was not in the Benson"**: Wyatt Earp to Walter Noble Burns, Vidal, CA, March 15, 1927. Wyatt told John Flood that he was dealing faro on the night of the robbery and Doc was playing against him. John Flood notes, group 3, box 1, Josephine Earp Collection, Tombstone Courthouse.

126 **games in the club room**: "Grand Reopening," *Tombstone Epitaph*, March 29, 1881.

127 **"Well, here comes the stage robber"**: As quoted in Ed Bartholomew, *Wyatt Earp, 1879–1882: The Man and the Myth, A Sequel to "The Untold Story"* (Toyahvale, TX: Frontier Book Company, 1964), 146.

127 **Doc eventually got off easy**: Tanner, *Doc Holliday*, 152.

127 **"He was his own worst enemy"**: Wyatt Earp to Walter Noble Burns, Vidal, CA, March 15, 1927.

128 **"fine specimens of the frontier"**: "The Vendetti," *Arizona Daily Star* (Tucson), March 26, 1882.

128 **"I told him that he could not"**: Testimony of Wyatt Earp, Spicer hearing typescript, 120, and *Tombstone Epitaph*, Nov. 17, 1881.

129 **Frank and Tom McLaury**: The best treatment of the McLaurys is Paul Lee Johnson, *The McLaurys in Tombstone, Arizona: An O.K. Corral Obituary* (Denton, TX: University of North Texas Press, 2012).

130 "They were both well educated": "The Vendetti," *Arizona Daily Star* (Tucson), March 26, 1882.

130 part of the Cowboy network: Breakenridge, *Helldorado*, 105.

130 "were a tough lot of rustlers": The man offering this opinion was none other than former Cochise County sheriff Johnny Behan. "Men Met in Hotel Lobbies," *The Washington Post*, Nov. 16, 1897.

131 "We tracked the mules": Testimony of Wyatt Earp, Spicer hearing typescript, 113, and *Tombstone Epitaph*, Nov. 17, 1881.

131 the lieutenant posted a notice: *Tombstone Epitaph*, July 30, 1880.

131 "If I thought you did": "Arizona Affairs," *The Daily Examiner* (San Francisco), May 28, 1882.

131 "They tried to pick a fuss": Testimony of Wyatt Earp, *Tombstone Epitaph*, Nov. 17, 1881.

131 "I told them," Wyatt recalled: Ibid.

131 promised another thousand dollars: Testimony of Joseph I. Clanton, Spicer hearing typescript, 70; and "The Vendetti," *Arizona Daily Star* (Tucson), March 26, 1882.

132 buy the ranch or get off: Testimony of Virgil Earp, Spicer hearing transcript, 137.

132 "Here are three of you": Ibid., 138.

132 the answer to his wire: Testimony of Joseph I. Clanton, Spicer hearing typescript, 68.

133 "both determined men": *Tombstone Epitaph*, June 9, 1881.

133 a way to lure the stage robbers: Testimony of Wyatt Earp, Spicer hearing transcript, 114.

134 "wished someone would shoot him": "Sent to Meet His God," *Tombstone Epitaph*, June 18, 1881.

134 "The country is well rid": Ibid.

135 their secret was out: Frederick R. Bechdolt to William M. Breakenridge, Carmel, CA, Dec. 23, 1927, box 19, Houghton Mifflin Company correspondence and records, MS Am 1925, Houghton Library, Harvard University, Cambridge, MA.

135 "Clanton, of course, immediately": Wyatt Earp narrative.

135 rumored to have been hanged: "Arizona Items," *The Evening Express* (Los Angeles), April 6, 1881; and "False Alarm," *Tombstone Epitaph*, April 1, 1881.

135 Jim Crane and several comrades: "The Cowboys," *The Daily Examiner* (San Francisco), March 23, 1882; and W. Lane Rogers, ed. *When All Roads Led to Tombstone*, 50–51. See also Roy B. Young, "The Other Ike and Billy: The Heslet Brothers in Grant County, New Mexico," *A Wyatt Earp Anthology*, 286–301.

135 "never saw such a dreadful sight": "End of the Cow-Boy Tragedy," *Tombstone Epitaph*, June 22, 1881.

135 "they shunned us": Testimony of Wyatt Earp, *Tombstone Epitaph*, Nov. 17, 1881.

136 "was in a place where taste": "Oriental Club Rooms," *Tombstone Epitaph*, June 15, 1881.

136 the Oriental was on fire: For the Tombstone fire of June 22, 1881, see Bailey, ed., *Tombstone from a Woman's Point of View*, 29–31; "The Tombstone Fire," *The Daily Examiner* (San Francisco), June 24 and 27, 1881; "The Fiery Ordeal," *Arizona Weekly Star* (Tucson), June 30, 1881; and Bailey, ed., *A Tenderfoot in Tombstone*, 155–57.

137 "I was very much surprised": Wyatt Earp narrative.

138 "We have not heard of": "Thursday's Gleanings," *Tombstone Epitaph*, June 24, 1881.

138 Doc was indicted: Criminal Register of Actions, Territory of Arizona v. J. H. Holliday, May 27, 1881, reproduced in Traywick, *Historical Documents and Photographs of*

Tombstone, 137; *Tombstone Epitaph*, May 29, 1881; and *Arizona Weekly Star* (Tucson), June 2, 1881.

138 **mask with a rope beard:** "The Vendetti," *Arizona Daily Star* (Tucson), March 26, 1882.

139 **Behan arrested Doc:** "Important Arrest," *The Weekly Arizona Miner* (Prescott), July 15, 1881.

139 **"Whenever [Behan's crowd]":** Stephens, ed. *Wyatt Earp Speaks!*, 195–96.

139 **"to block them":** Mary K. Cummings Recollections. For a much different account by Kate, in which she makes no mention of her affidavit or Doc's subsequent arrest, see Bork and Boyer, "The O.K. Corral Fight at Tombstone," 77–78.

139 **Virgil arrested her for being drunk:** Ibid.; and Roberts, *Doc Holliday*, 154.

139 **"he was personally satisfied":** As quoted in Roberts, *Doc Holliday*, 156.

139 **Spicer was happy to do:** *Tombstone Epitaph*, July 10, 1881.

140 **"It took all the persecution":** Mary K. Cummings Recollections.

EIGHT: BOLD TALK

141 **"The Cowboys as a class":** Joseph Bowyer to John J. Gosper, Galeyville, A.T., Sept. 17, 1881, Cowboy Depredations in Arizona, Microfilm 2061, UA. This is National Archives microfilm containing correspondence from Record Group 60, Records of the Department of Justice.

141 **Gray-bearded Old Man Clanton:** My narrative of the Mexican attack on Clanton and his fellow Cowboys is drawn from "Story of an Eye-Witness," *Arizona Weekly Star*, (Tucson), Sept. 1, 1881; "Arizona: Serious Trouble on the Border," *Sacramento Daily Record-Union*, Aug. 18, 1881, reprinting a story from the *Tombstone Epitaph*; "Horrible Butchery," *The Omaha Daily Bee*, December 16, 1881, reprinting a story from the *Tombstone Daily Nugget*; "Arizona: The Border War," *Sacramento Daily Record-Union*, Aug. 19, 1881; "Tombstone Topics," *Arizona Weekly Citizen*, Aug. 28, 1881; and letter of W. B. Hicks to Frederick R. Bechdolt published in *Adventure Magazine* 37 (Nov. 1927): 183.

142 **two thousand silver pesos:** Details on the booty captured by the Cowboys comes from a 1927 letter written by W. B. Hicks, cited above. This Hicks was known at the time as Bill Hicks, and he was a member of the Cowboys. A letter written from Galeyville, Arizona, a popular Cowboy hangout, reported that the take from the smugglers' pack train amounted to "$4,000 in Mexican coin, silver bullion, mescal, horses, and cattle." Joseph Bowyer to John J. Gosper, Galeyville, A.T., Sept. 17, 1881.

142 **"This killing business":** Bailey, ed. *A Tenderfoot in Tombstone*, 167. See also Bailey, ed. *Tombstone from a Woman's Point of View*, 40.

142 **"Serious international complications":** *Sacramento Daily Record-Union*, Aug. 18, 1881.

143 **"The Cowboys will come to control":** John J. Gosper to James G. Blaine, Prescott, AZ, Sept. 20, 1881, Cowboy Depredations in Arizona, Microfilm 2061, UA.

143 **The robbery and Wyatt's posse:** "Stage Robbery," *Tombstone Epitaph*, Sept. 10, 1881.

144 **appointed a deputy US marshal:** There's been much discussion as to whether Wyatt was indeed a deputy US marshal at this time. Wyatt says that he was, and so did his brother Virgil. He's also identified as a deputy US marshal by both the *Daily Nugget* and the *Tombstone Epitaph*. Wyatt Earp narrative; "Arizona Affairs," *The Daily Examiner* (San Francisco), May 28, 1882.; "The Stage Robbery," *Arizona Weekly Citizen* (Tucson), Sept. 18, 1881, reprinting a story from the *Tombstone Daily Nugget* of Sept. 13; "In

the Tolls Again," *Tombstone Epitaph*, Oct. 14, 1881; and Gary Roberts, "Was Wyatt Earp Really a Deputy U.S. Marshal," *True West* (Feb./March 2021), available online at https://truewestmagazine.com/article/was-wyatt-earp-really-a-deputy-u-s-marshal/.

144 **Those who started out of town:** Three participants in the manhunt, Wyatt, Fred Dodge, and William Breakenridge, left accounts of the chase, and they all conflict with one another on a number of details. See "Sage Robbery," *Tombstone Epitaph*, Sept. 10, 1881; Wyatt Earp narrative; "Wyatt Earp Tells Tales of the Shotgun-Messenger Service"; Lake, ed. *Under Cover for Wells Fargo*, 13–15 and 245–46; and Breakenridge, *Helldorado*, 139–41. Breakenridge was an Earp detractor and admitted that he fleshed out his original manuscript considerably after getting access to historic Tombstone newspapers at the Arizona Pioneers' Historical Society. One wonders, then, just how much of his book is truly his own personal recollections of the events and people he describes. William Breakenridge to Ira Rich Kent, Tucson, AZ, Nov. 22 and Dec. 6, 1927, Houghton Mifflin Company correspondence.

144 **Frank Stilwell and Pete Spence:** For Stilwell, "The Fatal Bullet," *Arizona Weekly Citizen* (Tucson), March 26, 1882; Young, *Cochise County Cowboy War*, 120; and Lynn R. Bailey and Don Chaput, *Cochise County Stalwarts: A Who's Who of the Territorial Years*, 2 vols. (Tucson: Westernlore Press, 2000), 2: 141–42. For Spence, Roy B. Young, *Pete Spence: "Audacious Artist in Crime"* (Apache, OK: Young & Sons Enterprises, 2000).

145 **asked for the old heels:** Fred Dodge writes that he found a single detached boot heel on the trail and that he subsequently saw a new heel on one of Frank Stilwell's boots. Wyatt, however, makes no mention of a detached heel, instead stating that Stilwell had both heels replaced in Bisbee so that the screws in the old heels would not link him to the robber's boot prints. Testimony of the Bisbee shoemaker confirms Wyatt's version: He removed and replaced both heels. "The Stage Robbery Trial," *Tombstone Epitaph*, Oct. 23, 1881.

146 **"if it turns out as now anticipated":** "Important Capture," *Tombstone Epitaph*, Sept. 13, 1881.

146 **"I have threatened you boys' lives":** Testimony of Wyatt Earp, Spicer hearing transcript, 115, and *Tombstone Epitaph*, Nov. 17, 1881.

146 **a report reached Tombstone:** "Fighting in the Dragoons," *Tombstone Epitaph*, Oct. 5, 1881.

146 **twenty heavily armed men:** "The Flying Renegades," *Tombstone Epitaph*, Oct. 6, 1881.

147 **lost fourteen head of horses:** Berndt Kühn, *Chronicles of War: Apache & Yavapai Resistance in the Southwestern United States and Northern Mexico, 1821–1937* (Tucson: The Arizona Historical Society, 2014), 250.

147 **"was Arizona's most famous outlaw":** Bailey, ed. *A Tenderfoot in Tombstone*, 182.

147 **shot in the neck:** "Curly Bill," *Arizona Weekly Star* (Tucson), May 26, 1881.

147 **"Do not be too handy":** "A Life for a Life," *Arizona Weekly Star* (Tucson), July 14, 1881.

148 **"My boots and spurs":** Bailey, ed. *A Tenderfoot in Tombstone*, 184.

148 **dismissed by Justice Spicer:** "Justice's Court," *Tombstone Epitaph*, Oct. 6, 1881; and "Arrival of Mail Robbers," *Arizona Weekly Star* (Tucson), Oct. 20, 1881.

149 **Wyatt rearrested Stilwell:** "In the Tolls Again," *Tombstone Epitaph*, Oct. 14, 1881.

149 **"very bitter towards me":** Wyatt Earp narrative.

149 **"I understand you are raising":** Testimony of Virgil Earp, *Tombstone Epitaph*, Nov. 23, 1881. Here and elsewhere, I have corrected the spelling of surnames.

150 **back her on a bank loan:** Mary K. Cummings Recollections.

150 **hearing occurred over two days:** Coverage of the hearing is found in the *Tombstone Epitaph*, Oct. 22 and 23, 1881.

150 **"the favorite resort":** *Arizona Weekly Citizen*, Sept. 4, 1881.

150 **"to keep the peace":** Testimony of Virgil Earp, Spicer hearing transcript, 132.

150 **four to five hundred patrons:** "Bloody Deeds," *Tombstone Epitaph*, Dec. 30, 1881, reprinting an article from the *Kansas City Evening Star* (MO).

150 **Clanton found Wyatt one day:** Testimony of Wyatt Earp, *Tombstone Epitaph*, Nov. 17, 1881.

151 **a faro bank in Congress Hall:** Mary K. Cummings Recollections.

151 **"I will come after you tomorrow":** Bork and Boyer, "The O.K. Corral Fight at Tombstone," 79; and Mary K. Cummings to Lillie Raffert, March 18, 1940.

151 **"using his name":** Testimony of Joseph I. Clanton, *Tombstone Epitaph*, Nov. 13, 1881, and Inquest on the Bodies of William Clanton, Frank McLaury, and Thomas McLaury, Doc. No. 45, District Court of the 1st Judicial District, Cochise County, A.T., typescript, 8, box 2, folder 1, Glenn Boyer Wyatt Earp Collection, MS 752, UA. Hereafter cited as Clanton/McLaury inquest typescript.

151 **"Doc's vocabulary of profanity":** Lake, ed. *Under Cover for Wells Fargo*, 26.

152 **"to go to fighting":** Testimony of Joseph I. Clanton, *Tombstone Epitaph*, Nov. 10, 1881, and Spicer hearing transcript, 64.

152 **faro game he needed to close:** Testimony of Wyatt Earp, Spicer hearing transcript, 115.

152 **"about time to fetch it to a close":** Testimony of Wyatt Earp, *Tombstone Epitaph*, Nov. 17, 1881.

152 **"because there was no money in it":** Testimony of Wyatt Earp, Spicer hearing transcript, 116.

153 **"consider it necessary in their business":** "Another Tragedy," *Ford County Globe* (Dodge City, KS), April 8, 1879.

154 **"The damned son of a bitch":** Testimony of Virgil Earp, *Tombstone Epitaph*, Nov. 20, 1881.

NINE: THIRTY SECONDS

155 **"It is foolish to think":** Mary K. Cummings to Lillie Raffert, March 18, 1940.

155 **"You better get up":** Testimony of Virgil Earp, *Tombstone Epitaph*, Nov. 23, 1881.

155 **"as soon as those damned Earps":** Testimony of Wyatt Earp, *Tombstone Epitaph*, Nov. 17, 1881.

156 **"If God lets me live long enough":** Mary K. Cummings Recollections.

156 **"I hear you are hunting":** Testimony of Wyatt Earp, *Tombstone Epitaph*, Nov. 17, 1881.

157 **"I will get even with you":** Ibid.

157 **"You have threatened my life":** Testimony of R. J. Campbell, *Tombstone Epitaph*, Nov. 24, 1881.

157 **"You fellows haven't given me":** *Tombstone Epitaph*, Oct. 27, 1881.

157 **wouldn't tolerate any fuss:** Testimony of Wyatt Earp, *Tombstone Epitaph*, Nov. 17, 1881.

158 **"If you want to make a fight":** Ibid.

158 **revolver from the large side pocket:** Testimony of Appollinor Bauer, *Tombstone Epitaph*, Nov. 11, 1881. Some gunmen were known to have coats with large side pockets to

accommodate revolvers and also prevent a revolver's hammer from catching on the pocket when withdrawn. According to one source, Wyatt's coat had a pocket lined with canvas to facilitate sliding his revolver in and out. It was also common to have "pistol pockets" sewn into trousers. See "The Pistol Pocket in the U.S.," *The Clothier & Furnisher* 18 (June 1889): 39–40; "Your Pistol, How People Carry Firearms in the West and in the East," *The Wichita Daily Beacon*, March 8, 1894; and William B. Shillingberg, *Wyatt Earp & the "Buntline Special" Myth* (Tucson, AZ: Blaine Publishing Company, 1976), 48.

158 **"I could kill the son of a bitch":** Ibid. Bauer testified that McLaury told Wyatt he wasn't armed. Wyatt, however, stated that he could plainly see a pistol on the Cowboy's right hip.

158 **fined Ike $25 plus costs:** "Yesterday's Tragedy," *Tombstone Epitaph*, Oct. 27, 1881.

158 **"Anywhere where I can get them":** Testimony of Virgil Earp, *Tombstone Epitaph*, Nov. 20, 1881.

158 **He first found a doctor:** Testimony of William F. Claiborne, Clanton/McLaury inquest typescript, 20.

158 **he dressed in a gray suit:** Testimony of C. H. Light, Clanton/McLaury inquest typescript, 18; Tanner, *Doc Holliday*, 118 and 165; and Roberts, *Doc Holliday*, 193.

159 **at Baron's Barber Shop:** Testimony of John H. Behan, Clanton/McLaury inquest typescript, 1.

159 **reached out and shook his hand:** Testimony of Joseph I. Clanton, Clanton/McLaury inquest typescript, 9; and Testimony of William Allen, Spicer hearing typescript, 28.

159 **"What did he hit Tom for?":** Testimony of William Allen, Spicer hearing typescript, 28.

160 **"I see two more of them":** Testimony of Virgil Earp, *Tombstone Epitaph*, Nov. 23, 1881.

160 **short-barreled ten-gauge shotgun:** Ibid.

160 **lighting a cigar:** Testimony of Wyatt Earp, *Tombstone Epitaph*, Nov. 17, 1881.

160 **putting cartridges in their gun belts:** Ibid.; and testimony of Virgil Earp, *Tombstone Epitaph*, Nov. 23, 1881.

160 **A group of miners approached:** Ibid.; and testimony of Virgil Earp, *Tombstone Epitaph*, Nov. 20, 1881.

161 **the Cowboy's bloody bandage:** Testimony of Joseph I. Clanton, *Tombstone Epitaph*, Nov. 15, 1881.

161 **enter the Dexter Stables:** Testimony of Wyatt Earp, *Tombstone Epitaph*, Nov. 17, 1881. The Dexter Stables had been purchased by John Dunbar and his partner, Johnny Behan, in June 1881. See the *Tombstone Epitaph*, June 15, 1881.

161 **"There is to be trouble":** Testimony of John H. Behan, Clanton/McLaury inquest typescript, 1.

161 **they could have it:** Testimony of John H. Behan, *Tombstone Epitaph*, Nov. 3, 1881.

161 **persuaded Virgil to join him:** Testimony of P. H. Fellehy, Clanton/McLaury inquest typescript, 11. Former Pima County sheriff Charles Shibell was with Behan when he invited Virgil to a drink in the saloon.

161 **"They won't hurt me":** Testimony of Virgil Earp, *Tombstone Epitaph*, Nov. 20, 1881.

161 **"to lay off their arms":** Ibid.

161 **The purpose of the Committee:** John Clum to Stuart Lake, Los Angeles, Jan. 31, 1929, box 2, folder 21, Stuart N. Lake Papers.

161 **twenty-five armed volunteers:** Testimony of Virgil Earp, *Tombstone Epitaph*, Nov. 23, 1881.

162 **"a stripling belonging to":** Joseph Bowyer to John J. Gosper, Galeyville, A.T., Sept. 17, 1881.

162 **"Is your name Earp?":** Testimony of Virgil Earp, *Tombstone Epitaph*, Nov. 23, 1881; and testimony of H. F. Sills, *Tombstone Epitaph*, Nov. 23, 1881.

162 **"You're not going to leave me":** Wyatt Earp narrative. Authors and historians, from Stuart Lake to the present day, have Wyatt telling Doc it's not his fight and Doc, offended, responding with, "That's a hell of a thing for you to say to me." This line apparently appears in a version of John Flood's Earp biography, but it's not in two versions of Flood that I have access to, nor is it in the Wyatt Earp narrative dictated to Flood. See Lake, *Wyatt Earp*, 288; Roberts, *Doc Holliday*, 194; Flood, "Wyatt Earp," 228; and Wyatt S. Earp, *Wyatt Earp* (Sierra Vista, AZ: Yoma V. Bissette, 1981), 228.

162 **handed him the shotgun:** Testimony of Virgil Earp, *Tombstone Epitaph*, Nov. 23, 1881.

162 **"They have horses":** Testimony of Wyatt Earp, *Tombstone Epitaph*, Nov. 17, 1881.

163 **"It was our intention":** Wyatt Earp narrative.

163 **a winter storm was coming:** Bailey, ed. *A Tenderfoot in Tombstone*, 188.

163 **eighteen-foot-wide vacant lot:** Estimates of the lot's width range from fifteen to twenty feet.

163 **"For God's sake, boys":** This is what was heard by eyewitness Mrs. J. C. Collier, but there are many variations of Behan's words. Virgil Earp testified that Behan said "For God's sake, don't go down there, or they will murder you!" "Bloody Deeds," *Tombstone Epitaph*, Dec. 30, 1881, reprinting an article from the *Kansas City Evening Star* (MO); and testimony of Virgil Earp, *Tombstone Epitaph*, Nov. 20, 1881.

164 **pushed the holster around:** Ibid.; and testimony of Virgil Earp, Clanton/McLaury inquest typescript, 134.

164 **Wyatt placed his pistol:** Testimony of Wyatt Earp, *Tombstone Epitaph*, Nov. 17, 1881.

164 **Tom McLaury's hand gripped:** Testimony of Virgil Earp, *Tombstone Epitaph*, Nov. 20, 1881.

164 **"Boys," Virgil said, "throw up your hands":** Ibid.

164 **meant to take him out first:** Testimony of Wyatt Earp, *Tombstone Epitaph*, Nov. 17, 1881.

164 **the slightest of pauses:** Testimony of J. H. Lucas, *Tombstone Epitaph*, Nov. 29, 1881, and Clanton/McLaury inquest typescript, 161.

165 **"Don't kill me!":** Wyatt Earp narrative.

165 **"The fight has now commenced":** Testimony of Wyatt Earp, *Tombstone Epitaph*, Nov. 17, 1881.

165 **revolver over the animal's back:** Testimony of Virgil Earp, *Tombstone Epitaph*, Nov. 20, 1881. Eyewitness Mrs. J. C. Collier said she saw the gun being fired from beneath the horse's neck. "Bloody Deeds," *Tombstone Epitaph*, Dec. 30, 1881, reprinting an article from the *Kansas City Evening Star* (MO).

165 **"I am shot":** Testimony of Robert S. Hatch, *Tombstone Epitaph*, Nov. 18, 1881. In a letter dated February 4, 1882, Morgan's wife, Louisa, wrote that Morgan "was shot through both shoulders, both shoulder blades were broken and the spinal column was slightly injured." As quoted in Monahan, *Mrs. Earp*, 114.

165 **striking the horse in the withers:** Wyatt Earp narrative; and "How Wyatt Earp Routed a Gang of Arizona Outlaws."

165 **Tom clutched his chest:** Testimony of William Allen, Clanton/McLaury inquest typescript, 31.

165 **started to run down Fremont:** Testimony of R. F. Coleman, Ibid., 6.

165 **couldn't get the gun to go off:** Mary K. Cummings Recollections; Mary K. Cummings to Lillie Raffert, March 18, 1940; and testimony of John H. Behan, *Tombstone Epitaph*, Nov. 4, 1881. Kate Elder claimed to have watched the gunfight from the Fly boardinghouse window. She said that Doc fired one barrel of the shotgun, "but after that something went wrong. He threw the gun on the ground and finished the fight with his revolver." The fact that Tom McLaury was found to have twelve buckshot wounds in a very tight group supports this scenario. According to a 1901 article, Wells Fargo express messengers of this period typically used shot shells that held thirteen buckshot. Thus, if Doc had fired both barrels at once, as some authors have written, the coroner would have found twice the number of wounds in McLaury's body. See Charles Michelson, "Stage Robbers of the West," *Munsey's Magazine* 25 (July 1901): 452.

166 **toward the street with his horse:** Testimony of James Kehoe, Clanton/McLaury inquest typescript, 37.

166 **the police chief stood back up:** Testimony of H. F. Sills, *Tombstone Epitaph*, Nov. 23, 1881; and "Yesterday's Tragedy," *Tombstone Epitaph*, Oct. 27, 1881.

166 **tiny piece of Wyatt's coat:** Flood, "Wyatt Earp," 232.

166 **struggled to get the Winchester:** Testimony of Wesley Fuller, *Tombstone Epitaph*, Nov. 8, 1881.

166 **"I've got you now":** "A Desperate Street Fight," *Arizona Weekly Citizen* (Tucson), Oct. 30, 1881, reprinting a story from the *Tombstone Daily Nugget* of Oct. 27.

166 **slid down against the corner:** Testimony of Wesley Fuller, Clanton/McLaury inquest typescript, 41; and *Tombstone Epitaph*, Nov. 8, 1881.

166 **rested the revolver on his leg:** Testimony of C. H. Light, Clanton/McLaury inquest typescript, 18.

166 **"Give me some more cartridges":** Testimony of Robert S. Hatch, *Tombstone Epitaph*, Nov. 18, 1881.

166 **"The son of a bitch has shot me":** Testimony of P. H. Fellehy, Clanton/McLaury inquest typescript, 12.

167 **"I will have to arrest you":** Testimony of William Cuddy, Ibid., 16–17.

167 **"I won't be arrested":** Testimony of R. F. Coleman, Ibid., 6–7.

167 **"a commotion, and looking up":** Wyatt Earp narrative.

167 **"We won't have to disarm that party":** Testimony of John H. Behan, *Tombstone Epitaph*, Oct. 29, 1881.

168 **"Oh, this is just awful":** Bork and Boyer, "The O.K. Corral Fight at Tombstone," 80.

TEN: AN EYE FOR AN EYE

169 **"We went into Tombstone":** "Virgil W. Earp," *The Daily Examiner* (San Francisco), May 27, 1882.

169 **"Wyatt Earp stood up and fired":** "Yesterday's Tragedy," *Tombstone Epitaph*, Oct. 27, 1881.

170 **"a word of complaint"**: "A Desperate Street Fight," *Arizona Weekly Citizen* (Tucson), Oct. 30, 1881, reprinting a story from the *Tombstone Daily Nugget* of Oct. 27.

170 **"They have murdered me!"**: Testimony of Thomas Keefe, *Tombstone Epitaph*, Nov. 11, 1881.

170 **"only on the face of"**: "A Desperate Street Fight," *Arizona Weekly Citizen* (Tucson), Oct. 30, 1881.

171 **"Shooting Affray at Tombstone"**: *Los Angeles Daily Herald*, Oct. 27, 1881.

171 **"Cowboys try to run Tombstone"**: *Oakland Daily Evening Tribune*, Oct. 27, 1881.

171 **"the liveliest street battle"**: *The Weekly Bee* (Sacramento), Oct. 29, 1881.

171 **"Murdered in the Streets of Tombstone"**: Johnson, *The McLaurys in Tombstone, Arizona*, 187.

171 **horse-drawn creped wagons**: Ibid.; and "The Funeral," *Tombstone Epitaph*, Oct. 28, 1881.

172 **"a public manifestation of sympathy"**: Bailey, ed. *Tombstone from a Woman's Point of View*, 43.

173 **A woman and her two children**: "Bloody Deeds," *Tombstone Epitaph*, Dec. 30, 1881.

173 **"You may meet one man"**: Bailey, ed. *Tombstone from a Woman's Point of View*, 43.

173 **He swore out a complaint**: "Justice's Court," *Tombstone Epitaph*, Oct. 30, 1881.

174 **Spicer set bail at $10,000 each**: Ibid.; and "Arrested," *Arizona Weekly Citizen* (Tucson), Nov. 6, 1881, reprinting an article from the *Tombstone Daily Nugget* of Oct. 30, 1881.

174 **the Earps and their wives moved**: Wyatt Earp narrative.

174 **"as cold-blooded and foul"**: As quoted in Johnson, *The McLaurys in Tombstone, Arizona*, 211.

174 **"I haven't got anything, boys"**: Testimony of William F. Claiborne, *Tombstone Epitaph*, Nov. 9, 1881.

175 **"Let them have it!"**: Testimony of Martha J. King, *Tombstone Epitaph*, Nov. 5, 1881.

175 **began turning against the Earps**: "Devotees of Crime," *St. Louis Globe-Democrat*, Nov. 8, 1881.

175 **remanded Wyatt and Doc**: *Tombstone Epitaph*, Nov. 8, 1881.

175 **"The scoundrels are in jail"**: As quoted in Johnson, *The McLaurys in Tombstone, Arizona*, 212.

175 **"the sheriff had been as active"**: *Tombstone Epitaph*, Nov. 8, 1881.

176 **"I could not tell"**: Testimony of Addie V. Borland, Clanton/McLaury inquest typescript, 153.

176 **"would have to kill them or else"**: Testimony of Joseph I. Clanton, *Tombstone Epitaph*, Nov. 13, 1881.

176 **Attorney Thomas Fitch quizzed Behan**: Testimony of John H. Behan, *Tombstone Epitaph*, November 5, 1881; and Casey Tefertiller, "Behan's Lies," in *A Wyatt Earp Anthology*, 405–6.

177 **Williams, subsequently testified**: Testimony of Winfield S. Williams, *Tombstone Epitaph*, Nov. 29, 1881.

177 **"When I went as deputy marshal"**: Testimony of Wyatt Earp, *Tombstone Epitaph*, Nov. 17, 1881.

177 **"from our knowledge of him"**: Ibid.

178 **"the gratification of revenge"**: "Devotees of Crime," *St. Louis Globe-Democrat*, Nov. 8, 1881.

178 **set at $10,000 each:** *Tombstone Epitaph*, Nov. 24, 1881. Wyatt said that "at least fifty persons came forward and offered to give bond."

178 **"In fact, as the result plainly proves":** "The Decision," *Tombstone Epitaph*, Dec. 1, 1881.

179 **"with a very bad grace":** Bailey, ed. *Tombstone from a Woman's Point of View*, 47.

179 **Henry Holliday received a letter:** *The Valdosta Times* (GA), June 24, 1882.

179 **this time for firing a pistol:** Roberts, *Doc Holliday*, 223.

179 **a reputation as a brazen rustler:** A letter writer in Galeyville, a young silver mining camp northeast of Tombstone, referred to Ringo as a "notorious Cowboy." Joseph Bowyer to John J. Gosper, Galeyville, A.T., Sept. 17, 1881.

179 **"always looked neat":** Mary K. Cummings Recollections.

180 **described him as a heavy drinker:** Breakenridge, *Helldorado*, 134.

180 **prepared a "death list":** John Clum to Stuart Lake, Los Angeles, Jan. 31, 1929.

180 **"more genial clime":** "A Cheerful Letter," *Tombstone Epitaph*, Dec. 18, 1881.

180 **conduct a raid on Tombstone:** "Bloody Deeds," *Tombstone Epitaph*, Dec. 30, 1881; and John Clum to Stuart Lake, Los Angeles, Jan. 31, 1929.

181 **the stage contained no bullion:** "Attempted Assassination of Hon. John P. Clum, *Daily Arizona Citizen* (Tucson), Dec. 16, 1881, typescript in box 2, folder 21, Stuart N. Lake Papers.

181 **"as it is a well-known fact":** Ibid.

181 **no rifle shell casings:** "Attempted Assassination of Hon. John P. Clum, *Daily Arizona Citizen* (Tucson), Dec. 16, 1881.

181 **"Your favorite method":** *Tombstone Daily Nugget*, December 16, 1881, as quoted in Ben T. Traywick, *Wyatt Earp: Angel of Death* (Honolulu, HI: Talei Publishers, Inc., 2007), 412.

182 **Stilwell was granted bail:** "The Fatal Bullet," *Arizona Weekly Citizen* (Tucson), March 26, 1882; and Shillingberg, *Tombstone, A.T.*, 276.

182 **Frank Stilwell, seated nearby:** Wyatt Earp narrative.

182 **saw Frank run into an adobe:** Ibid.; and Wyatt Earp to Stuart Lake, n.d., folder 39, box 3, Stuart N. Lake Papers.

182 **four loud blasts:** Bailey, ed. *A Tenderfoot in Tombstone*, 198. Some accounts say five shots. See "Midnight Assassins," *Tombstone Epitaph*, Dec. 29, 1881.

182 **shattered the bone in his arm:** Virgil's injuries are detailed in "Attempted Assassination," *Sacramento Daily-Record Union*, Dec. 30, 1881; *Tombstone Epitaph*, Dec. 30, 1881; and Virgil W. Earp pension application abstracted in Irvine, comp., *Data on the Earp Family*, installment for July 30, 1958.

182 **"I want him myself":** Wyatt Earp narrative.

183 **"I almost fainted":** Reidhead, *Travesty*, 410.

183 **"It's hell, isn't it!":** Bailey, ed. *A Tenderfoot in Tombstone*, 199.

183 **removed his elbow joint:** Ibid.; and *Tombstone Epitaph*, Dec. 30, 1881.

183 **nineteen pellets hit:** "Midnight Assassins," *Tombstone Epitaph*, Dec. 29, 1881.

183 **suspects included Curly Bill, Will McLaury:** Bailey, ed. *A Tenderfoot in Tombstone*, 199.

183 **"Virgil Earp was shot":** "Another Chapter in the Earp-Holliday History," *The Weekly Arizona Miner* (Prescott), Dec. 30, 1881.

184 **"spare no expense in discovering":** As quoted in Roberts, *Doc Holliday*, 233. The *Daily Nugget* reported on January 3 that Dake telegraphed the "appointment of Deputy

United States Marshal vice Virgil Earp." The use of "vice" here means "in the place of." As has been seen, Wyatt was already a deputy US marshal, but it would seem that Wyatt was replacing Virgil as the lead deputy US marshal for the area.

184 **Wyatt sold his interest:** Ibid., 236; and Shillingberg, *Tombstone, A.T.*, 297.

184 **bad blood had developed:** "Almost a Tragedy," *Arizona Weekly Citizen* (Tucson), Jan. 22, 1882, reprinting an article from the *Tombstone Daily Nugget.*

184 **Ringo's attentions to Kate:** Interestingly, Kate would claim that Ringo "was a loyal friend to my husband, Doc Holliday, and to myself." The two certainly weren't acting like friends on this day in Tombstone. Mary K. Cummings Recollections.

184 **"Holliday, you have been":** Wyatt Earp narrative. There are a number of versions of this near-gunfight between Holliday and Ringo. See Roberts, *Doc Holliday*, 236–38.

185 **arrested and fined $32:** *Tombstone Epitaph*, Jan. 18, 1882.

185 **"carries his death warrant":** John Church as quoted in "Arizona's Exhibit," *Rocky Mountain News*, June 27, 1882.

185 **Wyatt Earp and eight men:** "Flight of the Earps," *The Sun* (San Diego, CA), Jan. 26, 1882, reprinting an article from the *Tombstone Daily Nugget.*

185 **The men riding with Wyatt:** For members of the posse see Ibid.; Wyatt Earp to Walter Noble Burns, Vidal, CA, March 15, 1927; Peter Brand, *Wyatt Earp's Vendetta Posse Rider: The Story of Texas Jack Vermillion* (Meadowbank, Australia: Published by the author, 2012), 34–36; Peter Brand, "Wyatt Earp's Vendetta Posse," in *A Wyatt Earp Anthology*, 458–459; and Roberts, *Doc Holliday*, 233 and 239.

186 **arrested and fined $25:** Tanner, *Doc Holliday*, 282 n. 62.

186 **using McMaster as a spy:** Wyatt told John Flood that he "had a man engaged for the purpose of learning the whereabouts of 'Curly Bill' and 'Pony' Deal." When Flood asked the identity of this man, Wyatt said he was McMaster. Wyatt Earp narrative.

186 **each man received $5 a day:** Shillingberg, *Tombstone, A.T.*, 303.

186 **"as desperate men":** "Flight of the Earps," *The Sun* (San Diego, CA), Jan. 26, 1882, reprinting an article from the *Tombstone Daily Nugget.*

187 **connection to the Bisbee stage:** Wyatt Earp narrative.

187 **supposedly by Johnny Ringo:** Roberts, *Doc Holliday*, 239.

187 **"nearly paralyzing the business":** "'A Pestiferous Posse,' and the Daily Rustleiferous," *Tombstone Epitaph*, Jan. 28, 1882, reprinting an article from the *Tombstone Daily Nugget.*

187 **the Clantons surrendered:** "The Gentlemen Win," *Tombstone Daily Nugget*, Jan. 31, 1881, as quoted in Timothy W. Fattig, *Wyatt Earp, The Biography* (Honolulu, HI: Talei Publishers, Inc., 2002), 481–82.

187 **"would have to go back":** "The Clanton Trial," *Tombstone Epitaph*, Feb. 3, 1882.

187 **"much harsh criticism":** "Draw Your Own Inference," *Tombstone Epitaph*, Feb. 2, 1882.

188 **"private wrongs to avenge":** "Last Night's Meeting," *Tombstone Epitaph*, Feb. 1, 1882.

188 **he did not accept:** Fattig, *Wyatt Earp*, 488.

188 **"Cowboys are a great obstacle":** Jee, "The Arizona Cow-boys."

188 **"most emphatically declined":** As quoted in Johnson, *The McLaurys in Tombstone, Arizona*, 269.

188 **he filed a complaint:** J. B. Smith, Order for Arrest, Feb. 9, 1882, "Testimony, Earp-Clanton Murder Case," typescript, 171, box 2, folder 1, Glenn Boyer Wyatt Earp Collection, MS 752, UA; and *Tombstone Epitaph*, Feb. 11, 1882.

189 **"This was all planned"**: Wyatt Earp narrative.

189 **"armed to the teeth"**: Bailey, ed. *A Tenderfoot in Tombstone*, 206. See also *Tombstone Epitaph*, Feb. 15, 1882.

189 **"Your Honor, we have come"**: Forrestine Hooker, *An Arizona Vendetta: The Truth About Wyatt Earp*, Don Taylor, ed. (Old West Research & Publishing, 2011), 54.

189 **"I have got the Earps"**: The full letter is reproduced in Tanner, *Doc Holliday*, 174.

189 **considerable legal wrangling**: "The Final Disposition of the Earp Case," *Tombstone Epitaph*, Feb. 16, 1882.

189 **"A bad time is expected"**: Bailey, ed. *A Tenderfoot in Tombstone*, 206.

190 **"they were liable to get it"**: Testimony of Briggs Goodrich, Coroner's Inquest on Morgan Earp, March 22, 1882, reproduced in Ben T. Traywick, ed. *"Death's Doings in Tombstone"* (Tombstone, AZ: Red Marie's Books, 2002), 88.

190 **The appeal for Morgan**: Wyatt Earp narrative. Wyatt misremembered the name of the actress in his dictation.

190 **"remarkably trim and elegant"**: "Stolen Kisses," *Los Angeles Daily Herald*, March 11, 1882.

190 **play one game of pool**: Wyatt Earp narrative. My account of the shooting of Morgan Earp that follows is based on Wyatt's dictated narrative; the testimonies of J. M. Isaacs, Daniel G. Tipton, Patrick Holland, Dr. George Goodfellow, Sherman McMaster, Dr. William S. Millar, and Robert Hatch, in Coroner's Inquest on Morgan Earp, 86–108; Bailey, ed. *Tombstone from a Woman's Point of View*, 57; "Death of Morgan Earp, *Arizona Weekly Citizen* (Tucson), March 26, 1882; and "Morgan Earp Killed," *The Sunday Chronicle* (San Francisco, CA), March 19, 1882.

ELEVEN: ABOVE THE LAW

193 **"I there and then made a vow"**: Wyatt Earp narrative.

194 **"Now, Virgil"**: "He Is a Dude Now," *The Denver Republican*, May 14, 1893, as quoted in Stephens, ed., *Wyatt Earp Speaks!*, 140.

194 **Wyatt and his posse**: Ibid.; "Arizona Affairs," *The Daily Examiner* (San Francisco), May 28, 1882; Bailey, ed. *Tombstone from a Woman's Point of View*, 58; and Brand, *Wyatt Earp's Vendetta Posse Rider*, 42.

194 **"I thanked God I was takin' Virge"**: Reidhead, *Travesty*, 426.

194 **carrying a message for Wyatt**: In a May 1882 interview, Virgil stated that they were warned of a possible ambush in Tucson "on the road between Tombstone and Contention." See "Arizona Affairs," *The Daily Examiner* (San Francisco), May 28, 1882.

194 **Spence's wife, Marietta**: Testimony of Marietta Duarte Spence in Coroner's Inquest on Morgan Earp, 96–100.

194 **Wyatt was convinced they were**: Wyatt Earp narrative; "He Is a Dude Now," *The Denver Republican*, May 14, 1893, as quoted in Stephens, ed., *Wyatt Earp Speaks!*, 139; and "The Earp Brothers," *Daily News-Democrat* (Gunnison, CO), June 4, 1882.

195 **pulled into Tucson at dusk**: For the details of the shooting of Frank Stilwell that follows, I've drawn from the witness testimony taken during the coroner's inquest and published as "The Stilwell Inquest," *Arizona Weekly Citizen* (Tucson), April 2, 1882; Wyatt Earp narrative; "The Fatal Bullet," *Arizona Weekly Citizen*, March 26, 1882;

"Arizona Affairs," *The Daily Examiner* (San Francisco), May 28, 1882; "Virgil W. Earp," *The Daily Examiner*, May 27, 1882; and "Another Assassination," *Tombstone Weekly Epitaph*, March 27, 1882.

196 **"shot all over"**: Neil B. Carmony, ed. *Next Stop: Tombstone, George Hand's Contention City Diary, 1882* (Tucson, AZ: Trail to Yesterday Books, 1995), 10.

196 **"It's all right, Virge!"**: Reidhead, *Travesty*, 426.

197 **"Frank Stilwell's body"**: Bailey, ed. *A Tenderfoot in Tombstone*, 212.

197 **"only twenty-seven years"**: Bailey, ed. *Tombstone from a Woman's Point of View*, 58.

197 **"If one-twentieth part"**: "The Tombstone Baditti," *Arizona Daily Star* (Tucson), March 22, 1882.

197 **Mattie and Bessie left:** *Tombstone Epitaph*, March 24, 1882.

197 **using the name Sadie Mansfield:** Brand, "Josephine 'Sadie' Earp's Sordid Secrets and Lies," 31.

197 **Behan received a telegram:** "The Tombstone Vendetta," *Sacramento Daily Record-Union*, March 22, 1882.

198 **"Wyatt, I want to see you"**: "Does Misrepresentation Pay?" *Tombstone Weekly Epitaph*, March 27, 1882; and Bailey, ed. *Tombstone from a Woman's Point of View*, 58. Wyatt later told Stuart Lake that "when they came to arrest me, I just laughed at them and told them to just run away." Wyatt Earp to Stuart Lake, Los Angeles, Nov. 6, 1928, box 3, folder 39, Stuart N. Lake Papers.

198 **at a woodcutting camp:** My account of the killing of Indian Charley is drawn from the coroner's inquest testimony reproduced in Traywick, ed., *"Death's Doings in Tombstone*," 118–36; and "Another Murder by the Earp Party," *Arizona Daily Star* (Tucson), March 24, 1882.

199 **Florentino Sáiz:** Sáiz's first name was also given as Philomeno. See Brand, *Wyatt Earp's Vendetta Posse Rider*, 43.

199 **pointed to where he'd gone:** In his lengthy testimony for the coroner's inquest, which, curiously, wasn't filed until the following June, Judah failed to relate that he'd told Wyatt where Indian Charley had gone, which had sealed the man's fate. However, in an interview he gave to the *Epitaph* on March 23, he openly admitted to pointing Wyatt in the right direction. See "Still Another Killing," *Tombstone Epitaph*, March 23, 1882.

199 **"left stretched in his tracks"**: "He Is a Dude Now," *The Denver Republican*, May 14, 1893, as quoted in Stephens, ed., *Wyatt Earp Speaks!*, 142.

199 **a $10 per diem"**: S. J. Reidhead, ed., *A Church for Helldorado: The 1882 Tombstone Diary of Endicott Peabody & the Building of St. Paul's Episcopal Church* (Roswell, NM: Jinglebob Press, 2006), 62.

199 **strong contingent of Cowboys:** "Search for the Earp Party, *Tombstone Epitaph*, March 23, 1882; and Breakenridge, *Helldorado*, 179.

199 **Paul had been assured:** *Arizona Daily Star* (Tucson), March 28, 1882; *Los Angeles Daily Herald*, March 28, 1882; and Bailey, ed., *Tombstone from a Woman's Point of View*, 59. Years later, Paul would claim that he did ride with Behan's posse, at least for one day, and that he wanted to continue to assist Behan but was left out, all of which is in striking contrast to the information he was providing to the Arizona newspapers in March 1882. See "Story of Phin Clanton," *The Arizona Republican*, March 3, 1898.

199 **"If the truth were known"**: Bailey, ed. *A Tenderfoot in Tombstone*, 213.

200 **a lengthy interview:** "The Cowboys," *The Daily Examiner* (San Francisco), March 23, 1882.

200 **two posses were in the field:** "More About the Earps," *Tombstone Weekly Epitaph*, March 27, 1882; and *Arizona Weekly Citizen* (Tucson), March 26, 1882.

200 **"Sheriff Behan has turned all":** Bailey, ed. *A Tenderfoot in Tombstone*, 214.

201 **request $1,000 from friend:** Wyatt Earp narrative; and Flood, "Wyatt Earp," 295.

201 **remote but well-known spring:** In his later years, Wyatt always gave the name of the spring as Iron Springs. Stuart Lake wrote that the name of this water hole was later changed to Mescal Springs (also Spring). Lake, *Wyatt Earp*, 338. Modern-day researchers believe that the spring Wyatt referred to was actually Cottonwood Spring, which is just under one and a half miles west of Mescal Spring. Perhaps, but in Wyatt's earliest versions of the fight, there's no mention of cottonwoods, only willows. Coordinates for Mescal Spring are 31.7436830537705, -110.42813955520504. See Wyatt's handdrawn map of Iron Springs in Earp, *Wyatt Earp*, 306.

201 **Earp posse neared the spring:** Stuart Lake writes that Wyatt had instructed brother Warren to wait for Charlie Smith (and, presumably, Tipton as well) at a "fork in the trail" five miles from Iron Springs. However, Wyatt does not mention leaving Warren behind in either the Wyatt Earp narrative or his account of the Iron Springs fight published in *The Denver Republican*, May 14, 1893, reprinted in Stephens, ed., *Wyatt Earp Speaks!*, 144–45.

201 **The day had turned warm:** In his narrative, Wyatt says that the fight with Curly Bill occurred during the late fall and that "cold winds were coming from the north." Of course, the fight actually occurred in the spring, and, according to what Doc Holliday told a reporter just two months later, it was a warm day. Endicott Peabody wrote in his diary for March 24 that it was a "Beautiful early summer day." Wyatt Earp narrative; "Awful Arizona," *The Denver Republican*, May 22, 1882, as reprinted in Walling, *John "Doc" Holliday*, 12; and Reidhead, ed., *A Church for Helldorado*, 64.

201 **Wyatt said, "Hold!":** My account of the gunfight is drawn from Wyatt Earp narrative, Wyatt's 1893 interview in *The Denver Republican*, reprinted in Stephens, ed., *Wyatt Earp Speaks!*, 144–45; Doc Holliday's 1882 interview in "Awful Arizona"; and Frederick R. Bechdolt to William M. Breakenridge, Carmel, CA, Dec. 23, 1927. Wyatt's different versions vary considerably in the details.

203 **"There are fresh rumors":** "The Earps," *Tombstone Daily Nugget*, as reprinted in *Arizona Daily Star* (Tucson), March 29, 1882.

204 **"Apache Hank" Swilling:** Lake, *Wyatt Earp*, 345.

204 **meet brother Virgil:** *Arizona Daily Star* (Tucson), March 28, 1882.

204 **"friendly messenger":** "The Earp Party," *Tombstone Epitaph*, April 5, 1882; "The Earps," *Tombstone Daily Nugget*, as reprinted in *Arizona Daily Star* (Tucson), March 29, 1882; and "The Earp Party," *Tombstone Epitaph*, March 28, 1882.

204 **next afternoon, March 27:** "Facts of History," *Tombstone Epitaph*, April 14, 1882.

204 **cattle king of Arizona:** "Hooker's Ranche," *Arizona Weekly Citizen*, June 12, 1881.

204 **"a fine man":** Wyatt Earp to Walter Noble Burns, Vidal, CA, March 15, 1927.

204 **"You are doing good work":** Wyatt Earp narrative.

205 **$1,000 for Curly Bill:** *Tombstone Weekly Epitaph*, April 3, 1882. At the First National Convention of Cattle Growers held in St. Louis in 1884, Henry C. Hooker was a delegate representing both the Arizona Live Stock Ranchmen's Association and the

Southeastern Live Stock Association. See *Proceedings of the First National Convention of Cattle Growers of the United States* (St. Louis, MO: R. P. Studley & Co., 1884), 32.

205 **Tipton finally caught up:** "The Earps," *Tombstone Daily Nugget*, as reprinted in *Arizona Daily Star* (Tucson), March 29, 1882; and Wyatt Earp narrative.

205 **Earp posse now rode north:** A report circulated later that around this time, the Earp posse arrested an outlaw named Frank Jackson, believed to have been a member of the Sam Bass gang. This story was later declared to be false. See "Heard From," *Tombstone Epitaph*, April 5, 1882; and *Arizona Daily Star* (Tucson), April 9, 1882.

205 **"You must be upholding":** "Facts of History," *Tombstone Epitaph*, April 14, 1882.

206 **"Sheriff, every man you have":** Wyatt Earp narrative.

207 **watched Behan's posse:** "The Earp Party," *Tombstone Epitaph*, April 5, 1882.

207 **a mile to the west:** Wyatt Earp narrative. It's given as three miles in Hooker, *An Arizona Vendetta*, 94.

207 **"They told me to tell you":** Ibid.; and "The Earps," *Arizona Weekly Star* (Tucson), April 6, 1882.

207 **in the amount of $8,000:** *Arizona Weekly Citizen*, May 14, 1882. The Wyatt Earp narrative gives the figure as $12,000. Lake says it was $13,000 in *Wyatt Earp*, 352. However, a copy of a requisition in either amount has not been found to date. See Fattig, *Wyatt Earp*, 557 and 862 n. 31.

207 **"Mileage still counting":** Bailey, ed. *A Tenderfoot in Tombstone*, 213.

207 **Lewis Cooley arrived:** Wyatt Earp narrative; Lake, *Wyatt Earp*, 348; and Hooker, *An Arizona Vendetta*, 97 and 98.

208 **"too much property":** "James C. Earp," *Los Angeles Daily Times*, March 28, 1882.

208 **a strong desire to run:** "The Earp Brothers," *Daily News-Democrat* (Gunnison, CO), June 4, 1882.

208 **Ringo was in Charleston:** Wyatt Earp narrative.

208 **serving a twenty-day sentence:** "Indian 'Hank' Arrested," *Arizona Weekly Star* (Tucson), March 30, 1882.

208 **want of evidence on April 4:** *Arizona Daily Star* (Tucson), April 5, 1882; and *Tombstone Epitaph*, April 24, 1882.

209 **"well mounted and armed":** *New Southwest and Grant County Herald*, April 22, 1882, as quoted in Roberts, *Doc Holliday*, 267.

210 **"An Arizona Vendetta":** *The Daily Nonpareil* (Council Bluffs, IA), April 16, 1882.

TWELVE: YES, WE ARE FRIENDS

211 **"I'll camp upon creation's edge":** Amelia Josephine Burr, "Gypsy Heart," *Selected Lyrics* (New York: George H. Doran Company, 1927), 73.

211 **"bring a party of Cowboy":** "Downed at Last," *Albuquerque Evening Review*, May 13, 1882.

212 **"Doc Holliday became intoxicated":** *Tombstone Daily Nugget* as reprinted in *Los Angeles Daily Herald*, May 13, 1882.

212 **found in a letter written:** The letter, believed to have been written by Miguel A. Otero Jr., is reproduced in Chuck Hornung and Gary L. Roberts, "The Split: Did Doc & Wyatt Split Because of a Racial Slur?" *True West* 48 (Nov./Dec. 2001): 58–59. Otero wasn't always the most truthful chronicler.

212 **Wyatt's friendship with:** See Mark Dworkin, "Henry Jaffa and Wyatt Earp: Wyatt Earp's Jewish Connection, A Portrait of Henry Jaffa, Albuquerque's First Mayor," *Western Outlaw-Lawman History Association Journal* 13 (Fall 2004): 25–37.

214 **rode it as far as Trinidad:** A story in the *Epitaph* claimed that after the argument with Wyatt, Doc and Daniel Tipton left for Colorado separately from Wyatt and the rest of the posse. The *Albuquerque Evening Review* said only that "when Albuquerque was left, the party disbanded, Holliday going with Tipton." It should be noted, however, that the *Epitaph* piece also reported that Tipton was killed while with Doc. Wyatt stated that the posse traveled together to Trinidad. In the words of the *Epitaph*, "Much reliance must not be placed on rumors." "The Last Earp Row," *Tombstone Epitaph*, as reprinted in *Arizona Daily Star* (Tucson), May 11, 1882; *Albuquerque Evening Review*, May 13, 1882; and Wyatt Earp narrative.

214 **"few easily frightened people":** As quoted in *Arizona Weekly Citizen* (Tucson), May 14, 1882.

214 **former Tombstone resident:** Dick Seifred, *Colorado Daily Chieftain* (Pueblo), March 4, 1882.

214 **a man named Perry Mallon:** Ibid., May 17, 1882; and "Awful Arizona," *The Denver Republican*, May 22, 1882, as reprinted in Walling, *John "Doc" Holliday*, 12. For Mallon, see Peter Brand, *The Life and Crimes of Perry Mallon* (Meadowbank, Australia: Published by the author, 2006).

214 **"small, ferrety eyes":** "'Doc' Holliday," *Colorado Daily Chieftain* (Pueblo), May 17, 1882.

215 **"Throw up your hands!":** "The Cowboy's Capture," *The Kansas City Daily Times*, May 19, 1882, reprinting a story from the *Denver Tribune*.

216 **out of his own pocket:** Roberts, *Doc Holliday*, 294; "Sheriff Mallen's Card," *Rocky Mountain News*, May 25, 1882; "Cochise Wants the Earps," *Arizona Daily Star* (Tucson), May 17, 1882; *Arizona Weekly Citizen*, May 21, 1882; and Fattig, *Wyatt Earp*, 592.

216 **"If I can catch the Earp party":** "Facts of History," *Tombstone Epitaph*, April 14, 1882.

216 **an incredible $40,000:** Casey Tefertiller, *Wyatt Earp: The Life Behind the Legend* (New York: John Wiley & Sons, Inc., 1997), 250.

216 **appointed Sheriff Bob Paul:** "Cochise Wants the Earps," *Arizona Daily Star* (Tucson), May 17, 1882, and "That Requisition," May 18, 1882; "The Earp Case," *Arizona Weekly Citizen*, May 21, 1882; and "Tombstone Tablets," *The Sun* (San Diego), May 18, 1882.

217 **The requisition, dated May 16:** *Journals of the Twelfth Legislative Assembly of the Territory of Arizona* (Lincoln, NE: Journal Company, 1883), 46.

217 **wanted to assassinate him:** "The Cowboy's Capture," *The Kansas City Times*, May 19, 1882, reprinting a story from the *Denver Tribune*.

217 **robbing a mark of $150:** "A Lively War," *Rocky Mountain News*, May 19, 1882.

217 **this all-important certification:** "Paul's Return," *Tombstone Epitaph*, June 10, 1882; and "The Legal Fact," *Arizona Daily Star* (Tucson), June 3, 1882.

217 **"the revised statues":** *Arizona Daily Star* (Tucson), June 27, 1882.

218 **in the amount of $300:** Ibid.; "Gave Bail," *Las Vegas Daily Gazette* (NM), June 2, 1882; and "The End," *Colorado Daily Chieftain* (Pueblo), June 1, 1882.

218 **this one was "flawless":** John Flood notes, group 1, box 2, Josephine Earp Collection, Tombstone Courthouse.

218 **$12,000 playing faro:** "The Exploits of Col. Crummy," *Silver World*, Jan. 10, 1880.

218 **"Governor, can you drive":** John Flood notes, group 1, box 2, Josephine Earp Collection, Tombstone Courthouse.

218 **"to deliver the parties":** *Journals of the Twelfth Legislative Assembly of the Territory of Arizona*, 47.

219 **"I promised my brother":** "The Earp Brothers," *Daily News-Democrat* (Gunnison, CO), June 4, 1882.

219 **"Do you see that man":** "A Man of Sand," *Daily News-Democrat* (Gunnison, CO), June 18, 1882.

220 **a devil incarnate:** "Doc Holliday," *The Cincinnati Enquirer*, May 29, 1882.

221 **"always wore two guns":** Judd Riley interview, typescript, box 11, folder 41, Stuart N. Lake Papers.

221 **"the liveliest, biggest":** "Leadville," *The Brooklyn Daily Times*, Sept. 27, 1882.

221 **"was subject to frequent fits":** "Death of John Ringo," *Tombstone Weekly Epitaph*, July 22, 1882.

222 **Johnny wasn't wearing boots:** Ibid.; and "Statement by Citizens in regards the death of Johnny Ringo, July 14, 1882," reproduced in Traywick, *Death's Doing in Tombstone*, 151–54.

222 **"trying the Indian dodge":** *The Daily Examiner* (San Francisco), Aug. 30, 1882.

222 **"There is more than one man living":** *Tombstone Prospector* as quoted in *Arizona Weekly Enterprise* (Florence), March 22, 1890.

222 **known movements that July:** Gunnison's *Daily News-Democrat* of July 15, 1882, reported that Wyatt and Warren planned to leave Gunnison for San Francisco "in a day or two." If this statement is correct, Wyatt was still in Gunnison at the time of Ringo's death. Also, Wyatt stated in an 1893 interview that he never got Ringo and that he was killed by someone else. "He Is a Dude Now," The *Denver Republican*, May 14, 1893, as quoted in Stephens, ed., *Wyatt Earp Speaks!*, 142–43.

222 **"It is highly improbable":** Eugene Manlove Rhodes to William MacLeod Raine, Pacific Beach, CA, Dec. 28, 1931, author's collection.

222 **the worst hit was Virgil's:** "A Raid on Faro Games," *Daily Evening Bulletin* (San Francisco), Aug. 2, 1882.

222 **"They are evidently":** *The Vallejo Evening Chronicle* (CA), Aug. 14, 1882.

223 **overdose of laudanum:** *The Arizona Silver Belt* (Globe), July 14, 1888; and *Arizona Weekly Enterprise*, July 7, 1888.

223 **"wrecked her life":** Mattie Earp inquest, July 21, 1888, reproduced in Traywick, *Death's Doing in Tombstone*, 199–208.

223 **shipped to her family in Iowa:** Boyer, *Suppressed Murder of Wyatt Earp*, 22.

223 **back in Colorado:** *The Solid Muldoon* (Ouray, CO), April 20, 1883.

223 **Arlington Saloon and Gambling Hall:** Roberts, *Doc Holliday*, 334.

223 **Trouble in Dodge City:** All the pertinent contemporary news reports pertaining to what became known as the Dodge City "war" are available in Miller and Snell, *Why the West Was Wild*, 520–62.

224 **"It has and always shall be":** The letter is reprinted in "The Dodge City Troubles," *Kansas City Daily Journal* (MO), May 24, 1883.

224 **"My God, Wyatt":** "Wyatt Earp's Tribute to Bat Masterson."

225 **let slide its ordinance:** "The Dodge City War," *Augusta Advance* (KS), June 20, 1883.

225 **appeared as an engraving:** "Dodge City's Sensation," *National Police Gazette* (NY), July 21, 1883.

226 **remembered two men riding up:** Wm. B. Shillingberg introduction, *Wyatt Earp, Tombstone, & the West from the Collections of John D. Gilchriese*, 9; and Roy B. Young, *Newton Jasper Earp: Mystery Brother of the Famous "Fighting Earps"* (Apache, OK: Young & Sons Enterprises, 2022), 29.

226 **"a thin, spare looking man":** "Leadville Sketches," *The Omaha Daily Bee*, May 10, 1883.

226 **"neither a lady's man":** E. D. Cowan, "Memories of the Bad Man," *The Salt Lake Herald* (UT), Nov. 14, 1898.

226 **began taking laudanum:** Tanner, *Doc Holliday*, 206.

227 **faro dealers was $6 a day:** "Leadville Sketches."

227 **she was Sister Mary Melanie:** Roberts, *Doc Holliday*, 340; "Convent of St. Peter and Paul," *The Atlanta Constitution*, Sept. 9, 1884; and "Profession of Novices," *The Atlanta Constitution*, Feb. 2, 1886.

227 **Johnny still held a grudge:** "Shooting Affray at Leadville," *St. Louis Globe-Democrat*, Aug. 20, 1884; and "Doc Holliday," *Arizona Weekly Citizen*, April 4, 1885. For more on Tyler, who also went by Jack, see his death notice in *The Examiner*, Jan. 25, 1891.

227 **several cronies accosted Doc:** *The Leadville Democrat*, July 22, 1884, as quoted in Roberts, *Doc Holliday*, 344.

227 **"I am afraid to defend myself":** "Holliday Shoots," *The Leadville Democrat*, Aug. 20, 1884, as reprinted in Walling, *John "Doc" Holliday*, 37.

228 **"Holliday, I'll give you 'till":** "Holliday Bound Over," *The Leadville Herald*, Aug. 26, 1884.

228 **"For God's sake":** Ibid.

228 **a hole in Allen's right arm:** "Holliday Shoots" and "At the Bar," *Carbonate Chronicle* (Leadville, CO), April 4, 1885.

228 **"It was not about the $5":** "Holliday Shoots."

229 **"the local bad men":** "Memories of the Bad Man."

229 **in an Aspen newspaper:** "How 'Doc' Holliday Collected a Debt," *The Aspen Daily Times*, June 12, 1885.

230 **reached "the end of his string":** "Buckshot and Bullets," *Carbonate Chronicle* (Leadville, CO), July 5, 1886. According to an obituary for Doc, Leadville's authorities asked him to leave town. See "Doc Holliday Dead," *The Butte Daily Miner*, Nov. 20, 1887.

230 **population of eighteen thousand:** *The Sun* (NY), Dec. 2, 1885.

230 **"wickedest city on earth":** As reprinted in *The Buffalo Commercial* (NY), June 3, 1886.

230 **Butte's Revere House:** *The Daily Town Talk* (Butte, MT), July 13, 1885.

230 **"Doc is well known":** Ibid.

230 **"habits are unchanged":** "Giles' Grindings," *Carbonate Chronicle* (Leadville, CO), Nov. 21, 1885.

230 **dance his best quickstep:** "Buffum an Old Knight of the Western Grip," *The Anaconda Standard* (MT), Nov. 8, 1905.

230 **"a cowardly attack":** "Doc Holliday Dead," *The Butte Daily Miner*, Nov. 20, 1887.

230 **"drawing and exhibiting":** "'Doc' Holliday Arrested," *Semi-Weekly Miner* (Butte, MT), Feb. 20, 1886.

230 **boarding a morning train:** "Where Is 'Doc' Holliday?" Ibid.

231 **"Doc Holliday has come"**: Ibid.

231 **Wyatt and Sadie checked into**: "At the Hotels," *Rocky Mountain News*, June 7 and 11, 1886.

231 **"I have never seen a man"**: Josephine (Sadie) Earp, "She Married Wyatt Earp," typescript, box 1, folder 5, Glenn Boyer Wyatt Earp Collection, MS 752, UA. The quotes that follow, and all the details of the meeting, are from this manuscript.

232 **"tinhorn gamblers, confidence men"**: "After the Worthless Characters," *Rocky Mountain News*, Aug. 4, 1886.

232 **into a paddy wagon**: "'Doc Holliday' in Jail," *Denver Tribune-Republican*, as reprinted in Walling, *John "Doc" Holliday*, 47.

232 **boarded the Kit Carson stage**: Angela K. Parkison with Donald H. Parkison, *Hope and Hot Water: Glenwood Springs from 1878 to 1891* (Glenwood Springs, CO: Glenwood Springs Legacy Publishing, 2000), 93.

232 **Ike Clanton's death**: *The St. Johns Herald* (AZ), June 9, 1887.

233 **couldn't get out of bed**: "Death of J. [H.] Holliday," *Ute Chief* (Glenwood Springs, CO), Nov. 12, 1887, as reprinted in Walling, *John "Doc" Holliday*, 49–50.

233 **took up a collection**: "Local Laconics," *Leadville Evening Chronicle*, Nov. 10, 1887.

233 **"This is funny"**: Burns, *Tombstone*, 259. Burns does not give a source for this quote. He did research his subjects thoroughly, but he is also known to have embellished and created dialogue in his works. Doc may never have said this, but without additional evidence, the possibility that he did say it should not be dismissed.

EPILOGUE: IMMORTALITY

234 **"For truly, when a man shall end"**: Austin Dobson, "Fame Is a Food That Dead Men Eat," *The Century Magazine* 73 (Nov. 1906): 18.

234 **mark his grave**: Doc's burial site in Linwood Cemetery was not recorded, and the stone monument for Holliday present today is only a memorial. A story that Doc's remains were later disinterred and sent to Georgia lacks evidence. An 1896 news piece on Doc from Valdosta, Georgia, notes that Doc's father "died in this city three years ago, and was buried in our city cemetery." If Doc was also buried in Valdosta, why was only his father mentioned as being buried there? See "'Doc' Holliday," *The Morning News* (Savannah, GA), Jan. 23, 1896.

234 **His personal possessions**: Recollections of Mary Holliday; and Tanner, *Doc Holliday*, 221–22.

235 **"many excellent qualities"**: "Holliday Death," *The Denver Republican*, Nov. 10, 1887, as reprinted in Walling, *John "Doc" Holliday*, 48.

235 **living in San Diego**: For Wyatt and Sadie's time in San Diego, see Garner A. Palenske, *Wyatt Earp in San Diego, Life After Tombstone* (Santa Ana, CA: Graphic Publishers, 2011).

235 **"His remarkable career"**: "He Has Killed Ten Men," *The San Francisco Call*, Dec. 19, 1886.

236 **"had treated themselves"**: "Echos of the Big Fight," *The Kansas City Star* (MO), Dec. 7, 1896.

237 **"a product of the frontier gambler"**: *The Western Grazier* (Wilcannia, New South Wales, Australia), Sept. 5, 1900.

237 **accepted an assignment:** Robert K. DeArment, *Bat Masterson: The Man and the Legend* (Norman: University of Oklahoma Press, 1979), 380.

237 **"Much has been written":** Masterson, "Wyatt Earp," *Human Life*, 22.

238 **"selfish and had a perverse":** Masterson, Doc Holliday. The *Human Life* series on gunfighters also appeared in *The Washington Post* and the *El Paso Times*, thus bringing Masterson's stories broader exposure than just the magazine had.

238 **"Damon did no more":** Ibid.

238 **"The real story of":** Lake, *Wyatt Earp*, foreword.

238 **"After Holliday died":** Ibid., 193.

239 **"The story of Wyatt Earp":** Wyatt Earp to H. Maule, Doubleday, Page & Company, Los Angeles, CA, May 24, 1927, box 7, folder 1, Burns Papers, UA.

239 **he crafted a section:** See Burns, *Tombstone*, vii–ix.

239 **"a brave and fearless officer":** Breakenridge, *Helldorado*, 179.

239 **"If there ever was":** Wyatt Earp to Stuart Lake, Los Angeles, Nov. 6, 1928, box 3, folder 39, Stuart N. Lake Papers.

240 **The *Daily Nugget* refused:** *Tombstone Weekly Epitaph*, April 3, 1882.

240 **"All of which is very interesting":** Wyatt Earp to Stuart Lake, Los Angeles, Nov. 30, 1928, box 3, folder 39, Stuart N. Lake Papers.

240 **citizens of Galeyville:** "More Good Cowboys," *Tombstone Epitaph*, Dec. 15, 1881.

241 **"stilted and florid":** Ann Johnston to William S. Hart, Indianapolis, IN, Feb. 21, 1927, group 1, box 2, folder 6, Josephine Earp Collection, Tombstone Courthouse.

241 **proposing they collaborate:** Stuart Lake to Wyatt Earp, Dec. 25, 1927, box 6, folder 44, Stuart N. Lake Papers.

241 **"I was pumping, pumping":** Stuart Lake to Burton Rascoe, Jan. 9, 1941, box 8, folder 13, Stuart N. Lake Papers.

241 **She told a reporter:** "Earp Buried By Old West," *Los Angeles Times*, Jan. 17, 1929.

242 **"altogether too much personal":** Ira Rich Kent to Stuart Lake, Boston, Aug. 29, 1930, box 4, folder 47, Stuart N. Lake Papers.

242 **"in such a uniformly":** Ira Rich Kent to Stuart Lake, Boston, March 17, 1931, box 4, folder 47, Stuart N. Lake Papers.

242 **"Did he really talk":** Ira Rich Kent to Stuart Lake, Boston, Aug. 30, 1929, box 4, folder 47, Stuart N. Lake Papers.

242 **"I've often wondered":** Stuart Lake to Burton Rascoe, Jan. 9, 1941, box 8, folder 13, Stuart N. Lake Papers.

242 **"more as that of the blood":** Josephine Earp to Stuart Lake, Los Angeles, Jan. 27, 1931, box 3, folder 36, Stuart N. Lake Papers.

242 **"nice, clean story":** Ira Rich Kent to Stuart Lake, Boston, Oct. 23, 1930, box 4, folder 47, Stuart N. Lake Papers.

242 **"Mr. Earp was not":** "Widow of Early Day Kansas Marshal Here to Visit a Relative," *The Wichita Eagle*, Oct. 5, 1930.

244 **"a piece of fiction":** Frank Waters, *The Colorado* (New York: Rinehart & Company, 1946), 226.

244 **Home for Aged and Infirm:** Big Nose Kate materials, box 1, folder 1, Glenn Boyer Wyatt Earp Collection, MS 752, UA.

244 **married a prospector:** "Cummings-Horoney," *The Avalanche* (Carbondale, CO), March 5, 1890.

244 **"I am the only one alive"**: Bork and Boyer, "The O.K. Corral Fight at Tombstone," 75.

244 **"the wildest and most"**: Mary K. Cummings Recollections.

244 **a whopping $3,750:** Paul Andrew Hutton, "Showdown at the Hollywood Corral: Wyatt Earp and the Movies," *Montana, the Magazine of Western History* 45 (Summer 1995): 9.

244 **to help write it:** Mabel Earp Cason to Eleanor B. Sloan, Whitmore, CA, May 20, 1959, Mabel Earp Cason Papers, MS 138, AHS; and Mabel Earp Cason to Mrs. William Irvine, Whitmore, CA, Feb. 5, 1959, as quoted in Boyer, *Suppressed Murder of Wyatt Earp*, 81.

245 **"I will tell all":** "Wyatt Earp's Widow Visits Tombstone," *The El Paso Times*, March 1, 1937.

245 **publisher wanted to know:** Mabel Earp Cason to Eleanor B. Sloan, Whitmore, CA, May 20, 1959.

246 **visited Doc one last time:** Mabel Earp Cason to Mrs. William Irvine, Whitmore, CA, Feb. 13, 1959, as quoted in Boyer, *Suppressed Murder of Wyatt Earp*, 84.

INDEX

References to illustrations are in *italics*. Page numbers with *n* refer to the notes; *nn* refers to multiple notes on the same page.

ABOUT THE AUTHOR

MARK LEE GARDNER is a recipient of the Frank Waters Award for Literary Excellence. His bestselling books, many of them award winners, include *The Earth Is All That Lasts*, *Rough Riders*, *Shot All to Hell*, and *To Hell on a Fast Horse*. An authority on the American West, Mark appeared on the hit Netflix docuseries *Wyatt Earp and the Cowboy War*. His YouTube video for *Wired*'s Tech Support, where Mark answers questions from the Internet about the Wild West, has received several million views. A native of Missouri, he holds an MA in American Studies from the University of Wyoming and lives with his family at the foot of Pikes Peak.